The Superhero Symbol

The Superhero Symbol

MEDIA, CULTURE, AND POLITICS

Edited by Liam Burke, Ian Gordon, and Angela Ndalianis

RUTGERS UNIVERSITY PRESS
New Brunswick, Camden, and Newark, New Jersey, and London

Library of Congress Cataloging-in-Publication Data

Names: Burke, Liam (Liam P.), editor. | Gordon, Ian, 1954– editor. |
Ndalianis, Angela, 1960– editor.
Title: The super hero symbol : media, culture, and politics / edited by
Liam Burke, Ian Gordon, and Angela Ndalianis.
Description: New Brunswick : Rutgers University Press, 2019. |
Includes bibliographical references.
Identifiers: LCCN 2019010257 | ISBN 978-0-8135-9716-4 (paperback) |
978-0-8135-9717-1 (hardback) | 978-0-8135-9718-8 (ebook)
Subjects: LCSH: Superheroes—Social aspects. | Comic books, strips,
etc.—History and criticism. | Comic strip characters in motion pictures. |
Superhero films—History and criticism. | Superheroes in literature. |
Heroes in motion pictures. | Heroes in mass media.
Classification: LCC PN6714 .S83 2019 | DDC 741.5/351—dc23
LC record available at https://lccn.loc.gov/2019010257

A British Cataloging-in-Publication record for this book is available
from the British Library.

♾ The paper used in this publication meets the requirements of the American
National Standard for Information Sciences—Permanence of Paper for
Printed Library Materials, ANSI Z39.48–1992.

www.rutgersuniversitypress.org

Manufactured in the United States of America

CONTENTS

The Superhero Symbol

Introduction

"Everlasting" Symbols

LIAM BURKE

Unmasking Superheroes and Their Shifting Symbolic Function

"As a man, I'm flesh and blood, I can be ignored, I can be destroyed; but as a symbol . . . as a symbol I can be incorruptible, I can be everlasting."[1] In the 2005 reboot of the then dormant Batman film franchise, *Batman Begins*, Bruce Wayne articulates how the figure of the superhero can serve as a transcendent icon. It is hard to imagine a time when superheroes have been more pervasive in our culture. Today, superheroes are intellectual property jealously guarded by media conglomerates, icons co-opted by grassroots groups as a four-color rebuttal to social inequities, masks people wear to more confidently walk convention floors and city streets, and bulletproof banners that embody regional and national identities. From activism to cosplay, understanding how these different groups and interests have made use of this powerful icon is essential to unmasking the appeal of superheroes and their wider impact. To address this interest, *The Superhero Symbol* brings together scholars from a range of disciplines, alongside key industry figures. Collectively, these contributions provide fresh perspectives on how these costume-clad heroes have engaged with media, culture, and politics, thereby becoming the "everlasting" symbols to which a wayward Bruce Wayne once aspired.

Defining Superheroes

With their high-flying heroics, superheroes are easy to identify but more difficult to define. Much of superhero scholarship has wrestled with this dilemma, with Peter Coogan cautioning in his 2006 book *Superhero: The Secret Origin of a Genre* that a "sloppy definition of the superhero makes it more difficult to examine the way the superhero genre embodies cultural mythology and narratively animates and resolves cultural conflicts and tensions."[2] While some scholars have welcomed this "taxonomic rigor,"[3] strict definitions have also been criticized for "arbitrary boundary marking."[4]

Comic scholars Charles Hatfield, Jeet Heer, and Kent Worcester link the "genre's murkiness" to the lack of consensus as to when superheroes first emerged. Chris Gavaler opens his eon-hopping study *On the Origin of Superheroes* by tracing a broad history of superheroes that includes Gilgamesh, Maui, and Horus, arguing, "Humans have been thinking about superheroes for over seventeen millennia."[5] Other scholars have located the superhero's origins to more recent social bandits, pulp heroes, and comic strip strongmen.[6] Although there is little agreement on the earliest example of a superhero, Superman's first appearance on the cover of *Action Comics* #1 in 1938 is often credited with codifying and popularizing a character type that was ideally suited to the challenges of the time as well as the opportunities of the fledgling comic book form.

A pioneer in the study of popular culture, John G. Cawelti observed how heroic types come with expiration dates: "New periods seem to generate new adventure formulas while to some extent still holding on to earlier modes. Adventure situations that seem too distant either in time or in space tend to drop out of the current catalog of adventure formulas."[7] With a proclivity for vigilante justice, the Western gunslinger is often considered the superhero's immediate forebear, with cartoonist Robert C. Harvey arguing that the superhero is the "Western heroic persona elevated to near omnipotence."[8] However, as the Machine Age progressed and the Great Depression took root, the cowboy was increasingly out of step with contemporary interests, with Ramzi Fawaz distinguishing the superhero from the Western gunfighter through the superhero's "mutually constitutive relationship to twentieth-century science and technology."[9] Similarly, Ben Highmore argues that superheroes are "a species that has adjusted to the modern city and overcome its obstacles."[10] Superman demonstrated this Machine Age resilience on his first cover by effortlessly smashing a car against a rock face, a feat he bettered on the story's first page in which he hurdled a twenty-story building and outpaced an express train.[11] Cartoonist Jules Feiffer recalls how growing up in the 1930s superheroes seemed inevitable given the pressures of modernity: "When *Superman* at last appeared, he brought with him the deep satisfaction of all underground truths: Our reaction was less 'How original!' than 'But, of course!'"[12]

As Chris Murray notes, when Jerry Siegel and Joe Shuster created Superman their innovation was not inventing superheroes but organizing an idea that already existed but was "not fully conceptualized."[13] While tracing a longer history of superheroes, Chris Gavaler remarks of Superman's first appearance, "After him, the hourglass widens into a spacious ball of imitation and evolution."[14] Although adopting a critical stance, philosopher Walter Ong similarly described Superman as a "raw, elemental prototype, constructed on a monumentally primitive pattern," observing that he "is the leader of a swarm of satellites separated from him only by a copyright."[15] As Gavaler and Ong suggest, each superhero that came after Superman was indebted to the Man of Steel, whether as a continuation of the type (Captain Marvel, Wonder Man) or a contrast (Batman, Wonder Woman). Despite this cycle of repetition and variation, some scholars prefer to treat the superhero as a wider archetype rather than a distinct genre, with Gavaler suggesting these heroes are "all-swallowing über-characters that consume other genres like black holes."[16] Murray makes a similar argument, proposing that the superhero defies easy definition because it "was a blend of influences from the start."[17]

The superhero's debt to Westerns, science fiction, crime, fantasy, and a host of other genres is well established, but these costume-clad characters distilled and reworked these antecedents into a new model that many recognize as a dedicated genre. For instance, in what is often considered the first book-length study of the topic, *Super Heroes: A Modern Mythology*, Richard Reynolds extrapolates from Superman's first appearance in *Action Comics* #1 to arrive at a "working definition of the superhero genre" that he organizes under seven headings: "Lost Parents," "The Man-God," "Justice," "The Normal and the Superpowered," "The Secret Identity," "Superpowers and Politics," and "Science as Magic."[18] Coogan offers his own dictionary-ready definition of the superhero, which echoes Reynolds through a focus on a "pro-social mission," "superpowers," and a "transformation" from a civilian identity.[19] Thus, it is possible to link demigods, nocturnal vigilantes, and rage monsters through a distinct set of generic conventions. However, what is more interesting than how these characters are the same is how they are different.

Cultural Thermometers

In his essay "Batman, Deviance and Camp" media scholar Andy Medhurst describes the avuncular Batman that appeared in the conservative comics of the 1950s as a "cultural thermometer, taking the temperature of the times."[20] Indeed, every superhero story is inflected by the time and culture in which it was produced, and it is this sociopolitical relevance that is a central interest of this collection. For instance, in his first appearance Superman took on not only the challenges of modernity but also social problems such as abusive husbands and crooked Washington lobbyists—an attitude that would have chimed with readers struggling through the tail end of the Depression. The other heroes who populated the comic book industry's Golden Age were similarly shaped by their context. Batman was indebted to the pulp tradition of mystery men that traded blows with heightened versions of real-world gangsters; Wonder Woman was positioned by her creator, pop psychologist William Moulton Marston, as a corrective to the "bloodcurdling masculinity" of comics[21]; while a number of comic creators sought to hasten U.S. involvement in World War II, with Joe Simon and Jack Kirby introducing their new hero, Captain America, by having him punch Hitler on the jaw almost a full year before the United States entered the war.

Politics and culture scholar Alex Evans describes how superheroes are particularly useful to cultural studies because they are a "mythic palimpsest."[22] In 1945 Walter Ong argued that such mythological allusions were an unconvincing attempt to disarm criticisms of comic book heroes: "Only say that the comics are like folk tales, and all misgivings vanish."[23] However, after decades of sustained publication, reboots, and adaptation superheroes have escaped their paper-and-ink origins and float more freely as mythological archetypes. As a number of contributions to this collection demonstrate, these superpowered symbols are often enlisted to comprehend, even mollify, societal anxieties.

In many ways it is the industrial simplicity of superhero stories that makes them a reliable reflection of social change. For instance, former Spider-Man editor Danny Fingeroth argues that the genre's "lack of self-consciousness may enable us to read cultural signposts that would be harder to discern in a cultural vein more knowingly developed,"[24] while Gavaler explains that superheroes "reflect a lot about us. And since superheroes have been flying for decades, they document our evolution too."[25] Indeed, long after the comic industry's Golden Age superheroes continued to serve as Medhurst's "cultural thermometer." In the early 1960s the heroes who populated the burgeoning Marvel Universe, such as the Fantastic Four, Incredible Hulk, and Spider-Man, gained their abilities in disastrous space missions or science experiments gone awry. These irradiated icons were equally cursed and blessed by their newfound gifts, thereby articulating the conflicting attitudes to the rapid technological innovation of the time. Fawaz notes of this period how the superhero transformed from a "nationalist champion to a figure of radical difference mapping the limits of American liberalism and its promise of universal inclusion in the post–World War II period."[26]

This process continued into the 1970s, when Wonder Woman found herself a symbol of Women's liberation when longtime fan Gloria Steinem put the satin suffragette on the first cover of feminist magazine *Ms.* Steinem described how when she was growing up Wonder Woman "rescued" her from a steady diet of male heroes, adding, "If we had all read more about Wonder Woman and less about Dick and Jane, the new wave of the feminist revolution might have happened less painfully and sooner"—a sentiment shared by cartoonist Trina Robbins in her interview for this collection.[27] This back-and-forth between fiction and reality has helped maintain the superhero genre's currency, even while some interactions warrant greater scrutiny.

In the 1980s a rise in inner-city violence gave antihero the Punisher renewed relevance, with the vigilante headlining several comic books. The Punisher's skull logo, with its tendril-like teeth and permanent grimace, became synonymous with a zero-tolerance approach to crime, with police and the military in the real world emblazoning their uniforms, equipment, and vehicles with the controversial superhero symbol.[28] Examples such as this seem to validate wider fears of the corrupting influence of superheroes. In their 2002 book *The Myth of the American Superhero* Lawrence and Jewett rework Joseph Campbell's monomyth to reflect American exceptionalism, noting, "It would not be long before the American monomyth became a subculture of Planet Earth, managing especially the consciousness of youth and adults, evoking a wide array of imitative behaviors."[29]

This type of critique was particularly prevalent during the postwar years when superheroes were linked to a number of social problems. In 1954 psychiatrist Dr. Fredric Wertham published his influential book *Seduction of the Innocent* in which he linked a post–World War II rise in juvenile delinquency to comic books. Wertham considered superhero books to be a particularly "harmful" type of crime comic that inspired a range of dangerous reader responses. For instance, Wertham argued that Superman compelled teenagers to drive recklessly and break speeding limits, adding, "The superman conceit gives boys and girls the feeling that ruthless go getting based on physical strength or the power of weapons or machines is the desirable way to behave."[30] In a pre-web version of Godwin's law, it was inevitable that these social guardians would connect comic books' superpowered protagonists to Hitler and other fascist leaders. Writing in 1945, Ong cautioned, "We do not have to look far in the present comic field to discover a strong crosscurrent of those forces which the German, and other, super states have found useful."[31] Wertham made similar comparisons: "In these children there is an exact parallel to the blunting of sensibilities in the direction of cruelty that has characterized a whole generation of central European youth fed on the Nietzsche-Nazi myth of the exceptional man who is beyond good and evil."[32]

Although these readings might today be dismissed as the reactive rhetoric of scholars fresh from the experience of World War II, anxieties about the imitative potential of superhero power fantasies persist. Furthermore, while the methods and the conclusions of these social scientists turned moral guardians have been criticized, much like other media disciplines, these detractors were the first to give comics and superheroes sustained scholarly attention.[33] Thus, it is unsurprising that many of the issues raised by Ong and Wertham reappear in this collection, a study that is indebted to a field of scholarship that they unknowingly helped establish.

Tied to these critiques is concern over the propensity for simplification in superhero stories. Despite being an advocate of the star-spangled hero, Steinem noted, "The Wonder Women stories are not admirable in all ways," adding, "her wartime adventures sometimes had highly jingoistic and even racist overtones."[34] The Manichean morality that facilitated such stereotypes also served to rationalize the superhero's code of ethics. Reynolds identifies "justice" as a key convention of the superhero, explaining, "Superman's devotion to 'those in need' involves coming to the help of those victimized by a blind though well-intentioned state."[35] Many heroes act in the gaps left by that state while still upholding its higher principles. As Lawrence and Jewett note, this convention transmutes "lawless vigilantism into a perfect embodiment of law enforcement."[36] However, as Neal Curtis reminds us in his contribution to this collection, this simple equivalency is complicated at times when the principles of the state are unclear or the actions of those in power chafe with the baked-in morality of superheroes. For example, Reynolds challenges "narrowly nationalistic" interpretations of Superman's mission "Truth, Justice, and the American Way," arguing, "The third term has stood for the ideals enshrined in the US constitution. Superheroes have been better Americans—as the founding fathers would have understood the term—than most of America's modern political leaders."[37] Similarly, Fawaz recognizes that superheroes embody a tension, which he identifies as "the central tension of American liberal democracy" between liberalism's "individual agency" and democracy's "collective solidarity."[38] How the superhero navigates this tension can provide further insight into the time in which the stories are (re)told.

When the first feature-length film adaptation of Spider-Man broke box office records in 2002, cultural commentators looked to the zeitgeist to provide a reason for the unprecedented popularity of superhero movies, and they did not have to look far. Heroes on the comic book page were never more popular than when they were turning over Axis tanks. This superpowered response to a real-world threat found many in the popular press and scholarly community linking the more recent success of cinema's heroes to the escape they offered American audiences rocked by 9/11, with Hagley and Harrison contending that the "post–September 11 resurrection of the superhero genre, particularly in film, is a direct response to the feelings of helplessness and terror that Americans experienced in the days and years following the attack."[39] However, how the superhero responded to the terrorist attacks provides a potent illustration of the conflicting attitudes to 9/11 and, in particular, the subsequent War on Terror.

Where once superheroes reflected anxieties such as the impact of scientific research, post-9/11 there was an emphasis on militarization. For instance, the Marvel characters relaunched under the publisher's Ultimate imprint in 2002 gained a militaristic dimension, with heroes such as Captain America, Thor, Iron Man, and Hulk now working for the government and wearing costumes that more greatly resembled army fatigues. Celebrated artist Jim Lee noted of this development, "In some ways, the government is now our version of radiation. Radiation used to be the reason why people got superpowers. Now the government is."[40] This militarization was also evident in films such as Christopher Nolan's *Dark Knight* trilogy, where the hero's arsenal is cherry-picked from Wayne Enterprises' military prototypes, with cultural studies scholar Justine Toh arguing that the Batsuit and Batmobile became "emblems of the military-industrial-entertainment complex."[41]

In contrast to this seeming endorsement of military response, these films also invite more liberal readings, particularly in those moments where the motives of the hero are questioned. Discomfort bordering on anxiety looms over many superhero movies, with it frequently suggested that the actions of the hero create the conditions for further violence. For instance, in both *The Dark Knight Rises* and *Iron Man* billionaires Bruce Wayne and Tony Stark maintain a personal armory while simultaneously moving their companies away from military contracts to focus on renewable energy. Furthermore, supporting characters regularly voice concerns regarding vigilantism (Alfred and Rhodey) and escalation (Gordon and Fury). Given this uncertainty these films are a good example of what Alan Sinfield describes as "faultline stories" in that "they address the awkward, unresolved issues, the ones in which the conditions of plausibility are in dispute."[42] Scholars Will Brooker and Alex Evans have applied Sinfield's approach to Batman and Superman, respectively.[43] Evans suggests that in a cultural materialist paradigm "no ideological domination is total" and that we should view these heavily reinterpreted heroes as faultline texts, which are more than simply "a tool of hegemony and imperialism but also a site of considerable resistance and conflict."[44] Similarly, historian Ian Gordon argues that Superman is more of "a process, rather than a static, fixed phenomenon."[45] The contributions to this collection examine how from cosplaying fans to global media conglomerates superheroes have been enlisted to respond to a range of societal imperatives, industrial pressures, and unresolved conflicts. These varied uses have given the superheroes greater cultural presence than probably any other time in their history, but why has this particular moment proven so fertile for superhero stories?

Why the World Needs Superheroes

Although they may have faced threats from moral guardians and new heroic types, superheroes have maintained a presence in popular culture since the comic book industry's Golden Age. However the visibility of superheroes since 2000 goes beyond popularity to an unprecedented level of pervasiveness. Many of the factors that fostered the increased production of comic book film adaptations can also be attributed to the purchase superheroes now have on cultural and political life.[46] For instance, since *Superman: The Movie* first promised audiences that "You'll Believe a Man Can Fly," a surge in superhero movies has been linked to new filmmaking technologies. In his 2006 book Coogan suggests one of the limitations of live-action adaptations of superheroes has been the difficulty in achieving an "equivalent surface realism" because in the comic book all the elements "are made out of the same material (ink, paper, color)."[47] This semiotic gap has been narrowed in the digital age as the screen artifacts are increasingly, often exclusively, composed of the same material (ones and zeroes rather than paper and ink). In this pixel-populated environment, gun-toting raccoons and purple aliens can convincingly share the screen with live-action actors. Thus, the digital age made the once impossible images of comics achievable, thereby helping to facilitate today's superhero movies, TV shows, videogames, and other audiovisual adaptations.

This technological shift has also found the boundaries between media platforms blurring. For instance, a superhero TV show such as *Inhumans* can be exhibited on large-format IMAX screens, while a fan might catch ten minutes of a blockbuster film on their phone. This media convergence has been embraced by conglomerates such as WarnerMedia and Disney, which are eager to find "spreadable media" that will work seamlessly across multiple media platforms.[48] Superheroes, with their readily identifiable iconography, cross-generational appeal, and never-ending quests for justice, lend themselves to transmedia strategies. Given these imperatives, it is easy to understand why Disney acquired Marvel in 2009 for four billion dollars. Similarly, while Disney's acquisition of Twentieth Century Fox in 2019 was about a lot more than regaining the rights to Marvel characters such as Fantastic Four and X-Men, adding a few more transmedia stars to Disney's already bustling lineup would have been an incentive.

As former DC Entertainment president Diane Nelson describes in her interview for this collection, superheroes bound effortlessly from one medium to the next. These cross-platform extensions have had an impact on the superhero's relationship to its native form: comics. The comic book and classical superhero were twinned from birth.[49] In the late 1930s the recently established four-color medium was the only format capable of fully capturing the heightened heroics of these exciting new creations. Conversely, in superheroes comic books found what celebrated creator Grant Morrison describes as their "defining content."[50] Many scholars have remarked on this seemingly inseparable link, with Gavaler identifying comics as the superhero's "most enduring home."[51] However, Fingeroth notes how, since the peaks of the 1940s and 1950s, comic books have become the "pastime of a rarefied audience" with the number of people getting their superhero content through movies, TV, and videogames increasingly dwarfing comic books.[52]

Much like a young Kal-El leaving his ailing planet of Krypton, superheroes have flourished in their adopted homes. However, the increased distance between the comic book form and its traditional standard bearer may also benefit the U.S. comic book industry, with comic scholar Brad Brooks suggesting "that since now movies can use CGI, there is no need for comics to have superheroes in them."[53] Writing in 1992 Richard Reynolds noted how the superhero dominance of the U.S. comic book industry frustrated many writers and artists who "would like to bring the wider possibilities of the comic book (or graphic novel) to the attention of the general public."[54] Indeed, since the superhero movie boom, a wider range of genres such as science fiction (*Saga*), horror (*The Walking Dead*), and crime (*Kill or Be Killed*) have begun to sit confidently on comic store shelves that were once uniformly costume clad. These alternative approaches have even started to filter into the long-standing superhero books, where rigid practices are being rethought.

Traditionally the U.S. comic book industry was populated by (usually male) fans who managed to turn "their avocation into their vocation,"[55] but since the mid-2000s a more eclectic approach to comic creators has rejuvenated the mainstream industry. These fresh perspectives have given the superhero greater relevance and wider reach. This is particularly evident in the convention of the superhero's transformation from a secret identity to a costumed crime fighter.

Several decades before Quentin Tarantino arrived at the same conclusion in *Kill Bill: Volume 2*, Jules Feiffer argued that Clark Kent was "Superman's opinion of the rest of us, a pointed caricature of what we . . . were really like."[56] Similarly, Steinem wondered how Wonder Woman could "bear to be like Diana Prince? Did that mean that all women really had to disguise their true selves in weak feminine stereotypes in order to survive?"[57] Although the secret identity could be seen as the hero's critique of humanity, many commentators argue that the transformation from a mild-mannered citizen into an indestructible icon is the superhero's most admirable trait and central to their appeal. For instance, Gavaler describes how "gods may look or act human, but superheroes bridge the divine-mundane chasm. . . . They are humans who become gods but then choose to be human."[58]

Reflecting on this careful balance, Morrison identifies Clark Kent as the "ultimate reader identification figure," while semiotician Umberto Eco suggests that Clark "personifies fairly typically the average reader."[59] The implication is that Clark Kent, Peter Parker, and all the other bespectacled civilians who hide costumes under their daywear are so innocuous that they invite the reader's self-identification. However, these secret identities are far from universal character types. As Trina Robbins noted of Golden Age superheroes before the appearance of Wonder Woman, "Aside from their brightly colored longjohns, the one thing these heroes had in common was their gender."[60] Politics professor Carolyn Cocca recently reiterated Robbins's argument in her book *Superwomen: Gender, Power, and Representation*, where she also pointed out the limited representation in ethnicity, sexual orientation, and disability: "The word 'superhero' pretty much assumes that the hero in question is male, and white, and heterosexual, and able-bodied."[61]

As demonstrated in this collection, fans who did not identify with the historically narrow demographic makeup of superhero stories found inventive ways to challenge and critique this lack of representation. Yet moving into the second decade of the millennium there was a sustained attempt on the part of the comic book industry to redress this disparity by reworking the secret identities of some of their most high-profile characters, with female heroes taking over the mantles of Wolverine and Thor, Korean American Amadeus Cho serving as the Hulk's alter ego, and Pakistani American Kamala Khan becoming the new *Ms. Marvel* when the previous title holder, Carol Danvers, received her overdue promotion to the rank of *Captain Marvel*.

Wider audiences might have missed these changes as they took place in the pages of the comic books rather than on-screen, yet after years in which every superhero seemed to be played by a white guy named Chris (Evans, Hemsworth, Pratt) some of this diversity began to seep into superheroes on screen. Superhero shows like *Jessica Jones*, *Luke Cage*, *Supergirl*, and *Black Lightning* provided a greater array of heroic types, while the box office grosses of *Wonder Woman*, *Black Panther*, *Aquaman*, and *Captain Marvel* have hopefully dispelled the misconception that women or people of color cannot lead superhero movies. In the introduction to *Superwomen*, Carolyn Cocca succinctly describes why such representation matters: "You are more likely to imagine yourself as a hero if you see yourself represented as a hero."[62] With a wider audience feeling greater ownership of these characters, they are increasingly weaved into the fabric of cultural and political life. This symbolic use might be as simple as a branded T-shirt or online avatar, but, as Henry Jenkins demonstrates in his chapter, often these characters are pressed into some form of civic engagement.

Superheroes are inherently passive. They camp on rooftops or brood in subterranean lairs waiting for a reason to spring forth. Reflecting on this inactivity, Reynolds went so far as to suggest that superheroes can be "summoned like a genie from a bottle in order to redress all moral imbalances."[63] As Jason Bainbridge explores in his contribution to this collection, traditionally it is the appearance of a villain that creates the need for superheroes, with Coogan suggesting "villains are proactive and heroes are reactive."[64] As has been discussed, from the Great Depression to 9/11, this pattern was reflected in the wider world where superheroes were enlisted to respond to times of uncertainty or unease.

Often this ritualistic return to superheroes at times of crisis is positioned as escapism. As Grant Morrison succinctly wrote, "Scary times and superhero movies go together like dirt and soap," while Henry Jenkins proposed in his analysis of 9/11 comic books that "for some, Superhero comics hark back to simpler times and get consumed as comfort food."[65] Such pleasures are often met with derision. Escapism was cited by Chinese officials in 1978 as the reason for removing *Superman: The Movie* from cinemas only one day after its release, with the *Beijing Evening News* describing the character as a "narcotic the capitalist class gives itself to cast off its serious crises."[66] Similarly, in the elegiac superhero movie *Logan*, the onetime Wolverine dismisses superhero comics as "ice cream for bed-wetters," explaining, "In the real world, people die, and no self-promoting asshole in a fucking leotard can stop this."[67]

Reynolds challenges the criticisms frequently leveled against superheroes: "Far from being as 'escapist' as is claimed, most superhero comics are intensely grounded in the normal and everyday."[68] This potent contrast between the familiar and the fantastic has better enabled superheroes to have a "real-world" impact. Political geographer Jason Dittmer believes that superheroes are not merely reflective of prevailing sentiment but can be active in changing opinion. Dittmer uses the example of Captain America promoting an "interventionist attitude" prior to official U.S. involvement in World War II, but one might also point to the impact of Wonder Woman on generations of feminists or how X-Men addressed pertinent topics like civil rights that most popular media avoided.[69] From inventive Internet memes and clever protest banners to costumed culture jamming, today social activism is often made more relatable (and colorful) through the use of the superhero symbol.

Technological and industrial changes have given superheroes a wider reach than ever before. Embracing that opportunity, the once rigid icon has become a more inclusive symbol that has maintained the tradition of responding to and reflecting our world. The diversity, intentions, and impact of this symbolic use are the focus of this collection.

The Superhero Symbol

The Superhero Symbol is divided into four thematic sections, which are punctuated with industry interviews. Collectively these perspectives offer a rounded understanding of how the transcendent symbol of the superhero has been used under different industrial, social, and cultural conditions. Henry Jenkins opens the first part of the book, "Superheroes, Politics, and Civic Engagement," with a question posed by *Astro City* writer Kurt Busiek: "If a superhero can be such a powerful and effective metaphor for male adolescents, then what else can we do with them?" Building on his recent research on youth activism, Jenkins provides a vibrant account of how grassroots groups from a variety of backgrounds make use of superhero symbols. Using examples from undocumented immigrants, Muslim comic creators, equal rights campaigners, and environmental activists, Jenkins makes a convincing argument that superheroes are now a vital element in our collective civic imagination. This opening chapter establishes many themes that are addressed across the collection, including responsibility, ethics, and political capital.

With the provocative chapter title "America Is a Piece of Trash," Neal Curtis uses a *What If?* story in which Captain America is revived in a fascist America as a springboard to examine how *Captain America* comics have consistently engaged with patriotism, nationalism, and fascism. Curtis, citing Dittmer, argues that such analysis is important given the co-constitutive relationship between political discourses of nationhood and cultural artifacts like comics. To bring these topics into focus Curtis examines Captain America's battles with his many evil alternates such as Bad Cap, Super Patriot, Nuke, and Anti-Cap. As Curtis illustrates, these conflicts animate debates about what it means to be American.

Moving from heroes to villains, Jason Bainbridge considers the function of supervillains. Bainbridge contends that like their heroic alternates villains can symbolize wider attitudes. For example, Lex Luthor's transition from a mad scientist in the 1950s to an unscrupulous politician in the early 2000s was reflective of changing societal concerns. Bainbridge argues that this topic demands greater attention as a more thorough investigation of the supervillain provides a fuller understanding of the complex sets of associations around the legality, sovereignty, and politics of the superhero's actions.

The first section concludes with an interview with Trina Robbins. As an artist, writer, and "herstorian" Robbins has worked tirelessly since the late

1960s to increase the visibility of women in comics. From a childhood reading Wonder Woman comics to her participation in the 2017 Women's March (where she carried a Wonder Woman–themed banner) the celebrated creator reflects on the interplay between superheroes and politics as well as how superheroes can inspire and inform civic engagement.

While Superman might profess that his emblem means hope, the readily recognizable logo has also become a brand every bit as powerful as golden arches or a stylized swoosh. In this way superheroes have come to symbolize a complex array of commercial interests. The book's second part, "The Superhero as Brand," unmasks how these properties are maintained and exploited. For instance, in opening this part Mitchell Adams reveals the secret commercial identity of superheroes. Through a detailed analysis of trademark applications filed by Marvel and DC Comics, Adams demonstrates how a focus on intellectual property can reveal how creative organizations commercialize superheroes as well as the global distribution of these properties.

Adams notes how Superman is protected with over five hundred registered trademarks, but in his chapter Ian Gordon shifts our attention to a brand that may not be registered but nonetheless was instrumental in the development of the Last Son of Krypton: Siegel and Shuster. Gordon revisits the oft-discussed creation of Superman with a critical lens, challenging accounts of Siegel and Shuster as creators cast aside by a greedy corporation. Gordon notes how in the early years of Superman DC Comics was eager to market the character as a "Siegel and Shuster" creation, and how it was only after a 1947 challenge from Siegel to regain ownership of the character that DC Comics began to obfuscate the pair's contribution. Gordon goes on to describe how the brand of "Siegel and Shuster" gained new currency with the rise of fan culture in the 1970s, visibility Siegel was able to leverage to regain authorial recognition.

The complex legal wrangling that surrounds these money-spinning characters is the focus of Tara Lomax's chapter, "Practicing Superhuman Law." With a particular focus on the 2017 film *Spider-Man: Homecoming*, which found the webslinger join the Marvel Cinematic Universe (MCU), Lomax demonstrates how licensing and other legal considerations shape the creative process. In an inventive allegory, this chapter unpacks the relationship between superheroes and franchising through a focus on "Superhuman Law," the fictitious legal field that appears in self-aware comics such as Marvel's *She-Hulk*.

Due to their origins on the comic book page, music is an oft-ignored aspect of the superhero brand. However, as Dan Golding explores in his chapter, with the adaptation of superheroes to audiovisual media the theme music these characters received often became as familiar as their capes and cowls. Concentrating on the many screen versions of Batman and Superman, Golding notes how superhero identity is articulated through music. For instance, Golding identifies continuity between the music found in the Fleischer animated Superman serials of the 1940s and John Williams's iconic score for *Superman: The Movie*, which he locates around the perfect fifth interval typically found in patriotic fanfares.

When Harry Potter brand manager Diane Nelson replaced comic book fan and creator Paul Levitz as the head of DC Comics in 2009, it underscored the growing importance of superheroes as brands. During her tenure as president of DC Entertainment Nelson oversaw the extension of these characters across multiple media platforms. In her interview, which closes the book's second section, Nelson discusses why these characters are fertile enough to sustain multiple interpretations. Nelson also describes how superheroes can address societal concerns and how she used these familiar symbols to bring awareness to social causes.

As discussed, one of the central tenets of the superhero genre is the hero's transformation from an unassuming civilian to an impenetrable icon. The collection's third part, "Becoming the Superhero," examines the many ways that audiences can re-create this trajectory and assume the mantle of a hero. One of the most potent platforms for this superheroic transformation is videogames, which afford the player a degree of interactivity absent in other media. Through best-selling games like *Injustice: Gods among Us*, players can become their favorite heroes. Yet Steven Conway identifies in his chapter the disparity between the superhuman competences of these characters and the player's inevitable mistakes. Focusing on *Batman: Arkham Knight*, Conway notes how the developer, Rocksteady Studios, managed to reconcile this tension through inventive game design that put the Joker in control.

In her contribution Claire Langsford picks up on the first section's focus on social activism. She cautions that scholars should not treat fan activists as a homogenous group with a common goal simply because they have a shared enthusiasm for superheroes. Langsford demonstrates the diverse actors inevitable in any fan community by focusing on a group who don their favorite hero's costumes, cosplayers. She contrasts the superhero cosplay community's supposed inclusivity with the hierarchies and divisions that often emerge.

Moving from the convention floor to city streets, Vladislav Iouchkov and John McGuire look at the recent phenomenon of "real-life superheroes," individuals who patrol their neighborhoods in superhero costumes and often intervene in crimes and social welfare injustices. Drawing on dozens of interviews with real-life superheroes Iouchkov and McGuire contrast the homemade heroes' activities and motivations with those of their fictional inspirations. The chapter identifies many points of comparison, such as traumatic origin stories, as well as many points of difference, in particular how most real-life superheroes want to work within the limits of the law.

The emergence of real-life superheroes stems from a desire to have our favorite heroes intervene when we need them most or to find that courage in ourselves. Keeping with this theme, an interview with the award-winning writer Paul Dini closes this part on "Becoming the Superhero." Dini is perhaps best known as the writer of Batman across animation, comics, and videogames, as well as cocreator of fan-favorite antihero Harley Quinn. However, in 1993, at the height of the popularity of *Batman: The Animated Series*, Dini was mugged and viciously beaten blocks from his home. Dini depicts the attack in his best-selling memoir *Dark Night: A True Batman Story*. In his interview Dini describes how he imagined Batman swooping down on his attackers, and how during his recovery he could hear the Dark Knight's voice challenging him to get back on his feet. Ultimately, Dini explains how he found his hero's resolve and rediscovered the importance of escapist fantasy figures like Batman.

Like jazz and baseball, comic books are often described as an American artform, and the medium's most popular character, the superhero, did much to affirm that link with dozens of star-spangled heroes created during the industry's Golden Age. However, this increasingly global icon has been reimagined in a range of contexts to respond to local cultures, politics, and traditions. From the superhero's birthplace in America, to Ireland, Germany, China, and Australia, the book's final part examines "Superheroes and National Identity."

Picking up on Curtis's contribution to the collection's first section, Naja Later examines how the retroactive continuity and reboots common to all comic book superheroes are made textually explicit in Captain America comics with characters frequently reflecting on the unreliability of memory as well as official accounts of wartime heroics. Later argues that this indeterminacy allows Captain America comics to subvert national ideologies, particularly those linking war and heroism. With a focus on the many origins of Captain America and Bucky, this chapter also suggests that this unreliable narration opens up Captain America comics for queer readings that challenge the conservative narratives often associated with the all-American hero.

Crossing the Atlantic, I look at how superhero stories featuring Irish characters tend to perpetuate Victorian-era stereotypes about Ireland designed to undermine Irish claims for self-government. The chapter traces these conventions from nineteenth-century political cartoons to modern U.S. comics, where stories featuring Irish and Irish American characters such as Banshee, Daredevil, and Captain America tend to rely on heavily circulated (and outdated) depictions of Ireland. I argue that the emergence of a modest comic book industry in Ireland (with its own cadre of nationally themed superheroes) is serving as a corrective to these wider representations.

Ireland is not the only country that has recently welcomed the arrival of local superheroes. Demonstrating the international reach of these costumed crime fighters, Paul Malone charts the recent emergence of German-speaking heroes. In his chapter Malone identifies the reasons for this late development, including fears of cultural imperialism and resistance to a character type that echoed the Nazis' strongman tactics. The chapter demonstrates how historical distance from World War II coupled with the growing global popularity of the superhero has facilitated the emergence of German-speaking superheroes such as Captain Berlin, Tracht Man, and Captain Austria, Jr., who leads the Austrian Super Heroes.

Shan Mu Zhao examines how the increasingly globalized icon of the superhero has resulted in a number of movie coproductions with the world's second largest film market, the People's Republic of China (PRC). Concentrating on *Iron Man 3*, which was partially funded by China's DMG Entertainment, Zhao notes how producers sought to link Tony Stark's techno-positivism with China's industrial and technological development. The chapter describes how some audiences in China greeted the film's purported Chinese content with skepticism, developing online responses that used moments from the film to critique the unintended consequences of China's seemingly unfettered progress.

As Malone noted in his contribution, many nations sought to offset the "corrupting" influence of U.S. popular culture following World War II. With their four-color fisticuffs and star-spangled optimism, comic book superheroes provoked this cultural imperialism anxiety. In his chapter Kevin Patrick provides a historical account of little-known Australian heroes created during 1940s and 1950s such as Captain Atom and the Crimson Comet. Patrick argues that the creation of these characters was indicative of Australia's tentative embrace of Cold War modernity and its complex relationship with Britain and the United States. Ultimately, like the other contributions to this part, this chapter provides a fuller understanding of how the American superhero became a transnational phenomenon.

Staying in Australia, the final interview in this part and the larger collection is with Ryan Griffen, the creator of the superhero TV show *Cleverman*, and its star Hunter Page-Lochard. Set in a near-future Australia, *Cleverman* draws on Aboriginal mythology to create a uniquely Australian superhero. Featuring a largely indigenous cast, the show was developed by Griffen as a direct response to the lack of diversity in superhero stories.

Using the broadly appealing framework of the superhero genre, *Cleverman* serves as a provocative allegory for the many social injustices faced by Australia's first nations people.

By confronting audiences with social issues they might otherwise avoid, *Cleverman* is a potent example of the civic imagination Jenkins explores in the collection's opening chapter. Indeed, *Cleverman* and this collection's diverse contributions testify to the many ways superheroes have been used to respond to social and industrial demands. As the superhero becomes more embedded in media, culture, and politics, acknowledging and studying this symbolic use becomes essential. Through an array of disciplinary perspectives and industry interviews, this collection helps us better understand the reach and power of the superhero symbol.

Notes

1 Christopher Nolan, dir., *Batman Begins* (Burbank, CA: Warner Bros. Pictures, 2005).

2 Peter Coogan, *Superhero: The Secret Origin of a Genre* (Austin, TX: MonkeyBrain Books, 2006), 59–60.

3 Charles Hatfield, Jeet Heer, and Kent Worcester, eds., *The Superhero Reader* (Jackson: University Press of Mississippi, 2013), 3.

4 Jason Dittmer, *Captain America and the Nationalist Superhero: Metaphors, Narratives, and Geopolitics* (Philadelphia: Temple University Press, 2013), 6.

5 Chris Gavaler, *On the Origin of Superheroes: From the Big Bang to Action Comics No. 1* (University of Iowa Press, 2015), 18.

6 Coogan, *Superhero*, 165; Gerard Jones, *Men of Tomorrow: Geeks, Gangsters, and the Birth of the Comic Book* (London: Arrow, 2006), 86; Chris Murray, *The British Superhero* (Jackson: University Press of Mississippi, 2017), 12.

7 John G. Cawelti, *Adventure, Mystery, and Romance: Formula Stories as Art and Popular Culture* (Chicago: University of Chicago Press, 1976), 40–41.

8 Robert C. Harvey, *The Art of the Comic Book: An Aesthetic History* (Jackson: University Press of Mississippi, 1996), 65.

9 Ramzi Fawaz, *The New Mutants: Superheroes and the Radical Imagination of American Comics* (New York: New York University Press, 2016), 6.

10 Ben Highmore, *Cityscapes: Cultural Readings in the Material and Symbolic City* (New York: Palgrave Macmillan, 2005), 124.

11 Jerry Siegel and Joe Shuster, *Action Comics* #1 (New York: DC Comics, June 1938).

12 Jules Feiffer, *The Great Comic Book Heroes* (1965; Seattle: Fantagraphics Books, 2003), 9.

13 Murray, *British Superhero*, 12.

14 Gavaler, *On the Origin of Superheroes*, 8.

15 Walter Ong, "The Comics and the Super State" (1945), in Hatfield, Heer, and Worcester, *Superhero Reader*, 35–36.
16 Gavaler, *On the Origin of Superheroes*, 3.
17 Murray, *British Superhero*, 12.
18 Richard Reynolds, *Super Heroes: A Modern Mythology* (Jackson: University Press of Mississippi, 1994), 12–16.
19 Coogan, *Superhero*, 30.
20 Andy Medhurst, "Batman, Deviance and Camp," in *The Many Lives of the Batman: Critical Approaches to a Superhero and His Media*, ed. Roberta E. Pearson and William Uricchio (New York: Routledge, 1991), 154.
21 Jill Lepore, *The Secret History of Wonder Woman* (Melbourne: Scribe, 2015), 187.
22 Alex Evans, "Superman *Is* the Faultline: Fissures in the Monomythic Man of Steel," in *Reframing 9/11: Film, Popular Culture and the "War on Terror,"* ed. Jeff Birkenstein, Anna Froula, and Karen Randell (New York: Continuum, 2010), 121.
23 Ong, "Comics and the Super State," 42.
24 Danny Fingeroth, *Superman on the Couch: What Superheroes Really Tell Us about Ourselves and Our Society* (New York: Continuum, 2005), 56.
25 Gavaler, *On the Origin of Superheroes*, 1.
26 Fawaz, *New Mutants*, 3.
27 Gloria Steinem, "Wonder Woman" (1972), in Hatfield, Heer, and Worcester, *Superhero Reader*, 208.
28 Abraham Riesman, "Why Cops and Soldiers Love the Punisher," *Vulture*, November 16, 2017, www.vulture.com/2017/11/marvel-punisher-police-military-fandom.html.
29 John Shelton Lawrence and Robert Jewett, *The Myth of the American Superhero* (Grand Rapids, MI: Eerdmans, 2002), 83.
30 Fredric Wertham, *Seduction of the Innocent* (London: Museum Press, 1955), 97.
31 Ong, "Comics and the Super State," 35.
32 Wertham, *Seduction of the Innocent*, 97.
33 Fredric Wertham's work has been criticized since the publication of *Seduction of the Innocent*. In 2010 the sources for Wertham's study were made widely available, with Carol Tilley arguing in her "Seducing the Innocent" that Wertham manipulated evidence. Carol L. Tilley, "Seducing the Innocent: Fredric Wertham and the Falsifications That Helped Condemn Comics," *Information and Culture: A Journal of History* 47, no. 4 (2012): 383–413.
34 Steinem, "Wonder Woman," 205–207.
35 Reynolds, *Super Heroes*, 14.
36 Lawrence and Jewett, *Myth of the American Superhero*, 46.
37 Reynolds, *Super Heroes*, 74.
38 Fawaz, *New Mutants*, 7.
39 Annika Hagley and Michael Harrison, "Fighting the Battles We Never Could: The Avengers and Post–September 11 American Political Identities," *PS: Political Science & Politics* 47, no. 1 (2014): 120.
40 Tom DeFalco, *Comics Creators on Fantastic Four* (London: Titan Books, 2005), 190.

41 Justine Toh, "The Tools and Toys of (the) War (on Terror): Consumer Desire, Military Fetish, and Regime Change in Batman Begins," in Birkenstein, Froula, and Randell, *Reframing 9/11*, 128.
42 Alan Sinfield, *Faultlines: Cultural Materialism and the Politics of Dissident Reading* (Berkeley: University of California Press, 1992), 47.
43 Will Brooker, *Hunting the Dark Knight: Twenty-First Century Batman* (London: I.B. Tauris, 2012), 209; Evans, "Superman *Is* the Faultline," 117–126.
44 Evans, "Superman *Is* the Faultline," 117–122.
45 Ian Gordon, *Superman: The Persistence of an American Icon* (New Brunswick, NJ: Rutgers University Press, 2017), 3.
46 In *The Comic Book Film Adaptation: Exploring Modern Hollywood's Leading Genre* (Jackson: University Press of Mississippi, 2015), I identify a number of the factors that gave rise to the "Golden Age of Comic Book Filmmaking" in the early 2000s, including cultural traumas, technological advancements, conglomerate ownership, and the rise of a generation of fans to positions of power in media industries. Many of these factors could be reapplied to the popularity of superheroes during that time.
47 Coogan, *Superhero*, 168.
48 Henry Jenkins, Sam Ford, and Joshua Green, *Spreadable Media: Creating Value and Meaning in a Networked Culture* (New York: New York University Press, 2013), 2.
49 In 1933 US comic strips, which had been popular since the turn of the century, finally made the move to their own format with the publication *Famous Funnies: A Carnival of Comics*—a repackaging of popular newspaper strips. The success of this format soon necessitated the production of original material, a demand that was met by collections such as the appropriately titled *New Comics* in 1935. Three years later *Action Comics* #1 was published with Superman as its cover star. Ron Goulart, *Comic Book Encyclopedia: The Ultimate Guide to Characters, Graphic Novels, Writers, and Artists in the Comic Book Universe* (New York: HarperEntertainment, 2004), 4.
50 Grant Morrison, *Supergods: Our World in the Age of the Superhero* (London: Jonathan Cape, 2011), 4.
51 Gavaler, *On the Origin of Superheroes*, 18.
52 Fingeroth, *Superman on the Couch*, 170.
53 Aldo J. Regalado, "Unbreakable and the Limits of Transgression," in *Film and Comic Books*, ed. Ian Gordon, Mark Jancovich, and Matthew P. McAllister (Jackson: University Press of Mississippi, 2007), 118.
54 Reynolds, *Super Heroes*, 8.
55 Randy Duncan and Matthew J. Smith, *The Power of Comics: History, Form, and Culture* (London: Continuum, 2009), 171.
56 Feiffer, *Great Comic Book Heroes*, 13.
57 Steinem, "Wonder Woman," 208.
58 Gavaler, *On the Origin of Superheroes*, 21.
59 Morrison, *Supergods*, 9; Umberto Eco, "The Myth of Superman," *Diacritics* 2, no. 1 (1972): 15.

60 Trina Robbins, "The Great Women Superheroes" (1996), in Hatfield, Heer, and Worcester, *Superhero Reader*, 54.
61 Carolyn Cocca, *Superwomen: Gender, Power, and Representation* (New York: Bloomsbury Academic, 2016), 6.
62 Cocca, *Superwomen*, 3.
63 Reynolds, *Super Heroes*, 50–52.
64 Coogan, *Superhero*, 110.
65 Morrison, *Supergods*, 375; Henry Jenkins, "Captain America Sheds His Mighty Tears," in *Terror, Culture, Politics: Rethinking 9/11*, ed. Daniel J. Sherman and Terry Nardin (Bloomington: Indiana University Press, 2006), 79.
66 Martin Pasko, *The DC Vault: A Museum-in-a-Book Featuring Rare Collectibles from the DC Universe* (Philadelphia: Running Press, 2008), 157.
67 James Mangold, dir., *Logan* (Century City, CA: Twentieth Century Fox, 2017).
68 Reynolds, *Super Heroes*, 74.
69 Dittmer, *Captain America and the Nationalist Superhero*, 10–11.

Bibliography

Batman Begins. Directed by Christopher Nolan. Warner Bros. Pictures, 2005.

Brooker, Will. *Hunting the Dark Knight: Twenty-First Century Batman*. London: I.B. Tauris, 2012.

Buck, Scott, writer. "Behold . . . the Inhumans." In *Inhumans*. ABC, September 29, 2017.

Burke, Liam. *The Comic Book Film Adaptation: Exploring Modern Hollywood's Leading Genre*. Jackson: University Press of Mississippi, 2015.

———. *Superhero Movies*. Harpenden: Pocket Essentials, 2008.

Cawelti, John G. *Adventure, Mystery, and Romance: Formula Stories as Art and Popular Culture*. Chicago: University of Chicago Press, 1976.

Cocca, Carolyn. *Superwomen: Gender, Power, and Representation*. New York: Bloomsbury Academic, 2016.

Coogan, Peter. *Superhero: The Secret Origin of a Genre*. Austin, TX: MonkeyBrain Books, 2006.

DeFalco, Tom. *Comics Creators on Fantastic Four*. London: Titan Books, 2005.

Dini, Paul, and Eduardo Risso. *Dark Night: A True Batman Story*. Burbank, CA: DC Comics, 2017.

Dittmer, Jason. *Captain America and the Nationalist Superhero: Metaphors, Narratives, and Geopolitics*. Philadelphia: Temple University Press, 2013.

Duncan, Randy, and Matthew J. Smith. *The Power of Comics: History, Form, and Culture*. London: Continuum, 2009.

Eco, Umberto. "The Myth of Superman." *Diacritics* 2, no. 1 (1972): 14–22.

Evans, Alex. "Superman *Is* the Faultline: Fissures in the Monomythic Man of Steel." In *Reframing 9/11: Film, Popular Culture and the "War on Terror,"* edited by Jeff Birkenstein, Anna Froula, and Karen Randell, 117–126. New York: Continuum, 2010.

Fawaz, Ramzi. *The New Mutants: Superheroes and the Radical Imagination of American Comics*. New York: New York University Press, 2016.

Feiffer, Jules. *The Great Comic Book Heroes*. 1965. Seattle: Fantagraphics Books, 2003.
Fingeroth, Danny. *Superman on the Couch: What Superheroes Really Tell Us about Ourselves and Our Society*. New York: Continuum, 2005.
Gavaler, Chris. *On the Origin of Superheroes: From the Big Bang to Action Comics No. 1*. Iowa City: University of Iowa Press, 2015.
Gordon, Ian. *Superman: The Persistence of an American Icon*. New Brunswick, NJ: Rutgers University Press, 2017.
Goulart, Ron. *Comic Book Encyclopedia: The Ultimate Guide to Characters, Graphic Novels, Writers, and Artists in the Comic Book Universe*. New York: HarperEntertainment, 2004.
Hagley, Annika, and Michael Harrison. "Fighting the Battles We Never Could: The Avengers and Post–September 11 American Political Identities." *PS: Political Science & Politics* 47, no. 1 (2014): 120–124.
Harvey, Robert C. *The Art of the Comic Book: An Aesthetic History*. Jackson: University Press of Mississippi, 1996.
Hatfield, Charles, Jeet Heer, and Kent Worcester, eds. *The Superhero Reader*. Jackson: University Press of Mississippi, 2013.
Highmore, Ben. *Cityscapes: Cultural Readings in the Material and Symbolic City*. New York: Palgrave Macmillan, 2005.
Jenkins, Henry. "Captain America Sheds His Mighty Tears." In *Terror, Culture, Politics: Rethinking 9/11*, edited by Daniel J. Sherman and Terry Nardin. Bloomington: Indiana University Press, 2006.
Jenkins, Henry, Sam Ford, and Joshua Green. *Spreadable Media: Creating Value and Meaning in a Networked Culture*. New York: New York University Press, 2013.
Jones, Gerard. *Men of Tomorrow: Geeks, Gangsters, and the Birth of the Comic Book*. London: Arrow, 2006.
Lawrence, John Shelton, and Robert Jewett. *The Myth of the American Superhero*. Grand Rapids, MI: Eerdmans, 2002.
Lepore, Jill. *The Secret History of Wonder Woman*. Melbourne: Scribe, 2015.
Logan. Directed by James Mangold. Twentieth Century Fox, 2017.
Medhurst, Andy. "Batman, Deviance and Camp." In *The Many Lives of the Batman: Critical Approaches to a Superhero and His Media*, edited by Roberta E. Pearson and William Uricchio, 149–163. New York: Routledge, 1991.
Morrison, Grant. *Supergods: Our World in the Age of the Superhero*. London: Jonathan Cape, 2011.
Murray, Chris. *The British Superhero*. Jackson: University Press of Mississippi, 2017.
Ong, Walter. "The Comics and the Super State." 1945. In *The Superhero Reader*, edited by Charles Hatfield, Jeet Heer, and Kent Worcester, 34–44. Jackson: University Press of Mississippi, 2013.
Pasko, Martin. *The DC Vault: A Museum-in-a-Book Featuring Rare Collectibles from the DC Universe*. Philadelphia: Running Press, 2008.
Regalado, Aldo J. "Unbreakable and the Limits of Transgression." In *Film and Comic Books*, edited by Ian Gordon, Mark Jancovich, and Matthew P. McAllister, 116–136. Jackson: University Press of Mississippi, 2007.

Reynolds, Richard. *Super Heroes: A Modern Mythology.* Jackson: University Press of Mississippi, 1994.

Riesman, Abraham. "Why Cops and Soldiers Love the Punisher." *Vulture*, November 16, 2017. www.vulture.com/2017/11/marvel-punisher-police-military-fandom.html.

Robbins, Trina. "The Great Women Superheroes." 1996. In *The Superhero Reader*, edited by Charles Hatfield, Jeet Heer, and Kent Worcester, 53–60. Jackson: University Press of Mississippi, 2013.

Sinfield, Alan. *Faultlines: Cultural Materialism and the Politics of Dissident Reading.* Berkeley: University of California Press, 1992.

Steinem, Gloria. "Wonder Woman." 1972. In *The Superhero Reader*, edited by Charles Hatfield, Jeet Heer, and Kent Worcester, 203–210. Jackson: University Press of Mississippi, 2013.

Tilley, Carol L. "Seducing the Innocent: Fredric Wertham and the Falsifications That Helped Condemn Comics." *Information and Culture: A Journal of History* 47, no. 4 (2012): 383–413.

Toh, Justine. "The Tools and Toys of (the) War (on Terror): Consumer Desire, Military Fetish, and Regime Change in Batman Begins." In *Reframing 9/11: Film, Popular Culture and the "War on Terror,"* edited by Jeff Birkenstein, Anna Froula, and Karen Randell, 127–140. New York: Continuum, 2010.

Wertham, Fredric. *Seduction of the Innocent.* London: Museum Press, 1955.

Part 1

Superheroes, Politics, and Civic Engagement

1

"What Else Can You Do with Them?"

Superheroes and the Civic Imagination

HENRY JENKINS

In his comic book *Astro City*, writer Kurt Busiek asks, "If a superhero can be such a powerful and effective metaphor for male adolescents, then what else can we do with them?"[1] Busiek rejects the premise that the superhero saga suffers from genre exhaustion,[2] proposing other allegories to explore: "Could you build a superhero story around the metaphor of female adolescence? Around mid-life crisis? Around the changes adults go through when they become parents? Sure, why not? And if a superhero could exemplify America's self-image at the dawn of World War II, could a superhero exemplify America's self-image during the less-confident 1970s? How about the emerging national identity of a newly independent African nation? Or a non-national culture, like the drug culture, or the 'greed-is-good' business culture of the go-go Eighties? Of course. If it can do one, it can do the others."[3] This chapter asks what superheroes can stand for, seeking to identify what political meanings they can carry in contemporary culture. Around the world, activists, struggling for immigrant rights, battling rape culture, questioning the police state, or condemning wealth inequality, deploy superhero iconography and mythology. Superheroes are now a vital element in our collective civic imaginations. Before they can change the world, civic agents need to imagine what a better world might look like: they need to believe that change is possible; they need to see themselves as capable of making change; and they need to develop a sense of solidarity with others whose experiences differ from their own. The civic imagination describes the shared mental constructs that inspire social and political change.

Recent research on participatory politics suggests that today's civic imagination is being fueled by popular culture, especially among youths.[4] Historically mass-media superheroes have been understood as speaking to an audience largely of white males from the West, but within this expanded space of the civic imagination, others also desire heroic narratives that they can share with their children. Busiek's question animates this chapter: what else can society do with superheroes?

Origin Story

In *On the Origin of Superheroes*, Chris Gavaler traces several cultural streams that merged around this popular icon, suggesting that the debates that shaped the superhero genre took root well before the launch of Superman and Batman in the 1930s.[5] Gavaler links superheroes to the mythology of Guy Fawkes within British radical politics. Gavaler also sees early signs of superhero mythology in the figure of Robin Hood, who directly inspires DC's Green Arrow character. This trajectory of rebel leader to superhero leads from swashbucklers—the Man in the Iron Mask and the Scarlet Pimpernel—through to the masked avenger figures—Zorro or the Shadow—in early pulp novels. Keep in mind that in the most repeated version of his origin story, Bruce Wayne's parents were killed coming out of a cinema screening of *The Mark of Zorro*, DC's acknowledgment of the influence of this earlier protagonist. Gavaler summarizes this trajectory: "When God retired from politics, Superman claimed the empty throne. . . . Even when the star-spangled warriors of World War II fought for democracy, they never represented it. Peel back Captain America's flag costume and you find Guy Fawkes and Oliver Cromwell, revolutionary radicals championing their own self-defined liberty. Today we call them terrorists."[6] With great power comes great responsibility, but who defines the superhero's responsibility and acceptable tactics?

The superhero genre allows a broad ethical range. The original Superman was described as "champion of the oppressed, the physical Marvel who has sworn to devote his existence to helping those in need."[7] In these early stories Superman is accountable only to his own conscience: he protects women against abusive spouses, mine workers against exploitative owners, and the public against corrupt politicians. By the time America entered World War II Superman was waging "a never ending fight for truth, justice, and the American way!"[8] Thomas Andrea tells us, "[As of this period] Superman no longer operates outside the law but is made an honorary policeman. . . . His struggle against evil becomes confined to the defense of private property and extermination of criminals; it is no longer a struggle against social injustice, and attempts to aid helpless and the oppressed."[9]

His powers are frightening as he is an alien with unknown loyalties, therefore Superman must become an establishment figure.

And it is in this role that he and other supermen in capes performed as professional mourners in the wake of 9/11.[10] In one poster from the period Superman stands before the burning towers, clutching a tattered Star-Spangled Banner as he weeps for America's lost innocence. As DC and Marvel artists confronted the traumas surrounding the terrorist attack, the publishers' most iconic figures—Superman in the case of DC, Captain America in the case of Marvel—were often depicted paying tribute to the first responders, these mighty men now subordinate to both local and national authorities. Strikingly, post-9/11 superheroes did not punch America's overseas enemies, as they might have during World War II, but stood against domestic intolerance, suggesting a different model for the American way. Questioning what it means to be an American hero ultimately led Superman to denounce his American citizenship and fight, at least briefly, on behalf of the United Nations.[11]

In *The New Mutants: Superheroes and the Radical Imagination of American Comics*, Ramzi Fawaz reclaims the radical potential of the superhero genre, suggesting the ways that the superheroes of the 1960s and 1970s embraced countercultural identity politics. Fawaz writes, "The superhero comic book expanded who got counted as legitimately human within liberal thought by valuing those bodies that were commonly excluded from liberal citizenship, including gender and sexual outlaws, racial minorities, and the disabled. . . . [It also suggested] a need for a political common ground that would bind people across multiple identities and loyalties."[12] As Fawaz notes, the X-Men and other Marvel mutants often operated as multifunctional metaphors for those who felt excluded from the American mainstream. But DC during this period also provided narratives where Green Arrow and Green Lantern, embodying different ideological perspectives, set off on the road together to better understand America during this tumultuous time. In one key story an angry black man confronts Green Lantern: "I've been reading about you. . . . How you work for the blue skins. . . . And how on a planet someplace you helped out the orange skins. . . . And you done considerable for the purple skins! Only there are skins you never bothered with. . . . The black skins! I want to know how come?!"[13] Recall that other iconic narrative about setting out in search of America—*Easy Rider* (1969)—that paid tribute to the superhero stories by nicknaming Peter Fonda's iconic red, white, and blue chopper "Captain America."

Superheroes have accumulated conflicting meanings since their conception, whether they were understood as championing the oppressed or performing policing functions. Their individualism created a tension within

Figure 1.1. Like other superheroes, Superman served as a professional mourner in the wake of 9/11. DC Comics.

a democratic culture, where they either must apply their own standards or accept subordination to the public will. Superheroes perform these duties most explicitly during times of national crisis, such as World War II or 9/11. Stories may expose these political tensions, or the narrative could mask them as the characters choose how to apply their power within particular tales.

#black(super)livesmatter

Truth: Red, White & Black suggests how far a major publisher might be willing to go toward offering a radical political vision for one of their anchor characters.[14] Comic book writers Robert Morales and Kyle Baker explore the ethical dimensions of the Tuskegee experiments through the lens of Captain America's supersoldier program, suggesting the first Captain was a black man whom the government experimented on without his consent. This Afrocentric comic paved the way for subsequent experimentation with diversifying Marvel's superheroes (for example, Afro-Hispanic Miles Morales as Spider-Man; African American woman Riri Williams as Iron Man; America Chavez, a Latina, as Miss America). David Gabriel, Marvel's vice-president of sales, sparked heated backlash in 2017 when he blamed a decline in their readership on these experiments in diversity: "What we heard was that people didn't want any more diversity."[15] Critics have attempted to debunk Gabriel's claim, suggesting that titles such as *Black Panther*, the top-selling Marvel title in 2016, and *Ms. Marvel*, another best-selling title, demonstrate a robust market for more inclusive stories reflecting today's social justice struggles.[16]

Marvel hired Ta-Nehisi Coates, an author noted for his scathing critiques of U.S. racial politics, to write and reimagine Black Panther. This new Black Panther comic was published at the same time the traditionally secondary character was due to be introduced to the Marvel Cinematic Universe in the 2016 film *Captain America: Civil War*. Coates described his boyhood experience reading comics in the projects: "I think if you are a young man in West Baltimore and all around you is a considerable amount of powerlessness, you probably have an attraction to people with power."[17] Coates sees superhero comics as a means of passing wisdom on to today's black youth, embodying new forms of black power. Consider the image Netflix offered of Luke Cage confronting the police on behalf of his community, wearing a bullet-hole-sprayed hoodie as gunfire bounces off his impenetrable chest. *The Root* suggested that Cage possesses "the power that many black parents wish they could bestow upon their children today."[18] Beyond this vivid image of a black man defending his community against organized crime, the series deployed intertextual references to a larger history of black culture (Ralph Ellison) and politics (Shirley Chisholm).

Also consider American Muslim Sana Amanat, a Marvel series editor. Echoing Fawaz's arguments about the progressive politics underlying the mutant metaphor, Amanat explains the significance of the X-Men: "These people were the little girl's safe space. . . . The X-Men embraced who they were. They owned it. . . . On Saturday mornings when she would race down to watch that show, she felt different, a little less alone because they filled a

Figure 1.2. The superhero TV series *Luke Cage* uses its bulletproof superhero to make references to black culture. Netflix, Marvel Studios, and ABC Studios.

need for her to see herself in the world outside."[19] Amanat was one of the primary architects behind *Ms. Marvel,* which placed a Pakistani American girl, Kamala Khan, in her own superhero narrative.

Superman's renouncing of his American citizenship raised questions for Dreamers, the undocumented immigrants fighting for citizenship and education rights in the United States.[20] If ever there was an illegal alien, it was Kal-El from the planet Krypton. His parents sent him away to a new world in search of a new life. He entered the country without authorization and was adopted by an Anglo family from Kansas who taught him to hide who he is and where he is from. Nevertheless, Superman embodies "truth, justice, and the American way," even as he wears proudly ethnic garb; his costume was made from the swaddling blanket his parents wrapped him in when they sent them forth. When exactly did Superman become an American citizen? Did Superman have a green card? Or was he like the Dreamers, living within a shadow economy, fearful of what happened when the "wrong" people (Lex Luther perhaps) discover his identity? Dreamers found Superman's saga a powerful tool for explaining their own experiences to those who might otherwise not be sympathetic to their arguments for citizenship.[21] As they did so, they connected back to a larger history of immigration politics, as Superman was created by Jerry Siegel and Joe Shuster, two second-generation Eastern European Jewish immigrants.

The Civic Imagination

These stories about Coates, Amanat, and the Dreamers suggest the powerful resources the superhero provides for the civic imagination as people of diverse backgrounds construct fantasies about having the power to change their world. For the book *By Any Media Necessary*, my research team interviewed more than two hundred young activists, seeking to better understand their political lives, documenting their deployment of popular culture references as shared political capital.[22] Many told us that the language of American politics was broken. It is too exclusive, speaking only to policy wonks, and too repulsive, as most political rhetoric served only partisan purposes. References to popular culture, including superheroes, allow young activists to wage politics on their own terms, using shared stories that speak to their generation. As we've sought to understand the ways these popular references work for them, my research team has consolidated insights from writers variously describing "the public imagination," "the radical imagination," "the political imagination," and "popular fantasy."

One starting point was Harry Potter author J. K. Rowling's graduation speech at Harvard in 2008. Rowling challenged Harvard students to use their voices in human rights advocacy: "We do not need magic to change the world. We carry all the power we need inside ourselves already. We have the power to imagine better."[23] We interpret Rowling as calling for her young fans to "imagine better" in two distinctive senses: to do a better job of imagining and to imagine a better world that embraces human rights and social justice. Rowling offers a point of entry into a larger conversation about deploying the imagination for social change.

Stephen Duncombe has long argued that the left needs to reassess its facts-oriented approach and find better ways to capture the public imagination: "We need utopian thinking because without it, we are constrained by the tyranny of the possible."[24] Often activists are overwhelmed by real-world conditions, urgent problems, and current limitations on social action. They lose track of what they are fighting for in the face of an all-too-vivid picture of the forces they are combatting. The civic imagination helps activists to move beyond current constraints, mapping the contours of a more just society. Utopia literally means "no place," so utopian fictions offer impossible fantasies, provocations for reflection and resources against which to measure the strengths and limits of contemporary society: "Utopia offers a goal to reach and a vision to be realized. For the reformer, it provides a compass point to determine which direction to move toward and a measuring stick to determine how far one has come. . . . Without a vision of an alternative future, we can only look backwards nostalgically to the past or unthinkingly maintain what we have."[25] Duncombe further discusses a potential blending of the roles of fan and activist: "Fandom provides a space to explore fabricated worlds that operate according to different norms than those we experience in our real lives. . . . This ability to imagine alternatives and build community, not coincidentally, is a basic prerequisite for political activism."[26]

Gianpaolo Baiocchi and Elizabeth A. Bennett offer a sociological account of how community organizers think about change making. These scholars' approach to the civic imagination is more literal minded than what presently concerns us, identifying what activists must believe to be true in order to choose their course of action. However, these ideas can be applied to our present concerns. For Baiocchi and Bennett, "The civic imagination consists of the ways in which people individually and collectively envision better political, social, and civic environments. Civic imaginations are people's theories of civic life. They are cognitive roadmaps, moral compasses, and guides that shape participation and motivate action."[27] These authors recognize numerous functions of the civic imagination: "identifying problems and solutions, envisioning better societies and environments, and developing a plan to make those visions of a better future into reality."[28]

How do we move from the fantastical narratives offered by superhero comics to this more plausible plan of action? When does "escapism" become a dead-end rather than a means of sidestepping obstacles and inspiring our will to overcome? The Institute for the Future stresses the shared rather than individualistic nature of what they call the public imagination: "Any democracy requires a thriving public imagination, in order to make visible, shareable and understandable to all people new ideas, new models, new potential policies. We cannot make any kind of collective decision unless the collective can understand what is at stake."[29] In their discussion of the radical imagination, Max Haiven and Alex Khasnabish take this idea a step further: "The radical imagination is not something that we have as individuals; it's something that we do and that we do together. . . . The radical imagination forces us to reimagine our relationship with those who suffer and to imagine the ways our own suffering or fortune is tied to the suffering or fortune of others. . . . The radical imagination takes us from sympathy to solidarity."[30]

Put all this together and we can identify some core functions of the civic imagination:

1. Before we can change the world, we have to imagine what a better world looks like.
2. We have to envision the process of social change that will help us achieve our goals.

3. We have to envision ourselves as agents capable of making political change.
4. We have to see ourselves as sharing interests with a larger collective, something like Benedict Anderson's "imagined community,"[31] though I prefer the more active form of an "imagining community."
5. We have to experience empathy or solidarity with people whose perspective and life experiences are different from our own.
6. For those who lack access to power and resources, there is a need to develop a compelling vision of freedom and equality before they are directly experienced.

Each of these functions of the civic imagination demands an imaginative leap beyond the literal, the plausible, and the realistic.

Why Superhero Stories Matter?

These functions often depend upon political storytelling, even as the stories told differ across generations. For example, there is a statue in the Smithsonian Institution of George Washington wearing a toga. This is not a literal representation of a specific moment in the life of the first American president. Rather the statue is suggestive of the ways the U.S. Founding Fathers saw the American Revolution as a rebirth of Athenian democracy. Such stories reflected the shared culture at America's emerging elite institutions of higher learning, such as William & Mary, Harvard, and Princeton, part of the liberal arts training of the white landed gentry who wrote the founding documents. Similarly, the American civil rights movements of the 1950s and 1960s spoke the shared language of the black church and, in particular, the narrative of Moses's exodus from Egypt.[32]

Contemporary popular culture provides young activists with similar resources for the civic imagination. Often these young activists share a common experience of growing up in digital culture, immersed in superhero comics and young adult novels, and they have their own visions of social change. Around the world committed activists paint themselves blue like the Na'vi in *Avatar* to rally for environmental justice, or fight against wealth inequality and totalitarianism by flashing the three-finger salute from *The Hunger Games* trilogy. Ironically, Hollywood's dominance over the global media marketplace results in a shared reservoir of cultural narratives and symbols that enable people in different contexts to make common causes. But popular Hollywood culture is not unique in offering resources for the civic imagination. Witness the number of protests deploying Bollywood dance as a form of collective expression,[33] or across Latin America, luchador wrestlers (such as SuperBario) are champions of the oppressed.[34]

A decade ago our dominant understanding of the relationship between activism and popular culture would have reflected the "culture jamming" paradigm.[35] Seeing no hope of inserting themselves into popular culture, activists sought to disrupt the flow, block the signal, and hijack signs. Culture jamming assumed that there was no underlying progressive politics encoded in the original stories. Yet as we have seen in the case of the superhero, popular culture often represents a site of contradiction. In one of the foundational texts of cultural studies as an academic discipline, cultural theorist Stuart Hall rejects, on the one hand, the idea that the people are simply dupes of a powerful media industry and, on the other, what he describes as the "heroic alternative," a "whole, authentic, autonomous" popular culture outside "cultural power and domination."[36] Rather, Hall writes, "Popular culture is one of the sites where this struggle for and against a culture of the powerful is engaged: it is also the stake to be won or lost in that struggle. It is the arena of consent and resistance."[37] If the culture jamming position emphasized the hegemonic function of popular culture, contemporary activists are choosing to struggle for control over popular fantasies that constitute shared passions and common experiences. They have no illusion that these stories unambiguously support their causes, but they appropriate these stories to speak truths that have been historically excluded from mass culture: for example, wealth inequality (as signified by *The Hunger Games* salute) or Palestinian rights (as embodied by the Na'vi-dressed protestors). They are asserting ownership over these popular fantasies as a fan might lay claim to a favorite cult media text. They are also seeking to tap into global awareness of these properties, even as they reshape their circulation to serve other purposes.

Because these forms of the civic imagination build on preexisting cultural materials, it matters whose narratives provide the raw materials. It matters that the world now has a Pakistani American Ms. Marvel, that Jessica Jones is confronting rape culture, and that police bullets can't stop Luke Cage. It matters that Superman represents an immigrant narrative and that Wonder Woman has a complex history of engagement with issues of female power and women's rights.[38] And it matters that the superhero figure traces its roots back to Robin Hood, Guy Fawkes, and other champions of the oppressed. But we also can't disentangle the superhero narrative from other associations, such as the fascist assumption that might makes right, the legacy of a universe dominated by strong white males, and the subordination of the superhero to the nation-state.

Let us focus a bit more on what resources superhero comics offer young activists. Superheroes are culturally pervasive, and thus handy for political deployment. They offer a shared vocabulary for talking about the relationship between personal and cultural identity. Different superheroes embody different conceptions of justice and the social good; these missions evolve over time in response to changed social and economic realities. The superhero genre deals directly with issues of power and its responsible use. Superheroes change the world and never doubt their capacity to make a difference. Superhero comics provide alternative conceptions of the social good and different models for how to make change. The superhero comic articulates who the good guys are and what they are fighting for, as well as who the bad guys are and what they are fighting against. This political drama unfolds in bright primary colors, often lacking the nuances necessary to foster real-world change—but such fantasies provoke debates about possible alternatives to the status quo.

Redrawing the Superhero

The superhero iconography and genre conventions surface across a range of different social movements. For example, LGBTQ activists have found that secret identity politics offer an ideal metaphor for the process of coming out of the closet. In a number of representative images the superhero rips open his shirt to reveal a rainbow flag or the marriage equality symbol. A feminist website depicts women with a diverse array of skin colors and body types all dressed like Amazons.[39] The news website Colorlines offers its readers advice on how to become a "racial transformer" with different social skills mapped as superpowers: "open mind," "alert eyes," "strong backbone," "loving heart," "rolled up sleeves," "outstretched arms," and "decoder ring."[40] Rebecca Cohen, an artist in the Black Lives Matter movement, depicts Bree Newsome, a thirty-year-old activist who climbed a flagpole outside the South Carolina Statehouse and lowered the Confederate flag, in Wonder Woman garb. As Cohen explained, "I liked the immediate associations invoked by the Wonder Woman iconography—the all-Americanness, the feminism, empowered women . . . I like the idea of blending that established character with this sort of real-life superhero."[41]

In this regard fans and activists are exploring similar ground. The American news media have been preoccupied with white male backlash against black stormtroopers and female Ghostbusters, giving the media industry every reason to go slow for fear of alienating their core base, but other fans have been modeling what diverse casting in superhero movies might look like by fan casting actors of color as the imagined protagonists in popular superhero franchises. For example, Korean American actor John Cho is imagined as Iron Man. The feminist Hawkeye project redrew and gender-swapped superhero comics art to challenge sexist representations of female characters.[42] The Black Kirby Project involves an Afrocentric/Afro-futurist reimagining of vintage comic book art with a portrait that places a

Magneto helmet on top of an image of Malcolm X, suggesting strong parallels in political tactics and orientation.[43] In these and many other ways, fans are asserting themselves into struggles over cultural representation and inclusion.

If superhero iconography allows both activists and fans to frame alternative conceptions of the heroes, the figure of the supervillain offers a way of representing what they are struggling against. American conservatives opposing health care reform created a controversial image of a white-faced Barack Obama modeled after the Heath Ledger version of the Joker. More recently, another meme captured Donald Trump's unpredictable antisocial impulses by associating him with the Jared Leto version of the Joker from *Suicide Squad.* Street artists around the world have depicted superheroes opposing Trump. In Mexico Birdman slaps Trump for his anti-immigrant positions, while Swedish artist Herr Nilsson pits a cock kicker against the self-proclaimed pussy grabber. These examples barely scratch the surface, as will be seen by anyone running a Google search for superhero activism.[44]

Performing the Superhero

Haiven and Khasnabish tell us, "The radical imagination is not just about thinking differently, it is about acting differently."[45] So what does it take to get someone to act upon their particular superhero fantasies in the real world? Consider the case of Vishaljit Singh, who has become a public figure through his opposition to New York City's "see something say something" campaign, which encourages subway riders to call police attention toward anyone they think looks suspicious, which, more often than not, means brown people carrying backpacks. Determined to take action against such prejudices, Singh dresses as a bearded and turban-wearing Captain America. He encourages subway riders to take a more critical perspective about what people like him contribute to U.S. society.[46]

Performing the superhero constitutes what Marie Dufrasne and Geoffroy Patriarche describe as a genre of participation. Genres of participation consist of "a type of communicative action recognized by a community . . . as appropriate to attain a specific objective."[47] The conventions surrounding a genre of participation address core questions about why, how, what, when, and where social action is to take place. These conventions provide participants with a "shared purpose and practice."[48] In cities across the world, inspired no doubt by such films as *Super* and *Kick-Ass*, everyday people are becoming superheroes, dressing in costumes, working in teams, and patrolling the streets to protect their communities from "evildoers." Brisbane's Captain Australia defines his mission as "acting as a deterrent by actively patrolling and thus intimidating the criminal element."[49] Many people assume that these real-world superheroes confuse fantasy with reality, but Captain Australia's mission statement makes clear that he sees his role as performative, a provocation to imagine a different social contract: "To inspire normal people to be better, by demonstrating a level of moral excellence that I hope will serve as an example to the people I meet. If all else fails, I can accept simply amusing or shocking people—having ordinary citizens lighten their hearts by amusement or surprise." Not unlike the Sikh Captain America, Captain Australia wants to challenge people to think more deeply about how to improve the world around them.

Real-world superheroes act on an implicit understanding of those conventions that comics scholar Peter Coogan says define the iconic figure—the mission, the powers, the persona, the alter ego, and the origin story.[50] They choose symbolically rich identities, assemble their own armored costumes, articulate their own social missions, and form alliances via social networking sites, all actions they believe will make their cities a better place to live. Being a real-life superhero represents one of the many ways that fantasies animating the civic imagination can be translated into civic action. If nothing else, they get people talking.

A Global Phenomenon

There would have been a time when being a superhero was distinctly American. But the recent wave of Marvel- and DC-related television series and feature films is reaching international audiences on an unprecedented scale, leading international communities to create superheroes who speak for their own experiences. For example, a video shot inside a Syrian refugee camp shows Batman as a playmate and friend for a young Arab boy, getting water from the well, kicking a football, strumming a musical instrument, and carrying the lad on his back.[51] In the video's closing moments Batman dissolves into a refugee father carrying his son on a long march into the future, as we watch smoke billowing from the neighboring village and hear the blades on a helicopter: "Unfortunately, for some, fantasy is the only way to escape reality. . . . Help the children of war." Here Batman represents a shared cultural reference point between Syrian refugees and their Western benefactors, a means of spreading a message that might otherwise not be heard.

The documentary *Girls Rising* shares an Egyptian girl's story in which her fantasies of becoming a superhero enable her to survive a sexual assault. As she tells her story to a local policeman, it remains ambiguous whether she fought back against her oppressor or simply endured what happened to her: "Yasmin has done what many marginalised fans do when engaging

Figure 1.3. In Pakistan, the Burka Avenger fights those who would disrupt the education of girls. Unicorn Black.

the superhero genre, they make space: placing themselves behind the masks and writing themselves into the stories."[52] This video is simply one among many projects across the developing worlds that use the superhero genre to educate people about women's issues. In Pakistan the Burka Avenger fights those who would disrupt the education of girls. Aaron Haroon Rashid, a producer of this highly successful animated series, explains that the burka is used here not as a sign of repression but as a form of empowerment: "She is using the burka to hide her identity like other superheroes. Since she is a woman, we could've dressed her up like Catwoman or Wonder Woman, but that wouldn't work in Pakistan."[53] This cartoon series has now been exported across the Islamic world.

Often what fuels the production of these regionally specific superhero narratives is the desire to offer more empowered fantasies for their own children. Naif Al-Mutawa, creator of *The 99*, an Islamic-themed superhero series, explains that his comics emerged from a sense of being underrepresented in popular culture: "In a world where Muslims were just evil characters, these offer another way of seeing Muslims. . . . The only way to combat the extremism is through arts and culture—appealing to the young through stories."[54] A similar impulse inspired Australia's Ryan Griffen, creator of the *Cleverman* television series, which borrows from multiple genres, including superhero sagas, to represent contemporary Aboriginal struggles: "We were playing Ninja Turtles and in that moment I certainly wished we had something cultural—something Aboriginal—you could cling to with as much excitement as he [his son] did with this. . . . I wanted a character that would empower him to take a stand and fight when presented with racism."[55] Jide Martin of Nigeria's Comic Republic tells a similar story: "There was a moral vacuum in the present generation, a general lack of icons. People stopped believing in the institutions of old. . . . That is why we are here. . . . To give us a place in this genre and to show the world what Africans are capable of. . . . To put more of our own stories out there by any means possible."[56]

In each of these instances the desire to pass along cultural values around empowerment and responsibility to their young leads local creative artists to create hybrid works that merge Western influences (in particular, superhero sagas) with regional mythologies. In each case the hope is that such stories will inspire their youth to question and change poor conditions in their lives while remaining proud of who they are and where they come from. Here again we see the civic imagination at work, with popular culture resources inspiring struggles for democracy and social justice. For women in the developing world such fantasies constitute the radical imagination since they are being asked to anticipate rights systematically denied them outside of fantasy. As these texts travel they also inspire solidarity between struggles taking place across the planet, helping us to see connections between groups that might otherwise be held apart.

Not Always Champions of the Oppressed

So far this chapter has focused on how localized superhero stories speak for the powerless and challenge institutionalized constraints on the dispossessed. Yet just as America's Superman sometimes gets subjugated to the U.S. military-industrial complex, superhero narratives also respond to powerful institutional imperatives. For example, the 2017 film *Guardians* appropriated the X-Men series into the service of Russian nationalism. During the Cold War a secret organization ran a supersoldier program, transforming representatives from various Soviet republics. For years the heroes hide their identity, but in hard times they reemerge to fight for their country. One superhero strongman has the face and physique of a bear, while another yields a hammer and sickle. Here the superhero narrative seeks to restore Russian national pride damaged since the collapse of the communist state. *Guardians* lacks the recognition of multiple kinds of mutant identity that Ramzi Fawaz found in the 1960s' comics. These mutants are not outcasts but supreme embodiments of the superiority of the Russian state—and they are totally subordinate to its needs. This example should be a reminder that there is nothing inherently progressive about the pathway that leads from popular culture to the civic imagination. Consider the eastern Kentucky police force, which put the Punisher's logo, along with the "Blue Lives Matter" slogan (a pro-police message), on their cop cars, only to confront public protest that this particular icon implies that they are seeking to use deadly force to control the neighborhood.[57]

Popular appropriations of ideologically contradictory narratives can yank these resources in various directions depending on our political goals and social context. We certainly should be concerned by the brute force and simple logics shaping some popular narratives. In the wrong hands the superhero can embody a more robust, more masculinized image of the American nation-state ready to enforce its will on the rest of the world. Media scholar Ethan Zuckerman asked us to consider the consequences of relying on simple popular stories as the basis for political change movements: "If we need simple narratives so people can amplify and spread them, are we forced to engage only with the simplest problems? Or to propose only the simplest of solutions?"[58] Haiven and Khasnabish's work on the radical imagination suggests some paths forward: "The radical imagination is not simply one thing; it emerges from tensions, arguments, debates and differences. . . . But if we work hard, and re-create intentional spaces, we can synchronize our imaginations, like the common beat of many different drums."[59]

Here fans might have something to teach activists: fans have spent decades debating how superheroes deploy their power to what purposes and under which ethical limits. Any given superhero at any moment may offer only a simple narrative with clear moral answers, but as that character has evolved with different authors and artists exploring different dimensions of his or her core contradictions, a more complex picture of this figure emerges. Fans often debate the morality of these popular fantasies and in the process ask core questions about what constitutes social good. Such debates constitute an intersubjective context from which the civic imagination grows, providing a shared vocabulary through which to debate alternative paths forward. Activists need to be similarly committed to working through the metaphors they deploy as they struggle for social change, looking at them from multiple angles, imagining alternative perspectives that might inform and inspire their struggles.

Notes

1 Kurt Busiek, "Introduction," in *Astro City: Life in the Big City* (New York: Image, 1999), 7–8.

2 See, for example, Henry Jenkins, "'Just Men in Tights': Rewriting Silver Age Comics in an Era of Multiplicity," in *The Contemporary Comic Book Superhero*, ed. Angela Ndalianis (London: Routledge, 2009), 16–43.

3 Busiek, "Introduction," 7–8.

4 See Henry Jenkins, Sangita Shresthova, Liana Gamber-Thompson, Neta Kligler-Vilenchik, and Arely M. Zimmerman, *By Any Media Necessary: The New Youth Activism* (New York: New York University Press, 2016).

5 Chris Gavaler, *On the Origin of Superheroes: From Big Bang to Action Comics #1* (Iowa City: University of Iowa Press, 2015).
6 Gavaler, *On the Origin of Superheroes*, 48.
7 Jerome Siegel and Joe Shuster, "Superman," in *Superman: From the Thirties to the Eighties*, ed. E. Nelson Birdwell (New York: Crown, 1983), 24.
8 Ian Gordon notes that the "American way" was added for the radio serial in August 1942. Ian Gordon, *Superman: The Persistence of an American Icon* (New Brunswick, NJ: Rutgers University Press, 2017), 43.
9 Thomas Andrea, "From Menace to Messiah: The History and Historicity of Superman," in *American Media and Mass Culture: Left Perspectives*, ed. Donald Lazere (Berkeley: University of California Press, 1987), 131.
10 See Henry Jenkins, "Captain America Sheds His Mighty Tears: Comics and September 11," in *Terror, Culture, Politics: Rethinking 9/11*, ed. Daniel J. Sherman and Terry Nardin (Indianapolis: Indiana University Press, 2006), 69–102.
11 See Jenkins et al., *By Any Media Necessary*.
12 Ramzi Fawaz, *The New Mutants: Superheroes and the Radical Imagination of American Comics* (New York: New York University Press, 2016), 13.
13 Dennis O'Neil and Neal Adams, "No Evil Shall Escape My Sight!," in *Green Lantern/Green Arrow* (New York: DC, 1970), 15.
14 Robert Morales and Kyle Baker, *Truth: Red, White & Black* (New York: Marvel, 2004).
15 Beth Elderkin, "Marvel VP of Sale Blames Women and Diversity on Sales Slump," *Io9*, April 1, 2017, http://io9.gizmodo.com/marvel-vp-blames-women-and-diversity-for-sales-slump-1793921500.
16 Kelly Kanayama, "Marvel Is Wrong about Diversity," *Nerdist*, 2017, http://nerdist.com/marvel-diversity-comics-david-gabriel-wrong/.
17 *Atlantic*, "Ta-Nehisi Coates on Writing Marvel's Black Panther," YouTube March 17, 2016, www.youtube.com/watch?v=OSTuUs-HVE8.
18 Lawrence Ware, "Luke Cage: A Bulletproof Black Man in the Black Lives Matter Era," *The Root*, 2016, www.theroot.com/luke-cage-a-bulletproof-black-man-in-the-black-lives-m-1790857029.
19 Sana Amanat for TedXTeen 2014, "Myths, Misfits and Masks," YouTube, March 17, 2014, www.youtube.com/watch?v=o9lev9739zQ.
20 See Jenkins et al., *By Any Media Necessary*.
21 For more information, see Henry Jenkins, Sangita Shresthova, Liana Gamber-Thompson, and Neta Kligler-Vilenchik, "Superpowers to the People! How Young Activists Are Tapping the Civic Imagination," in *Civic Media: Technology/Design/Practice*, ed. Eric Gordon and Paul Mihailidis (Cambridge, MA: MIT Press, 2016), 295–220.
22 See Jenkins et al., "Superpowers to the People!"
23 J. K. Rowling, "The Fringe Benefit of Failure and The Importance of the Imagination," *Harvard Magazine*, June 5, 2008, http://harvardmagazine.com/2008/06/the-fringe-benefits-failure-the-importance-imagination.
24 Stephen Duncombe, "Introduction: Open Utopia," *Open Utopia*, http://theopenutopia.org/full-text/introduction-open-utopia/.

25 Duncombe, "Introduction."

26 Stephen Duncombe, "Imagining No Place," *Transformative Works and Cultures* 10 (2012), http://journal.transformativeworks.org/index.php/twc/article/view/350/266.

27 Gianpaolo Baiocchi and Elizabeth A. Bennett, *The Civic Imagination: Making a Difference in American Political Life* (New York: Routledge, 2014), 55.

28 Baiocchi and Bennett, *Civic Imagination.*

29 Institute for the Future, "Framework: Public Imagination," Re:Constitutional Convention (2013), http://reconcondev.govfutures.org/?recent_works=frameworks8.

30 Max Haiven and Alex Khasnabish, "Lessons from Social Movements: Six Notes on the Radical Imagination," *Truthout*, August 9, 2014, www.truth-out.org/news/item/25411–lessons-from-social-movements-six-notes-on-the-radical-imagination.

31 Benedict Anderson, *Imagined Communities: Reflections on the Origin and Spread of Nationalism* (London: Verso, 1983).

32 Robin D. G. Kelley, *Freedom Dreams: The Black Radical Imagination* (Boston: Beacon, 2013).

33 Sangita Shresthova, "Dance It, Film It, Share It: Exploring Participatory Dance and Civic Potential," in *Artistic Citizenship: Artistry, Social Responsibility and Ethical Praxis*, ed. David Elliott, Marissa Silverman, and Wayne Bowman (Oxford: Oxford University Press, 2016), 146–162.

34 Heather Levi, "The Mask of the Luchador: Wrestling, Politics, and Identity in Mexico," in *Steel Chair to the Head: The Pleasure and Pain of Professional Wrestling*, ed. Nicholas Sammond (Durham, NC: Duke University Press, 2005), 96–131.

35 See, Marilyn DeLaure and Moritz Fink, eds., *Culture Jamming: Activism and the Art of Cultural Resistance* (New York: New York University Press, 2017).

36 Stuart Hall, "Notes on Deconstructing the Popular," in *Cultural Theory and Popular Culture: A Reader*, ed. John Storey (1981; London: Routledge, 2008), 512.

37 Stuart Hall, "Notes on Deconstructing the Popular," 518.

38 Matt Yockey, "Wonder Woman for a Day: Affect, Agency and Amazons," *Transformative Works and Cultures* 10 (2012).

39 Sarah Satrun and Catherine Satrun, "We Are All Wonder Woman," *Satrun Twins' Art Shop, Etsy* (2012), www.etsy.com/shop/SatrunTwinsArtShop.

40 Hatty Lee and Terry Keleher, "How to Be a Racial Justice Hero, on MLK Day and All Year Long," *Colorlines*, January 16, 2012, www.colorlines.com/content/how-be-racial-justice-hero-mlk-day-and-all-year-long.

41 Jared Goyette, "Artists Explain Why Bree Newsome Became an Internet Superhero after Taking down SC's Confederate Flag," *PRI*, June 30, 2015, www.pri.org/stories/2015-06-30/artists-explain-why-bree-newsome-became-internet-superhero-after-taking-down.

42 Suzanne Scott, "The Hawkeye Initiative: Pinning Down Transformative Feminisms in Comic Book Culture through Superhero Crossplay Fanart," *Cinema Journal* 55, no. 1 (Fall 2015): 150–160.

43 John Jennings and Stacey Robinson, *Black Kirby: In Search of the Motherboxx Connection* (San Francisco: Cedar Grove, 2013).
44 Lee Moran, "A Tremendous Roundup of Street Art Ridiculing Donald Trump," *Huffington Post*, February 2, 2017, www.huffingtonpost.com/entry/anti-trump-street-art_us_58820c24e4b070d8cad1ead2.
45 Haiven and Khasnabish, "Lessons from Social Movements."
46 Jenkins et al., ""Superpowers to the People!"
47 Marie Dufrasne and Geoffroy Patriarche, "Applying Genre Theory to Citizen Participation in Public Policy Making: Theoretical Perspectives on Participatory Genres," *Communication Management Quarterly* 21 (2011): 65.
48 Dufrasne and Patriarche, "Applying Genre Theory."
49 Nicholas Underhill, "Not So Black and White," *Outlook*, n.d., www.uow.edu.au/alumni/outlook/4/UOW222421.html.
50 Peter Coogan, "The Definition of a Superhero," in *Superhero: The Secret Origin of a Genre* (Austin, TX: MonkeyBrain Books, 2006), chap. 3.
51 Alyssa Braithwaite, "Batman Visits Syrian Refugee Camp in This Moving Video," *SBS*, July 14, 2016, www.sbs.com.au/topics/life/family/article/2016/07/12/batman-visits-syrian-refugee-camp-moving-video.
52 Ellen Kirkpatrick, "'I'm a Superhero': Seeing Ourselves in Unlikely Spaces," *In Media Res*, November 17, 2015, http://mediacommons.futureofthebook.org/imr/2015/11/17/im-superhero-seeing-ourselves-unlikely-spaces.
53 Associated Press, "Forget Wonder Woman and Supergirl, Meet Burka Avenger," *National*, July 28, 2013, www.thenational.ae/world/asia/forget-wonder-woman-and-supergirl-meet-burqa-avenger-1.291463?videoId=5587173110001.
54 Arifa Akbar, "The All-Islamic Superheroes: Muslim Children Love the 99 Comics but Hardliners Loathe Their Creator—Whose Trial for Heresy Is Looming," *Independent*, March 11, 2015, www.independent.co.uk/arts-entertainment/books/features/the-all-islamic-super-heroes-muslim-children-love-the-99-comics-but-hardliners-loathe-their-creator-10101891.html.
55 Underhill, "Not So Black and White."
56 David Barnett, "African Avengers: The Comic Book Creators Shaking Up the Superhero Genre," *Guardian*, February 3, 2016, www.theguardian.com/books/2016/feb/03/african-avengers-comic-books-superhero-diversity-nigeria.
57 Beth Elderkin, "Kentucky Police Remove Punisher Logo from Cop Cars after People Rightfully Point Out He's a Murderer," *Io9*, February 24, 2017, http://io9.gizmodo.com/kentucky-police-remove-punisher-logo-from-cop-cars-afte-1792720736.
58 Ethan Zuckerman, "Unpacking Kony 2012," *My Hearts in Accra* (2012), www.ethanzuckerman.com/blog/2012/03/08/unpacking-kony-2012/.
59 Haiven and Khasnabish, "Lessons from Social Movements."

Bibliography

Akbar, Arifa. "The All-Islamic Superheroes: Muslim Children Love the 99 Comics but Hardliners Loathe Their Creator—Whose Trial for Heresy Is Looming."

Independent, March 11, 2015. www.independent.co.uk/arts-entertainment/books/features/the-all-islamic-super-heroes-muslim-children-love-the-99-comics-but-hardliners-loathe-their-creator-10101891.html.

Amanat, Sana, for TedXTeen 2014. "Myths, Misfits and Masks." YouTube, March 17, 2014. www.youtube.com/watch?v=o9lev9739zQ.

Anderson, Benedict. *Imagined Communities: Reflections on the Origin and Spread of Nationalism*. London: Verso, 1983.

Andrea, Thomas. "From Menace to Messiah: The History and Historicity of Superman." In *American Media and Mass Culture: Left Perspectives*, edited by Donald Lazere, 124–138. Berkeley: University of California Press, 1987.

Associated Press. "Forget Wonder Woman and Supergirl, Meet Burka Avenger." *National*, July 28, 2013. www.thenational.ae/world/asia/forget-wonder-woman-and-supergirl-meet-burqa-avenger-1.291463?videoId=5587173110001.

Atlantic. "Ta-Nehisi Coates on Writing Marvel's Black Panther." YouTube, March 17, 2016. www.youtube.com/watch?v=OSTuUs-HVE8.

Baiocchi, Gianpaolo, and Elizabeth A. Bennett. *The Civic Imagination: Making a Difference in American Political Life*. New York: Routledge, 2014.

Barnett, David. "African Avengers: The Comic Book Creators Shaking Up the Superhero Genre." *Guardian*, February 3, 2016. www.theguardian.com/books/2016/feb/03/african-avengers-comic-books-superhero-diversity-nigeria.

Braithwaite, Alyssa. "Batman Visits Syrian Refugee Camp in This Moving Video." *SBS*, July 14, 2016. www.sbs.com.au/topics/life/family/article/2016/07/12/batman-visits-syrian-refugee-camp-moving-video.

Busiek, Kurt. "Introduction." In *Astro City: Life in the Big City*, 7–8. New York: Image, 1999.

Coogan, Peter. *Superhero: The Secret Origin of a Genre*. Austin, TX: MonkeyBrain Books, 2006.

DeLaure, Marilyn, and Moritz Fink, eds. *Culture Jamming: Activism and the Art of Cultural Resistance*. New York: New York University Press, 2017.

Dufrasne, Marie, and Geoffroy Patriarche. "Applying Genre Theory to Citizen Participation in Public Policy Making: Theoretical Perspectives on Participatory Genres." *Communication Management Quarterly* 21 (2011): 61–86.

Duncombe, Stephen. "Imagining No Place." *Transformative Works and Cultures* 10 (2012). http://journal.transformativeworks.org/index.php/twc/article/view/350/266.

———. "Introduction: Open Utopia." *Open Utopia*. http://theopenutopia.org/full-text/introduction-open-utopia/.

Elderkin, Beth. "Kentucky Police Remove Punisher Logo from Cop Cars after People Rightfully Point Out He's a Murderer." *Io9*, February 24, 2017. http://io9.gizmodo.com/riticiz-police-remove-punisher-logo-from-cop-cars-afte-1792720736.

———. "Marvel VP of Sale Blames Women and Diversity on Sales Slump." *Io9*, April 1, 2017. http://io9.gizmodo.com/marvel-vp-blames-women-and-diversity-for-sales-slump-1793921500.

Fawaz, Ramzi. *The New Mutants: Superheroes and the Radical Imagination of American Comics*. New York: New York University Press, 2016.

Gavaler, Chris Gavaler. *On the Origin of Superheroes: From Big Bang to Action Comics #1*. Iowa City: University of Iowa Press, 2015.

Gordon, Ian. *Superman: The Persistence of an American Icon*. New Brunswick, NJ: Rutgers University Press, 2017.

Goyette, Jared. "Artists Explain Why Bree Newsome Became an Internet Superhero after Taking down SC's Confederate Flag." *PRI*, June 30, 2015, www.pri.org/stories/2015-06-30/artists-explain-why-bree-newsome-became-internet-superhero-after-taking-down.

Haiven, Max, and Alex Khasnabish. "Lessons from Social Movements: Six Notes on the Radical Imagination." *Truthout*, August 9, 2014. www.truth-out.org/news/item/25411-lessons-from-social-movements-six-notes-on-the-radical-imagination.

Hall, Stuart. "Notes on Deconstructing the Popular." In *Cultural Theory and Popular Culture: A Reader*, edited by John Storey, 455–466. 1981. London: Routledge, 2008.

Institute for the Future. "Framework: Public Imagination." Re:Constitutional Convention, 2013. http://reconcondev.govfutures.org/?recent_works=frameworks8.

Jenkins, Henry. "Captain America Sheds His Mighty Tears: Comics and September 11." In *Terror, Culture, Politics: Rethinking 9/11*, edited by Daniel J. Sherman and Terry Nardin, 69–102. Bloomington: Indiana University Press, 2006.

———. "'Just Men in Tights': Rewriting Silver Age Comics in an Era of Multiplicity." In *The Contemporary Comic Book Superhero*, edited by Angela Ndalianis, 16–43. London: Routledge, 2009.

Jenkins, Henry, Sangita Shresthova, Liana Gamber-Thompson, and Neta Kligler-Vilenchik. "Superpowers to the People! How Young Activists Are Tapping the Civic Imagination." In *Civic Media: Technology/Design/Practice*, edited by Eric Gordon and Paul Mihailidis, 195–220. Cambridge, MA: MIT Press, 2016.

Jenkins, Henry, Sangita Shresthova, Liana Gamber-Thompson, Neta Kligler-Vilenchik, and Arely M. Zimmerman. *By Any Media Necessary: The New Youth Activism*. New York: New York University Press, 2016.

Jennings, John, and Stacey Robinson. *Black Kirby: In Search of the Motherboxx Connection*. San Francisco: Cedar Grove, 2013.

Kanayama, Kelly. "Marvel Is Wrong about Diversity." *Nerdist*, 2017. http://nerdist.com/marvel-diversity-comics-david-gabriel-wrong/.

Kelley, Robin D. G. *Freedom Dreams: The Black Radical Imagination*. Boston: Beacon, 2013.

Kirkpatrick, Ellen. "'I'm a Superhero': Seeing Ourselves in Unlikely Spaces." *In Media Res*, November 17, 2015. http://mediacommons.futureofthebook.org/imr/2015/11/17/im-superhero-seeing-ourselves-unlikely-spaces.

Lee, Hatty, and Terry Keleher. "How to Be a Racial Justice Hero, on MLK Day and All Year Long." *Colorlines*, January 16, 2012. www.colorlines.com/content/how-be-racial-justice-hero-mlk-day-and-all-year-long.

Levi, Heather. "The Mask of the Luchador: Wrestling, Politics, and Identity in Mexico." In *Steel Chair to the Head: The Pleasure and Pain of Professional Wrestling*, edited by Nicholas Sammond, 96–131. Durham, NC: Duke University Press, 2005.

Morales, Robert, and Kyle Baker. *Truth: Red, White & Black.* New York: Marvel, 2004.

Moran, Lee. "A Tremendous Roundup of Street Art Ridiculing Donald Trump." *Huffington Post*, February 2, 2017. www.huffingtonpost.com/entry/anti-trump-street-art_us_58820c24e4b070d8cad1ead2.

O'Neil, Dennis, and Neal Adams. "No Evil Shall Escape My Sight!" In *Green Lantern/Green Arrow.* New York: DC, 1970.

Rowling, J. K. "The Fringe Benefit of Failure and the Importance of the Imagination." *Harvard Magazine*, June 5, 2008. http://harvardmagazine.com/2008/06/the-fringe-benefits-failure-the-importance-imagination.

Satrun, Sarah, and Catherine Satrun. "We Are All Wonder Woman." *Satrun Twins' Art Shop, Etsy*, 2012. www.etsy.com/shop/SatrunTwinsArtShop.

Scott, Suzanne. "The Hawkeye Initiative: Pinning Down Transformative Feminisms in Comic Book Culture through Superhero Crossplay Fanart." *Cinema Journal* 55, no. 1 (Fall 2015): 150–160.

Shresthova, Sangita. "Dance It, Film It, Share It: Exploring Participatory Dance and Civic Potential." In *Artistic Citizenship: Artistry, Social Responsibility and Ethical Praxis*, edited by David Elliott, Marissa Silverman, and Wayne Bowman, 146–162. Oxford: Oxford University Press, 2016.

Siegel, Jerome, and Joe Shuster. "Superman." In *Superman: From the Thirties to the Eighties,* edited by E. Nelson Birdwell. New York: Crown, 1983.

Underhill, Nicholas. "Not So Black and White." *Outlook*, n.d. www.uow.edu.au/alumni/outlook/4/UOW222421.html.

Ware, Lawrence. "Luke Cage: A Bulletproof Black Man in the Black Lives Matter Era." *The Root*, 2016. www.theroot.com/luke-cage-a-bulletproof-black-man-in-the-black-lives-m-1790857029.

Yockey, Matt. "Wonder Woman for a Day: Affect, Agency and Amazons." *Transformative Works and Cultures* 10 (2012). http://journal.transformativeworks.org/index.php/twc/article/view/318.

Zuckerman, Ethan. "Unpacking Kony 2012." *My Heart's in Accra*, 2012. www.ethanzuckerman.com/blog/2012/03/08/unpacking-kony-2012/.

2

"America Is a Piece of Trash"

Captain America, Patriotism, Nationalism, and Fascism

NEAL CURTIS

The quote in the title of this chapter is a comment Captain America makes in the story "What If Captain America Were Revived Today" from *What If?* #44, published in 1984. The comic is part of an alternative universe series where creators explore worlds unconstrained by character and narrative continuity. This particular issue offered one of the starkest engagements with the right-wing politics that have been an ongoing feature in *Captain America* comics since their inception in 1941. In this alternative world America has become a fascist state under a white-supremacist senator who successfully runs for president, and with the help of a paramilitary police force securing the streets he encloses Harlem behind a giant wall. In the context of Donald Trump being elected president of the United States in 2016 on a ticket that many saw to be xenophobic, if not racist, against both Muslims and Mexicans, and whose presidency both displays authoritarian tendencies and appears to have emboldened white supremacist groups, *What If?* #44 has an added resonance when reading it today.[1] Further details of the story will be set out below as part of a brief evaluation of how *Captain America* comics have consistently engaged the subjects of patriotism, nationalism, and Nazism.

While *Captain America* comics have consistently taken these particular strains of politics as a theme, they are also broader cultural explorations of national identity. Here, I agree with Jason Dittmer, who has argued that superheroes are not simply a reflection of a preestablished identity but become "a discourse *through which* the world becomes understandable."[2] He goes on to argue that because "geopolitical orders are themselves stories," there is a strong relationship between political discourses of nationhood and cultural artifacts like comics. In other words, they inform and shape each other, or are "*co-constitutive*."[3] However, in the introduction to *Nation and Narration*, an earlier collection of essays on this same topic, Homi Bhabha had already problematized this relationship, arguing this narrative element in the conception of nationhood introduces an "ambivalence that haunts" it.[4] Different, often competing stories about a nation introduce a significant level of indeterminacy around the concept and have the potential to destabilize an idea that many hold to be true, certain, and incontrovertible (a topic that is very clearly demonstrated in Naja Later's chapter in this volume). Contrary to assumptions that Captain America (as the name implies) is a jingoistic defender of America at all costs, the character has been an ongoing exercise in this narrative ambivalence or "conceptual indeterminacy," with the comics often "wavering between vocabularies" of familiar comfort and alien disturbance.[5]

This chapter argues that the narrative ambivalence around the concepts of both nation and the patriotism it calls upon is played out in the comics through a form of doubling, as seen in Captain America's regular encounters with authoritarian right-wing patriots, or zealous versions of his own idealism. For Sigmund Freud (after Otto Rank), the double, in the form of a statue or an image, was originally used by the Ancient Egyptians as insurance against mortality, but in modern literary treatments the double has become "the uncanny harbinger of death."[6] Its appearance is also an image of criticism and censure, a sign that the protagonist is at fault or has lost their way. The double is consequently important in the production of the uncanny, a feeling that Freud notes is a simultaneous sense for the familiar *and* the unknown.[7] The uncanny nature of the double activates a sense for something that therefore belongs to "two set of ideas" that are not necessarily contradictory.[8] In the context of a comic like Captain America it can evoke the uncanny sense (and a warning) that a nation can be an agent of both inclusive protection *and* exclusionary violence, an avatar of justice *and* injustice.[9]

The chapter therefore contends that despite the enormous amount of ideological work that comics do in support of an ideal image of America, they also periodically evoke the uncanny sense that the familiar language of patriotism and nationalism hides a dark side by pitting Captain America against a variety of zealous doubles. Depending on the story being told, both nation and patriot can speak to ideas of hospitality and xenophobia, law and violence, freedom and authority, and these competing narratives permanently struggle over the meaning or status of national identity. In Captain America comics battles with characters like Bad Cap, Super Patriot, Nuke, and Anti-Cap have been used to engage in the debate over what it means to be American. Against those who would readily appropriate Captain America for more belligerent politics, liberal writers have regularly sought to tie Captain America and therefore the American nation to a narrative of openness, tolerance, and multiculturalism. More recently, however, and especially in response to the anabolic militarism of the Bush Doctrine and the War on Terror,[10] writers of Captain America have explicitly accentuated the uncanny ambivalence and indeterminacy of this national icon with interesting political effect. This became most pronounced with Trump's presidency, when Nick Spencer used retroactive continuity to tell a story in which Captain America was shown to have been a Hydra agent and therefore some variant of a fascist or a Nazi from the very beginning. This chapter contends that the "Hydra Cap" story was in keeping with the comic's use of uncanny doubles to criticize zealous nationalism, but also asks if this radical "othering" of the character ultimately bypasses the familiarity necessary to evoke the uncanny that haunts national identity and therefore failed as an attempt to engage with the rise of far-right sentiment in the United States, signaled by the triumph of Donald Trump.

Captain America, Nationalism, and Patriotism

Knowing what was happening in Europe, Joe Simon and Jack Kirby created Captain America in 1941 as a piece of propaganda designed to encourage America to enter World War II. The cover of the first issue is famous for its depiction of Captain America punching Hitler in the face. Over the years, and in an echo of Simon and Kirby's own heritage as sons of Jewish immigrants, Steve Rogers's origin has been updated to include his status as the son of Irish immigrants, tying the symbol of American authority and virtue to the powerful story of the nation's openness to those looking for a new home. Simon and Kirby were trying to counter the reluctance of an American public uncertain about entering another Word War, but what is less well recognized is that among the many reasons for U.S. isolationism was a small group of white nationalists who openly advocated support for German National Socialism and found the image of Captain America punching Hitler deeply offensive. As Joe Simon wrote in his memoir, "There was a substantial population of anti-war activists in the country. 'American Firsters' and other non-interventionist groups were well organized. Then there was the German American Bund. They were all over the place, heavily financed and effective in spewing their propaganda of hate; a fifth column of Americans following the Third Reich party line. . . . Our irreverent treatment of their Fuehrer infuriated them. We were inundated with a torrent of raging hate mail and vicious, obscene telephone calls. The theme was 'death to the Jews.'"[11] From the beginning, then, the comic has directly challenged Nazism and exclusionary nationalism and has been engaged in conflicting debates of what America is or should be.

The original run of the comic lasted eight years but could not survive the downturn in interest in superheroes after the war, and the comic stopped in 1949 with Captain America seemingly dying in action. The comic was brought back in 1953 when Captain America returned as a "Commie Smasher," but this was also a failure, lasting only three issues. He resurfaced again (literally floating to the surface of the ocean in a block of ice) in 1964 when writer Stan Lee brought him back in *The Avengers* #4. Although he was still a soldier, this era in comic book history is what Phillip Cunningham has called a "period of pacification" in which Captain America refrained from using guns and was written as a man out of time, a New Deal Democrat with a deep sense of social justice.[12]

The problem for Stan Lee's vision of Captain America, however, was that the comic often needed to do important ideological work in support of a belligerent foreign policy, and the patronym in his name regularly enabled crude, nationalistic appropriation. The ease with which Captain America could be used to support the idea of the United States as the world's savior is clearly set out in Robert Jewett and John Shelton Lawrence's argument about the "Captain America complex" and its role in valorizing the redemptive violence of U.S. foreign policy in the tireless battle of absolute good against absolute evil.[13] So as this third iteration of the character became popular, writers had to find ways to establish the liberal, social democratic, and internationalist credentials they had now set for the character. To do this writers regularly pitted Captain America against arch-nationalists in order to make it clear what the hero thought "America" meant.

The first of these was William Burnside, a man whose introduction was also used to explain the gap in the character's continuity, and the appearance of "Commie Smasher" Captain America in 1953. In *Captain America* #153 from 1972, Steve Englehart wrote a story in which a new Captain America appears while Steve Rogers is on vacation. He is highly aggressive and racist, referring to Sam Wilson as "boy," and believes the "pinko" Steve Rogers is weak, ineffectual, and ultimately unfit to carry on the fight against America's enemies,[14] whom we find out in Issue 155 are anyone who is not "*pure-blooded*" American.[15] When Steve Rogers stops him, it is explained that this Captain America is the zealous impostor from the 1950s who tried to fill in for the national icon presumed dead.

As a patriotic fan of Steve Rogers, Burnside used plastic surgery to make himself look and sound like Steve. Burnside also stole a batch of the super-soldier serum that turned the weakling Steve Rogers into the superhero Captain America. However, without the stabilizing supplement of the vita rays, the serum made him "demonstrably insane."[16] He was taken down and locked away in a special containment unit, only to be revived by a disgruntled "patriot" years later. While this is a brilliant way to explain the gap in Captain America's story, it is also a simple tale in which zealotry, violence, prejudice, and racist myths of belonging—which were integral to the racist southern strategy that contributed to Nixon's presidential win that year—are presented as alien to the proper construction of American nationhood and are shown to be the ideas of "costumed bigots."[17] However, the ambivalence around the idea of America was also explicitly recognized in this arc. In Issue 156 Steve Rogers reflects on how the fight was difficult: "I've never had to fight the *evil side* of my *own* nature."[18] Here, rather than Burnside simply being dismissed as a madman, he is acknowledged as a dangerous element of national identity, prone as it is to discriminatory and exclusionary violence. By saying Bad Cap is actually part of himself, Captain America articulates the dangers presented by the different vocabularies available to national narrators.

In another story collected under the title *The Captain*, first published in 1987, Steve Rogers goes before a Senate commission, and concerned that he is being asked to act as a government stooge to fight America's proxy wars, he resigns. This is one of numerous times Captain America makes an explicit distinction between the government that made him and the nation he now represents. This is also an excellent example of the way Marvel constantly negotiates competing visions of America (a topic taken up by Henry Jenkins in his chapter that opens this part). On the one hand Steve Rogers expresses "left" politics in his concern that he will be sent to fight with the Contras, a right-wing group sponsored by the United States to overthrow the democratically elected government in Nicaragua, while on the other hand his criticism of the commission rests clearly with a general suspicion of government on the political "right."

While this is taking place a terrorist known as Warhead threatens to detonate a nuclear device if the government does not go to war on "somebody" in order to strengthen "national character."[19] As Steve Rogers weighs up how he should act as a national symbol, in steps John Walker, also known as Super-Patriot, to take down Warhead and quickly assume the vacant Captain America title. Despite his passionate love for his country, Walker's dogmatic belief in America first, together with his own involvement with a campaign of retribution and revenge, shows him to be wholly unfit to assume the mantle. His own superhero name is also a loaded one within the Marvel universe due to an earlier version of the character appearing in *Nick Fury: Agent of S.H.I.E.L.D.* #13 in 1969. This first version was an explicit racist who promoted anti-immigration policies and then met his end when he tripped himself up on an American flag he had draped himself in and fell to his death. The message is simple: this advocate of exclusionary nationhood is undone by the Star-Spangled Banner that we are asked to believe represents the exact opposite. Here the faultline of ambivalence and indeterminacy in the narration of nationhood is exposed. The uncanny sense for the alien within the familiar is allowed to briefly do its work before the indeterminacy over whether the American nation should be inclusive or exclusive is swiftly covered over in a story promoting multicultural tolerance.

Another character used to differentiate Captain America's patriotism from obedient and zealous nationalism is Frank Simpson, also known as Nuke. Introduced by Frank Miller in *Daredevil* #232 in 1986, Nuke is an enhanced soldier and Vietnam veteran, pharmaceutically controlled to do the dirty work of U.S. covert operations around the world. He is also a mercenary for hire, and as such he represents the dark underbelly of American foreign policy. Nuke is despised by Captain America because he literally "wears the flag,"[20] having had it tattooed onto his face. The need for another such character reemerged almost thirty years later in 2004, when the "with us or against us" politics of the War on Terror made a "liberal" Captain America seemingly irrelevant. In a story titled "Two Americas," which directly plays on the ambivalence this chapter is highlighting, Christopher Priest introduced Anti-Cap, a new Captain America minus the "messy scruples or moral centre."[21] He was engineered to obey orders without question. He was a "true believer," but his power, combined with his lack of conscience and a war that, like Vietnam, once again undermined America's moral authority, collapsed the distinction between hero and villain, and he, too, needed to be taken down. When Captain America does defeat Anti-Cap, the imposter's shield is broken to symbolize his illegitimacy. This is also an important moment of ideological recuperation showing that blind obedience is not the American way.

Captain America, Authoritarianism, and Fascism

In light of Captain America's regular criticism of the dangers of crude nationalism and his defense of liberal multiculturalism, we might refer to him as a "constitutional patriot," a phrase referring to "the idea that political attachment ought to center on the norms, the values, and, more directly the procedures of a liberal democratic constitution."[22] The greatest threat to which is, of course, Nazism. Since Steve Rogers's return as Captain America in 1964, the comic has regularly set out the slippery slope from love of country to exclusionary identity and persecutory violence. Two of the most important stories in this regard have both involved Bad Cap, aka William Burnside. In *Captain America* #231 we are introduced to a neo-Nazi group known as National Force, whose leader, the Grand Director, is campaigning for strong national identity through racial purity and the purging of all nonwhites. We later find out the Grand Director is Burnside, whose own brand of zealous nationalism makes him susceptible to brainwashing by the Nazi Dr. Faustus. However, by Issue 234 Captain America also comes under the spell of the fascist psychiatrist. In this issue, we see Captain America chanting the name of National Force and brandishing his shield now adorned with a swastika. Fortunately, he is freed from the spell in a fight with Daredevil where the leaked contents of a barrel of oil act as a paint stripper to reveal his true shield beneath the fake. This vision of the star in place of the swastika is enough to break his trance and undermine this particular bid by Faustus to seize power.

In *What If?* #44, the comic with which this chapter opened, Burnside is not brainwashed by a Nazi. Rather, his zealous, discriminatory nationalism leads to the formation of a fascist government in the United States. In this timeline Steve Rogers was not found in 1964, and a disgruntled "patriot" releases Burnside from his 1950s' slumber to reinvigorate the nation. At this time Quentin Harderman, head of the Committee to Regain America's Principles (CRAP), has thrown his support behind the white supremacist Norman Chadwick's campaign for Senate. After being successfully elected, Chadwick sets up the Federal Jobs Bureau and introduces an anti-immigration identity card that discriminates against minority groups looking for work. Riots ensue and martial law is introduced, policed by a new paramilitary security force that assumes the name Sentinels of Liberty—the volunteer group Captain America asked the nation's young people to join in his very first issue in 1941.

As unrest grows the Harlem Wall is erected and a ghetto created behind it. When Steve Rogers is finally discovered he joins the resistance behind the wall, and he eventually confronts Bad Cap at a rally for Norman Chadwick's America First Party. After the obligatory Cap on Cap battle, the victorious Steve Rogers makes yet another great Captain America speech. Possibly the most radical, he declares, "*America is nothing!* Without its ideals—its commitment to the freedom of all men, America is a piece of *trash!*"[23] Then he explains why he volunteered to fight the fascism that has now taken hold in 1980s America: "I fought Adolf Hitler not because America was great but because it was fragile!"[24] Interpreting this statement in relation to the subject at hand, it might be said that America is fragile, despite the seeming power of its institutions, precisely because America is only an idea supported by stories and different narrators have the power to bring about very different realities. In all of these stories it is not just that America is positioned in opposition to Nazism: the use of other patriotic figures, and the susceptibility of Captain America himself to its influence, is used to show the dangerous proximity of authoritarian and discriminatory

Figure 2.1. In *Captain America* vol. 1 #234 the hero falls under the influence of a fascist psychiatrist (New York: Marvel, June 1979).

violence to both patriotism and nationalism. Here political work is done by producing a sense of uncanny disturbance through the use of the double. With Captain America fighting recognizable and familiar yet also alien versions of himself, we are shown how the nature of the country he represents is very much dependent upon the way the story of national identity is told. Enter Hydra Cap.

Hydra Cap

After being stripped of his youth and powers by Arnim Zola, a Nazi biochemist originally created by Jack Kirby in 1977, Steve Rogers is unable to continue as Captain America, and he hands over the title and his shield to Sam Wilson, his partner since 1969. This was a significant moment as Sam Wilson is black and the first ever specifically African American superhero (Black Panther was African). When Nick Spencer took over writing duties for the comic in 2015, Sam Wilson's history as a onetime crook turned Harlem social worker, who had strongly identified with militant civil rights activism, made him the perfect candidate to confront the racism and xenophobia that defined Donald Trump's rise to prominence during the Republican primaries in that year.

In Spencer's first issue, and immediately working on the "conceptual indeterminacy" of what America means, Sam Wilson directly challenged Trump's agenda by traveling to the U.S.-Mexico border where he rescued illegal immigrants from a group of right-wing vigilantes known as the Sons of the Serpent, who were kidnapping Mexicans for use in genetic experiments. The story immediately grabbed the attention of Fox News, which claimed Captain America's new enemy was conservatism. Spencer continued to write a politically topical comic focused primarily on the issues motivating the Black Lives Matter movement, but it soon became apparent he always planned the return of Steve Rogers to the role of Captain America to celebrate the seventy-fifth anniversary of the character. A black Captain America was an important component in Marvel's shift toward better representation in its comics, and Sam Wilson as the *only* Captain America at this time would have been a powerful message about race in America, but Marvel decided this wasn't going to be the story.

Steve Rogers's return was dramatic. In the first issue of the new story it was revealed he was a Hydra agent and had been all along. There was a mixed reaction, with those thinking his alignment with Marvel's fascist terror organization made no sense in relation to the character's lifelong fight against Nazism and that it was an insult to his two Jewish creators. However, it can also be interpreted as a radical political statement. With the rise of Trump on an "anti-establishment" ticket that was also racist and xenophobic and was clearly giving legitimacy to white supremacism and America's own proto-Nazi movement that goes by the name of the "alt-right," Spencer seemed to be saying that fascism was no longer an alien threat emanating from some foreign field: it was now in the heart of the American body politic. The question remained, though, once Trump became president, how effective was this realignment of Captain America as a means of challenging Trump's deeply chauvinistic brand of nationalism?

When Captain America said "Hail Hydra" at a time when Trump's white nationalist agenda carried an echo of the Grand Director's call for America to be purged, the comic was continuing a long tradition of engagement with far-right politics. However, by the time the story was expanded into the *Secret Empire* event where Hydra took over the U.S. government, the threat had become alien and foreign, rather than domestic and familiar. As Captain America teamed up with a range of old foes, including Baron Zemo, Arnim Zola, Madame Hydra, Gorgon, Kraken, Dr. Faustus, and the Hive, to bring the Hydra plan for a perfect world to fruition, Captain America was now very clearly in the category of villain. The familiarity required for the conceptual ambivalence around nation to do its political work was undone. With the character no longer recognizable as Captain America, this story about the proximity of fascism to a particular brand of nationalism could easily be rejected. Unlike previous stories in which Captain America's doubles had all retained some aspect of a commitment to country that readers might identify with, Hydra Cap was too remote. However, this is not to say that over the course of the story arc there have not been moments of serious political critique. In the one-shot titled *The Oath*, for example, Captain America takes over as head of S.H.I.E.L.D. and under emergency powers assumes executive control of the country, thereby becoming the de facto president. The issue was on the shelves in the same week as Trump's inauguration, with the swearing in of the fascist Captain America made to look uncannily like the real inauguration that had just taken place in Washington.

The story also became problematic in that people were having debates about whether Hydra were actually fascists, nitpicking over terminology in the same way members of the "alt-right" were trying to pretend they were not fascists. This was compounded by some disturbing iconography in the book itself where Captain America raises aloft Thor's hammer—a popular symbol in the contemporary fascist's manual—and declares himself to be worthy. The character was also rendered unrecognizable by the decision to have Captain America execute his longtime friend and onetime sidekick Rick Jones, which pushed the character deep into the category of supervillain. In these moments Captain America is so radically "othered" that the political critique traditionally based on an uncanny proximity to a recognizable

Figure 2.2. In the one-shot comic *Civil War II: The Oath*, Captain America takes over as head of S.H.I.E.L.D. (New York: Marvel, March 2017).

identity loses its efficacy. The stories involving Bad Cap, Super-Patriot, Nuke, and Anti-Cap all articulate some avowed element of the American national myth, no matter how perverse. Hydra Cap, by contrast, has no connection to American nationalism but is committed to a global authoritarian cult that predates even the Nazism Captain America was created to fight against. To return to the ambivalence that provides powerful political critique we need to conclude with another story.

Uncanny Patriotism

It has traditionally been the case that Captain America comics have articulated the uncanny only as a means of overcoming conceptual indeterminacy and ideologically tying the meaning of America to a particular vision of pacific, liberal cosmopolitanism. This has been the function of all of Captain America's doubles presented so far. Since the beginning of the War on Terror, however, writers have increasingly evoked the uncanny in order to allow it to do significant disruptive work. This can be seen in John Rieber's Captain America comic *The New Deal*, first published in 2002, that asks readers to think about the destruction of "9/11" through the lens of what allied bombers did to the civilians of Dresden in 1945. Perhaps the most disturbing story, however, is *Ultimate Captain America*, a four-part story by Jason Aaron set in the alternative (now defunct) Marvel Ultimate universe. Taking his lead from the portrayal of a more belligerent and jingoistic Captain America presented by Mark Millar in his Ultimate universe take on the Avengers from 2002, Aaron depicts a Captain America that is far more nationalistic and whose patriotism is unreflexive and uncritical, unlike the Captain America of the regular universe. This different status is shown through Ultimate Cap using guns and killing people. Since his period of "pacification," one of the most powerful ideological disavowals in the comic has been Captain America's refusal to use a gun. Instead, in a perverse articulation of the ambivalence around this subject, it is his young sidekick Bucky who acts as his proxy and does the killing, allowing Cap to retain his veneer of using only defensive, nonlethal violence. In *Ultimate Captain America*, however, this duplicity is done away with, but the violence of American foreign policy becomes the explicit subject of the book.

In an echo of *Apocalypse Now*, Captain America is sent to track down Nuke, who has gone AWOL. In doing so Captain America is captured by Nuke's group of newfound disciples, and the comic opens at the point where Nuke is about to execute him. On his knees, Captain America starts to pray. Nuke hears this and mocks him, deciding to leave him in his cell for a further five minutes to see if Cap's God will come and rescue him. In the meantime the book takes us on a lengthy flashback through Nuke's own

Figure 2.3. Nuke introduces Ultimate Captain America to enhanced interrogation, *Ultimate Comics Captain America* #3 (New York: Marvel, May 2011).

epiphany, and his attempts to reeducate Captain America about the true horrors of American foreign policy. In the Ultimate universe Captain America was lost for much longer. To fill him in Nuke starts to teach him about Nixon and U.S. actions in Indonesia, Laos, and Chile, among other places. In Issue 3 we also see Nuke treating Cap to some of the latest U.S. techniques for enhanced interrogation. Nearly drowning him, Nuke says, "Just keep telling yourself waterboarding isn't torture." At the end of the issue, when the story returns to Cap in his cell, we hear him pray and ask God to show him "there was a purpose" to his mission. At which point he suddenly sees "the hand of God."[25]

In Issue 4 we see that a cobra has appeared in the corner of the cell. Cap kills the snake and uses its poison to overpower Nuke, who after a lengthy fight is taken down by Cap and later arrested by S.H.I.E.L.D. At home and relaxing with fellow Avenger Hawkeye, Cap explains, "God wasn't done with me . . . so he sent down a miracle and saved me." To which Hawkeye reminds Cap that snakes "aren't really the big guy's style,"[26] and asks him how he knows it was not the work of the devil. The book then closes with Cap denying the possibility that his mission is anything but good, and having refused to hear the truth from Nuke, he sits next to the now restrained prisoner and reads him the Bible, seemingly to reaffirm his and America's manifest destiny.

This is an unnerving Captain America story precisely because it so brilliantly evokes the uncanny ambivalence, indeterminacy, and wavering vocabularies that haunt the narration of nation, and it does this precisely because it uses the double to make the familiar strange. Not only do Captain America and Nuke mirror each other as images of patriotic soldiers; this mirroring also inverts both characters as they have been used in earlier stories. Most importantly, however, the indeterminacy of the snake as "hand of God" or "work of the Devil" exemplifies the ambivalence in our acts of narration, or the multiple ways we can represent events and ideas in the stories we choose to tell. Captain America's struggle to protect the nation will, of course, go on, and it does so at a time when the struggle over how to tell the story of that nation seems especially acute.

Notes

1 Jonathan Blitzer, "A Scholar of Fascism Sees a Lot That's Familiar with Trump," *New Yorker*, November 4, 2016; Ameer Hasan Loggins, "Is It Wrong to Call Trump a White Supremacist?," *Guardian*, September 16, 2017.

2 Jason Dittmer, *Captain America and the Nationalist Superhero: Metaphors, Narratives, and Geopolitics* (Philadelphia: Temple University Press, 2013), 2, emphasis original.

3 Dittmer, *Captain America and the Nationalist Superhero*, 124–125, emphasis original.
4 Homi Bhabha, *Nation and Narration* (London: Routledge, 1990), 1.
5 Bhabha, *Nation and Narration*, 2.
6 Sigmund Freud, *Art and Literature* (London: Penguin, 1990), 356.
7 Freud, *Art and Literature*, 346.
8 Freud, *Art and Literature*, 345.
9 This also applies to processes, rituals, institutions, and media that are both commemorative and forgetful at the same time. So often the story a nation celebrates is written at the expense of all manner of actions and events it would rather deny, repress, censor, or erase.
10 The War on Terror was defined by a set of policies known as the Bush Doctrine that promoted preemptive strikes, the legitimation of torture, imprisonment without trial, and a permanent state of emergency.
11 Joe Simon and Jim Simon, *The Comic Book Makers* (Middlesex, NJ: Vanguard Productions, 2003), 45.
12 Phillip L. Cunningham, "Stevie's Got a Gun: Captain America and His Problematic Use of Lethal Force," in *Captain America and the Struggle of the Superhero: Critical Essays*, ed. Robert G. Weiner (Jefferson, NC: McFarland, 2009), 183.
13 See Robert Jewett and John Shelton Lawrence, *Captain America and the Crusade Against Evil: The Dilemma of Zealous Nationalism* (Grand Rapids, MI: Eerdmans, 2003).
14 Steve Englehart and Sal Buscema, *Captain America and the Falcon*, #153 (New York: Marvel, September 1972), n.p.
15 Steve Englehart and Sal Buscema, *Captain America and the Falcon*, #155 (New York: Marvel, November 1972), n.p.
16 Steve Englehart and Sal Buscema, *Captain America and the Falcon*, #156 (New York: Marvel, December 1972), n.p.
17 Englehart and Buscema, *Captain America* #156, n.p.
18 Englehart and Buscema, *Captain America* #156, n.p.
19 Mark Gruenwald, Tom Morgan, et al., *Captain America* #332 (New York: Marvel, August 1987), n.p.
20 Frank Miller and David Mazzucchelli, *Daredevil* #233 (New York: Marvel, August 1986), n.p.
21 Christopher Priest and Bart Sears, *Captain America and The Falcon* #4 (New York: Marvel, June 2004), n.p.
22 Jan-Werner Müller and Kim Lane Scheppele, "Constitutional Patriotism: An Introduction," *International Journal of Constitutional Law* 6, no. 1 (January 2008): 67.
23 Peter Gillis and Sal Buscema, *What If?* #44 (New York: Marvel, 1984), n.p.
24 Gillis and Buscema, *What If?*, n.p.
25 Jason Aaron and Ron Garney, *Ultimate Captain America* #3 (New York: Marvel, May 2011), n.p.
26 Jason Aaron and Ron Garney, *Ultimate Captain America* #4 (New York: Marvel, June 2011), n.p.

Bibliography

Aaron, Jason, and Ron Garney. *Ultimate Captain America* #3. New York: Marvel, 2011.

———. *Ultimate Captain America* #4. New York: Marvel, June 2011.

Bhabha, Homi. *Nation and Narration*. London: Routledge, 1990.

Blitzer, Jonathan. "A Scholar of Fascism Sees a Lot That's Familiar with Trump." *New Yorker*, November 4, 2016.

Cunningham, Phillip. L. "Stevie's Got a Gun: Captain America and His Problematic Use of Lethal Force." In *Captain America and the Struggle of the Superhero: Critical Essays*, edited by R. G. Weiner, 176–189. Jefferson, NC: McFarland, 2009.

Dittmer, Jason. *Captain America and the Nationalist Superhero: Metaphors, Narratives, and Geopolitics*. Philadelphia: Temple University Press, 2013.

Englehart, Steve, and Sal Buscema. *Captain America & The Falcon* #153. New York: Marvel, September 1972.

———. *Captain America & The Falcon* #155. New York: Marvel, November 1972.

———. *Captain America & The Falcon* #156. New York: Marvel, December 1972.

Freud, Sigmund. *Art and Literature*. London: Penguin, 1990.

Gillis, Peter, and Sal Buscema. *What If?* #44. New York: Marvel, 1984.

Gruenwald, Mark, Tom Morgan, et al. *Captain America* #332. New York: Marvel, August 1987.

Jewett, Robert, and John Shelton Lawrence. *Captain America and the Crusade Against Evil: The Dilemma of Zealous Nationalism*. Grand Rapids, MI: Eerdmans, 2003.

Loggins, Ameer Hasan. "Is It Wrong to Call Trump a White Supremacist?" *Guardian*, September 16, 2017.

Miller, Frank, and David Mazzucchelli. *Daredevil* #233. New York: Marvel, August 1986.

Müller, Jan-Werner, and Kim L. Scheppele. "Constitutional Patriotism: An Introduction." *International Journal of Constitutional Law* 6, no. 1 (January 2008): 67–71.

Priest, Christopher, and Bart Sears. *Captain America and The Falcon* #4. New York: Marvel, June 2004.

Simon, Joe, and Jim Simon. *The Comic Book Makers*. Middlesex, NJ: Vanguard Productions, 2003.

3

"This Land Is Mine!"

Understanding the Function of Supervillains

JASON BAINBRIDGE

Almost as soon as he announced that he was running for president of the United States, many popular commentators drew comparisons between Donald Trump and Superman supervillain Lex Luthor.[1] The parallels between the two men seemed clear: both were billionaire industrialists in the 1980s who helped shape the skylines of their respective cities, New York and Metropolis, and both have named every subsidiary of their company after themselves. The cover of Lex Luthor's 1989 *Unauthorized Biography* deliberately homages the cover of Trump's 1987 book *Trump: The Art of the Deal*,[2] and, most significantly, both men became U.S. president, with Luthor assuming office in 2000 in the DC Universe and Trump following suit in the real world in 2017. Furthermore, both men successfully ran presidential campaigns on platforms of paranoia and xenophobia directed at "aliens." Late-show mashups of Trump interviews with footage of an animated Lex Luthor,[3] a dramatically underlit photo of Trump standing over an illuminated globe of the world,[4] and even photos taken beside then-campaign director Kellyanne Conway dressed as Supergirl at a Heroes and Villains costume party only invited further comparisons with Luthor.[5]

Of course it is somewhat easier to imagine a supervillain than a superhero actually existing in our world. Superheroes are invariably defined via superhuman powers, like Superman, Thor, and Wonder Woman; superior abilities, like Batman or Green Arrow; augmentation via technology, like Iron Man and Green Lantern; or genetic change, like Spider-Man, Hulk, or the X-Men. In contrast supervillains can, in addition to these categories, be considered supervillains simply by virtue of their superior intellect, such as Lex Luthor; madness, as with the Joker; or vast resources such as committed followers and/or technology, like Doctor Doom. These aspects are much easier to replicate in our world. This creates a strange dichotomy in the James Bond franchise, for example, where few would argue that Bond himself is a superhero while Blofeld, Doctor No, Oddjob, Jaws, and any number of his antagonists could reasonably qualify as supervillains. This is because while the superhero acts as a screen that we (not unproblematically) project our hopes onto, the supervillain acts as a mirror for our worst traits, matched with an innate belief in their own superiority and the force of will to impose that superiority onto everyone else.

At first glance superheroes and supervillains would seem to embody the simple binaries of law scholar Robert Cover's *nomos*, a normative universe where we "constantly create and maintain a world of right and wrong, of lawful and unlawful, of valid and void."[6] As Cover describes it, "Understood in the context of narratives that give it meaning, law becomes not merely a system of rules to be observed, but a world in which we live."[7] Here the rules of law and legal institutions form only a small part of this larger normative universe. It is only within "narratives that locate [law] and give it meaning,"[8] like superhero and supervillain narratives, that we can truly understand the role of law and how it is articulated, for it is these stories that act as "a bridge linking a concept of reality to an imagined alternative."[9]

With the expansion of superhero narratives from comic books to multiple television series and feature films,[10] superheroes have arguably reached beyond their comic book origins to become the exemplars of justice in popular culture more generally, "a bridge linking a concept of reality to an imagined alternative" that attract enormous audiences and are capable of being regularly mobilized in various forms of civic engagement, as Henry Jenkins demonstrates in his chapter opening this part. Supervillains, on the other hand, have been largely dismissed as little more than foils for superheroes or used as shorthand analogies for arrogant presidents. But a closer analysis of the supervillain reveals their importance in these Coverian definitions of *nomos* and points to a more nuanced reading of their narrative functioning. This chapter focuses on three villains who regularly top polls for most popular villains and who serve as primary antagonists for their respective heroes—Lex Luthor, the Joker, and Doctor Doom.[11] While there are many different types of villains, these prolific examples provide an understanding of the classic archetype that more recent versions have continued and challenged. Through these case studies of male supervillainy, the narrative, thematic, and political function of the supervillain in superhero narratives is explored.[12]

What Is a Supervillain?

Sherlock writer Steven Moffat refers to Sherlock Holmes's nemesis Moriarty as the "original supervillain," claiming that "all who follow are in his shadow."[13] While the notion of Moriarty being the "first" supervillain can be disputed, the character does clearly articulate several of the defining traits of supervillainy for our purposes in this chapter.

First, and as I have argued elsewhere, just as the superhero offers a critique of our society, most often speaking to the deficiencies in our legal system and the widening gap between law and justice, supervillains too speak to societal fears by individualizing them.[14] As Moffat explains, for Arthur Conan Doyle Moriarty was a supervillain precisely because he represented what *The Strand*'s Victorian readers most feared: organized crime, as Moriarty was in part based on the real-world underworld figure Jonathan Wild.[15] In the same way *Sherlock*'s modern-day Moriarty (Andrew Scott) represents society's present-day fears around online hate groups and suicide bombers. Second, as revealed in his sole canonical appearance in December 1893, and expanded upon in any number of media adaptations over the years, Moriarty is a disruptor of the social order, inverting it in favor of a criminal empire with himself at the center.[16] He thereby becomes someone to whom the hero must respond. Third, Moriarty sees himself as innately superior, and he has the will to make others accept that by whatever means are at his disposal. This chapter argues that by exploring each of these three traits in turn we can better understand the overall function of the supervillain.

Individualizing Societal Fears

Given the long history of comic books, supervillains have the capacity to embody any number of societal fears directly relevant to their readerships across changing eras. Lex Luthor is perhaps the best example of this fluidity, representing the fear of the foreigner in his first appearance as a flame-haired despot in 1940;[17] the fear of science throughout the 1950s and 1960s; the fear of the criminal genius in the 1970s, particularly in the real-estate-obsessed Gene Hackman depiction of Luthor in 1978's *Superman: The Movie*;[18] the fear of technology in the early 1980s, when both Luthor and fellow Superman villain Brainiac were "upgraded" to be more robotic in appearance;[19] the fear of big business in the mid-1980s and 1990s; the fear of unfettered governmental power in the early 2000s; and the fear of subversive groups in the 2010s, when, following his presidency, Luthor went to ground.[20] In this way the supervillain's personification of fear serves to make sense of what could otherwise be considered meaningless suffering.[21]

Even villains who have remained largely consistent in their portrayal show some capacity for reflecting the anxieties of different eras. For example, scholar Mark Edward DiPaolo refers to the Joker as a "sane, Moriarty figure" when he first appeared in the 1930s, when he was presented as a typical crime boss with a bad complexion.[22] This persona is very different from the psychopath of 1988's graphic novel *The Killing Joke* and other comics of the present day, even if the character looks the same.[23] Similarly, we can find points in the Joker's timeline when he individualizes specific fears, be they fears around contaminated consumer products, illustrated in his toxins and "Laughing Fish" storyline; the Middle East, as seen during the 1988–1989 *A Death in the Family* storyline; or random acts of terrorism, as in Christopher Nolan's 2008 *The Dark Knight* film.[24]

The Joker also points to another societal fear projected onto almost all supervillains: the idea that crime itself may be motiveless, that people may simply *be* evil without justification or reason. Interestingly, the comic industry itself engendered this fear. In an attempt to regulate content following widespread criticism of comics due to the medium's links to juvenile delinquency, the Comics Code Authority (CCA) Code for Editorial Matter was imposed on comic publications, commencing on October 26, 1954. As Jack Fennell explains,

> General Standards Part A of the Code mandated that "Crimes shall never be presented in such a way as to create sympathy for the criminal, to promote distrust of the forces of law and justice, or to inspire others with a desire to imitate crimes." Thus, no comics were allowed to "present the unique details and methods" of any crime. . . . In short, crime was to be unpleasant and nasty, never profitable, objectively "evil," and totally unattractive, and there would be no logical reason given why anyone *should* engage in criminal activity. Crime simply happened because it was what "bad people" did; "evil" was the compulsion to engage in crime for its own sake. The CCA code thus indirectly mandated that ne'er-do-wells be depicted as sub-humans whose criminal nature is overt, visible, and therefore containable.[25]

What this meant was that the supervillain not only represented a societal fear but also *became* that fear, making it something that could be punched in the face, "solved," or otherwise addressed without looking for underlying causes or wider social responsibility. For the greater part of the code's duration, the superheroes' mission was therefore reduced to "fixing" their city, or "protecting" their society by foiling supervillains issue by issue, month by month, rather than addressing the broader societal concerns that had created these villains. This also resulted, again in Fennell's words, in the creation of a supervillain that was "much more unnerving than any real-world criminal, because he has no intelligible motive."[26] As the code was relaxed and eventually abolished, origins and justifications were retrofitted (retconned) to explain a supervillain's motivations. For example, Luthor gained abusive parents. However, these later revisions were to justify motivations that for two decades had been crafted as being self-evident, and, as Fennell concludes, where no motivation was retconned, as in the case of the Joker, it set the stage for "the emergence of truly psychotic villains."[27] This leads Fennell to conclude that the "much-reviled CCA Code" did produce one long-standing legacy: the creation of "a whole new class of *Homines Sacri* [defined below] by exaggerating that which already existed, and creating hate-figures without any real-world equivalent."[28] In this way the evil of supervillains became self-evident, legitimating the action of the superhero while simultaneously speaking to readers' fears that we can never truly understand evil, that we will never know why people do bad things, that we can never explain some actions or behaviors.

Disrupting the Social Order

Developing this idea of the supervillain *legitimating* the superhero brings us to a broader consideration of the overarching relationship between the superhero and the supervillain. Again, while it may be tempting to dismiss the supervillain as just someone whom the hero needs to fight, it was actually the supervillain who begot the superhero. Superman began as a bald, mad supervillain who could read and control minds in Shuster and Siegel's 1933 fanzine story "The Reign of the Superman," before being transformed into the handsome, costumed superhero Superman who first appeared in *Action Comics* #1.[29] This idea of supervillains *creating* superheroes even becomes a trope, particularly in various media adaptations. Both Tim Burton's 1989 *Batman* (Michael Keaton) and television's 1990 *The Flash* (John Wesley Shipp), for example, were created through the actions of supervillains leading to two memorable "you created me" / "no, you created *me*" exchanges.[30]

Superheroes are, with a few exceptions such as *The Authority*, essentially passive characters in that they do not try to change the status quo and act only when a supervillain threatens that status quo.[31] The supervillain is therefore the agent of change, the disruptor, active where the superhero is merely reactive. As Richard Reynolds puts it, it is "the villains [who] are concerned with change and the heroes with the maintenance of the status quo."[32] Fighting the villain therefore becomes the superheroes' way of justifying their own existence by constantly reframing their struggle in binaries between "the good and the bad, the just and the unjust," rather than simply one individual operating outside the law fighting another individual who also operates outside the law.[33]

Given that comics are serial, open-ended narratives, the narrative engine of most superhero comics is melodrama wherein the supervillain is driven by a morally negative motivation such as ambition, avarice, anger, jealousy, psychosis, or lust, and thus propels the narrative by assaulting the passively displayed superhero.[34] This usually commences with the "primal scene" caused by the supervillain that places the superhero's virtue and happy existence in peril, by enacting upon either the superhero directly or the society of which the superhero is a part.[35] The fact that the superhero does not act first but is instead acted upon maintains the melodramatic conceit that we are all innocent victims of a hostile world.[36] This is accentuated by focusing on the protagonist's suffering whereby virtue undergoes unbearable trials and endures extremes of pain and anguish to ultimately emerge successful at the narrative's end.[37]

The supervillain's individualization of societal fears makes the villain, as Tim Peters describes, a "something" rather than a "nothing" that can be confronted and fought by the superhero. "Without Evil to fight," writes Peters, "the superheroes would have little to do. Thus the superhero's role in restoring the social order—in fulfilling justice—can never actually be completely fulfilled. At the same point in time this also reflects the way the law itself is inherently tied to crime and acts of Evil."[38] In this way, the superhero becomes dependent upon the supervillain's disruption, the crisis that the supervillain creates. The supervillain thereby justifies both the superhero's existence and the reactions, which are framed as the pursuit of justice that the superhero must take to stop the villain.

These reactions by the superhero harken back to Foucauldian descriptions of "disciplinary societies," which are involved in marking the body through violence, as opposed to the Deleuzian conception of "societies of control" that are systematized and juridical.[39] Importantly, most supervillains are already branded in some way, be they scarred like Doctor Doom, disfigured like the Joker, or even prematurely bald like Luthor. As Fennell describes it, "This pre-emptive, almost karmic punishment makes the precise nature of their criminality physically manifest. . . . The implied logic of the motif is that these characters are innately *deserving* of this kind of punishment . . . the deformity of the villain emphasizes the hero's right to punish them."[40]

Being Superior

The supervillain individualizes societal fears, and by introducing those fears back into society the villain disrupts the social order, creating a crisis that the superhero must respond to and resolve. But there is a third element at play here, one that enables both the superhero and the supervillain to act: the failure of the state. It is the failure of the state to deal with the supervillain, through either inaction or inability, that implicitly validates the superhero's intervention. This failure is the point at which the juridical state processes (incorporating both due process and the accused's right to trial) give way to the disciplinary. As Chris Gavaler describes it, "In comics, government exists to be disrespected"[41]—and that disrespect comes from both the superhero *and* the supervillain. While the superhero seeks to maintain the "status quo," it is a status quo predicated on the consistent failure of the state and its institutions—failures that create a space (and a need) in which the superhero operates (and responds to).

Superhero and supervillain alike are linked by the prefix "super," which illustrates a shared sense of being superior to those around them. Scholars like Richard Reynolds and Audrey Anton suggest that rather than referring to "super powers," "super" here implies an element of relationality that works through contrast and comparison. "Being super entails being *superior*," says Anton. "In this sense, the state of being super seems to include a relative element: the relation to that which is not super."[42]

This word "superior" has also been used in the comic industry, but largely only in relation to supervillains. For example, Marvel Comics has developed a "superior" brand in titles such as *The Superior Spider-Man* and *The Superior Iron Man*, where the lead hero is taken over by a villain or displays out-of-character villainous tendencies.[43] Similarly, supervillains such as Lex Luthor and Doctor Doom frequently justify their actions in terms of being innately superior to others and thereby more deserving to rule society.

Superiority is also literalized in media adaptations. Special effects are reserved for the superheroes, and also occasionally superpowered supervillains, to make real the superiority of these characters. "You'll believe a man can fly," promised 1978's *Superman: The Movie* thanks to a flying rig, a blue screen, and front projection, while today Bruce Banner (Mark Ruffalo) becomes a CGI/motion capture character as the Hulk in 2012's *The Avengers*.[44] Lacking many of the superpowers of the superheroes, supervillains' superiority is more often literalized through celebrity casting. This trend commenced with the use of big-name stars in the 1960s Batman television series playing the rogues' gallery, such as Vincent Price, Liberace, Cesar Romero, and Burgess Meredith, through to top-billed celebrities in Warner Bros.' DC Films, such as Gene Hackman / Lex Luthor, Jack Nicholson / Joker, and Michelle Pfeiffer / Catwoman.[45] More recently, Marvel Studios has mobilized well-respected celebrity actors for their film villains too, with Michael Keaton as the Vulture, Josh Brolin as Thanos, and Cate Blanchett as Hela.

Of course the idea that "super" is a contraction of "superiority" is nothing new. The superhero and supervillain's ideological ancestor is Friedrich

Nietzsche's *Übermensch. Übermensch* translates as "superior man," with Nietzsche arguing that those who are "super" achieve such a status naturally and independently of those who are not.[46] According to Nietzsche, superiority here refers to *potential*, which is a set of uncommon skills and abilities that includes talent, strength, and "a will to power." It is this "will to power" that is most important for Nietzsche, as this is the life force that compels someone to control, to dominate, and to exploit resources. The prefix "super" in both the superhero and the supervillain is therefore more than just a label: it is a statement announcing how each category understands their relationship with the broader society, directed at both the citizenry *and* the state—and by extension the laws, rules, and policies that the state enacts. That is, superheroes and supervillains proclaim that they are *superior* to them.

Supervillains and the State

The state's power is largely based in its decision-making ability, as articulated through laws and policies. Legal theorist Carl Schmitt identifies this link between decision making and domination as *sovereign power*, referring back to a sovereign being the divine ruler of premodern societies. For Schmitt, "it is the essence of sovereignty both to decide the exception and to make the decisions appropriate to that exception,"[47] in other words, to decide what constitutes a crisis and when to operate in an exceptional relationship to the law to best respond to that crisis. However, sometimes the crisis becomes too much for the state to deal with, and here, where the state fails, it can be considered to have abdicated its sovereign power. Such abdication allows sovereign power to be appropriated by someone else, someone who views themselves as naturally superior and therefore deserving of that power: the superhero and the supervillain.

"Before the dawn of election ballots," writes Gavaler, "Kings represented God and so ruled by divine right. When God retired from politics, supermen claimed the empty throne. . . . They may act alongside law enforcement, even accepting deputy status if it makes officials feel better, but they're free agents."[48] Therefore, the superhero claims sovereign power by virtue of their legitimated role as protector of the people, stepping in to identify and declare a *state of exception*, which outlines the crisis requiring justice to be done. It is at this point, in the absence of governmental action, that the superhero appropriates the sovereign decision from the state, operating as the sovereign in the space of law suspended. As Schmitt describes it, such a person holds the sovereign power and therefore stands "outside the normally valid legal system" but "nevertheless belongs to it."[49] By way of example, many superheroes, such as Superman and Spider-Man, have often existed *outside* the society they defend, engaging with that society only through their secret identities Clark Kent and Peter Parker. However, as the state recognizes that only the superhero can deal with this crisis, the state will occasionally seek to co-opt or deputize the superhero to restore order. This is a recurrent feature of the Marvel Cinematic Universe, for example, with the films often exploring the dynamic between superheroic freedom and state control.

The supervillain appropriates sovereign power in order to overturn or invert the present legal system in favor of a new *grundnorm* (the order or rule that forms the basis for a legal system) that best serves their vision for how society should operate.[50] On the largest scale, this is true of supervillains like Doctor Doom or Luthor who seek to "take over the world" because they believe they would do a better job of running it. However, it is also true of villains like the Joker, who seeks to replace order with chaos, and supervillains like Vulture or Captain Cold, who think that they're entitled to a better life by virtue of their perceived superiority through artificial wings or a freeze ray and rob banks to give themselves the resources they need to make that better life a reality.[51] Whatever their intention, each and every supervillain represents an assault on sovereign power. As Michel Foucault notes, "Besides its immediate victim, the crime attacks the sovereign," both personally, in the sense that crime defies the sovereign's will, and physically, for as law constitutes "the force of the prince," so too does crime constitute "an opposed force that does violence to his royal agency."[52]

The *super* prefix in superhero and supervillain stands for *superiority*, so that the superhero and supervillain become competing wills to power, competing claims to be the sovereign. The "super" encapsulates both categories' belief that they have the right to take sovereign power from the state and to declare a state of exception in relation to law and due process. The struggle that exists between superheroes and supervillains, and is played out across comics, films, and TV shows, is this contestation for sovereign power by virtue of superior abilities, consistently presented against the backdrop of a state that has failed to intervene, to control crime, and to deliver justice to its citizenry. Neal Curtis's chapter in this collection, "'America Is a Piece of Trash': Captain America, Patriotism, Nationalism, and Fascism," offers another example of this ideological struggle, but framed by ideas of nationhood.

Giorgio Agamben challenges the logic of sovereignty that Schmitt outlines. He identifies such a legal position "to be outside and yet belong . . . [as] the topological structure of *the state of emergency*."[53] For Agamben, "what is specific for the state of emergency is not so much the confusion of powers as it is the isolation of the force of law from the law itself. The state of emergency defines a regime of the law within which the norm is valid but cannot be applied (since it has no force), and where acts that do not have the value of law acquire the force of law."[54] Applying these ideas to our own concerns, both the superhero and the supervillain challenge the state's right to articulate that sovereign power, and the superhero can neither execute law as authority nor transgress it as the supervillain does, but rather "inexecutes" the law within this state of exception.[55] That is, they act with the force of law even though they are not legal officers for (following Pindar) "the sovereign is the point of indistinction . . . the threshold on which violence passes over into law and law passes over into violence."[56] Or as comic book scholar Mervi Miettinen describes it, "In order to protect society, the superhero must inevitably become a criminal, a vigilante who breaks the law in order to save it when the more traditional state powers fail to do so."[57]

Once again, then, we return to this notion that it is the supervillain who legitimates the superhero. Both superhero and supervillain operate outside the law, but the superhero is *alegal*, operating in an area where no specific laws exist to make their acts expressly illegal, whereas the supervillain is *illegal*, acting in contravention of existing laws, but whose abilities place them outside of societal norms and thus beyond the reach of conventional law. The superhero is thus capable of recuperation (deputization) by the state, while the supervillain is truly irrecoverable.

Outside society, physically marked in some way so their evil becomes self-evident, the supervillain most clearly resembles Agamben's figure of the *homo sacer*. This is someone who has been expunged from society, living a "life that does not deserve to live."[58] Defining supervillains in this way, as *homines sacri*, makes the power of the superhero "totally benign, transmuting lawless vigilantism into a perfect embodiment of law enforcement," even as the superhero is actually using nondemocratic means to achieve democratic ends.[59] But as Neal Curtis writes in regard to the relationship between sovereignty and superheroes, "Rather than being unthinking celebrations of authority and order the comics regularly destabilize any simple or unqualified claim about the goodness of these sovereign prerogatives" so rather than providing "a justification of the need for *extra*-legal violence" they instead represent "the ambiguous realm of the law's own violence."[60] While the superhero frequently obscures their connection to violence and their complex relationship with the law and the state, it is through conflict with the supervillain that they are suddenly revealed.

Conclusion: "This Land Is Mine!"

The title of this chapter—"This Land Is Mine!"—comes from Issue 247 of Marvel Comics' *The Fantastic Four* by writer/artist John Byrne.[61] It is a story that speaks directly to the preoccupations of this chapter: supervillains, sovereign power, and the blurring of the boundaries between law and violence that underpins Cover's *nomos*. The story sees the superhero team the Fantastic Four dealing with the consequences of defeating the supervillain Doctor Doom in the sovereign state of the small European nation of Latveria some issues previously. Without Doom's iron-fisted rule, enacted to ensure that, in his view, his people were happy and productive, the nation has fallen into ruin. The Fantastic Four are therefore forced to question whether they have done the right thing, while Doom plots to take back the throne.

This idea of the supervillain as social disruptor is crucial. His function is not just to question and to critique society, the state, and how that state articulates its sovereign power as the superhero does, but also to unpack superheroes as justice figures themselves along with their relationships to law, sovereignty, and violence. Furthermore, it is the supervillain, most often generating or personifying the crisis or threat, that creates the state of emergency and maintains the state of exception in which superheroes operate and are legitimated. The supervillain's true purpose then is to expose these complex sets of associations around legality, sovereignty, violence, and punishment that undergird the superhero, but often go unseen. The supervillain's tragedy is that part of their role in legitimating the superhero means that they end up falling back into these binaries too. The superhero is truly legitimated only by triumphing after all, however short-lived that triumph may actually be. The supervillain has to fail. Superman must beat Luthor. The Joker must fall before Batman. Doom's scheme will be foiled by the Fantastic Four. However, to only focus on those failures rather than the struggle that is taking place would miss the nuances of what the supervillain is actually revealing about the hero and the lapsed society in which they both operate.

Notes

1 See, for example, Melissa Leon, "The Many Ways Donald Trump Is a Real-Life Lex Luthor," *Daily Beast*, August 14, 2016, www.thedailybeast.com/the-many-ways-donald-trump-is-a-real-life-lex-luthor; Kwame Opam, "Donald Trump Says He's Batman. He's Really Bizarro Lex Luthor," *Verge*, August 17, 2015, www.theverge.com/platform/amp/2015/8/17/9164469/donald-trump-batman-bruce-wayne-bizarro-lex-luthor; Eric Kleefeld, "Pop Culture Warned Us about Trump, Part 3: Lex Luthor!," *National Memo*, December 14, 2015, www.nationalmemo.com/pop-culture-warned-us-about-trump-part-3–lex-luthor.

2 Donald Trump and Tony Schwartz, *Trump: The Art of the Deal* (New York: Random House, 1987).

3 *Jimmy Kimmel Live!*, January 26, 2017, ABC.

4 "What Was That Glowing Orb Trump Touched in Saudi Arabia?," *New York Times*, May 22, 2017, www.mobile.nytimes.com/2017/05/22/world/middleeast/trump-glowing-orb-saudi.amp.html.

5 Jessica Chia, "Is It a bird? Is It a Plane? No, It's Kellyanne Conway: Trump's Right-Hand Woman Dons a Superwoman Outfit as They Attend Exclusive Costume Party Hosted by Influential Donors," *Daily Mail*, December 4, 2016, www.dailymail.co.uk/news/article-3998142/amp/Trump-mulling-Cabinet-picks-attends-lavish-costume-party.html.

6 Robert Cover, "Nomos and Narrative," in *Narrative, Violence and the Law: Essays of Robert Cover*, ed. M. Minnow, M. Ryan, and A. Sarat (Ann Arbor: University of Michigan Press, 1992), 95–172, 95.

7 Cover, "Nomos and Narrative," 96.

8 Cover, "Nomos and Narrative," 95.

9 Cover, "Nomos and Narrative," 101.

10 See, for example, Marvel Studios' Marvel Cinematic Universe film franchise (commencing 2008), DC Comics' "Arrowverse" television shows on the CW network (commencing 2012), DC Comics' DC Extended Universe film franchise (commencing 2013), and Netflix's Marvel Television Series (commencing 2015).

11 See, for example, www.dorkly.com/post/50525/the-25-greatest-comic-book-villains-of-all-time or www.ranker.com/crowdranked-list/best-comic-book-villains.

12 It should be noted that for reasons of clarity this chapter considers "superhero" and "supervillain" as complete, singular words, and therefore the inclusion of hyphens or plurals or any variation thereof does not change any of the central tenets of the argument.

13 Steven Moffat, "Sherlock: Script to Screen" (talk, Regent Theatre, Melbourne, November 23, 2015).

14 Jason Bainbridge, "'This Is the Authority. This Planet Is Under Our Protection': An Exegesis of Superheroes' Interrogations of Law," *Law, Culture and the Humanities* 3 (2007): 455–476.

15 Arthur Conan Doyle, *The Valley of Fear* (London: George H. Doran, 1915).

16 Arthur Conan Doyle, "The Adventure of the Final Problem," *Strand Magazine*, December 1893 (later collected as "The Final Problem," in *The Memoirs of Sherlock Holmes* [London: George Newnes, 1983]).

17 Jerry Siegel and Joe Shuster, *Action Comics* #23 (New York: DC Comics, April 1940).

18 *Superman: The Movie*, dir. Richard Donner (Warner Brothers, 1978).

19 Designed by George Perez and first appearing in Cary Bates, Curt Swan, and Murphy Anderson, *Action Comics* #544 (New York: DC Comics, June 1983).

20 Gail Simone and Dale Eaglesham, *Villains United* #1 (New York, July 2005).

21 Robert Jeffrey, *Evil and International Relations: Human Suffering in an Age of Terror* (New York: Palgrave Macmillan, 2008), 28–30.

22 Bill Finger and Bob Kane, *Batman* #1 (New York: DC Comics, April 25, 1940).

23 Alan Moore and Brian Bolland, *Batman: The Killing Joke* (New York: DC Comics, May 1988); Marc DiPaolo, "Terrorist, Technocrat, and Feudal Lord: Batman in Comic Book and Film Adaptations," in *Heroes of the Film, Comics and American Culture: Essays on Real and Fictional Defenders of Home*, ed. Lisa DeTora (Jefferson, NC: McFarland, 2009), 205.

24 Steve Englehart and Marshall Rogers, *Detective Comics* #475 (New York: DC Comics, February 1978); Jim Starlin and Jim Aparo, *Detective Comics* #426–429 (New York: DC Comics, May 1988–January 1989); *The Dark Knight*, dir. Christopher Nolan (Warner Brothers, 2008).

25 Jack Fennell, "The Aesthetics of Supervillainy," *Law Text Culture* 16, no. 1 (2012): 308–309.

26 Fennell, "Aesthetics," 309.

27 Fennell, "Aesthetics," 309.

28 Fennell, "Aesthetics," 325.

29 Jerry Siegel and Joe Shuster, "The Reign of the Superman," in *Science Fiction: The Advance Guard of Future Civilization* #3 (mimeographed fanzine, January 1933); Jerry Siegel and Joe Shuster, *Action Comics* #1 (New York: National Publications, later DC Comics, June 1938).

30 *Batman*, dir. Tim Burton (Warner Brothers, 1989); *The Flash* (CBS, 1990–1991).

31 Richard Reynolds, *Super Heroes: A Modern Mythology* (Jackson: University of Mississippi Press, 1994), 50–51.

32 Reynolds, *Superheroes*, 51.

33 Robert Cover, "The Supreme Court, 1982 Term." *Harvard Law Review* 97, no. 1 (1983): 8.

34 For more on the relationship between superheroes and melodrama, see Jason Bainbridge, "'Worlds within Worlds'—The Role of Superheroes in the Marvel and DC Universes," in *The Contemporary Comic Book Superhero*, ed. Angela Ndalianis (New York: Routledge, 2009), 64–85.

35 The primal scene in superhero narratives is a classic melodramatic trope. See Jerome Smith, *Melodrama* (London: Methuen, 1973).

36 Lea Jacobs, "The Women's Picture and the Poetics of Melodrama," *Camera Obscura* 31 (1993): 123.

37 Peter Brooks, *The Melodramatic Imagination* (London: Yale University Press, 1976).

38 Tim Peters, "Comic Book Mythology: Shymalan's Unbreakable and the Grounding of Good in Evil," *Law Text Culture* 16 (2016): 265.

39 Michel Foucault, *Discipline and Punish: The Birth of the Prison* (London: Penguin, 1991); Gilles Deleuze, "Postscript on the Societies of Control," *October* 59 (1992): 5.

40 Fennell, "Aesthetics," 322.

41 Chris Gavaler, *On the Origin of Superheroes: From the Big Bang to Action Comics No. 1* (Iowa City: Iowa University Press, 2015), 47.

42 Audrey Anton, "The Nietzschean Influence in *The Incredibles* and the Sidekick Revolt," in *The Amazing Transforming Superhero! Essays on the Revision of Characters in Comic Books, Film and Television*, ed. Terence R. Wandtke (Jefferson, NC: McFarland, 2007), 210, emphasis added.

43 Dan Slott, Ryan Stegman, Humberto Ramos, and Giuseppe Camuncoli, *The Superior Spider-Man* #1–33 (New York: Marvel Comics, January 2013–June 2014); Tom Taylor and Yildiray Cinar, *Superior Iron Man* #1–9 (New York: Marvel Comics, January 2015–August 2015).

44 *The Avengers*, dir. Joss Whedon (Marvel Studios / Disney, 2013).

45 *Batman* (ABC, 1966–1968).
46 Friedrich Nietzsche, *The Will to Power*, translated by R. J. Hollingdale and Walter Kaufman (New York: Vintage, 1968).
47 Carl Schmitt, *Political Theology: Four Chapters on the Concept of Sovereignty*, trans. George Schwab (1922; Chicago: University of Chicago Press, 2005), xii.
48 Gavaler, *On the Origin of Superheroes*, 48.
49 Schmitt, *Political Theology*, 7.
50 Hans Kelsen, *Pure Theory of Law* (1960; Berkeley: University of California Press, 1978).
51 For a more detailed account of the relationship between the Joker, madness, and law, see Neal Curtis, *Sovereignty and Superheroes* (Manchester: Manchester University Press, 2016), 65–66.
52 Foucault, *Discipline and Punish*, 47.
53 Giorgio Agamben, "The State of Emergency," *Generation Online* (2003), www.generation-online.org/p/fpagambenscmitt.html.
54 Agamben, "State of Emergency."
55 Giorgio Agamben, *Homo Sacer: Sovereign Power and Bare Life* (1995; Stanford, CA: Stanford University Press, 1998).
56 Agamben, *Homo Sacer*, 32.
57 Mervi Miettinen, "Representing the State of Exception: Power, Utopia, Visuality and Narrative in Superhero Comics," in *Images in Use: Towards the Critical Analysis of Visual Communication*, ed. Matteo Stocchetti and Karin Kukkonen (New York: John Benjamins, 2011), 269–290.
58 Agamben, *Homo Sacer*, 136.
59 J. S. Lawrence and R. Jewett, *The Myth of the American Superhero* (Grand Rapids, MI: Eerdmans, 2002), 46.
60 Curtis, *Sovereignty and Superheroes*, 6.
61 John Byrne, *The Fantastic Four* #247 (New York: Marvel Comics, October 1982).

Bibliography

Agamben, Giorgio. *Homo Sacer: Sovereign Power and Bare Life*. 1995. Stanford, CA: Stanford University Press, 1998.

———. "The State of Emergency." *Generation Online*, 2003. www.generation-online.org/p/fpagambenscmitt.html.

Anton, Audrey. "The Nietzschean Influence in *The Incredibles* and the Sidekick Revolt." In *The Amazing Transforming Superhero! Essays on the Revision of Characters in Comic Books, Film and Television*, edited by Terence R. Wandtke, 209–230. Jefferson, NC: McFarland, 2007.

Bainbridge, Jason. "'This Is the Authority. This Planet Is Under Our Protection': An Exegesis of Superheroes' Interrogations of Law." *Law, Culture and the Humanities* 3 (2007): 455–476.

———. "'Worlds within Worlds'—The Role of Superheroes in the Marvel and DC Universes." In *The Contemporary Comic Book Superhero*, edited by Angela Ndalianis, 64–85. New York: Routledge, 2009.

Brooks, Peter. *The Melodramatic Imagination*. London: Yale University Press, 1976.

Chia, Jessica. "Is It a Bird? Is It a Plane? No, It's Kellyanne Conway: Trump's Right-Hand Woman Dons a Superwoman Outfit as They Attend Exclusive Costume Party Hosted by Influential Donors." *Daily Mail*, December 4, 2016. www.dailymail.co.uk/news/article-3998142/amp/Trump-mulling-Cabinet-picks-attends-lavish-costume-party.html.

Cover, Robert. "Nomos and Narrative." In *Narrative, Violence and the Law: Essays of Robert Cover*, edited by M. Minnow, M. Ryan, and A. Sarat, 95–172. Ann Arbor: University of Michigan Press, 1992.

Cover, Robert. "The Supreme Court, 1982 Term." *Harvard Law Review* 97, no. 1 (1983): 1–306.

Curtis, Neal. *Sovereignty and Superheroes*. Manchester: Manchester University Press, 2016.

Deleuze, Gilles. "Postscript on the Societies of Control." *October* 59 (1992): 5.

DiPaolo, Marc. "Terrorist, Technocrat, and Feudal Lord: Batman in Comic Book and Film Adaptations." In *Heroes of the Film, Comics and American Culture: Essays on Real and Fictional Defenders of Home*, edited by Lisa DeTora, 194–217. Jefferson, NC: McFarland, 2009.

Doyle, Arthur Conan. "The Adventure of the Final Problem." *Strand Magazine*, December 1893. Later collected as "The Final Problem." In *The Memoirs of Sherlock Holmes*. London: George Newnes, 1983.

———. *The Valley of Fear*. London: George H. Doran, 1915.

Fennell, Jack. "The Aesthetics of Supervillainy." *Law Text Culture* 16, no. 1 (2012): 308–309.

Foucault, Michel. *Discipline and Punish: The Birth of the Prison*. London: Penguin, 1991.

Gavaler, Chris. *On the Origin of Superheroes: From the Big Bang to Action Comics No. 1*. Iowa City: University of Iowa Press, 2015.

Jacobs, Lea. "The Women's Picture and the Poetics of Melodrama." *Camera Obscura* 31 (1993): 123.

Jeffrey, Robert. *Evil and International Relations: Human Suffering in an Age of Terror*. New York: Palgrave Macmillan, 2008.

Kelsen, Hans. *Pure Theory of Law*. 1960. Berkeley: University of California Press, 1978.

Kleefeld, Eric. "Pop Culture Warned Us about Trump, Part 3: Lex Luthor!" *National Memo*, December 14, 2015. www.nationalmemo.com/pop-culture-warned-us-about-trump-part-3-lex-luthor.

Lawrence, J. S., and R. Jewett. *The Myth of the American Superhero*. Grand Rapids, MI: Eerdmans, 2002.

Leon, Melissa. "The Many Ways Donald Trump Is a Real-Life Lex Luthor." *Daily Beast*, August 14, 2016. www.thedailybeast.com/the-many-ways-donald-trump-is-a-real-life-lex-luthor.

Miettinen, Mervi. "Representing the State of Exception: Power, Utopia, Visuality and Narrative in Superhero Comics." In *Images in Use: Towards the Critical Analysis of Visual Communication*, edited by Matteo Stocchetti and Karin Kukkonen, 269–290. New York: John Benjamins, 2011.

Moffat, Steven. "Sherlock: Script to Screen." Talk, Regent Theatre, Melbourne, November 23, 2015.

Nietzsche, Friedrich. *The Will to Power.* Translated by R. J. Hollingdale and Walter Kaufman. New York: Vintage, 1968.

Opam, Kwame, "Donald Trump Says He's Batman. He's Really Bizarro Lex Luthor." *Verge*, August 17, 2015. www.theverge.com/platform/amp/2015/8/17/9164469/donald-trump-batman-bruce-wayne-bizarro-lex-luthor.

Peters, Tim. "Comic Book Mythology: Shymalan's Unbreakable and the Grounding of Good in Evil." *Law Text Culture* 16 (2016): 265.

Reynolds, Richard. *Super Heroes: A Modern Mythology.* Jackson: University of Mississippi Press, 1994.

Schmitt, Carl. *Political Theology: Four Chapters on the Concept of Sovereignty.* Translated by George Schwab. 1922. Chicago: University of Chicago Press, 2005.

Smith, Jerome. *Melodrama*. London: Methuen, 1973.

Trump, Donald, and Tony Schwartz. *Trump: The Art of the Deal.* New York: Random House, 1987.

"What Was That Glowing Orb Trump Touched in Saudi Arabia?," *New York Times*, May 22, 2017. www.mobile.nytimes.com/2017/05/22/world/middleeast/trump-glowing-orb-saudi.amp.html.

4

An Interview with Comics Artist, Writer, and "Herstorian" Trina Robbins

LIAM BURKE

Trina Robbins is a comics artist, writer, and "herstorian" who broke many boundaries while bringing attention to the often forgotten female creators who came before. Trina's career began in 1966 when she started creating comics for New York's iconic underground newspaper, the *East Village Other*. In 1970 she produced the very first all-woman comic book, *It Ain't Me, Babe*. In 1972 she was one of the founding mothers of *Wimmen's Comix*, the longest-lasting women's anthology comic book (1972—1992).

In the mid-1980s, tired of hearing publishers and editors say that girls don't read comics and that women had never drawn comics, she cowrote (with Catherine Yronwode) *Women and the Comics*, the first of what would become a series of histories of women cartoonists. In 1986 she became the first woman to draw a Wonder Woman comic book. In 2013 Trina was inducted into the Will Eisner Comic Book Hall of Fame.

LIAM BURKE What comics did you like to read growing up?

TRINA ROBBINS I was a lucky kid; first of all, my mother was a secondary school teacher and she taught me to read when I was four and I just dove into reading. Aside from giving birth to me, the greatest gift ever given to me, again by my mother, was teaching me to read, and I read everything. So when I read comics my parents were very permissive. This was a time when a lot of people thought comics were really bad for kids, but because I read

Figure 4.1. Trina Robbins with some of her key titles. Photo by Jessica Christian.

everything, I read books, I read comics, I read the back of the cereal boxes at breakfast; they were fine with me reading comics.

In those days you bought your comics at a candy store. You had to cross two streets for my local candy store. So as soon as I was old enough to cross two streets by myself I was buying comics there.

LB What types of comics were you particularly interested in?

TR Anything that starred a female character. Whether they were girls or women, as long as it was female I bought it. First choices were definitely Wonder Woman but also Sheena, Queen of the Jungle who I absolutely adored. I wanted to be her, I wanted to live in a tree house with my pet chimpanzee, I wanted to swing from vines. I loved Wonder Woman, but the one that I really wanted to be was Sheena.

LB Superhero comics have waxed and waned in terms of popularity over the years, what was it about that particular moment that made them the preferred choice?

TR I think that for kids comics were always popular. I don't think they ever waned, I think they were always popular. There were of course the movements in the fifties, which tried to tell kids not to read them because they were bad for you, but that didn't mean kids didn't read them anyway.

LB Were Sheena and Wonder Woman a bad influence on you?

TR Of course not. Even though I never did get to go live in the jungle and swing from vines, they certainly were not bad influences. Both of them fought the bad guys, they were always on the side of good. I liked Wonder Woman because she lives on a "Girls Only" island, there were no boys allowed, and I thought that was wonderful because when I was a kid it was really more of the "No Girls Allowed" time. Let's face it, even now it's "No Girls Allowed"—we had a woman run for president and she didn't win! So I loved the fact that there was an island that didn't allow boys for a change.

LB And talking about boys' clubs, how did you first become involved in comics as a creator?

TR As a kid I used to draw them. I always drew comics. Then when I hit high school age my mother talked me out of comics, she said, "That's kids' stuff and you're a teenager now so you shouldn't read comics anymore" and I believed her and I obeyed her, I was a very good daughter. So I gave away my collection, which of course if I had kept it would be worth thousands. It was just about then, because I needed something to take its place, it was just about then that I discovered science fiction.

So at about fourteen I started reading science fiction instead of comics. In the middle sixties I got reintroduced to comics. That was when Marvel came out with what I call the "Marvel Renaissance." All those new superheroes, such as the X-Men, Fantastic Four, Dr. Strange, Spider-Man, Thor. Suddenly, rather than kids' stuff, hippies and college students were reading them, and we thought they were really cool. Meanwhile I had never stopped drawing and I realized at that point that what I was drawing could easily be comics and that's when I started trying to do comics.

LB What was the impetus for the underground "comix" movement?

TR The thing about superhero comics, of course, was that everyone was very straight. All the guys had short hair and the few women that were there were very proper and very straight, and we were not, we were counterculture. So I just started immediately, I didn't even know that anyone else was doing it, I started trying to draw comics that reflected the life I was living in. I remember the very first comic I attempted to do, which I did not finish because I was still thinking in terms of superheroes. I came up with a comic where this scientist invents kind of a psychedelic that enables him to see through walls and to walk through walls, and it was all based on LSD. I didn't finish it because I'm simply not a superhero artist and I realized that after a couple of pages that I am not into drawing guys punching bad guys and stuff like that.

But immediately the comics that I wanted to do had to do with my world rather than the straight world, and I think that other people all over the country were thinking the same thing. I think it was 1965 or '66 that somebody showed me a copy of the *East Village Other*, which was an underground newspaper, and underground newspapers were happening and they were all about the counterculture, they were news for the counterculture rather than the straight news. Somebody showed me the *East Village Other* and it had comics in it and I went, "Whoa yes, that's what I want to do."

LB Your comics served as a corrective to some of the misogyny in the underground comic scene. Did you feel a responsibility to provide a response?

TR Well in the beginning it didn't even occur to me that they were all guys and that I was a woman. I just wanted to do comics and there were all these people doing comics and they happened to be guys, but I wasn't thinking in those terms. You have to also understand that in the very beginning they weren't really very misogynist, and it wasn't until about '68 or '69 that they became misogynist and I suddenly noticed the change and I noticed the misogyny in the comics and spoke up. Of course as soon as I would say, "But rape and torture and killing women isn't funny" and the guys would go, "You have no sense of humour."

LB So you responded by publishing *Wimmen's Comix*?

TR Yes, but that was a long way in the future. I was starting in '66 and in '66 I was doing strips for the *East Village Other* and the occasional longer comic. It wasn't until about '68 that they started getting really sexist and depicting rape and torture and murder of women as funny, and that was when I started objecting. So it wasn't until 1970 when I came to San Francisco from New York and there was a whole underground comic scene, but I was left out, I was not invited into that scene. I needed somewhere to publish, and I saw a copy of *It Ain't Me Babe*, which was America's first feminist newspaper. At the time I thought it was the first on the West Coast, but it turns out it was the very first in America. So of course I joined the staff and started doing comics with them.

LB Do you think the political engagement of the underground comics ever filtered back into the mainstream books?

TR I can't really think of when they started getting just vaguely political. I'm thinking of Neal Adams and that Green Lantern one with the black guy which was his attempt to be relevant, but I always found it incredibly embarrassing because it's so patronizing to black people that it's really disgusting, I think it's really insulting. They attempted to be relevant and to be political, but they were so tame.[1]

LB Do you think that superhero stories are not the best place to have those discussions?

TR I think you could do great things with superhero comics, but they simply weren't doing it, that's all.

LB You've dealt with serious issues in superhero comics, like the comic *Wonder Woman: The Once and Future Story* that addressed domestic violence. Why did you feel that was an appropriate way of dealing with that topic?[2]

TR It started with me simply wanting to do a story, kind of like a parallel because as you know the main character was not Wonder Woman, she was the real Princess Diana or whatever you want to call her from two thousand years ago, and then it occurred to me to parallel it with what was going on contemporarily. So it grew organically.

LB What was the reaction from readers?

TR I know the readers liked it. Over the past few years I've met people who talk about that and tell me that they were abused as kids and how this kind of thing made them stronger, just to know that it existed, that it wasn't just them. That of course is wonderful and these are usually times when the two of us are hugging and crying at the same time, it's very powerful. I guess the best thing that anybody ever said about it was Christie Marston who is the granddaughter of [Wonder Woman creator] William Marston. Christie told me that she felt that that book should be required reading in every high school in America. That's one of the most wonderful things anyone's ever said to me.

LB Why do you think these comic book characters, in particular superheroes, are often used for activist movements? For instance, in the demonstrations we've seen in the U.S. following Trump's election you sometimes see people wearing Wonder Woman outfits or carrying signs that use Wonder Woman or Princess Leia.

TR Princess Leia, yes, yes, yes, I love how she has become the symbol of the resistance. Wonder Woman of course she's iconic and she symbolizes female strength, so of course Wonder Woman.

LB Is there any kind of contradiction in the fact that these are often grassroots movements, but the characters they're using to articulate their protests are intellectual property owned by these huge corporations?

TR But you see that's what's so cool, they're intellectual property owned by mega corporations, but we adopt them. Nobody's going to sue for putting Princess Leia on a poster or Wonder Woman. When I marched in Washington last January I carried a poster. I marched for the group called "Comic Book Women" and this one woman had made all the posters, she's wonderful, and the one that she made that I immediately grabbed had Wonder Woman on it. Is DC going to sue me for marching with a Wonder Woman poster, of course not.

LB You've done a lot of work to get women reading comics. Why did you feel that was needed and important?

TR It's not so much promoting women reading comics, it's more like just the fact that women do read comics and women have always read comics and women have written comics and drawn comics. Really this century is when things finally changed, but all through the seventies, eighties, and nineties it was a line that they repeated, it was like a mantra that editors would repeat over and over again which was, "Girls don't read comics, women never drew comics" and I knew that was bullshit. So I've had to just introduce people to all these wonderful women who have drawn comics over this century.

LB Absolutely. You were the first woman to draw Wonder Woman, why did it take so long?

TR Why did it take so long is something you have to ask DC, not me.

LB That's true.

TR When I did it I wasn't even thinking in terms of being the first. Just like when I started drawing comics I wasn't thinking "Gee they're all guys and I'm the only woman", when I drew that Wonder Woman I wasn't thinking "Wow I'm the first woman to draw the Wonder Woman comic". My life has been a series of firsts for some reason, but I never think "oh this is a first," I just do it.

LB What was your approach to the character?

TR I did her as the Wonder Woman that I loved as a child because I did her as the Golden Age Wonder Woman imitating Harry G. Peter's style, the original artist for Wonder Woman.

LB Wonder Woman has enjoyed renewed interest in recent years. Why do you think she is so popular right now?

TR The movie was wonderful, my god, the movie was so good. I think again that she's a symbol. We have Trump to thank for this. Because of Trump women are standing up who never called themselves feminists before, women are standing up and calling themselves feminists and identifying as feminists, and that's because of Trump. So thanks Trump.

LB Wonder Woman was made an honorary UN ambassador in 2016, but then there were some protests that she is a hypersexualized character and therefore inappropriate, with the ambassadorship ending early. How do you feel about the protests and the fact that she then lost that honorary position?

TR I think the problem of course with Wonder Woman is that she is a comic character and she's owned by DC and she is a slave. She's a slave to whoever draws her and writes her. A lot of people who have drawn her have drawn her in a hypersexualized way, especially in the nineties, that was the worst of it, in these tiny little thong bikinis. The women who objected aren't really comic readers, so they don't know what Wonder Woman symbolizes or what she's done and how wonderful she can be, they've only seen the hypersexuality and the tiny little shrunken outfits that they put on her in the nineties and so they don't really understand. I can guarantee none of those women were Wonder Woman readers or comic readers probably.

LB Throughout your career you've drawn attention to the fact that women do read comics, and that there's been a lot of female creators. Today, there are a lot more titles starring and created by women, so do you feel that change and do you feel at least partly responsible for ushering it in?

TR I don't know how responsible I am, but I sure feel the change. It's more wonderful than my wildest dreams. All I used to hope for was that women would be included, and now it's more than women included, women are starring. I never dreamed, really in my wildest dreams I never dreamed that it would be this wonderful.

Notes

1 The 1970 *Green Lantern* story "No Evil Shall Escape My Sight!" began a series of comics written by Dennis O'Neil and drawn by Neal Adams that found the intergalactic hero and his costar Green Arrow engage with social and political problems. In this particular issue an elderly black man admonishes Green Lantern, "I been readin' about you . . . how you work for the blue skins . . . and how on a planet someplace you helped out the orange skins . . . and you done considerable for the purple skins! Only there's skins you never bothered with—! The black skins! I want to know . . . how come?! Answer me that, Mr. Green Lantern!" Dennis O'Neil, Neal Adams, et al., *Green Lantern* #76 (New York: DC, April 1970).

2 In the 1998 comic *Wonder Woman: The Once and Future Story*, Wonder Woman travels to Ireland to translate stone tablets written in ancient Greek that have recently been uncovered in an archaeological dig. The comic parallels the story of princess Artemis, detailed on the stones, with the abuse suffered by one of the archaeologists at the hands of her husband. Trina Robbins, Colleen Doran, et al., *Wonder Woman: The Once and Future Story* (New York: DC, August 1998).

Part 2

The Superhero as Brand

5

The Secret Commercial Identity of Superheroes

Protecting the Superhero Symbol

MITCHELL ADAMS

"Look up in the air: It's a bird! It's a plane! It's . . . a trademark!"[1] When writer Jerome Siegel and artist Joseph Shuster created Superman and saw his debut on the cover of *Action Comics* #1, they would never have imagined that over eighty years later their character would be protected with over five hundred registered trademarks. Decades following *Action Comics* #1, DC Comics and Marvel have both fiercely protected the intellectual property of their superheroes inside and outside of court.[2] Given the unprecedented number of adaptations of comic book characters to major film and television franchises over the last twenty years, the protection of a superhero's unique identity and image has become increasingly important to comic book creators and companies.[3] One way to secure rights in a superhero's identity is to obtain a registered trademark for their name, attributes of their image, or accompanying logo or indicia.[4] Trademark registration affords the owner a right to commercialize these attributes (including through licensing arrangements). It also provides the right to stop others from using these attributes in the course of trade without permission.[5] Additionally, trademark registration provides assurance to film and television studios, distributors and merchandisers, who invest in these film franchises.[6] More generally, trademark filing activity can be an indicator to the wider market of upcoming film releases and planned television shows.

In their essence, trademarks are words, symbols, figures, shapes, colors, or any combination thereof that identify goods or services that are offered by a particular person or company.[7] These signs help consumers to distinguish between goods and services that may come from different traders. Over time both Marvel and DC Comics have moved beyond the pages of comic books and incorporated their characters and attributes into products such as toys, clothing, confectioneries, and backpacks.[8] Trademark registrations facilitate the commercialization of these characters with merchandising licensing ventures depending on the protection of the trademark.[9]

Trademarks are not the only method that can be used to protect the assets of creative industries. Trademarks are part of the wider family of intellectual property rights.[10] The concept of copyright for instance is widely known to the public but is commonly confused with trademarks.[11] Copyright protection is intended to act as a reward for an author's creation of artistic works, including comic book publications, which, under copyright law, are considered artistic and literary works. Copyright facilitates the dissemination of such creative works, on consent from the author and during the term of protection.[12] The length of protection is typically the life of the author plus seventy years. Trademarks, on the other hand, are not built on a system of reward. Rather, trademark law is concerned with the interests of consumers and the avoidance of deception and confusion in the marketplace.[13] In contrast to copyright, trademark protection can last indefinitely.[14] With comic book publications consisting of copyrighted artistic and literary works (within its pages) and a trademarked title on the cover, an overlap of intellectual property protection occurs.[15] With copyright and trademark law protecting different subject matter and providing a different scope of protection, it is possible for owners to utilize both systems.

While the legal academic Irene Calboli has raised concern about such dual protection for characters, surprisingly there is little known about the actual extent to which creative organizations utilize intellectual property protection, particularly the trademark system, for characters.[16] This is notwithstanding the availability of data on trademark applications and registrations from a large number of countries. This chapter attempts to remove the cape and cowl of trademarks and reveal the secret commercial identity of superheroes. This study then fills a gap in the literature and presents empirical findings that emerge from the analysis of a dataset compiled based on the trademark applications filed by Marvel and DC and published by the World Intellectual Property Organization (WIPO) and the European Intellectual Property Office (EUIPO). In particular, this chapter examines the distribution of trademarks filed between Marvel and DC, the division of trademark applications between countries, the proportion of trademarks currently registered, the share of trademark applications and registrations between individual superhero characters, the nature of protecting individual superhero characters and the share of goods, and services covered by the trademark applications.

The findings are important, in particular to commentators and scholars, for two reasons. First, they shed light on the global distribution of intellectual property protection for individual character assets owned by creative organizations and thus the possible commercialization of the characters beyond their native comic book and film/television products. Second, they provide evidence on how creative industries use trademarks as a way of investing in reputational assets (as opposed to creative assets), which in turn is an important factor in determining international trading patterns.

The first section of this chapter provides a brief explanation of the methodology used in compiling the superhero dataset and its analysis. The second section establishes the key empirical findings that emerge from an analysis of the trademark application data. The final section concludes by discussing potential implications.

Methodology

Trademark applications and registrations are traceable from publicly available information published by national intellectual property offices. The last decade has seen the emergence of a range of easy-access intellectual property information services. Services include trademark application datasets from multiple national intellectual property offices compiled into single databases and bulk downloads of intellectual property information. Such services have enabled the collation of application data from specific applicants (i.e., individuals or companies filing trademarks with national intellectual property offices).

For this study, data from the World Intellectual Property Office and the European Union Intellectual Property Office were used to compile a dataset of trademark applications filed by Marvel Characters Inc. ("Marvel") and DC Comics Inc. ("DC").[17] The dataset spans trademark applications from over fifty-eight trademark offices including, inter alia, the United States, the European Union, the United Kingdom, Brazil, Japan, and Australia. It is important to emphasize that the data contained in this study have been compiled into a single snapshot for the ease of statistical analysis. The data collected are unique as they provide detailed information about aspects of individual trademark applications from both organizations.

Using the publicly available WIPO and EUIPO data, the dataset serves as a basis for the summary statistics and stylized facts reported in the upcoming section. The dataset contains 7,188 observations of trademark applications with filing dates from 1938 to 2016. Each record was examined, cleaned, and grouped based on the subject matter of the application.[18] For the purpose of this study, applications refer to the flow of new trademarks filed at individual trademark offices, while registrations refer to the stock of trademarks that are currently in force.

To specifically investigate the protection of superhero characters, applications for corporate or house brand trademarks of both Marvel and DC were excluded from further analysis.[19] This left a dataset of 6,172 trademark applications that relate to comic book characters, titles, and other indicia. This chapter surveys the trademark filing activity for Marvel and DC and identifies filing patterns for the protection of superhero characters.

Analysis of Trademark Applications and Registrations

Figure 5.1 shows the general trends in the number of trademark applications filed per year from 1938 to 2016 from Marvel and DC. The data show that over the past eighty years Marvel filed 3,135 trademark applications and DC filed 3,073 trademark applications in connection with superhero characters. DC holds the higher proportion of registered trademarks with 2,037 applications registered, or 67 percent of total applications filed. Marvel meanwhile has 1,604 trademarks currently registered, which is only 51 percent of the total applications filed. The trends in trademark applications shown in Figure 5.1 indicate that filing activity has dramatically increased in the past two decades. This greater activity unsurprisingly comes at a time when comic book characters and titles have been increasingly adapted for film and television. Marvel, in particular, has accelerated its trademark filing activity in the past decade.

DC dominated trademark applications filed between 1939 and 1965, filing trademarks for its characters as they related to magazines, periodicals, comic strips, and cartoons. The first peaks in Figure 5.1 emerge in 1966 and 1967 for DC and Marvel, respectively. Interestingly both peaks correspond to releases of television series, the first in 1966 for the live-action *Batman* television series and then in 1967 for the first Spider-Man animated series. A larger peak comes from DC in 1979, with sustained trademark activity over a five-year period. The majority of these trademarks related to Superman and again corresponded to the 1978 Superman film adaptation. Marvel also exhibited two peaks in the same period, which coincided with new adaptations of Fantastic Four, the Incredible Hulk, and Spider-Man to television.

Trademark filing activity accelerated from this point onward with major spikes corresponding to the 1989 and 1992 Batman film adaptations, the 1992 X-Men and 1994 Spider-Man animated television series, the 1996 Superman animated series, the 2000 X-Men film adaptation, the 2001 *Smallville*

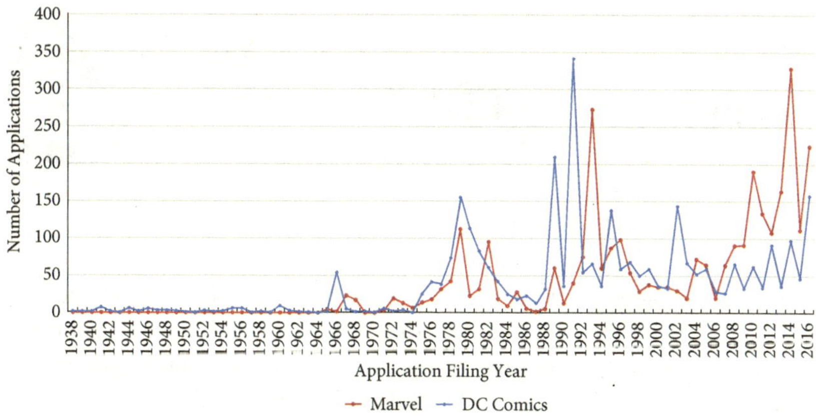

Figure 5.1. Applications per year by filing basis 1938–2016.

television series, the 2011 Captain America film adaptation, and the 2016 Wonder Woman film adaptation. The largest spike observed for Marvel corresponds to the announcement in 2014 of the "Phase 3" films in the Marvel Cinematic Universe.[20]

Where Do Marvel and DC File Their Trademarks?

The peaks shown in Figure 5.1 reveal increased filing activity not just in the United States, but also internationally for trademarks that cover classes of goods and services outside of comic book publications (discussed further below). For Marvel, trademark application activity was concentrated in the United States and made up 45 percent of their total filed trademark applications. This filing activity was then followed by applications to thirty-six other trademark offices, with the main jurisdictions being Brazil (10 percent of the total), Korea (6 percent), Mexico (4 percent), and the United Kingdom (4 percent). DC's portfolio is more diverse than Marvel's, and they filed trademarks in fifty-five different jurisdictions. The main jurisdictions were the United States (27 percent of the total), Korea (12 percent), Brazil (7 percent), Australia (4 percent), and Canada (4 percent). It is no surprise that this activity indicates an effort to merchandise the characters internationally alongside film and television adaptations.

What Are Marvel and DC Seeking to Protect?

While the main purpose of this chapter is to report the number of Marvel and DC trademark applications, it is also equally important to investigate the nature of the protection being sought for individual superhero characters.

Figure 5.2. Example of the different kinds of trademarks for "Superman." DC Comics.

As described above, a trademark can take the form of many different kinds of "signs." From the data it is clear that Marvel and DC have very different strategies for protecting their characters and ancillary elements. In general terms, the trademarks of Marvel and DC predominately take one of four kinds: a word(s), a stylized word(s), figures, or a combination of these. Figure 5.2 shows an example for Superman of these different kinds of trademarks.

The overall proportions of trademark applications based on each kind of "sign" are shown in Figures 5.3 and 5.4. It is clear that Marvel predominately sought to protect its superhero characters using word trademarks (for example, the superhero name or comic title), with 84 percent of the total trademark applications taking this form. On the other hand, DC diversified, also protecting the figure (or image) of their superhero characters either on their own or in combination with a stylized logo depicting the character's name. The larger proportion of DC figurative and combination trademark applications observed (21 percent and 23 percent, respectively) result from applications for the iconic Batman, Superman, and Wonder Woman emblems.

Batman is the subject of the largest number of trademark applications with 835, making up 27 percent of the total applications filed by DC. Following Batman, DC's portfolio is primarily composed of trademarks for DC's other "Trinity" characters, with Superman the subject of 739 applications (24 percent of the total) and Wonder Woman with 254 applications (8 percent of the total). Interestingly, Catwoman followed closely with 221 applications (7 percent of the total) and then the Penguin with 140 applications (5 percent of the total). Marvel, on the other hand, has invested in protecting a mixture of individual characters and groups of superhero characters. Spider-Man was subject to the highest number of applications with 408 applications, making up only 13 percent of Marvel's total portfolio. Following Spider-Man were 239 applications collectively for the X-Men (8 percent of the total), the Avengers collectively with 230 (7 percent of the total), the Fantastic Four collectively with 199 (6 percent of the total), and individually the Hulk with 158 (5 percent of the total).

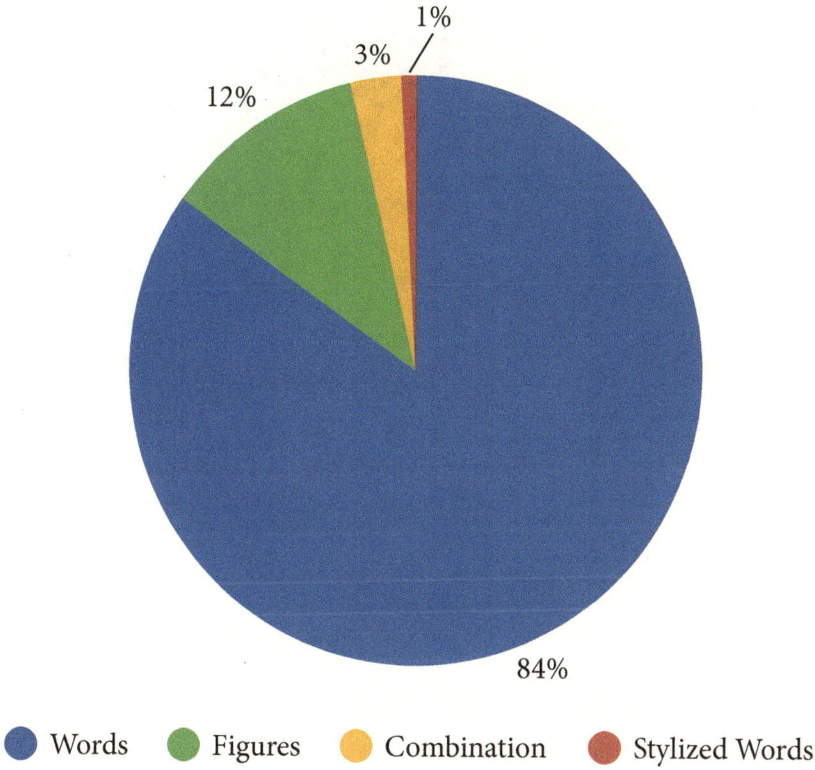

Figure 5.3. Proportion of Marvel trademarks by type.

Figures 5.5 and 5.6 show the peaks and troughs of total trademark applications made by both companies for their top characters or groups of characters. Again, it is evident from both figures that recent trademark activity corresponded to film and television adaptations. This activity indicates investment in the protection of not only the film and television titles, but also the identity of individual characters for merchandising and licensing efforts. To give a specific example, in 1991 DC made large volumes of trademark applications for Catwoman and the Penguin, both of which corresponded to the 1992 film *Batman Returns.* Although trademark application activity peaked the previous year for Batman trademarks (corresponding to the 1989 *Batman* film), the Catwoman and Penguin marks indicate a deliberate push to merchandise ancillary characters, including villains. For the most part, the investment made to protect both Batman and Spider-Man has been consistent over the period with filings occurring between adaptations.

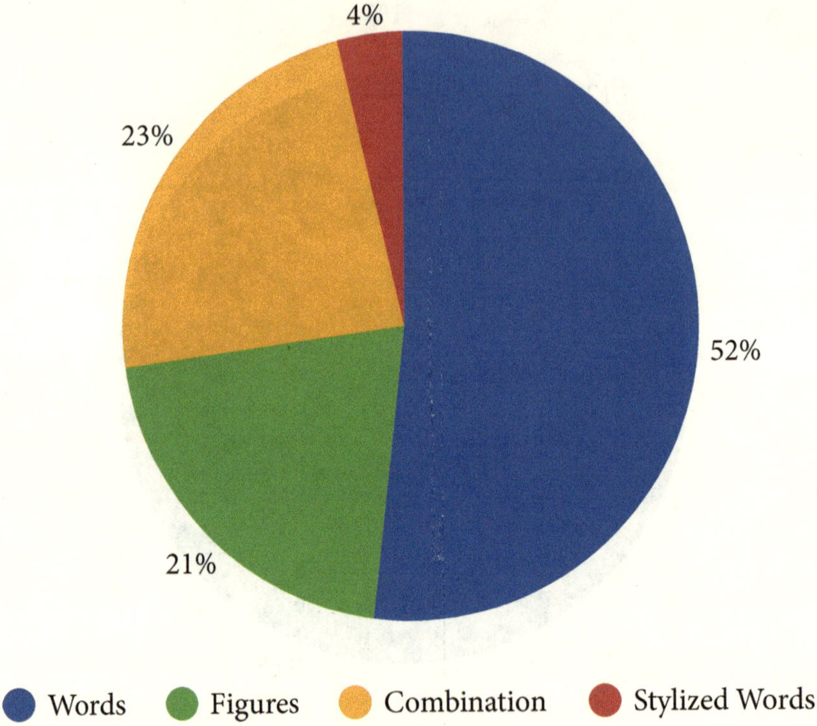

Figure 5.4. Proportion of DC trademarks by type.

What Categories of Goods and Services Are These Trademarks Applied For?

Finally, Table 5.1 sets out the number of claimed classes of goods and services for which Marvel and DC applications sought to register trademarks between 1938 and 2016.[21] The forty-five classes are from the international classification, or Nice Classification, which categorizes trademarks based on the goods and services applied for.[22] Marvel and DC can protect the same trademark in different classes of goods and services and, as such, they can request more than one class in an application. Therefore, there are typically more claimed trademark classes than the total number of trademark applications filed.

This aspect of trademark application data reveals the intentions of both companies to merchandise and apply their superheroes to an array of goods and services. Over this period DC claimed the highest number of classes of goods and services with 5,805, compared to Marvel with 5,096. Unsurprisingly, both Marvel and DC claim the same main class of goods and services, the most popular being class 16 for publications

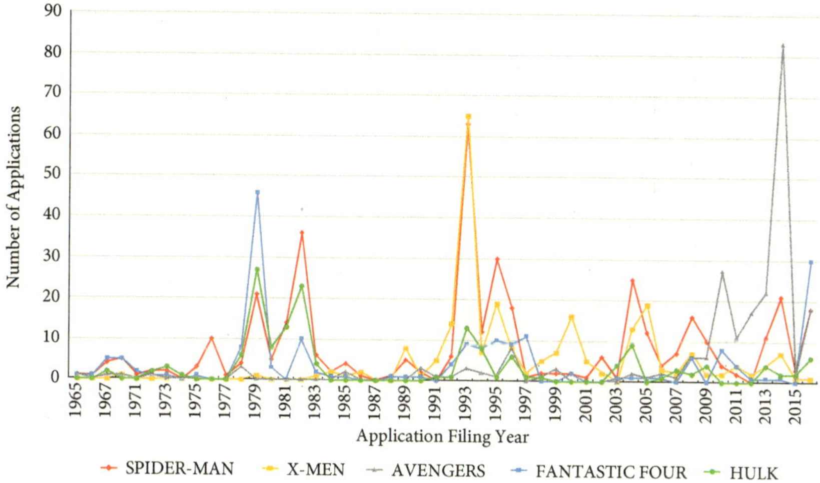

Figure 5.5. Applications per year by top Marvel character type.

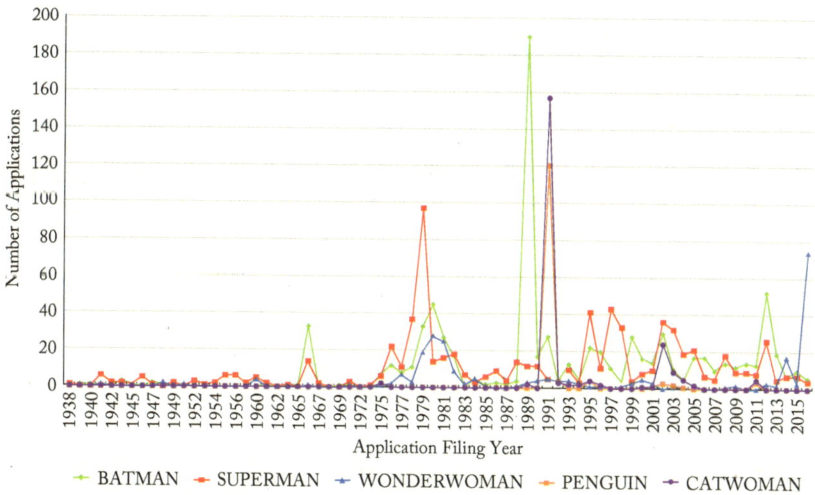

Figure 5.6. Applications per year by top DC character type.

(including comic books), making up 25.1 percent and 18.8 percent of Marvel and DC's portfolios, respectively. Most of these applications not only are the subject of the superhero character but also capture titles that feature the character, for example, trademarks for "THE AMAZING SPIDER-MAN."[23] Following publications, the companies also made applications covering classes for toys and sporting goods (class 28), instruments, software (including videogames), digital recording media

TABLE 5.1. Number of claimed classes of goods and services for which Marvel and DC applications sought to register trademarks between 1938 and 2016.

International Class		Marvel			DC		
		Number of Applications	*% of Total*	*Proportion Registered*	*Number of Applications*	*% of Total*	*Proportion Registered*
Classes of Goods							
1	Chemicals	1	0.02	0.00	29	0.50	1.00
2	Paints	1	0.02	0.00	9	0.16	0.78
3	Cosmetics and cleaning preparations	82	1.61	0.54	110	1.89	0.63
4	Lubricants and fuels	2	0.04	0.00	0	0.00	0.00
5	Pharmaceuticals	28	0.55	0.39	46	0.79	0.57
6	Common metals	24	0.47	0.75	22	0.38	1.00
7	Machinery	0	0.00	0.00	11	0.19	0.82
8	Hand tools	9	0.18	0.67	22	0.38	0.86
9	Instruments, software, digital recording media	637	12.50	0.70	735	12.66	0.79
10	Medical apparatus	8	0.16	1.00	16	0.28	1.00
11	Environmental control apparatus	19	0.37	0.58	17	0.29	0.71
12	Vehicles	17	0.33	0.59	22	0.38	0.64
13	Firearms	0	0.00	0.00	0	0.00	0.00
14	Jewelry	106	2.08	0.61	400	6.89	0.79
15	Musical instruments	1	0.02	1.00	7	0.12	1.00
16	Paper goods, publications	1279	25.10	0.58	1089	18.76	0.71
17	Rubber goods	5	0.10	0.80	4	0.07	1.00
18	Leather goods	214	4.20	0.72	160	2.76	0.63
19	Non-metallic building materials	11	0.22	0.73	5	0.09	1.00
20	Furniture	99	1.94	0.67	130	2.24	0.64
21	Housewares and glass	135	2.65	0.67	204	3.51	0.67
22	Cordage and fibers	6	0.12	1.00	13	0.22	1.00

23	Yarns and threads	0	0.00	0.00	0	0.00	0.00
24	Textiles and fabrics	155	3.04	0.75	127	2.19	0.72
25	Clothing and footwear	573	11.24	0.64	705	12.14	0.77
26	Fancy goods	34	0.67	0.59	117	2.02	0.71
27	Floor coverings	16	0.31	1.00	37	0.64	0.86
28	Toys and sporting goods	738	14.48	0.66	842	14.50	0.77
29	Meats and processed foods	46	0.90	0.50	78	1.34	0.65
30	Staple foodstuffs	190	3.73	0.67	245	4.22	0.70
31	Natural agricultural products	3	0.06	0.33	11	0.19	1.00
32	Beers and other nonalcoholic beverages	74	1.45	0.69	147	2.53	0.65
33	Alcoholic beverages (except beers)	1	0.02	1.00	9	0.16	1.00
34	Smokers' articles	0	0.00	0.00	0	0.00	0.00
Classes of Services							
35	Advertising and business	56	1.10	0.73	74	1.27	0.80
36	Insurance and financial	3	0.06	0.33	5	0.09	1.00
37	Building construction and repair	0	0.00	0.00	1	0.02	1.00
38	Telecommunications	8	0.16	0.00	10	0.17	0.70
39	Transport and storage	1	0.02	1.00	4	0.07	1.00
40	Treatment of materials	0	0.00	0.00	1	0.02	1.00
41	Entertainment and education	481	9.44	0.63	325	5.60	0.67
42	Technological and scientific	19	0.37	0.47	9	0.16	0.67
43	Providing food and drink	10	0.20	1.00	7	0.12	0.57
44	Medical, beauty, and agricultural	2	0.04	0.00	0	0.00	0.00
45	Personal and legal	2	0.04	0.50	0	0.00	0.00
	Total	5,096	100.00	0.64	5,805	100.00	0.74

(such as DVDs) (class 9), clothing and footwear (class 25), and entertainment services (class 41). While the majority of these applications are indicative of activities related to products produced by Marvel and DC, the vast array of goods and services claimed are also suggestive of an intention to extensively license their characters to merchandisers that sell a variety of goods.

Conclusion

This chapter is the first empirical study into the use of the international trademark system to protect superhero characters. It presents a rich history of trademark activity relating to superhero characters over the past eighty years. In summary, this chapter presents three main findings. First, superhero characters and titles, as the subject of trademark applications, have dramatically increased over the last two decades. Second, these trademark applications correspond to film and television adaptations for the same characters. Third, superhero trademarks are predominately applied in categories of nonmedia products. Overall, the activity is an indicator of merchandising and licensing efforts tied to film and television adaptations.

Historically Batman has been by far the most popular trademarked character, followed by Superman and Spider-Man. The data also show that DC has regularly sought protection for the "Trinity" of heroes (Batman, Superman, and Wonder Woman) in multiple forms, as a word, stylized word or words, stand-alone figure, or a combination of all three. These top-tier heroes' emblems were also prevalent. The data suggest Marvel employed a different strategy and predominately filed word trademarks for its characters and related titles.

The trademark application data show that since the release of the 1978 Superman film, there has been an new approach to trademark strategy for both DC and Marvel. Application activity has increased both in the United States and internationally for goods and services beyond comic book publications. Not only are film and television titles being protected, but there has also been an increase in protecting standalone characters and ancillary elements. This change reflects the shift in the business of superhero characters at the time.[24] Both companies have shifted away from comic book sales and concentrated on nonmedia products where the characters generate the greatest revenue.[25]

The data on trademark applications and registrations offer interesting insights into how superhero character assets are distributed, and how they are utilized in international commerce. The stylized facts presented in this chapter indicate that these characters do function as a "brand" or a "brand narrative."[26] The trademarks tie characters together alongside multiple media incarnations, which appear to be mutually reinforcing.[27] DC and Marvel's trademark applications and registrations represent a reach and influence far beyond that of comic books, and the companies intend them to be applied across an array of products. It is no surprise that these trademarks are considered valuable intellectual property assets, a value that is evident in the high proportion of trademarks Marvel and DC currently registered.

While this chapter is limited to providing a general overview of trademark applications from Marvel and DC, the data presented are designed to serve a larger purpose in that they provide a solid foundation for further research and investigation into the way intellectual property regimes have shaped superhero characters. This study and its findings, therefore, are an initial step toward a larger research undertaking on the commercialization of the identity of the superhero.

Notes

1 Thomas A. Crowell, *The Pocket Lawyer for Comic Book Creators: A Legal Toolkit for Comic Book Writers* (Burlington, VT: Focal Press, 2015): 360.

2 See, for example, DC Comics Inc. v. Powers, 465 F. Supp. 843 (SDNY 1978); DC Comics Inc. v. Crazy Eddie, Inc., aka U.L.S., Inc., and Edward Antar, 205 USPQ 1177 (1979); Marvel Characters Inc. v. Gary Charles, ATMO 92 (2011); DC Comics Inc. v. Cheqout Pty Ltd., FCA 478 (2013).

3 Joshua Saval, "Copyrights, Trademarks and Terminations: How Limiting Comic Book Characters in the Film Industry Reflects on Future Intellectual Property Issues for Character Law," *Florida International University Law Review* 9 (2014): 405.

4 For example, see Australian trademark 224025 and U.S. trademarks 87506117, 893770, and 885488.

5 See Trade Marks Act 1995 (Cth), sec. 20.

6 Thomas A. Crowell, *The Pocket Lawyer for Filmmakers: A Legal Toolkit for Independent Producers*, 2nd ed. (Oxford: Focal Press, 2007).

7 Trade Marks Act 1995 (Cth), secs. 6 and 17.

8 See, for example, "Spider-Man," Walmart, www.walmart.com/search/?query=spiderman.

9 Jane Gaines, *Contested Culture: The Image, the Voice and the Law* (Chapel Hill: University of North Carolina Press, 1991), 214.

10 For example, a cause of action for passing off is a form of intellectual property enforcement that can be used to prevent the unauthorized use of a fictional character in the absence of or along with a registered trademark. The law of passing off specifically prevents misrepresentations of association between two businesses to consumers. An action for passing off is useful where an action for trademark infringement is unlikely to be successful.

11 See, for example, "5 Everyday Things You Won't Believe Are Copyrighted," *Cracked*, October 16, 2012, www.cracked.com/article_20066_5-everyday-things-you-wont-believe-are-copyrighted.html; Jonathan Bailey, "Copyright, Trademark and Patents: A Guide for Journalists," *Plagiarism Today*, October 18, 2012, www.plagiarismtoday.com/2012/10/18/trademark-vs-copyright-guide-for-journalists/.

12 Andrew Stewart, Philip Griffith, Judith Bannister, and Adam Liberman, *Intellectual Property in Australia*, 5th ed. (Chatswood, NSW: LexisNexis, 2017), 131.

13 A trader's goodwill is also protected through the creation of a statutory property right against acts of infringement: Campomar Sciedad, Limitada v. Nike International Ltd., 202 CLR 45, 65 (2000).

14 Applicants who secure a registered trademark can renew the registration after every ten-year anniversary of filing the trademark application. See Trade Marks Act 1995 (Cth), sec. 77.

15 Equally, any creative elements can blur the boundaries. For example, pictures, graphics, figured characters, video clips, and songs could all be protected as trademarks and separately as subject matter capable of protection under copyright law. See Trade Marks Act 1995 (Cth), sec. 6.

16 Irene Calboli, "Overlapping Copyright and Trademark Protection: A Call for Concern and Action," *Illinois Law Review Slip Opinions* 1 (2014): 25. For a broad overview on intellectual property rights and licensing, see Nicole Sudhindra, "Marvel's Superhero Licensing," *WIPO Magazine*, June 1, 2012, www.wipo.int/wipo_magazine/en/2012/03/article_0005.html. For an exploration of trademark law and Superman, see Gaines, *Contested Culture*, 208. For an exploration of Superman as a brand, see Ian Gordon, *Superman: The Persistence of an American Icon* (New Brunswick, NJ: Rutgers University Press, 2017), 143.

17 "Global Brand Database," World Intellectual Property Organization, www.wipo.int/branddb/en/; "TMView," European Union Intellectual Property Office, www.tmdn.org/tmview/welcome. These two corporate entities predominantly hold ownership of the trademarks within the corporate structure of the parent companies, but other entities such as Marvel Entertainment Group Inc. and Cadence Industry Corporation (a former parent company of the Marvel Comics Group from 1968 to 1986) also hold trademarks belonging to Marvel. Applications that listed these companies as applicants were included in the dataset.

18 Where information was missing from the data, each trademark application was examined and detail added. A character group category was created when five or more trademarks appeared relating to one individual character or superhero team (e.g., Wonder Woman or the Fantastic Four).

19 For example, U.S. trademark application 74214397 and Australian trademark application 1468480. Trademarks that were also excluded were titles of comic book imprints (for example, Icon and Infinite Comics) and other commercial products offered by these companies, e.g., Marvel Unlimited and DC Universe

Online. Trademarks Marvel Characters Inc. and DC Comics Inc. jointly applying for the use of the word "SUPERHERO" were also excluded from the analysis.

20 Marc Strom, "Marvel Studios Announces Full Phase 3 Slate at Special Event," Marvel, October 28, 2014, https://news.marvel.com/movies/23547/marvel_studios_announces_full_phase_3_slate_at_special_event/.

21 Four hundred seventy-five applications were excluded from this part of the analysis as they did not contain Nice Class information. The is due to applications from jurisdictions that at the time of filing were not members of the Nice Agreement Concerning the International Classification of Goods and Services for the Purposes of the Registration of Marks. See "Nice Agreement," World Intellectual Property Organization, www.wipo.int/treaties/en/classification/nice/.

22 "Nice Classification," World Intellectual Property Organization, www.wipo.int/classifications/nice/en/.

23 See, for example, U.S. trademark 885910.

24 Gordon, *Superman*, 165.

25 Ian Gordon, "Refiguring Media: Tee Shirts as a Site of Audience Engagement with Superheroes," *Information Society*, 32, no. 5 (2016): 326–332.

26 Gordon, *Superman*, 170.

27 Gordon, *Superman*, 170.

Bibliography

Bailey, Jonathan. "Copyright, Trademark and Patents: A Guide for Journalists." *Plagiarism Today*, October 18, 2012. www.plagiarismtoday.com/2012/10/18/trademark-vs-copyright-guide-for-journalists/.

Calboli, Irene. "Overlapping Copyright and Trademark Protection: A Call for Concern and Action." *Illinois Law Review Slip Opinions* 1 (2014): 25–34.

Campomar Sciedad, Limitada v. Nike International Ltd., 202 CLR 45 (2000).

Crowell, Thomas A. *The Pocket Lawyer for Comic Book Creators: A Legal Toolkit for Comic Book Writers*. Burlington, VT: Focal Press, 2015.

———. *The Pocket Lawyer for Filmmakers: A Legal Toolkit for Independent Producers*. 2nd ed. Oxford: Focal Press, 2007.

DC Comics Inc v. Cheqout Pty Ltd., FCA 478 (2013).

DC Comics Inc. v. Crazy Eddie, Inc., aka U.L.S., Inc., and Edward Antar, 205 USPQ 1177 (1979).

DC Comics Inc. v. Powers, 465 F. Supp. 843 (SDNY 1978).

"5 Everyday Things You Won't Believe Are Copyrighted." *Cracked*, October 16, 2012. www.cracked.com/article_20066_5-everyday-things-you-wont-believe-are-copyrighted.html.

Gaines, Jane. *Contested Culture: The Image, the Voice and the Law*. Chapel Hill: University of North Carolina Press, 1991.

"Global Brand Database." World Intellectual Property Organization. www.wipo.int/branddb/en/.

Gordon, Ian. "Refiguring Media: Tee Shirts as a Site of Audience Engagement with Superheroes." *Information Society* 32, no. 5 (2016): 326–332.

———. *Superman: The Persistence of an American Icon*. New Brunswick, NJ: Rutgers University Press, 2017.

Marvel Characters Inc. v. Gary Charles, ATMO 92 (2011).

"Nice Agreement." World Intellectual Property Organization. www.wipo.int/treaties/en/classification/nice/.

Saval, Joshua. "Copyrights, Trademarks and Terminations: How Limiting Comic Book Characters in the Film Industry Reflects on Future Intellectual Property Issues for Character Law." *Florida International University Law Review* 9 (2014): 405–449.

"Spider-Man." Walmart. www.walmart.com/search/?query=spiderman.

Stewart, Andrew, Philip Griffith, Judith Bannister, and Adam Liberman. *Intellectual Property in Australia*. 5th ed. Chatswood, NSW: LexisNexis, 2017.

Strom, Marc. "Marvel Studios Announces Full Phase 3 Slate at Special Event." Marvel, October 28, 2014. https://news.marvel.com/movies/23547/marvel_studios_announces_full_phase_3_slate_at_special_event/.

Sudhindra, Nicole. "Marvel's Superhero Licensing." *WIPO Magazine*, June 1, 2012. www.wipo.int/wipo_magazine/en/2012/03/article_0005.html.

"TMView." European Union Intellectual Property Office. www.tmdn.org/tmview/welcome.

Trade Marks Act 1995 (Cth).

6

Siegel and Shuster as Brand Name

IAN GORDON

The stories of Superman's creation are multiple. Superman debuted in *Action Comics* #1 in June 1938, but had a long gestation. As Jerry Siegel told it he had a restless night in 1934 thinking of the character and in the morning ran over to Joe Shuster's house with the fully formed idea and scripts for a newspaper comic strip.[1] In telling this story Siegel left out earlier developments that he either forgot or did not see as relevant. Siegel neglected for instance his January 1933 story "The Reign of the Superman," authored under the pseudonym Herbert S. Fine, and published in his own fanzine *Science Fiction*, with unattributed illustrations by Shuster.[2] Likewise Siegel did not mention another 1933 version from August that was of interest to a Chicago comic book publisher that, unfortunately for Siegel, shortly after went bankrupt. Indeed in 1934, rather than having a sleepless night, Siegel approached Russell Keaton, a ghost artist on the *Buck Rogers* comic strip, and the two collaborated on some sample Superman comic strips. It was only in 1935 that Siegel returned to working with Shuster on trying to develop his character into a comic strip.[3]

Two things remain fairly constant in all these versions of Superman's origins: Jerry Siegel was the key driving force and his prime interest was in developing a comic strip not a comic book character. This background also tells us that Siegel was more instrumental in the development of Superman than was Shuster. Indeed, part of my argument in this piece is that notwithstanding Shuster's art in the very early days of *Action Comics* he was often quite marginal to the production of Superman comics. The notion that Siegel and Shuster created all the various Superman stories then was a myth, but one with remarkable staying power because of the way it became a brand name. Siegel's focus on developing a comic strip is important in understanding his later concern about the way he had handed over his intellectual property in Superman to DC Comics for $130 on March 1, 1938. Letters between Siegel and DC Comics, particularly the exchanges with Jack Liebowitz, show that Siegel almost immediately regretted signing over the rights to Superman.

Despite some renegotiated terms, once the character proved enormously popular, with a hefty chunk of money coming his way between 1938 and 1947, the desire to control his creation, to own the rights outright, featured heavily in Siegel's thinking and actions. Ultimately this led to Siegel's unsuccessful suit in 1947 for the return of his copyright.[4] Siegel's mind-set was shaped by the business model of comic strips in which the creator's name was as important a part of marketing a strip as its central characters, gags, or storylines. The author as a marketable property, and a series of legal cases in the early years of comic strips, resulted in some creators retaining a good deal of their rights in their characters. Indeed, DC Comics likewise understood the importance of the creators as part of marketing the character, and all the Superman stories from his debut in 1938 to 1948 carried the byline of Siegel and Shuster. After DC prevailed in the 1947 case the byline disappeared from Superman stories. The history of Jerry Siegel's pursuit of his Superman rights is as much the story of how the names Jerry Siegel and Joe Shuster functioned as a brand name as it is the story of other legal issues and the publication history of Superman.[5]

Rather than being treated as just a superhero character, Superman is often viewed as a brand unifying a range of products. However, this chapter takes such arguments further and suggests that "Siegel and Shuster" should be thought of as akin to a brand name. By examining the marketing of comic strip authors, this chapter shows that Siegel most likely had this concept of author-owner in mind when he created Superman. In a fledgling comic book industry that had no set business practices, DC Comics too followed this sort of comic strip business model of crediting authors and artists of stories. Indeed, they actively promoted Siegel and Shuster as the creators of Superman. At the same time though DC thought it essential to own the characters it published, and when challenged by Siegel in 1947, ownership was more important than promoting creators. Nonetheless, Siegel and Shuster as a brand name was not yet played out, and in the mid-1970s Siegel was able to take advantage of growing fan interest in the creators of comics to relaunch the brand name.

It is useful then to think of Siegel and Shuster through marketing and branding concepts. In recent years branding and marketing specialists have emphasized the importance of the brand narrative.[6] Essentially what that means is emphasizing the qualities in marketing that consumers are thought to have identified with the product and specifically the brand. Classic brand narratives that helped advertisers recognize this strategy of branding include Pepsi's creation of a youthful, or youthful-thinking, association with the Pepsi Generation campaign in the early 1960s and Marlboro switching from being a cigarette aimed at women to a rugged macho image through the Marlboro Man cowboy advertisements from the 1950s through to governments curtailing cigarette advertising in the 1990s. The Siegel and Shuster brand narrative has three key elements: creators of Superman, life-long pals, and victims of corporate greed. Since 1975 DC has tried to create a fourth element: beneficiaries of corporate recognition of their place in comics history. Both Siegel and DC were able to mobilize different configurations of these brand narrative elements at different times to sell Superman products and to profit from their sale. From 1938 to 1947 the interests of DC and Siegel converged, more or less, but not without tension. From 1947 to 1975 DC ignored the Siegel and Shuster brand. However, when Siegel managed to draw fan attention to the "victims of corporate greed" narrative, DC ultimately realigned itself with the Siegel and Shuster brand.

Comic Strips Creators as Brand Names

To understand the business model adopted by the fledgling comic book publishers as they tentatively created an industry based on the demand for comics in a new form, it is useful to look at the practices associated with comic strips from which comic books sprung.[7] The importance of an artist's byline on a comic strip stretches back to the earliest years of American comic strips. In the languid years of the mid-1890s, when these comic strips took shape in newspapers such as the *New York World* and the *New York American*, artists were wont to take summer breaks and had, it seems, little concern for production schedules or care about the place of their work in shaping the success of such newspapers. Even as successful an artist as Richard Outcault, whose Yellow Kid was the center of a considerable craze, did not keep a regular production schedule for his comic *Hogan's Alley*; at the height of the craze in early 1896 the Kid appeared only every other week in the *World*. But after the paper published a version of *Hogan's Alley* on May 31, 1896, drawn by George Luks, Outcault produced a weekly strip from June 7 to October 4, 1896. On September 6, 1896, Outcault appended a note to the strip proclaiming "Do Not Be Deceived None Genuine Without This Signature."[8] In doing this Outcault staked a claim to a link between the artist and the product of his labors. To Outcault the Yellow Kid belonged to him and him alone, and it was outrageous that the *World* had Luks create a version of his work. Outcault eventually abandoned the Yellow Kid precisely because he could not control the use of the character due to faults in his attempt to register copyright.[9]

Issues of artists trying to control the fruits of their labor through retaining intellectual property rights are of course important and indeed linked to the marketing of artists as a form of brand name. However, Outcault's move in insisting that no Yellow Kid was genuine in the absence of his signature put the question of the artist's right to be identified with their work in such a manner that it firmly tied the two together. Legally, though, matters did not always pan out in this fashion. For instance, when Outcault moved his second major comic strip character, Buster Brown, from the *New York Herald* to Hearst's newspapers he lost the right to name the strip because the *Herald* had copyrighted the name as part of protecting issues of the newspaper.[10] Fortunately for Outcault he had the foresight to purchase from the *Herald* all subsidiary rights to the name for two dollars and so retained control over its licensing.[11] Other artists also experienced this legal separation of their name from their characters. Rudolph Dirks, who for many years drew *The Katzenjammer Kids* for the Hearst papers, decided he wanted a few months' break from the strip, and when Hearst refused Dirks attempted to take his work to the rival papers of Joseph Pulitzer. Dirks could not use the title but continued to draw his characters under the new title *The Captain and the Kids*.[12] Harry "Bud" Fisher fared better in his dealings with Hearst over his comic strip *Mutt and Jeff* because he had copyrighted versions released prior to any contract with Hearst.[13]

These particular instances of conflict happened mostly in the early years of comic strips in American newspapers. There were conflicts between artists and publishers later, but by the 1920s the contours of the comic strip business had settled into place, and in return for high salaries artists were relatively content with their lot. By 1935, when Siegel returned to working with Shuster on a Superman comic strip, despite the Depression many artists were earning handsome amounts that were widely reported. For instance, *The Gumps* artist Sydney Smith, who famously died in a car accident that year just after signing a new contract, earned over a hundred thousand dollars at a time when the presidential salary was seventy-five thousand. Smith's salary was one-fifth of the highest reported salary earner of 1935, William Randolph Hearst, at half a million dollars. But Smith was on par with the president of DuPont, and his salary was close to twice those of famous reporters like Walter Lippmann and Walter Winchell.[14] The aforementioned Harry "Bud" Fisher was making close to the same money as Smith, as was Harold Gray of *Little Orphan Annie*. Not far off were a series of artists, including George McManus (*Bringing Up Father*, eighty thousand), Frank King (*Gasoline Alley*, seventy-five thousand), and Martin Branner (*Winnie Winkle*, fifty thousand). The value of this income in 2018 would range between one million and close to two million dollars. For artists like Gray, much of the money came from the favorable syndication deal that gave him 50 percent of the fees.[15] Promoting the success and earnings of comic strip artists was one way of promoting the comic strips themselves, with newspaper comics carrying the artist's signature or at the very least byline.

Many of the new publishers who flocked to the developing comic book market in the mid-1930s simply followed the practice of having artists and authors sign their comic book stories. For instance, the first issue of *Detective Comics* in 1937 had stories carrying the byline of Malcolm Wheeler-Nicholson (also the publisher), Creig Flessel, Homer Fleming, and Jerome Siegel and Joe Shuster.[16] This practice was simply a carryover from comic strips and in part happened because the first comic books were reprints of strips that of course carried the bylines. On the other hand comic book writers and artists were paid flat rates and signed over their copyrights, thereby relinquishing any control over their characters, including the opportunity to benefit from any subsequent republication or monetarization of the character in another fashion. These sorts of practices help explain why for several years Jerry Siegel withheld his Superman character from comic books, with an eye to profiting from a newspaper syndication deal.

Making the Siegel and Shuster Brand Name

From 1938 to 1947 Siegel and DC were in constant conflict. Much of this had to do with DC's demands that Siegel regulate production by providing story synopses, meet deadlines, and on the whole take charge of the production process for the comic book and later comic strip adventures of Superman. DC also tried to address defects in Siegel's command of standard written English and rein in his boundless enthusiasm for his character that had him promoting Superman outside the sanctions of DC's publicity operations. The success of Superman in *Action Comics* led to a newspaper comic strip version syndicated by McClure. Siegel and Shuster did not enjoy as favorable terms as many of the aforementioned comic strip artists, but they did profit from the venture, earning the equivalent (in 2018 dollars) of close to two and a half million dollars between 1938 and 1947 from the comic strip alone.[17] The strip version exacerbated the preexisting problems, and Siegel's abilities to manage the organizational aspects associated with a successful comic strip were severely challenged.

Much of the correspondence between Siegel and DC in this period has become public due to litigation between the two parties beginning in 1947. This correspondence reveals the mutual dissatisfaction of the two parties and also how marginal Joe Shuster was to the management and indeed the production of Superman. Siegel chafed at DC's control of Superman and its efforts to impose order on him. At the same time Siegel complained to

DC in a letter of March 8, 1942, about how little work Shuster performed and displayed some regret at treating him as an equal partner.[18] Nonetheless Siegel still felt some obligation to Shuster since he made no move to discard him. In any case all the contracts with DC and McClure were between Siegel and Shuster. So as much as Siegel thought that Shuster was creating problems for him in the production of Superman stories for the comic book and strip, he was bound to him legally and the byline Siegel and Shuster remained a hallmark of the character.

DC was also tied to the byline of Siegel and Shuster, if not legally, then as a marketing strategy, and it appeared on every Superman story published until March 1948. Such was the strength of Superman that DC attempted to launch new characters from Siegel. Various advertisements for these new characters appeared in DC Comics. The Spectre was advertised in *Action Comics* #21 as "a startling new and really different feature written by Jerry Siegel author of Superman." The Star-Spangled Kid was advertised in *Action Comics* #41 as "the Star Spangled Kid and Stripesy—slam banging comrades in combat from the pen of Jerry Siegel creator of Superman." None of these characters enjoyed much success, let alone the runaway enthusiasm Superman engendered in readers. Shuster did not participate in any of these features, and the artists who drew these strips—Bernard Bailey and Hal Sherman respectively—were not among the various assistants who drew Superman for Shuster. Yet another Siegel character, Robotman, drawn by Leo Nowack and Paul Cassidy, appeared unheralded and unsigned in *Star Spangled Comics* #7 in April 1942. Dubbed "the Man of Metal" by Siegel, the character drew a private comment from DC editor Whitney Ellsworth that it resembled "Superman too closely," which might account for it being unsigned.[19]

Nonetheless DC understood the value of the Siegel and Shuster byline. During World War II, when Siegel was unable to provide many stories due to his military service in Hawaii, the company continued to pay him his normal page rate for stories he had no hand in.[20] Likewise, even though Joe Shuster at best did limited work on Superman (often as little as drawing Superman's face), he too received his page rate. DC made these payments despite the fact that the company had taken on the organization of the regular production of Superman for the comic strip and comic book. DC's commitment to the Siegel and Shuster byline was part of their contract but also a sign of the comics being the genuine article. Nonetheless, there was an array of other Superman iterations, such as a radio serial and several animated cartoons, which did not always reference Siegel and Shuster as the creators of Superman. In these early days of characters appearing across media forms the concept of some sort of uniformity in various iterations had not yet developed. DC's respect for the Siegel and Shuster byline began to wane during World War II. With Siegel serving in the army, other hands wrote many of the Superman stories, and DC controlled production directly for the first time. In January 1945 DC published the first Superboy story in *More Fun Comics* #101, and although they apparently used a script by Jerry Siegel and it was drawn by Joe Shuster, neither received credit. Earlier in October 1944 Shuster wrote to Siegel to tell him he had just completed the story from a Superboy script Siegel had submitted a year earlier.[21] In a 1947 letter to Jerry Siegel Jack Liebowitz of DC made it clear that the company believed Superboy to be simply a derivative of Superman and so not requiring any permission from Siegel to use. That may well have been the case, but it is unclear why the story appeared unsigned when Siegel and Shuster created it, particularly since stories that month in both *Action Comics* and *Superman*, on which they had no creative input, carried their signatures. It is unclear why DC took this course of action. There is no available record of how Siegel responded to the 1944 letter from Shuster. It seems that for the rest of the war and until early 1947 Siegel hoped to get a better deal from DC, and a letter of September 6, 1946, from Siegel to Liebowitz suggests some contract negotiation on Superboy took place. But by early 1947 the ground shifted and Siegel and Shuster launched legal action against DC. The result of this legal action was the end of Siegel and Shuster's association with DC and the removal of their byline from the comic.[22]

Shuster's 1944 letter draws attention to a strain in the relationship with Siegel. Shuster had not heard from Siegel in over a year. It is noteworthy also that the only new creative project Shuster worked on with Siegel was at the behest of DC and then without the knowledge of Siegel. The point here is that part of the cachet of the Siegel and Shuster brand name was the notion of the two boyhood pals from Cleveland who created not just the preeminent superhero but a whole industry of superhero comics. Just how good of pals they were by the mid-1940s is questionable.

Reinventing the Brand

From 1948 the Siegel and Shuster brand name was mostly dormant. In 1948 Siegel launched a new character, Funnyman, that had a brief run in comic books and a strip that year. Shuster provided the layouts for the comic book version, but John Sikela and Dick Ayers drew much of the art. After this character flopped Siegel and Shuster went their separate ways. Siegel worked in the comics industry in various capacities, even for a time in the 1960s returning to DC anonymously, but by 1975 Siegel was poverty-stricken and working as a file clerk in Los Angeles. Shuster lived with his brother in an apartment in Queens, New York. Apparently the two had had little or no direct contact in years, possibly dating back to 1948.

The standard story of 1975 and the recovery of the two from obscurity goes something like this: After reading about a Superman film in production, Jerry Siegel wrote a lengthy "press release" memo condemning DC's treatment of him and Joe Shuster over the years. He cursed the movie. Prominent comics artists Neal Adams and Jerry Robinson became aware of their plight as a result of this memo and began campaigning on Siegel and Shuster's behalf for some sort of pension from DC. However the story is somewhat larger than this version, and as Brad Ricca, the biographer of Siegel and Shuster, tells it, DC began paying Siegel regularly sometime earlier, around 1974 or 1975, after prompting from Siegel's wife Joanne. Moreover, Joanne Siegel reached out to Joe Shuster to bring the two back together.[23] How well Joanne Siegel understood what she was doing is unclear, although I think she probably had a firm sense of it because of her subsequent actions, but in effect she relaunched the Siegel and Shuster brand name. The name no longer stood for a writer and artist so much as for people wronged by a large corporation. The narrative associated with that name became the two childhood friends, lifelong buddies done wrong by DC and left penniless, with the artist, tragically, almost blind. That Siegel and Shuster had made considerable sums of money up to 1948 disappeared from this narrative. In a stroke of genius Joanne Siegel inserted herself into this brand name, revealing that she had been the original model for Lois Lane. Prior to 1975 this relationship to Lois Lane had not been mentioned, a fact the Siegels themselves told interviewers at the San Diego Comic-Convention in August 1975. Ricca argues that this interview at Comic-Con and interviewers Murray Bishoff and Alan Light's interest in the legal travails of Siegel and Shuster gave Siegel the impetus and confidence to launch a campaign for justice, in which his memo was the opening salvo.[24]

There is a strong possibility that behind Siegel's action lay the hand of his wife. In 1957, when Siegel was struggling to find work, Joanne Siegel contacted Jack Liebowitz at DC and persuaded him to employ Jerry again, although anonymously. Given the acrimony between the two men, this must have taken some doing and conjures a vision of Joanne Siegel as a force of nature not easily swayed from her course. The story goes that she played on Liebowitz's fear of poor publicity around Siegel's poverty to get her way.[25] In 1975, when DC started sending checks, it is entirely possible that Joanne saw opportunities to step up the campaign to pitch for better treatment out of fear of bad publicity by adding Joe Shuster. Effectively Joanne Siegel turned the Siegel and Shuster brand name on DC and recaptured it. She introduced herself into the equation as Lois Lane, whether or not she was in fact the model for the character in the 1930s. Journalist Larry Tye questions this version of Joanne Siegel as the model for Lois Lane in his history of Superman. Joanne and Jerry had only reconnected, or connected, in 1947

Figure 6.1. Jerry, Joanne, and Laura Siegel at San Diego Comic Con, 1976. Photo by Alan Light.

at an artist ball. They married in 1948, and Joanne took six years off her age on the marriage certificate. Tye wonders why she would do this if they had known each other in the thirties.[26] That the Siegels themselves mentioned the Lois Lane model story was unheard before 1975 also raises some questions about its authenticity. As history the story is a little dubious, but as marketing it was genius. A publicity shot from 1975 shows Joanne holding a notebook and pen wearing a T-shirt marked Lois Lane; Jerry is unbuttoning his shirt to reveal a Superman logo; and the bespectacled Joe strikes an inquisitive pose, evoking Clark Kent. Alan Light's photo of the Siegels from the 1975 San Diego Comic-Con is signed by "Superman—Jerry Siegel" and "Joanne Siegel (Lois Lane)." In public relations terms these reports and photographs look very much like on-message talking points.

The tone of the campaign waged by the Siegels and their supporters was captured in a 1975 *New York Times* article: "Two 61-year-old men, nearly destitute and worried about how they will support themselves in their old age, are invoking the spirit of Superman for help. Joseph Shuster, who sits amidst his threadbare furniture in Queens, and Jerry Siegel, who waits in his cramped apartment in Los Angeles, share the hope that they each will get pensions from the Man of Steel."[27] Numerous newspapers across the country picked up the story of Siegel and Shuster's plight. The pair appeared on Tom Snyder's NBC *Tomorrow Show* on December 1, 1975. Cartoonists such as Milton Caniff, Jules Feiffer, Al Capp, Charles Schulz, Irwin Hasen, and

Burne Hogarth offered public support for the cause. Another *New York Times* story struck a tone of despair about the pair's plight and picked up the Joanne Siegel as the original Lois Lane angle.[28] Coverage of the story in another newspaper had Jerry Siegel "haunted' by Superman and physically ill at the mere sight of him. Nonetheless Siegel added that "Superman still stands for truth, justice, and the American Way. Yet, Joe and I have been deceived, treated unjustly and persecuted. I pray that isn't the American Way."[29] This clever evocation of Superman's best-known catch phrase was so good his daughter used it again in 2012 at the end of another lengthy legal battle with DC. The irony is that Siegel did not write the words, as they had originated in the 1940s radio serial.[30]

This positioning of Siegel and Shuster was very effective. Within four months of the Siegels' visit to the San Diego Comic-Con Warner Communications, the parent company of DC, decided to grant the pair a "pension" and medical benefits. The reason DC-Warner capitulated was that the *Superman* (1978) film was in the works and the corporation had planned an extensive licensing program that might have been undermined by bad publicity. After some negotiation DC also agreed to restore the Siegel and Shuster byline to all printed matter, television, and movies. Significantly the negotiations were handled on DC-Warner's side by Jay Emmett, Jack Liebowitz's nephew. Emmett had built the licensing arm of DC, the Licensing Corporation of America, into a powerhouse on the back of Superman, Batman, and additional characters the firm represented such as James Bond and Howdy Doody. Emmett was a vice president at Warner and responsible for licensing efforts. The decision to accede to Siegel's demands then was based on marketing.[31] If done reluctantly at first, the restoration of the credit, which cost the corporation nothing, added value in the years to come. Part of that value was the intangible and hard-to-quantify feel-good reputation that came from having done the right thing. But the Siegel and Shuster brand name also helped hold together disparate elements of the Superman brand, even to the point where the Superman name and logo were almost entirely absent. Jerry Siegel and Joe Shuster's byline appeared throughout the entire ten seasons of the television series *Smallville* (2001–2011), a show in which several important elements of Superman's character, such as his name, his powers, and his distinctive superhero costume, were absent. The Siegel and Shuster brand was one way of ensuring audiences that *Smallville* was indeed part of the Superman mythos. It may well be that the point has come where Superman, DC, and Siegel and Shuster have all reached mythic dimensions so that any mention of one reinforces the other. The truism that there is no such thing as bad publicity in this case means that even the long legal battle against DC by Siegel and Shuster and their heirs, which truly seems like one of Superman's never-ending battles, generated interest in the character to the benefit of DC, but I would suggest that benefit is hard to separate from the names Siegel and Shuster.

Notes

1 Siegel v. Warner Bros. Entm't, Inc., 542 F. Supp. 2d 1098 (CD Cal. 2008), LEXIS 27217, 4.
2 Jerry Siegel, "The Reign of the Superman," *Science Fiction: The Vanguard of Future Civilization*, January 1933, https://archive.org/details/ReignOfThe Superman.
3 Ian Gordon, *Superman: The Persistence of an American Icon* (New Brunswick, NJ: Rutgers University Press, 2017), 95–98.
4 Gordon, *Superman*, chap. 4.
5 Gordon, *Superman*, chap. 4.
6 See, for instance, Micael Dahlen, Fredrik Lange, and Terry Smith, *Marketing Communications: A Brand Narrative Approach* (Hoboken, NJ: John Wiley, 2009), and Laurence Vincent, *Legendary Brands: Unleashing the Power of Storytelling to Create a Winning Market Strategy* (Chicago: Dearborn, 2002).
7 Jean-Paul Gabilliet, *Of Comics and Men: A Cultural History of American Comic Books* (Jackson: University Press of Mississippi, 2010).
8 Ian Gordon, *Comic Strips and Consumer Culture, 1890–1945* (Washington, DC: Smithsonian Institution Press, 1998), 31.
9 Gordon, *Comic Strips and Consumer Culture*, chap. 2.
10 New York Herald Co. v. Star Co., 146 Federal Reporter 204 (1906); Outcault et al. v. New York Herald, 146 Federal Reporter 205 (1906), and 146 Federal Reporter 1023 (1906).
11 Outcault et al. v. Lamar, 119 NYS 930 (1909).
12 Star Company, Respondent, v. The Press Publishing Company and Rudolph Dirks, 147 NYS 579 (1914).
13 Star Company, Plaintiff, v. Wheeler Syndicate, Inc., 155 NYS 782 (1916); Harry C. Fisher, Respondent v. Star Company, 231 NY 414 (1921).
14 "Leading Salary Payments of 1935 Disclosed: Business Men, Movie Stars," *Chicago Tribune*, January 7, 1937, 23.
15 "Funnies: Colored Comic Strips in the Best of Health at Forty," *Newsweek*, December 1, 1934, 26–27; and W. E. Berchtold, "Men of Comics," *New Outlook*, April 1935, 34–40; May 1935, 43–47.
16 *Detective Comics* #1 (New York: Detective Comics, March 1937).
17 Statement of payments made to Siegel and Shuster by DC from 1947 copyright case, reproduced in Siegel v. Warner Bros. Entm't, Inc., No. 2:04-cv-08400-SGL-RZ, Document 353-4, www.scribd.com/user/3105491/Jeff-Trexler.
18 Letter reproduced in Lauren Agostino and A. L. Newberg, *Holding Kryptonite: Truth, Justice and America's First Superhero* (New York: Holmes and Watson, 2014).

19 Ellsworth to Siegel December 5, 1941, reproduced in Agostino and Newberg, *Holding Kryptonite.*

20 Sigel shipped out June 28, 1943. Brad Ricca, *Super Boys: The Amazing Adventures of Jerry Siegel and Joe Shuster* (New York: St. Martin's, 2013), 211–212, 223.

21 Joe Shuster to Jerry Siegel, October 1, 1944, reproduced in Agostino and Newberg, *Holding Kryptonite.*

22 Jerry Siegel to Jack Liebowitz, September 6, 1946, reproduced in Agostino and Newberg, *Holding Kryptonite*; Siegel v. National Periodical Publications, Inc., 364 F. Supp. 1032 (1973).

23 Jerry Siegel revealed to journalist Ira Berkow that the two had "lost contact." "Superman Haunts Creator Jerry Siegel," *Sarasota Journal*, December 17, 1975.

24 Gerard Jones, *Men of Tomorrow: Geeks, Gangsters and the Birth of the Comic Book* (New York: Basic Books, 2005), 249–251; Ricca, *Super Boys*, 271–275; Jerry Siegel, Joanne Siegel, and Laura Siegel, "Superman Grew Out of Our Personal Feelings about Life," interviewed by Murray Bishoff and Alan Light, *Alter Ego* 56 (February 2006): 7.

25 Jones, *Men of Tomorrow*, 283; Ricca, *Super Boys*, 243.

26 Larry Tye, *Superman: The High-Flying History of America's Most Enduring Hero* (New York: Random House, 2012), 311.

27 Mary Breasted, "Superman's Creators, Nearly Destitute, Invoke His Spirit," *New York Times*, November 22, 1975.

28 Murray Bishoff, "The Siegel & Shuster Deal at 30," *Alter Ego* 65 (February 2007): 38; David Vidal, "Mild-Mannered Cartoonists Go to the Aid of Superman's Creators," *New York Times*, December 10, 1975.

29 Berkow, "Superman Haunts Creator Jerry Siegel."

30 Eriq Gardner, "Superman Heir Pens Letter to Fans about Fight with Warner Bros," *Hollywood Reporter*, October 12, 2012, www.hollywoodreporter.com/heat-vision/superman-heir-pens-letter-fans-378793; Robert Maxwell and Olga Druce created the catch phrase; Gordon, *Superman*, 115.

31 Jones, *Men of Tomorrow*, 320–323, offers an account of the negotiations based on conversations with Jerry Robinson who acted for Siegel and Shuster; Gordon, *Superman*, chap. 6; Mitchell Adams, this volume.

Bibliography

Agostino, Lauren, and A. L. Newberg. *Holding Kryptonite: Truth, Justice and America's First Superhero.* New York: Holmes and Watson, 2014.

Berchtold, W. E. "Men of Comics." *New Outlook*, April 1935, 34–40; May 1935, 43–47.

Berkow, Ira. "Superman Haunts Creator Jerry Siegel." *Sarasota Journal*, December 17, 1975.

Bishoff, Murray. "The Siegel & Shuster Deal at 30." *Alter Ego* 65 (February 2007): 34–39.

Breasted, Mary. "Superman's Creators, Nearly Destitute, Invoke His Spirit." *New York Times*, November 22, 1975.

Dahlen, Micael, Fredrik Lange, and Terry Smith. *Marketing Communications: A Brand Narrative Approach.* Hoboken, NJ: John Wiley, 2009.

"Funnies: Colored Comic Strips in the Best of Health at Forty." *Newsweek*, December 1, 1934, 26–27.

Gabilliet, Jean-Paul. *Of Comics and Men: A Cultural History of American Comic Books*. Jackson: University Press of Mississippi, 2010.

Gardner, Eriq. "Superman Heir Pens Letter to Fans about Fight with Warner Bros." *Hollywood Reporter*, October 12, 2012. www.hollywoodreporter.com/heat-vision/superman-heir-pens-letter-fans-378793.

Gordon, Ian. *Comic Strips and Consumer Culture, 1890–1945*. Washington, DC: Smithsonian Institution Press, 1998.

———. *Superman: The Persistence of an American Icon*. New Brunswick, NJ: Rutgers University Press, 2017.

Harry C. Fisher, Respondent v. Star Company, 231 NY 414 (1921).

Jones, Gerard. *Men of Tomorrow: Geeks, Gangsters and the Birth of the Comic Book*. New York: Basic Books, 2005.

"Leading Salary Payments of 1935 Disclosed: Business Men, Movie Stars." *Chicago Tribune*, January 7, 1937.

New York Herald Co. v. Star Co., 146 Federal Reporter 204 (1906).

Outcault et al. v. Lamar, 119 NYS 930 (1909).

Outcault et al. v. New York Herald, 146 Federal Reporter 205, and 146 Federal Reporter 1023 (1906).

Ricca, Brad. *Super Boys: The Amazing Adventures of Jerry Siegel and Joe Shuster*. New York: St. Martin's, 2013.

Siegel, Jerry. "The Reign of the Superman." *Science Fiction: The Vanguard of Future Civilization*, January 1933. https://archive.org/details/ReignOfTheSuperman.

Siegel, Jerry, Joanne Siegel, and Laura Siegel. "Superman Grew Out of Our Personal Feelings about Life." Interviewed by Murray Bishoff and Alan Light. *Alter Ego* 56 (February 2006): 3–18.

Siegel v. National Periodical Publications, Inc., 364 F. Supp. 1032 (1973).

Siegel v. Warner Bros. Entm't, Inc., 542 F. Supp. 2d 1098 (CD Cal. 2008), LEXIS 27217, 4 (2008).

Star Company, Plaintiff v. Wheeler Syndicate, Inc., 155 NYS 782.

Star Company, Respondent v. The Press Publishing Company and Rudolph Dirks, 147 NYS 579.

Tye, Larry. *Superman: The High-Flying History of America's Most Enduring Hero*. New York: Random House, 2012.

Vidal, David. "Mild-Mannered Cartoonists Go to the Aid of Superman's Creators." *New York Times*, December 10, 1975.

Vincent, Laurence. *Legendary Brands: Unleashing the Power of Storytelling to Create a Winning Market Strategy*. Chicago: Dearborn, 2002.

7

Practicing Superhuman Law

Creative License, Industrial Identity, and Spider-Man's Homecoming

TARA LOMAX

The industrial conditions concerning ownership and licensing of intellectual property (IP) are central to the development of creative content in contemporary media franchising. Similarly, the licensing relationships between comic book publishers and Hollywood studios have a dynamic impact on the creative development and industrial identity of superhero properties. For example, in the late 1990s Marvel Comics regained its economic stability following bankruptcy by licensing high-profile superhero properties like Spider-Man and the X-Men to Hollywood studios.[1] This licensing strategy saw Marvel forfeit creative control of a number of its characters. Media and cultural studies scholar Derek Johnson notes that such licensing agreements gave Hollywood studios "creative and economic control over production, marketing, and sublicensing," and thus Marvel "struggled to maintain creative power over the direction of its comic book films."[2] This creative-industrial tension is at the foundation of Marvel Studios' organizational identity as a movie production company conceived to self-produce its remaining superhero properties. As president of Marvel Entertainment Alan Fine explains, in setting up Marvel Studios "we wanted to control the destinies of our own characters. *We* wanted to decide when, how, and in which ways we would bring them to filmed-entertainment."[3] Therefore, Marvel Studios is founded as an industrial intervention into the conventional structures of ownership and licensing relations between Hollywood and the American comic book industry.

Marvel Studios' objective to self-produce its own superhero properties is realized in the development of what it has branded the Marvel Cinematic

Universe (MCU): a transmedia franchise that maintains interconnecting diegetic continuity across multiple installments and media platforms. The MCU positions the Avengers as its narrative and character centerpiece and draws from the rich catalogue of Marvel comic book characters that are not already bound up in license agreements with other Hollywood movie studios. This creative strategy balances solo superhero installments and franchise series around characters like Captain America, Thor, and Iron Man with ensemble movies like *The Avengers* and *Guardians of the Galaxy*. This approach has been extended to television, where characters from individual Netflix series such as *Daredevil*, *Luke Cage*, and *Jessica Jones* team up in the crossover show *The Defenders*, while the broadcast series *Agents of S.H.I.E.L.D.* also exists in and contributes to the same diegetic universe by incorporating subtle to obvious crossovers.[4] The MCU is therefore significant as a creative-industrial pursuit because it can be characterized as both a complex creative initiative, through its experimentation with diegetic continuity, and an industrial venture, since it uses this interconnecting creative strategy in its brand as a studio that self-produces its own IP.

Due to preexisting licenses with Fox, Sony, and Universal, Marvel's IP portfolio has been fragmented across multiple Hollywood studios. While Marvel Studios is largely distinguished by the characters and franchises located "inside the MCU"—namely the Avengers—it is also unavoidably associated with franchises that have been produced by other studios "outside the MCU," like Spider-Man and X-Men. This means that the MCU is characterized by both what it is and what it is not. This not only risks creative confusion between the MCU and other franchises adapted from Marvel Comics through licensing but also incidentally complicates the strategic development of its interconnected diegetic continuity. Spider-Man is a productive example of a superhero property that has been developed as a franchise "outside (and prior to) the MCU," and has now been incorporated "inside the MCU." Spider-Man was previously off-limits to Marvel Studios due to a licensing agreement made in 1999 between Marvel and Sony Pictures Entertainment; however, these circumstances have recently changed since Sony agreed to loan Spider-Man to Marvel for inclusion in the MCU. As president of Marvel Studios Kevin Feige revealed, "Marvel's involvement [in producing these new Spider-Man movies] will hopefully deliver the creative continuity and authenticity that fans demand from the MCU."[5] First occurring with a cameo appearance in *Captain America: Civil War*, Spider-Man's full welcome into the MCU was heralded with a solo movie sentimentally titled *Spider-Man: Homecoming*.[6] At the heart of this industrial collaboration between Marvel and Sony, therefore, is the celebration of creative continuity and the affective sentiments of "returning home." *Homecoming* is thus the result of two competing studios "collaborat[ing] on a new creative direction for the web slinger."[7] Previously divorced from the creative and economic control of Marvel Studios, Spider-Man's incorporation into the MCU, and into the same diegetic world as the Avengers is a significant creative industry occurrence. Indeed, this chapter argues that *Homecoming* sets a precedent for understanding the complex creative and industrial dynamics of superhero franchises. As this chapter discusses below, *Homecoming* is not simply a new beginning for Spider-Man, Marvel, or Sony, but is discursively inscribed with Marvel Comics' turbulent economic history of bankruptcy, license farming, and the interplay of creative and industrial priorities in constructing the company's organizational identity.

In examining the nature and function of superhero properties within the context of media franchising, this chapter demonstrates that superhero franchises constitute both a proprietary function *and* a creative mode of expression. The interplay of these impulses is fundamental to understanding media franchising as a dominant mode of production in contemporary screen media. Johnson conceptualizes this interaction as a process of creative license, which he defines as "franchising as a mediation of creativity" through licensing relations.[8] This chapter considers this "mediation of creativity" through the notion of industrial identity; this conceptualizes how various franchise properties are inscribed with a distinct identity as a result of ownership structures and licensing relations, in tandem with the strategies of creative development. For example, prior to *Homecoming* Spider-Man's industrial identity had been shaped by its estranged licensed relationship, including various reboots and genre reimaginings under different creative teams and actors: Sam Raimi and Marc Webb as directors, and Tobey Maguire and Andrew Garfield as actors. Spider-Man's industrial identity, therefore, is currently under revision with his foray into the MCU, in which he is played by actor Tom Holland. This chapter considers the concept of creative license as a process through which a superhero property's industrial identity is also negotiated and shaped. As such, this approach understands superhero franchises as being inherently constituted by creative and industrial priorities.

The intersection between creativity and business is a premise that Marvel Comics has already previously explored with the introduction of the metatextual concept of "superhuman law" in comic book writer Dan Slott's run on *She-Hulk*.[9] As explained in *She-Hulk*, superhuman law is "a new and unchartered territory for legal pioneers" that caters to the litigious requirements of superheroes and other comic book characters, with clients ranging from Spider-Man to Howard the Duck.[10] In *She-Hulk*, superhuman law constitutes the professional setting for the character She-Hulk, aka Jennifer Walters, who is offered a job at the prestigious law firm of Goodman,

Lieber, Kurtzberg & Holliway (GLK&H), on the condition that she practice her job as Walters, not She-Hulk. For Walters, superhuman law and the offices of GLK&H are merely a backdrop for her to gain a better understanding of herself as human and superhuman; just as compelling, however, is that this character journey works in tandem with how the premise of superhuman law legalizes the dual nature of superheroes and supervillains as both fictional characters and legal entities. In the series Walters learns that in the practice of superhuman law comic books constitute legal case files that are "admissible in *any* court of law" and "most Marvel books are licensed from the *real* heroes."[11] In this legal practice comic book origin issues are approved by each superhero before being filed in long boxes and kept as legal documents in the basement of GLK&H.[12] For these reasons, it is not She-Hulk (or Walters) that is of interest for this chapter, but rather the practice of superhuman law. Superhuman law is a metafictional practice in which Marvel Comics demonstrates awareness of its own ownership histories and the complex industrial conditions of its characters; as such, it is a compelling metaphor through which to consider the relationship between the superhero genre and the franchise mode of production. However, superhuman law is not called on here as evidence of Marvel's legal practices or to necessarily support conclusions about the company's approach to creativity in superhero franchises; rather, it is a metafictional reflection of the complex process of creative license in developing superhero franchises.

Superhuman Law and Intellectual Property

Marvel Comics uses the notion of superhuman law as a metafictional narrative practice to playfully acknowledge the ownership histories of Marvel and the legalization of superhero identities as licensed properties in the contemporary entertainment industries. Operating out of offices at Timely Plaza in New York City—an allusion to Marvel's founding name of Timely Comics—the name Goodman, Lieber, Kurtzberg & Holliway explicitly refers to key Marvel figures: founder Martin Goodman and key creators Stan Lee (born Stanley Lieber) and Jack Kirby (born Jacob Kurtzberg). This reference to extradiegetic figures as partners of a diegetic law firm acknowledges the legacy of ownership and authorship in Marvel's history. The fourth partner, Holden Holliway, manages the firm within the diegesis and, it is assumed, liaises with the other partners, although this is never depicted in the comic series. Through this nod to Marvel's past, superhuman law is practiced at a metafictional law firm where its principal partners cross textual boundaries between reality and fiction, thus establishing a metatextual dialogue between the inside and outside of the text.

Superhuman law thus presents a playful but compelling creative reflection on the superhuman dimensions and procedures of entertainment law and the creative industries. This association between superhuman law and entertainment law complements Mitchell Adams's chapter in this collection, which considers how trademark law protects the secret commercial symbolism of superhero properties. In *She-Hulk*, superhuman law is used by comic book characters in the negotiation of movie sequel contracts. For example, in one side panel, Howard the Duck employs GLK&H to sue George Lucas for failing to produce a successful trilogy with the license to his property (Figure 7.1).[13] This is a comical allusion to Lucasfilm's critically and commercially disappointing production of a *Howard the Duck* film adaptation in 1986, while also satirically conveying how creative license inevitably involves some tension between licensee and licensor.[14] With this example there is also a conscious association made between the practice of superhuman law and the institutional ownership structures and licensing relations of the entertainment industry. Indeed, the conditions of IP and licensing relations in media franchising are metaphorically akin to the practice of superhuman law in Marvel Comics—that is, superhuman law is constituted by an interaction of metafiction and legal practice, which can also serve to function as a symbolic narration of creative license.

As a legal practice within the diegesis of Marvel Comics, superhuman law protects the legal interests of superheroes and negotiates the exceptional legal circumstances concerning superhero identities. The first client depicted in this *She-Hulk* series is Danger Man / Daniel Jermain, who acquires powers as the result of a workplace chemical accident. Using his uncontrollable super strength Daniel injures his family and damages his home.[15] His insurance company does not cover superhuman incidents, and so neither Daniel nor his family can receive health coverage. Superhuman law is employed here to argue that Danger Man's "origin story" resulted in the death of Daniel, and subsequently his family is eligible for his death insurance. Another noteworthy client of GLK&H is Spider-Man, who attempts to sue newspaper publisher J. Jonah Jameson for libel, but must settle out of court when the case inadvertently implicates Spider-Man's secret identity—Peter Parker—as Jameson's photographer.[16] Both these cases suggest that the practical function of superhuman law is not to achieve or strengthen coherence in superhero identities but to negotiate legal boundaries between superheroes and their secret identities. Indeed, American studies scholar Adam Capitanio describes She-Hulk and her practice of superhuman law as a "disrupter of continuity, someone who battles the narrative status quo."[17] This observation is consistent with the Danger Man and Spider-Man cases, which result in compromises despite and/or because of the disruptions caused by their secret and dual identities. Similarly, Capitanio's under-

Figure 7.1. At the superhuman law offices of Goodman, Lieber, Kurtzberg & Holliway, Marvel Comics character Howard the Duck confronts producer George Lucas about his failure to produce a successful trilogy with the license to his comic book property, *She-Hulk* #9 (New York: Marvel Comics, January 2005).

standing of superhuman law as a "disrupter of continuity" also productively describes the creative disruption that can occur as a result of real-world licensing agreements, as I have noted above in relation to the licensed outsourcing of Marvel's superhero IP.

A consideration of real-world IP via the metafictional practice of superhuman law paradoxically validates and questions the function of comic books as legal property. Moreover, it reflects on the legality of tangible comic books, which occupy a contentious space as both material object and immaterial IP. This undertaking not only delineates the contested definition of creative ideation as economic property but also implicates IP in questions of subjectivity, multiplicity, and storytelling conventions. The practice of superhuman law in *She-Hulk* provides Marvel with a diegetic creative space in which to explore and self-regulate the boundaries and interpretations of its own IP and licensing relations. Capitanio considers how Slott harnesses superhuman law as a metacomic device through which to engage in a revisionist exploration of the superhero comic book genre.[18] Capitanio says that, in *She-Hulk*, Slott experiments with the tropes of superhero storytelling conventions and thus represents the superhero genre's "sort of 'identity crisis'" in the new millennium.[19] Superhuman law is, therefore, also an analogy for Marvel's own struggle with developing and maintaining control of its own creative and industrial identity. As Capitanio points out, in *She-Hulk* "comic book storylines take on the force of legal rulings, which therefore set boundaries around the way that any subsequent storyline might unfold."[20] Superhuman law thus functions as a creative strategy for Marvel to self-consciously reflect on the conditions of the contemporary comic book industry and its storytelling conventions.

In a further congruous association with superhuman law, the nature and conditions of real-life IP and licensing are often defined in metaphysical dimensions. The objective of IP law, as law scholar Alexandra George describes it, is to protect the "intangible," "incorporeal," and "imaginary" "object" of the intellect.[21] In this way, the negotiation of such dimensions is also unavoidably subjective, and it defines "the boundaries of an intellectual property object as fuzzy."[22] This infers a potential for creative difference and interpretation. As George continues, "An intellectual property object's boundaries are multi-dimensional, and they are usually impossible to determine except when measured against the scope of other (actual or potential) intellectual property objects."[23] The conceptual nature of IP is thus fundamentally inscribed with an abstract dialectic between the immaterial phenomena of the intellect and the tangible object of property. The boundaries that define the IP object also shape its creative interpretation across multiple media forms, creators, corporations, and storylines. This space facilitates a mechanism for media production that is driven by an interaction of IP boundaries and creative development, as well as the collaborative processes of creative license that will be expanded on below.

Such a mechanism also corresponds with, and even inarguably contributes to, the superhero genre's shifting conditions from continuity to multiplicity. Media scholar Henry Jenkins notes that within this structural movement "difference is felt much more powerfully *within* a genre than *between* competing genres."[24] Similarly, English scholar Molly Hatcher identifies a comparable mechanism driving the relationship between IP structures, which "encourage greater creative possibilities *within* a particular character's story, [and] it also promotes exciting exchanges *between* characters from different stories."[25] The Spider-Man franchise is an example of how genre conventions can shift *within* the same franchise, in which the various reboot attempts have represented the source of Spider-Man's powers in different genre terms. For example, in Sam Raimi's 2002 film *Spider-Man*—the hero's first cinematic origin story—his web-shooting powers are rendered fantastical from a radioactive spider bite.[26] Conversely, in Marc Webb's rebooted movie origin *The Amazing Spider-Man*, the character's web-shooting capabilities are the result of Peter's technological genius, which reimagines the source of Spider-Man's powers in science fiction terms and in line with the character's comic book origin story.[27] This multifarious adaptation of the Spider-Man IP object also correlates with Hatcher's contention that "the intellectual property structure of these companies creates an avenue for the development of multi-layered narrative and images that combine old and new."[28] In one sense the different generic sources of Spider-Man's web-slinging powers serve to differentiate character branding across the different versions, with different creative approaches. In another sense the need to rejuvenate the brand and the creative desire to reimagine the character, while still working within the limitations and allowances of a license, results in an interaction between genre conventions and licensing conditions.

Creative License and Marvel's Organizational Identity

As a movie production company, Marvel Studios has consciously constructed an organizational identity around the dynamic between creativity and business. In their comprehensive analysis of Marvel Studios, film and popular culture scholars Martin Flanagan, Andrew Livingstone, and Mike McKenny identify Marvel as an "organization of storytellers" that actively works to construct an organizational identity that strategically facilitates and encourages the process of creative license.[29] As such, they describe Marvel's approach to creative development as a negotiation of art and commerce, in which "creative individuals are afforded the freedom they require, so long as the financial implications balance."[30] This speaks to the interaction between creativity and business that this chapter is concerned with and highlights the role of authorial process in Marvel's industrial organization. As Flanagan, Livingstone, and McKenny also contend, this organizational identity is defined by "Marvel's inherent capacity to tell stories—and its historic precedent of harbouring decision makers that are at once businessmen *and* storytellers."[31] This is most explicitly exemplified by Feige as franchise runner who manages both the creative and economic directions of Marvel Studios and the MCU. Flanagan, Livingstone, and McKenny consider Feige as "more like a film producer in the mould of an EIC [editor-in-chief]."[32] Similarly, Liam Burke regards Marvel for being the first to "appl[y] the collaborative authorship and editorial supervision commonplace in comics to a blossoming transmedia franchise."[33] These understandings of Marvel's organization identity also describe how Marvel's approach to creative development occupies the threshold between comic book publishing and movie production.

Marvel's organizational identity is also inscribed with its history of license outsourcing. As mentioned above, such licensing arrangements are central to the economic practices of the American comic book industry and its relationship with other dominant media industries like Hollywood. Communications professor Mark C. Rogers describes how the comic book industry has a long history operating as a licensing farm, in which comic book narratives function primarily "to develop and maintain characters that can be sold for use in other media."[34] As Rogers and Johnson have comprehensively documented, Marvel Comics' role as a licensing farm is central to its turbulent industrial history: its rapid horizontal expansion strategy of the 1990s led to its bankruptcy, and, as explained above, Marvel relinquished creative authority over its most high-profile superhero characters as a viable strategy for its economic replenishment.[35] The incidental paradox of this licensing arrangements is that, as Johnson states, the "licenses sold by Marvel had effectively given away the comic book company's position of creative authority and industrial authority over talent and labor."[36] Even though this strategy helped rescue the company from bankruptcy, it was at a creative cost. It is for this reason that the industrial identity of the MCU is intertwined with each comic book property's litigious boundaries and licensing relations. Spider-Man is one such example of a licensed property that plays a fundamental role in understanding Marvel's own organizational identity. Spider-Man's licensed distance and estrangement from Marvel not only is economically significant but also influences the strategic development of its own creative continuity and cohesion.

Spider-Man Is "Home"

When Marvel Studios and Sony officially announced a coproduction that would welcome Spider-Man into the same diegetic universe as the MCU, some critics, celebrities, and popular audiences lamented over the release of "yet another Spider-Man movie."[37] Indeed, in an interview at the time actress Emma Thompson even confessed to wanting to end her own life at the news of another Spider-Man movie.[38] Such a response suggests that the creative-industrial significance of *Homecoming* is obscured by the reboot logic that has characterized previous Spider-Man incarnations. *Homecoming* is the sixth solo Spider-Man installment within fifteen years—but it is not an origin story and does not retrace any of the previous plot elements or secondary characters of previous installments (except Aunt May, although even she has been reimagined within the MCU).[39] Therefore, *Homecoming* is creatively and industrially distinct from previous cinematic iterations of the iconic superhero property. Feige reveals that he is "excited for the opportunity to have Spider-Man appear in the MCU, something which both we at Marvel, and fans alike, have been looking forward to for years."[40] This is exemplified by "Homecoming" as the choice of subtitle: with the thematic sentiments of home, belonging, and identity associated with Marvel as the property's ultimate creator and owner. Therefore, the movie's subtitle reinforces and extends the intersection of creativity and industry

Figure 7.2. Spider-Man disarms Captain America of his shield in *Captain America: Civil War*, in the character's iconic costumed entry into the Marvel Cinematic Universe (Walt Disney Company, 2016).

that Flanagan, Livingstone, and McKenny characterize as central to Marvel's organizational identity.

While Marvel and Sony have renegotiated the terms of their licensing arrangement to relocate Spider-Man "inside the MCU," they have also reconfigured the terms of their industrial relationship: from that of licensor and licensee to creative collaboration. This plays out in *Homecoming* via two important textual elements: the opening studio logo and the appearance of the Avengers and its icons. *Homecoming* opens with Sony-Columbia's dual studio logo and is followed by a prologue scene set "eight years ago," which depicts the cleanup operations following *The Avengers*.[41] In its opening moments, *Homecoming* situates itself as first and foremost a Sony production, but then immerses itself into a pivotal historical moment in the MCU: the aftermath of the Battle of New York, which takes place in *The Avengers*. As the moment when the Avengers first "assembled," the Battle of New York could be regarded as the MCU's first creative milestone: the culmination of the first phase of its interconnected storytelling strategy. When the Marvel Studios logo finally appears in *Homecoming*, there is a significant addition to the familiar MCU images that project across the Marvel Studios logo: the image of Spider-Man holding Captain America's shield in *Civil War* (see Figure 7.2). By this stage the plot has not yet begun, but the logic of collaboration has been paratextually exemplified by the opening studio logos.

Even though the creative strategy of the MCU is based on the premise of an interconnected diegetic universe, not all MCU installments (e.g., *Guardians of the Galaxy* and *Doctor Strange*) explicitly identify the presence of the Avengers in their diegesis.[42] By contrast, *Homecoming* places the world of the Avengers at the forefront of its plot, setting, and publicity. For example, during the film's promotion one of the most successful anticipation-building posters features Spider-Man lying in front of the New York City skyline with the Avengers Tower in the background. This poster contains no movie title: the iconicity of Spider-Man in frame with the Avengers Tower is perhaps thought to be enough to visually signify the title "Spider is Home." There are many examples throughout *Homecoming* that emphasize Spider-Man's presence in the same diegetic universe as the Avengers: the prominent role of Tony Stark and the return of Happy Hogan from the Iron Man franchise; the prerecorded educational video of Captain America, dressed in an earlier version of his costume from *The Avengers*, viewed at Peter's high school during gym class and detention; and a number of scenes set inside the Avengers Tower, which was previously featured in *Avengers: Age of Ultron*.[43]

In *Homecoming* an ATM robbery sequence plays with the idea of a pseudo-appearance of the Avengers, as Spider-Man fights a group of four burglars wearing cheap masks of Iron Man, Hulk, Thor, and Captain America with an "Identity Theft" poster on the bank's wall. This scene almost channels the metafictional style of *She-Hulk* in its playful questioning of the nature of legal and creative identities: Spider-Man quips "it's great to finally meet you guys," then after being attacked by stolen Chitauri technology he adds, "I'm starting to think you're not the real Avengers." Similarly, a "Made by Peter Parker" video diary sequence that opens the film reveals behind-the-scenes footage of Peter's experience fighting members of the Avengers in *Civil War*, thus reinforcing that *Homecoming* is not considered tangential but is textually inscribed into the MCU. Indeed, in this way *Homecoming* makes deliberate effort to herald itself as being in the same world as the Avengers while, ironically, Peter always feels at an arms-length away as he awaits their call.

Although this chapter argues that *Homecoming* is not *just* another Spider-Man movie, it is still indeed *another* Spider-Man movie. The distinction here is important: *Homecoming* is significant both in its distinctiveness as the first solo Spider-Man movie "inside the MCU" *and* in its derivation from previous incarnations that sit "outside the MCU." This corresponds with how media scholar William Proctor defines the reboot strategy, which "does not render past narratives obsolete and irrelevant, regardless of industry intention, but rather reactivates them within an increasingly complex web."[44] *Homecoming* thus contributes to the fluid and multidimensional industrial identity of the Spider-Man property, which is constituted by various media producers and creative outputs, many managed by license agreements: over five decades of comic books series; six solo movie installments and a growing number of supporting roles; multiple animated and live-action television series produced in the United States and Japan; countless videogames by different developers; toys; various tie-ins; and a Broadway musical. These creative and commercial iterations of the Spider-Man property are an inevitable result of licensing agreements, which have been creatively achieved and negotiated using various comic book storytelling strategies, such as rebooting, seriality, and retroactive continuity to rejuvenate and keep the property viable. Therefore, *Homecoming* is not *just* another Spider-Man movie but a creative-industrial event of superhuman proportions that finally brings Spider-Man *home* to Marvel.

Conclusion

The significance of the MCU as a transmedia franchise with an interconnected diegetic continuity has attracted critical and mainstream attention to the industrial conditions of superhero property licensing. As such, the creative-industrial identity of Marvel's self-produced interconnected franchise strategy is discursively inscribed with the historical licensing arrangements between Marvel Comics and various Hollywood studios. For this reason the creative development of the MCU is centered on the Avengers, but it is also just as much defined by the absence of the X-Men and the Fantastic Four, and more recently the contingent inclusion of Spider-Man in *Homecoming.* The release of *Avengers: Infinity War* has intensified the MCU's interconnected premise, as it brings together the Avengers with the Guardians of the Galaxy for the first time in a movie adaptation.[45]

This chapter has argued that owned and licensed IP superhero franchises are shaped by a complex negotiation of industrial conditions *and* creative expression across multiple media and serialized iterations. As superhero franchises increasingly pervade contemporary screen culture and continue to expand across multiple media and franchises, the dynamic between creativity and business will become inevitably more complex. Such attention is likely to intensify in the future as media conglomerates continue to reconfigure and negotiate their IP portfolios, through either new licensing agreements or company acquisitions. For example, the Walt Disney Company's acquisition of Twenty-First Century Fox in early 2019 raises potential questions about what this means for the future of the MCU franchise strategy since superhero properties like the X-Men and Fantastic Four have returned to Marvel's creative control.[46]

The creative and industrial significance of Disney's acquisition of Fox is undoubtedly compatible with the metaphor of superhuman law called on in this chapter. In drawing on the diegetic practice of superhuman law, I have argued that Spider-Man's incorporation into the MCU is a creative-industrial feat of superhuman dimensions. In this way, Spider-Man's Homecoming expresses a creative-industrial nexus that is facilitated by the collaboration of two major movies studios, Sony and Marvel, through the processes of creative licensing. With *Homecoming,* not only does the Spider-Man character occupy the same diegesis as the Avengers, but the Spider-Man property is renegotiated as a shared industrial property. The creative-industrial identity of Spider-Man is multiple, contingent, and historically discursive. *Homecoming* therefore signals a tipping point in the creative and industrial history of the Spider-Man franchise and the further possibilities of the MCU. Indeed, *Homecoming* and Spider-Man's inclusion "inside the MCU" can be considered a feat of superhuman law.

Notes

1 Under this licensing strategy, Marvel licensed Spider-Man to Sony Pictures, the X-Men and Fantastic Four to Twentieth Century Fox, and Hulk to Universal Studios.

2 Derek Johnson, "Cinematic Destiny: Marvel Studios and the Trade Stories of Industrial Convergence," *Cinema Journal* 52, no. 1 (2012): 1–24, 9, 10.

3 *Marvel Studios: Assembling a Universe*, produced by Marvel Television in association with ABC Studios and Marvel Studios, TV Movie, aired March 18, 2014, on ABC. Fine's emphasis in dialogue.

4 *Marvel's Agents of S.H.I.E.L.D.*, executive produced by Joss Whedon, Jed Whedon, and Maurissa Tancharoen (Burbank, CA: Marvel Television, ABC Studios, and Mutant Enemy Productions, 2013–).

5 "Sony Pictures Entertainment Brings Marvel Studios in the Amazing World of Spider-Man," *Marvel News*, February 9, 2015, https://news.marvel.com/movies/24062/sony_pictures_entertainment_brings_marvel_studios_into_the_amazing_world_of_spider-man/.

6 *Captain America: Civil War*, dir. Joe Russo and Anthony Russo (Marvel Studios, 2016); *Spider-Man: Homecoming*, dir. Jon Watts (Marvel Studios and Sony-Columbia, 2017).

7 "Sony Pictures Entertainment Brings Marvel Studios in the Amazing World of Spider-Man."

8 Derek Johnson, *Media Franchising: Creative License and Collaboration in the Culture Industries* (New York: New York University Press, 2013), 25.

9 Dan Slott, Juan Bobillo, and Adi Granov, "Class Action Comics!," *She-Hulk* #2 (New York: Marvel, April 2004), 8.

10 Slott, Bobillo, and Granov, "Class Action Comics!," 9.

11 Slott, Bobillo, and Granov, "Class Action Comics!," 11.

12 Slott, Bobillo, and Granov, "Class Action Comics!," 11.

13 Slott, Bobillo, and Granov, "Strong Enough," *She-Hulk* #9 (New York: Marvel, January 2005), 5.

14 *Howard the Duck*, dir. Willard Huyuck (Lucasfilm, 1986).

15 Slott, Bobillo, and Granov, "Class Action Comics!," 14.

16 Slott, Bobillo, and Granov, et al., "Web of Lies," *She-Hulk* #4 (New York: Marvel, June 2004), 21.

17 Adam Capitanio, "'You, on the Other Hand . . .': Dual Identity and Superhero Storytelling in Dan Slott's *She-Hulk*," in *The Ages of the Incredible Hulk: Essays on the Green Goliath in Changing Times*, ed. Joseph J. Darowski (Jefferson, NC: McFarland, 2015), 188.

18 Capitanio, "'You,'" 185.

19 Capitanio, "'You,'" 185.

20 Capitanio, "'You,'" 188.

21 Alexandra George, *Constructing Intellectual Property* (Cambridge: Cambridge University Press, 2012), 83.

22 George, *Constructing Intellectual Property*, 126.

23 George, *Constructing Intellectual Property*, 125–126.

24 Henry Jenkins, "'Just Men in Tights': Rewriting Silver Age Comics in an Era of Multiplicity," in *The Contemporary Comic Book Superhero*, ed. Angela Ndalianis (New York: Routledge, 2009), 17.

25 Molly Hatcher, "The Dark Knight under Revision," *Journal of Graphic Novels and Comics* 4, no. 2 (2013): 269–270.

26 *Spider-Man*, dir. Sam Raimi (Columbia Pictures, 2002).

27 *The Amazing Spider-Man*, dir. Marc Webb (Sony-Columbia, 2012).

28 Hatcher, "Dark Knight under Revision," 258.

29 Martin Flanagan, Andrew Livingstone, and Mike McKenny, *The Marvel Studios Phenomenon: Inside a Transmedia Universe* (New York: Bloomsbury, 2016), 72.

30 Flanagan, Livingstone, and McKenny, *Marvel Studios Phenomenon*, 60.

31 Flanagan, Livingstone, and McKenny, *Marvel Studios Phenomenon*, 60.

32 Flanagan, Livingstone, and McKenny, *Marvel Studios Phenomenon*, 72.

33 Liam Burke, "'A Bigger Universe': Marvel Studios and Transmedia Storytelling," in *Assembling the Marvel Cinematic Universe: Essays on the Social, Cultural and Geopolitical Domains*, ed. Julian C. Chambliss, William L. Svitavsky, and Daniel Fandino (Jefferson, NC: McFarland, 2018), 41.

34 Mark C. Rogers, "Licensing Farming and the American Comic Book Industry," *International Journal of Comic Art* 1, no. 2 (1999): 134.

35 Rogers, "Licensing Farming"; Derek Johnson, "Franchise Histories: Marvel, *X-Men*, and the Negotiated Process of Expansion," in *Convergence Media History*, ed. Janet Staiger and Sabine Hake (New York: Routledge, 2009).

36 Johnson, "Cinematic Destiny," 14.

37 Emma Dibdin, "Do We Really Need Another Spider-Man?," *Digital Spy*, February 14, 2015, www.digitalspy.com/movies/spider-man/feature/a628323/do-we-really-need-another-spider-man/; Brandon Griggs, "Do We Really Need Another 'Spider-Man,'?" *CNN Entertainment*, February 10, 2015, http://edition

.cnn.com/2015/02/10/entertainment/spiderman-reboot-marvel-garfield-feat/index.html.

38 Kyle Buchanan, "Emma Thompson's Wonderful Thoughts on Feminism, Ageism, Trump, and Teapots," *Vulture*, September 2, 2015, www.vulture.com/2015/09/emma-thompson-on-feminism-trump-and-teapots.html.

39 Previous installments are *Spider-Man* (Sam Raimi, 2002), *Spider-Man 2* (Sam Raimi, 2004), and *Spider-Man 3* (Sam Raimi, 2007), and the reboot series *The Amazing Spider-Man* (Marc Webb, 2012) and *The Amazing Spider-Man 2: Rise of Electro* (Marc Webb, 2014).

40 "Sony Pictures Entertainment Brings Marvel Studios in the Amazing World of Spider-Man.

41 *The Avengers*, dir. Joss Whedon (Marvel Studios, 2012).

42 *Guardians of the Galaxy*, dir. James Gunn (Walt Disney Company, 2014); *Doctor Strange*, dir. Scott Derrickson (Walt Disney Company, 2016).

43 *Avengers: Age of Ultron*, dir. Joss Whedon (Marvel Studios, 2015).

44 William Proctor, "Regeneration and Rebirth: Anatomy of a Reboot," *Scope* 22 (2012): 12, www.nottingham.ac.uk/scope/documents/2012/february-2012/proctor.pdf.

45 *Avengers: Infinity War*, dir. Joe Russo and Anthony Russo (Marvel Studios, 2018).

46 Walt Disney Company, "The Walt Disney Company Acquire Twenty-First Century Fox" (press release, December 14, 2017), www.thewaltdisneycompany.com/walt-disney-company-acquire-twenty-first-century-fox-inc-spinoff-certain-businesses-52-4-billion-stock/.

Bibliography

The Amazing Spider-Man. Directed by Marc Webb. Sony-Columbia, 2012.

The Avengers. Directed by Joss Whedon. Marvel Studios, 2012.

Avengers: Age of Ultron. Directed by Joss Whedon. Marvel Studios, 2015.

Avengers: Infinity War. Directed by Joe Russo and Anthony Russo. Marvel Studios, 2018.

Buchanan, Kyle. "Emma Thompson's Wonderful Thoughts on Feminism, Ageism, Trump, and Teapots." *Vulture*, September 2, 2015. www.vulture.com/2015/09/emma-thompson-on-feminism-trump-and-teapots.html.

Burke, Liam. "'A Bigger Universe': Marvel Studios and Transmedia Storytelling." In *Assembling the Marvel Cinematic Universe: Essays on the Social, Cultural and Geopolitical Domains*, edited by Julian C. Chambliss, William L. Svitavsky, and Daniel Fandino, 32–51. Jefferson, NC: McFarland, 2018.

Capitanio, Adam. "'You, on the Other Hand . . .': Dual Identity and Superhero Storytelling in Dan Slott's She-Hulk." In *The Ages of the Incredible Hulk: Essays on the Green Goliath in Changing Times*, edited by Joseph J. Darowski, 181–192. Jefferson, NC: McFarland, 2015.

Captain America: Civil War. Directed by Joe Russo and Anthony Russo. Marvel Studios, 2016.

Dibdin, Emma. "Do We Really Need Another Spider-Man?" *Digital Spy*, February 14, 2015. www.digitalspy.com/movies/spider-man/feature/a628323/do-we-really-need-another-spider-man/.

Doctor Strange. Directed by Scott Derrickson. Walt Disney Company, 2016.

Flanagan, Martin, Andrew Livingstone, and Mike McKenny. *The Marvel Studios Phenomenon: Inside a Transmedia Universe*. New York: Bloomsbury, 2016.

George, Alexandra. *Constructing Intellectual Property*. Cambridge: Cambridge University Press, 2012.

Griggs, Brandon. "Do We Really Need Another 'Spider-Man'?" *CNN Entertainment*, February 10, 2015. http://edition.cnn.com/2015/02/10/entertainment/spiderman-reboot-marvel-garfield-feat/index.html.

Guardians of the Galaxy. Directed by James Gunn. Walt Disney Company, 2014.

Hatcher, Molly. "The Dark Knight under Revision." *Journal of Graphic Novels and Comics* 4, no. 2 (2013): 257–277.

Howard the Duck. Directed by Williard Huyuck. Lucasfilm, 1986.

Jenkins, Henry. "'Just Men in Tights': Rewriting Silver Age Comics in an Era of Multiplicity." In *The Contemporary Comic Book Superhero*, edited by Angela Ndalianis, 16–43. New York: Routledge, 2009.

Johnson, Derek. "Cinematic Destiny: Marvel Studios and the Trade Stories of Industrial Convergence." *Cinema Journal* 52, no. 1 (2012): 1–24.

———. "Franchise Histories: Marvel, *X-Men*, and the Negotiated Process of Expansion." In *Convergence Media History*, edited by Janet Staiger and Sabine Hake, 14–23. New York: Routledge, 2009.

———. *Media Franchising: Creative License and Collaboration in the Culture Industries*. New York: New York University Press, 2013.

Marvel's Agents of S.H.I.E.L.D. Executive produced by Joss Whedon, Jed Whedon, and Maurissa Tancharoen. Marvel Television, ABC Studios, and Mutant Enemy Productions, 2013–.

Marvel Studios: Assembling a Universe. Produced by Marvel Television. ABC Studios, March 18, 2014.

Proctor, William. "Regeneration and Rebirth: Anatomy of a Reboot." *Scope* 22 (2012): 1–19. http://www.nottingham.ac.uk/scope/documents/2012/february-2012/proctor.pdf.

Rogers, Mark C. "Licensing Farming and the American Comic Book Industry." *International Journal of Comic Art* 1, no. 2 (1999): 132–142.

Slott, Dan, Juan Bobillo, and Adi Granov. "Class Action Comics!" *She-Hulk* #2. New York: Marvel, April 2004.

———. "Strong Enough." *She-Hulk* #9. New York: Marvel, January 2005.

———. "Web of Lies." *She-Hulk* #4. New York: Marvel, June 2004.

"Sony Pictures Entertainment Brings Marvel Studios in the Amazing World of Spider-Man." *Marvel News*, February 9, 2015. https://news.marvel.com/movies/24062/sony_pictures_entertainment_brings_marvel_studios_into_the_amazing_world_of_spider-man/.

Spider-Man. Directed by Sam Raimi. Columbia Pictures, 2002.

Spider-Man: Homecoming. Directed by Jon Watts. Marvel Studios and Sony-Columbia, 2017.

Walt Disney Company. "The Walt Disney Company Acquire Twenty-First Century Fox." Press release, December 14, 2017. www.thewaltdisneycompany.com/walt-disney-company-acquire-twenty-first-century-fox-inc-spinoff-certain-businesses-52-4-billion-stock/.

8

The Sound of the Cinematic Superhero

DAN GOLDING

The cinematic superhero identity is tied to music, and today no performance of a superhero is complete without it. In the words of rapper Kanye West, "Every superhero needs his theme music."[1] When I was a child my Batman figurines would do battle only to the hummed tune of Danny Elfman's 1989 Batman film theme. Later, as an adult, I remember attending an orchestral performance of John Williams's 1978 Superman music where the host pulled out a red cape and twirled around the stage, as though symbol and score were incomplete without the other. Acting out the superhero identity just does not quite make as much sense without music; they seem almost to conjure each other into being.

Superhero identity has regularly been articulated in a number of conspicuous ways. For instance, comics scholar Richard Reynolds opens his 1994 book *Super Heroes* with a "working definition of the superhero genre," a list of motifs that includes the superhero's powers, their devotion to justice, their extraordinary nature, and their alter ego.[2] These elements are also visually contained in the routine semiotics of the superhero: a mask, an identity theme, a costume, and a symbol. To this kind of list, and particularly in an age when screen superheroes are now dominant, we must also add music. Certain musical modes and even melodic intervals have become indelibly associated with particular superheroes. For example, John Williams's fanfare for 1978's *Superman* and Danny Elfman's gothic brass for the Tim Burton *Batman* films defined each character in the popular imagination almost as much as visual devices such as Superman's chest emblem or the Bat-Signal.

This chapter argues that the music of superheroes has become crucial to the contemporary articulation of their identities as popular culture icons. Further, it contends that although cinematic superheroes can have many different musical themes—just as each superhero can have an array of different visual and thematic articulations and styles—each has a central musical identity. These can be revised, but rarely have producers changed them completely.[3] This argument is illustrated through an analysis of the cinematic instances of Superman and Batman, two heroes who have gone through more musical periods and composers than any other heroes, yet generally still retain a core melodic and harmonic identity. In particular, this chapter focuses on how the composer Hans Zimmer's scores for the most recent cinematic incarnations of these characters manage to be both a radical musical departure and a clearly faithful rendition of core thematic identities. Additionally, this chapter also explores the origins of these musical identities and suggests some larger cultural frameworks for understanding the musical persistence of these superheroes.

Musical Themes and Brands

In the 1989 film *Batman* the theme, as film music scholar K. J. Donnelly writes, "functions directly as a fanfare for Batman, announcing his presence while being associated solidly with both film and character. Consequently, along with the overall style of the film's music, the theme works outside the film's context."[4] It is a brand for the character both within the world of the film and beyond it.

This is a musical technique called leitmotif, a method that theorists have long debated. Leitmotif is a system of musical identification usually associated with the composer Richard Wagner, and it signals a character, place, or theme that is given a musical idea, which is returned to and usually developed across the course of a musical work. After Wagner, the logic of the leitmotif gained popularity among European composers such as Richard Strauss and Claude Debussy, and it was brought to American film music via Viennese émigré composers Max Steiner (*King Kong* [1933], *Gone with the Wind* [1939]) and Erich Wolfgang Korngold (*Captain Blood* [1935], *The Adventures of Robin Hood* [1938]). Such early Hollywood music is generally characterized by long melodies of sixteen bars, sometimes even longer, which may be memorable and well-written, but which, due to their inflexible nature, often bulldoze through scenes with little concern for the beat-by-beat flow of emotion and dialogue.

Although leitmotif, especially when used in cinematic scores, provides audiences with an easy way to connect music with image, character, or place, it has not been without criticism. The philosopher Theodor Adorno, for example, staunchly criticized the technique of leitmotif, both in film and in the concert hall. Writing with the composer Hanns Eisler in 1947's *Composing for the Films*, he stated, "Standard configurations [film music] interprets the meaning of the action for the less intelligent members of the audience, somewhat in the way patent medicines are promoted by means of pseudo-scientific explanations."[5] In other words, leitmotif promotes a simplistic kind of film scoring solely linked to reinforcing the image. Much of Adorno and Eisler's book is concerned with trenchant criticism of the entire profession of film composing. For example, they write that "no serious composer writes for the motion pictures for any other than money reasons," despite the fact that Eisler himself wrote forty film scores.[6] Nonetheless, these ideas provide a useful framework for thinking about film music, not in the least because Adorno and Eisler draw attention to not just the material means of film production but also its labor.

That Adorno and Eisler should be attracted to the material and technical means of film music production and its labor is not particularly surprising, given both authors' Marxism. That film music has rarely been considered along similar lines either before or since is perhaps more surprising. Film music was tied to machines long before any other type of musical performance: in film, music had to be timed perfectly from scene to scene, locking into projection speeds and editing cuts in a way totally foreign to the vicissitudes of a concert hall performance. Even as early as the 1930s conductors were using metronomes and timepieces, as well as visual cues like streamers and punches to match their compositions to the needs of film makers. This development is significant as the history of the superhero theme this chapter traces is material as much as anything else, and the major musical shift for superhero music in the current century has come about largely through advances in technology.

In *Composing for the Films* Adorno and Eisler regularly refer to film music as "autonomous music." They argue that "there is no such thing as a motion picture independent of technical recording processes. . . . Because of the commercial character of the film industry it is impossible to separate its organizational from its technical aspects."[7] Adorno and Eisler mean this disparagingly; however, it is useful to reflect on the nature of film music through this lens. To return to leitmotif, to think of film music through Adorno and Eisler's technological lens is to think of it as ultimately a product, or perhaps even as something less: as an advertisement for a product. This is, significantly, the conclusion that Adorno and Eisler reach: "The whole form language of current cinema music derives from advertising. The motif is the slogan; the instrumentation, the standardized picturesque; the accompaniments to animated cartoons are advertising jokes; and sometimes it is as though the music replaced the names of the commercial articles that the motion pictures do not yet dare mention directly."[8] Adorno and Eisler's analysis, which is meant as derisory, rings true, particularly true when it comes to superhero music. Today we can easily see superhero themes as something akin to the superhero's cowl, their mask and cape, their bat-signal, or their emblem. When translating the superhero's identity to a sense of popular appeal, it is not very difficult to imagine, say, Williams's *Superman* melody as Superman's slogan; its melody replaces the name of the character who no longer needs to be mentioned directly when it is played. Indeed, theme music has become commonplace in advertisements for an entire array of tie-in products, such as Mountain Dew's "Gotham City" commercials tying in to the release of *The Dark Knight Rises*, which made extensive use of Hans Zimmer's score. Superhero film scores are themselves products in another very real sense: the dual LP releases of the *Batman* soundtrack in 1989, containing both Elfman's orchestral score and Prince's diegetic pop songs, proved lucrative for Warner Brothers.[9] Yet these themes are not just emblematic of the superhero, not just a symbol of their brand; they are also reflective of their power, their personality, and the entire mood of the world they inhabit and how they inhabit it. Superhero music is not merely representative in the way that advertising is; it is also constitutive. The relationship between superheroes and their music is complex.

Super Lineages

It is possible to map out a lineage of the musical superhero when it comes to the cinematic incarnations of Batman and Superman. Both of these cinematic scores have a basis in the longer term thematic articulation of these screen franchises and, beyond that, in musical culture more generally. The musical identity of these superheroes has changed across history according to shifts in aesthetics, technology, and the labor of film music, but it remains ultimately similar in a number of key ways.

There are certain similarities across multiple iterations of each hero's theme, what music theorists sometimes call a "topic." For musicologist Wye Jamison Allanbrook, the notion of a musical topic can dramatically aid in signifying meaning to an audience: "By recognizing a characteristic style, he can identify a configuration of notes and rhythms as having a particular expressive stance, modified and clarified, of course, by its role in its movement and by the uses made of it earlier in the piece. In short, he can articulate within certain limits the shared response a particular passage will evoke."[10] Each version of Batman musically conjures up an idea of Batman; each version of Superman articulates a certain Supermanness.

The composers for Batman and Superman have identified certain configurations or characteristics that, over time, continue to evoke their respective superheroes, regardless of the individual permutations required by the moment. Even if they are not the same melodies, any two good Batman themes should still sound like Batman, producing the sound of the cinematic superhero.

For example, Superman has almost always, since his first moving-image incarnations, been associated with musical melodies based around a perfect fifth interval, and it is this that forms the basis of his musical topic. A perfect fifth is two notes played five degrees apart in a major scale. For example, in C major this would be C and G. A perfect fifth is similar to a bugle call, or the opening of "Twinkle, Twinkle, Little Star." This is one of the fundamental building blocks of harmony in Western musical traditions: the two notes sound particularly consonant together, powerful and strong. It makes sense that for Superman, a character "more powerful than a locomotive," and who fights for truth and justice, that the strongest and arguably most heroic of all musical intervals should be his most common recurrence.

The first of such musical instances comes from the Fleischer animated series (1941–1942).[11] The theme, an old-fashioned march by Fleischer Studios' veteran composer Sammy Timberg, begins by sketching a rising major triad played by the brass: 1–3–5. The second phrase repeats the movement by dropping down, from above: 7b–6–5 (see Figure 8.1). Both opening phrases therefore place the fifth note of the major scale as the core of the melody; with his earliest theme, Superman is already drawn to this strongest of intervals.

Today, the most enduring Superman theme is John Williams's music for the 1978 Richard Donner film. Williams's score was at the time seen as an intentional pastiche or throwback to an earlier age of film scoring, along with Williams's other iconic cinematic themes such as *Jaws* and *Star Wars*.[12] The brazen naïveté of the *Superman* theme represented a recalling of the classical Hollywood musical style that had fallen out of fashion. In this period, Williams was "almost single-handedly responsible for bringing back the classical Hollywood sound, updating it to the requirements of the contemporary blockbuster film, and, more important, leading people to rediscover and appreciate the music of Hollywood's Golden Age."[13] In other words, Williams's *Superman* both drew on the cinematic era, in which the character made his first screen appearance, and updated it for the 1970s.

In some respects, this was again due to the clear and uncomplicated emphasis on the perfect fifth interval. Williams's theme—another brass

Figure 8.1. Superman music over time. Time signatures and keys have been simplified for comparison's sake. Key melodic similarities have been linked in red. All perfect fifth intervals are highlighted in green. Transcriptions by the author.

fanfare—heavily emphasizes the importance of the perfect fifth and rests much of the melody on it. The melody seems to constantly rise from the first note of the scale to the fifth (see Figure 8.1). Williams himself identifies the sound of this interval as recalling the past: "the interval of the perfect fifth also rattles our memories of antiquity."[14] Of course, this also links Williams's music with the Superman themes that had come before, particularly Timberg's theme for the Fleischer animations: again, it is the perfect fifth that leads the Superman musical topic. Williams augments this approach with some melodic experimentation; though each phrase usually incorporates the fifth, the melody also anchors itself to the sixth, forth, and, unusually, the major seventh sequentially (see Figure 8.1), giving a surprising and effective feeling of rising to victory.

The overall effect of Williams's theme is to dramatically embellish and more deeply embed the Superman musical topic. This is an open and straight-faced brass fanfare that, while it may contain traces of pastiche, does not ironically parody or nod to the audience in any way. "The style [of the music for *Superman*] is tonal and kind of ceremonious and heraldic," said Williams in a 1978 interview.[15] Yet it is also worth examining its antecedents and influences beyond the Superman musical mythos.

The first era of Superman music—the Fleischer animated series of the 1940s—coincides with a period of musical history when such fanfares and marches were popular. In particular the 1940s saw a drive for American patriotic fanfares due to the nation's entry into the Second World War, with a great number being commissioned around the country.[16] The most enduring of these, Aaron Copland's *Fanfare for the Common Man* (1942), bares a similarity to the many *Superman* musical identities that indicates a shared musical heritage in the patriotic, militaristic brass melodies that marked this particular era of heroism. Indeed, as music scholar Tom Schneller notes, "the shadow" of Copland's nationalist style, particularly as demonstrated in the *Fanfare*, "looms large in Williams' oeuvre."[17]

In this sense we can think of the music of Superman as drawing on a broader project of American cultural power that has its origins in the 1940s. Particularly, the kind of musical landscape employed by subsequent Superman composers illustrates an intellectual link between not just the Copland composition but also the larger discourse that surrounded it. Superman is, after all, the champion of "Truth, Justice, and the American Way." Copland's *Fanfare* was inspired by a speech given by Roosevelt's socialist vice president Henry A. Wallace, who proclaimed the century of the "Common Man" in response to the rise of Nazism in Europe: "The people's revolution aims at peace and not at violence, but if the rights of the common man are attacked, it unleashed the ferocity of a she-bear who has lost a cub. . . . The truth is that when the rights of the American people are transgressed, as those rights have been transgressed, the American people will fight with a relentless fury which will drive the ancient Teutonic gods back cowering into their caves. The Götterdämmerung has come for Odin and his crew."[18]

Inspired by this speech, Copland's *Fanfare* uses extensive perfect fourths and perfect fifths to convey a sense of the stately significance of the common man who pays his taxes and supports his community and nation. Copland is the quintessential New Deal composer at his most patriotic.[19] Yet this is a startlingly similar musical topic to what we find in Superman's music: music that is also stately, with a melody based around perfect fifths in the brass and concerned with "the American way." Through these connections we can further understand Superman's sound, his musical identity, his brand, and his subject. It persists across these iterations, and Zimmer develops it further in the 2010s, as will be discussed shortly.

The Bat-Melody

But first a brief detour to examine the music history of another superhero with a long cinematic history: Batman. The musical identity of Batman has always been markedly different from other superheroes. As scholar Matthew David Young points out, even in contrast to other serialized superheroes of the 1940s, such as Superman, Captain Marvel, and Captain America, the theme music for the 1943 *Batman* serial composed by Lee Zahler is "a dark mysterioso set in minor mode."[20] It is a similar story for the 1949 *Batman and Robin* serial, with theme music composed by Mischa Bakaleinikoff in a dark, minor, and foreboding tone.[21]

Brief expeditions into surf music in the Neil Hefti-penned theme for the 1960s television show and 1966 film notwithstanding, it is easy enough to see that the musical topic for Batman—his brand as a superhero—is darkly orchestrated brass in a minor key. This has been largely consistent throughout his moving image incarnations. This is doubly reinforced by the most famous of the orchestral Batman themes: Danny Elfman's music from the 1989 film. Elfman's Batman theme begins by drawing out a minor scale in low brass—1–2–3—before leaping to a flattened sixth, which descends to a fifth (see Figure 8.2).[22]

The mood of the music is "pure Gothic melodrama, using a large, dark and Wagnerian orchestral sound."[23] The influence of Wagner may not be coincidental: the design of Burton's *Batman* is heavily influenced by German Expressionism, suggesting that German aesthetics were on the filmmakers' minds.[24] Walter Ong has also discussed the links between Wagner, Nietzsche, Nazism, and the origins of the superhero in the twentieth century.[25] This goes well beyond a simple association of Germanness, however: Fritz Lang, a key influence on Burton, directed a monumental five-hour adaptation of Wagner's *Die Nibelungen* in 1924. There is even a musical similarity between Elfman's Batman theme and Wagner's "Siegfried" theme (see Figure 8.2).

We can also note the contrast readily offered by Wallace's "Common Man" speech where he thunders "the Götterdämmerung has come for Odin and his crew." Wallace's direct invocation of the final opera in Wagner's *Der Ring des Nibelungen* here provides a tempting opportunity to trace the musical lineage of Batman and Superman to Wagner and Copland, respectively. Here is a new kind of Batman versus Superman: gothic brass versus patriotic fanfares, Richard Wagner versus Aaron Copland.[26]

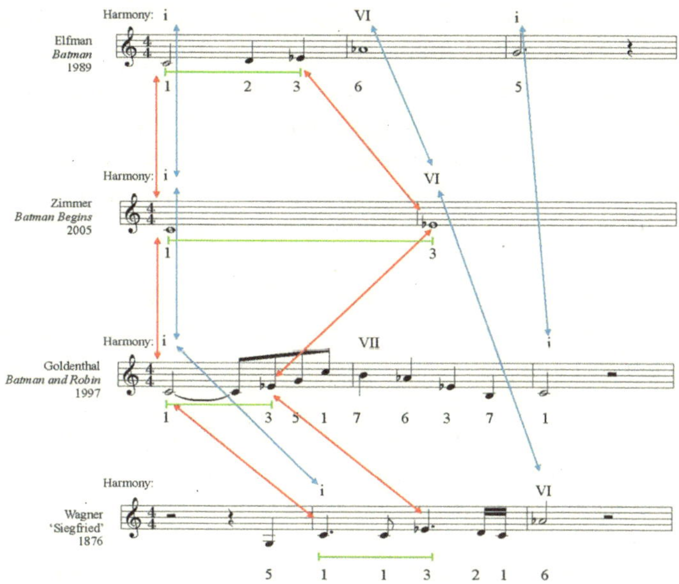

Figure 8.2. Batman music and its contexts over time. Time signatures and keys have been simplified for comparison's sake. Key melodic similarities have been linked in red. Key harmonic similarities have been linked in blue. All minor third intervals are highlighted in green. Transcriptions by the author.

The Superhero in the Age of the Hyperorchestra

In contemporary filmmaking the clearly identifiable melodies and musical traditions that have defined previous iterations of Batman and Superman are no longer *in vogue* in Hollywood, and the superhero's musical identity has accordingly been reworked. This is the result of both technological and cultural changes in Hollywood film composition, both of which have led to a move away from melody toward a film music aesthetic that emphasizes the textural and the structural.

Since the 1980s and 1990s, digital recording, mixing, and performance tools, as well as synthesizers and virtual instruments, have become prevalent in film scoring to the point where their use now animates the large majority of film scores without necessarily being perceptible to the average filmgoer. These are the material and labor aspects of composing for the films that Adorno and Eisler rightly called attention to. Scholar Sergi Casanelles calls this phenomenon the "hyperorchestra," which is "a specific medium, ontologically differentiated from the orchestra and other musical ensembles, due to its capability to transcend the physical world, achieving a result that could not be accomplished by physical means."[27] This has drastically altered the entire process of film scoring, and coupled the labor of music making for films to an entirely different array of machines.

This phenomenon is routinely combined with the influence of Hans Zimmer on the contemporary film music landscape, whose work was instrumental in popularizing the use of such a hyperorchestra.[28] Zimmer's own style has led the way in the truncation of melody, which can be traced from his initially tuneful scores such as *Rain Man* and *Driving Miss Daisy*, to the persistent emphasis on rhythmic complexity found in *Inception* and *Dunkirk*, the latter of which contains almost no melody to speak of.[29]

Accordingly, we cannot expect to find the similar melodic structures in Zimmer's work for Nolan's *Dark Knight* films and Zack Snyder's *Man of Steel* as we might in earlier decades of film music.[30] Surprisingly, however, the key musical topics already flagged in this chapter clearly persist: the superhero brand is resilient.

Zimmer's extension of the superhero's musical brand is achieved via a process of extreme melodic and harmonic compression. Where a musical idea might have been stated in twelve notes in the 1940s and six notes in the 1980s, in the modern era it may be given just two notes. Such is the case with Zimmer's Batman theme: it is simply two notes, a minor third apart, usually harmonized with I-VI chords (see Figure 8.2). Zimmer usually orchestrates these two notes as long brass swells, drawing out the drama and suspense while simultaneously reifying the Batman musical identity into perhaps the purest brand possible. Melodically and harmonically, these two notes and their standard harmonization are the perfect summation of all prior Batman themes in the way that they represent the distillation of the reoccurring features of the minor third interval and the I-VI harmony. In particular, Zimmer's theme seems to condense the Elfman music into just two notes: in the hands of Zimmer, Batman's music has become sublimated.

A similar process is at work with Zimmer's *Man of Steel*. Though Zimmer's Superman theme is played on slide steel guitar and synthesizers instead of the brass more standard to the Superman topic, the composer nonetheless persists with the perfect fifth in the opening interval to his theme. In fact, as music theorist Mark Richards points out, it seems that Zimmer's theme again matches the melodic structure of Williams's original in condensed form (see Figure 8.1): "These striking relationships create a connection between them that one could rightly call homage."[31] An homage it may well be, but also it is more striking evidence that the superhero can retain a coherent musical identity across vastly different film musical styles and eras. With both *The Dark Knight* and *Man of Steel*, the broader musical identity of these heroes endures, rearticulated through the constraints of the contemporary era of film music.

The leitmotif has been transformed beyond all recognition since Adorno and Eisler first discussed its possibilities as a kind of filmic advertising. It is now a digitally augmented and condensed musical brand in the hands of a composer such as Zimmer. Yet the superhero topic, at least in the case of Superman and Batman, persists, and it can clearly be refashioned within different eras of film music. Such a refashioning is complex: the contemporary context for film music has resulted in a radical, almost unrecognizable redrafting of the cinematic superhero sound, yet the fundamental topic for both superheroes has remained intact. It is not the complete break from the past it may otherwise appear.

The result is a new musical superhero identity formed by the mutation of these previous musical identities into contemporary minimal musical "brands." In augmenting the leitmotif through digital technology, we can see in Zimmer, the paradigmatic composer for this kind of approach to the sound of the cinematic superhero, a kind of musical iconography and branding that Adorno and Eisler could only gesture toward in their earlier and undeveloped critique of the structures of film music. By exploring the history of the cinematic superhero's music, this chapter has shed light on the practice of composing for superhero films as well as the larger role that music plays in the articulation and development of the superhero identity over time.

Notes

1 Kanye West, "Power," in *My Beautiful Dark Twisted Fantasy* (Def Jam, 2010).

2 Richard Reynolds, *Super Heroes: A Modern Mythology* (Jackson: University Press of Mississippi, 1994), 16.

3 Jim Collins, "Batman: The Movie, Narrative: The Hyperconscious," in *The Many Lives of the Batman: Critical Approaches to a Superhero and His Media*, ed. Roberta E. Pearson and William Uricchio (New York: Routledge, 1972), 64–181.

4 K. J. Donnelly, "The Classical Film Score Forever? Batman, Batman Returns and Post-classical Film Music," in *Contemporary Hollywood Cinema*, ed. Stephen Neale and Murray Smith (London: Routledge, 1998), 147.

5 Theodor Adorno and Hanns Eisler, *Composing for the Films* (New York: Oxford University Press, 1947), 60.

6 Adorno and Eisler, *Composing*, 54.

7 Adorno and Eisler, *Composing*, 90.

8 Adorno and Eisler, *Composing*, 60.

9 Donnelly, "Classical Film Score Forever?," 144–146.

10 Wye Jamison Allanbrook, *Rhythmic Gesture in Mozart: Le Nozze Di Figaro and Don Giovanni* (Chicago: University of Chicago Press, 1986), 6.

11 It is perhaps worth noting that the Superman radio serial that began in 1940 in its early years used no music in its opening credits, despite radio orchestras being commonplace at that time. Indeed, the great American composer Bernard Herrmann would transition from radio work with Orson Welles to composing music for Welles's *Citizen Kane* in 1941.

12 Donnelly, "Classical Film Score Forever?," 150–151; *Jaws*, dir. Steven Spielberg (Universal, 1975); *Star Wars*, dir. George Lucas (Twentieth Century Fox, 1977).
13 Emilio Audissino, *John Williams's Film Music:* Jaws, Star Wars, Raiders of the Lost Ark, *and the Return of the Classical Hollywood Music Style* (Madison: University of Wisconsin Press, 2014), 4–5.
14 As cited in Audissino, *John Williams's Film Music*, 75.
15 Derek Elley, "John Williams," *Films and Filming*, no. 28 (August 1978): 21.
16 Alex Ross, "Music for All: Music in FDR's America," in *The Rest Is Noise: Listening to the Twentieth Century* (New York: Picador, 2008), 284–332.
17 Tom Schneller, "Modal Interchange and Semantic Resonance in Themes by John Williams," *Journal of Film Music* 6, no. 1 (2013): 53.
18 Henry A. Wallace, "The Price of Victory," *War Information Center Pamphlets* 754 ([1942] 2016), 2.
19 For further discussion of this piece and its influences, see Ross, "Music for All."
20 *Batman*, dir. Lambert Hillyer (Columbia, 1943); Matthew David Young, "Musical Topics in the Comic Book Superhero Film Genre" (PhD diss., University of Texas, 2013), 113.
21 *Batman and Robin*, dir. Spencer Gordon Bennet (Columbia, 1949).
22 Where Williams looked to the Golden Age of Hollywood for his influence, Elfman looks slightly later, to the modernist film music of Bernard Herrmann and in particular the "Mountain Top/Sunrise" cue from his score to the 1959 Charles Brackett film *Journey to the Center of the Earth*—the opening of *Batman* is nearly identical.
23 Donnelly, "Classical Film Score Forever?," 147–148.
24 Peter C. Kunze, "The Use of German Expressionism and American Exceptionalism," in *Tim Burton: Essays on the Films*, ed. Johnson Cheu (Jefferson, NC: McFarland, 2016), 198–211.
25 Walter Ong, "The Comics and the Super State," in *The Superhero Reader*, ed. Charles Hatfield, Jeet Heer, and Kent Worcester (Jackson: University Press of Mississippi, 2013), 38.
26 Elliot Goldenthal's theme for *Batman Forever* (Joel Schumacher, 1995) and *Batman & Robin* (Joel Schumacher, 1997) conforms to a similar topic and is provided in figure 8.2 as a point of further comparison.
27 Sergi Casanelles, "The Hyperorchestra: A Study of a Virtual Musical Ensemble in Film Music That Transcends Reality" (PhD diss., New York University, 2015), 248.
28 In Craig Morgan's PhD survey of forty-six Australian screen composers, 86 percent of interviewed composers mentioned Zimmer, many in direct relation to the near ubiquity of digital tools. Craig Morgan, "The Use of Virtual Instruments by Australian Screen Composers" (PhD diss., University of Sydney, 2016), 134.
29 *Rain Man*, dir. Barry Levinson (United Artists, 1988); *Driving Miss Daisy*, dir. Bruce Beresford (Warner Bros., 1989); *Inception*, dir. Christopher Nolan (Warner Bros., 2010); *Dunkirk*, dir. Christopher Nolan (Warner Bros., 2017).
30 *The Dark Knight*, dir. Christopher Nolan (Warner Bros., 2008); *Man of Steel*, dir. Zack Snyder (Warner Bros., 2013).

31 Mark Richards, "Hans Zimmer's Score for Man of Steel," *Film Music Notes*, August 11, 2013, www.filmmusicnotes.com/hans-zimmers-score-for-man-of-steel/.

Bibliography

Adorno, Theodor, and Hanns Eisler. *Composing for the Films*. New York: Oxford University Press, 1947.

Allanbrook, Wye Jamison. *Rhythmic Gesture in Mozart: Le Nozze Di Figaro and Don Giovanni*. Chicago: University of Chicago Press, 1986.

Audissino, Emilio. *John Williams's Film Music:* Jaws, Star Wars, Raiders of the Lost Ark, *and the Return of the Classical Hollywood Music Style*. Wisconsin Film Studies. Madison: University of Wisconsin Press, 2014.

Batman. Directed by Lambert Hillyer. Columbia, 1943.

Batman and Robin. Directed by Spencer Gordon Bennet. Columbia, 1949.

Casanelles, Sergi. "The Hyperorchestra: A Study of a Virtual Musical Ensemble in Film Music That Transcends Reality." PhD dissertation, New York University, 2015.

Collins, Jim. "Batman: The Movie, Narrative: The Hyperconscious." In *The Many Lives of the Batman: Critical Approaches to a Superhero and His Media*, edited by Roberta E. Pearson and William Uricchio, 64–181. New York: Routledge, 1972.

The Dark Knight. Directed by Christopher Nolan. Warner Bros., 2008.

Donnelly, K. J. "The Classical Film Score Forever? Batman, Batman Returns and Post-classical Film Music." In *Contemporary Hollywood Cinema*, edited by Stephen Neale and Murray Smith, 142–165. London: Routledge, 1998.

Driving Miss Daisy. Directed by Bruce Beresford. Warner Bros., 1989.

Dunkirk. Directed by Christopher Nolan. Warner Bros., 2017.

Elley, Derek. "John Williams." *Films and Filming*, no. 28 (August 1978): 21.

Inception. Directed by Christopher Nolan. Warner Bros., 2010.

Jaws. Directed by Steven Spielberg. Universal, 1975.

Kunze, Peter C. "The Use of German Expressionism and American Exceptionalism." In *Tim Burton: Essays on the Films*, edited by Johnson Cheu, 198–211. Jefferson, NC: McFarland, 2016.

Man of Steel. Directed by Zack Snyder. Warner Bros., 2013.

Morgan, Craig. "The Use of Virtual Instruments by Australian Screen Composers." PhD dissertation, University of Sydney, 2016.

Ong, Walter. "The Comics and the Super State." In *The Superhero Reader*, edited by Charles Hatfield, Jeet Heer, and Kent Worcester, 34–45. Jackson: University Press of Mississippi, 2013.

Rain Man. Directed by Barry Levinson. United Artists, 1988.

Reynolds, Richard. *Super Heroes: A Modern Mythology*. Jackson: University Press of Mississippi, 1994.

Richards, Mark. "Hans Zimmer's Score for Man of Steel." *Film Music Notes*, August 11, 2013. www.filmmusicnotes.com/hans-zimmers-score-for-man-of-steel/.

Ross, Alex. "Music for All: Music in FDR's America." In *The Rest Is Noise: Listening to the Twentieth Century*, 284–332. New York: Picador, 2008.

Schneller, Tom. "Modal Interchange and Semantic Resonance in Themes by John Williams." *Journal of Film Music* 6, no. 1 (2013): 49–74.

Star Wars. Directed by George Lucas. Twentieth Century Fox, 1977.

Wallace, Henry A. "The Price of Victory." *War Information Center Pamphlets* 754 ([1942] 2016).

West, Kanye. "Power." In *My Beautiful Dark Twisted Fantasy*. Def Jam, 2010.

Young, Matthew David. "Musical Topics in the Comic Book Superhero Film Genre." PhD dissertation, University of Texas, 2013.

9

An Interview with Former President of DC Entertainment Diane Nelson

LIAM BURKE

In the past the presidents of Marvel and DC Comics have tended to be fans and creators who came up through the ranks to lead the companies. In a break with that tradition brand manager Diane Nelson was put in charge of DC Comics when the publisher was subsumed under DC Entertainment (DCE) in 2009. Nelson had previously overseen the company-wide brand management of *Harry Potter*, and her appointment was reflective of a changing approach to superheroes. These comic book characters were now the transmedia anchors of larger media conglomerates, appearing across a range of platforms.

This interview was conducted before Nelson resigned as president in 2018. As president Nelson led efforts to fully realize the potential of DC's brands, with the iconic characters becoming the basis of shared universes on TV (Arrowverse) and in film (DC Extended Universe). Nelson was also committed to raising the visibility of female characters and creators, a strategy that found Wonder Woman becoming an Honorary UN Ambassador for the Empowerment of Women and Girls, as well as receiving her long overdue feature-length film adaptation. Nelson's humanitarian work included the "We Can Be Heroes" campaign in which DC's most popular superheroes were enlisted to raise funds for hunger and drought relief in the Horn of Africa

LIAM BURKE Why do you think superheroes are so popular today?

DIANE NELSON I think there are several factors at play in the renaissance that superheroes are experiencing in popular culture.

Figure 9.1. Former President of DC Entertainment Diane Nelson. DC Entertainment.

Historically, superheroes and comics have been cyclical and often reflect or react to major social issues. The aspirational nature of superheroes offers role models that perhaps consumers are not experiencing in other aspects of their lives, or parents and individuals like to use them to represent the traits to which we should all aspire. This is true now certainly.

Additionally, I believe that the superhero renaissance is a testament to excellent creative storytelling in many new mediums.

Marvel, DC, and other independent publishers have been working to bring these characters to all screens and it is being done so well collectively that new audiences are experiencing and engaging with characters they may not have known, and comic fans are able to engage with characters they've loved in all sorts of new ways.

LB What is it about superheroes that make them amenable to cross-platform branding and why did that potential go untapped for decades?

DN I am not a fan of the notion of "cross platform branding" or "transmedia" as descriptors of what we are doing in comics. The success of any successful content is rooted in great characters and stories well told. For DC, we have the elasticity in many of our major characters to adapt them to various mediums for all ages and each adaptation works without creating confusion for consumers.

Additionally, our universes of characters are so broad and deep that we can effectively tap in to them with fresh new takes and extended stories without creating fatigue. But that's about great creative talent respecting the characters' integrity. What [*Arrow*, *Flash*, and *Supergirl* producer] Greg Berlanti has done with the television universe, what he has created on the CW, is a good example of this; strong lead characters and properties, but weekly stories introducing new and lesser known characters to extend the storytelling.

LB What aspects of the brand did you hope to realize and expand when taking on your role as President of DC Entertainment?

DN I believed then and continue to believe now that DC, inclusive of each of its brands (DC, Vertigo, and MAD), could fuel the creative engines of the various production and distribution businesses of Warner Bros. if managed effectively. There is great affinity for the DC brand with comic fans, but perhaps less so with what we refer to as casual fans. Bringing DC's characters to wide audiences and reinforcing both the characters and their relationship to DC (versus other publishers) was an opportunity that we are successfully addressing.

LB How do you reconcile the competing versions of characters such as the Flash appearing in comics, animation, TV, and now movies? Is there a need to emphasize brand continuity or do you embrace the difference?

DN We have always believed that many of our top characters have elasticity and can be adapted uniquely for various mediums. It always comes back to the right story with the right creator for the right medium. Greg Berlanti's adaptation of the Flash is wonderful and is introducing the character to a whole new generation. The WB Pictures adaptation of the Flash in films can and is being done well and uniquely by different creators. If the integrity of the character is maintained, which is the primary role of DC in working with our divisional partners and the creators with whom they work, there is room to tell different stories. We believe the problems can happen if the adaptations are too tightly controlled and connected (the film and TV universes being one, for example), because it constrains the storytelling latitude for the creators working in each medium. We embrace the difference in each of our businesses (film, TV, games, merchandise, DVDs, and digital content, etc.).

LB Is there tension between the transmedia ambitions for the characters and their long-standing history in comics?

DN No. Again, I do not believe in the concept of intentional transmedia adaptation. At DC, we understand the root characteristics and integrity of each of our characters and so long as that is protected, there is room to take latitude with stories in every medium, from publishing on.

LB Do you feel there is enough diversity in superhero stories? For instance, why did it take so long for a Wonder Woman film to be produced?

DN Diversity is an issue that is very consciously being addressed at DC and Warner Bros. and frankly, throughout the entertainment industry. Progress is being made, but there is still a long way to go. Our stories should reflect real life and everyone involved in the adaptation of our characters and storytelling with them is working to ensure that's true. *Wonder Woman* took the time it took to find the right director [Patty Jenkins] with her passion and vision for a film we believed in. It also hit the zeitgeist at exactly the right time, with an appetite among moviegoers for a strong female role model and a message of compassion, love, equality, and justice. We're very proud of the film and how it has resonated with audiences.

LB Has *Wonder Woman* set a template for future adaptations?

DN The only "template" is the reinforcement of choosing and supporting filmmakers with their own vision and passion for the character and its story. Hope and optimism were present in Patty Jenkins's vision and the tone of her film and that resonates particularly strongly right now and is inherently part of who many of our characters are.

LB Were you disappointed when Wonder Woman's tenure as an honorary UN Ambassador was cut short due to criticisms of how the character had been sexualized in the past? And what needs to be done to dispel the view of female superheroes, and Wonder Woman in particular, as "a pin-up girl"?

DN We are very proud of the many attributes that Wonder Woman represents—strength, compassion, equality, love, and beauty. Women are made up of some, many, or all of these characteristics and we believe Wonder Woman would have done a great job in extending awareness of the UN's global initiatives. Dispelling any misconceptions about female characters is showing people who they can be. Girls can't model what they don't see in front of them. I believe the success of the movie has illustrated this perfectly.

LB Superheroes are often used for social activism such as DC's philanthropic initiative We Can Be Heroes. Why do you think these fictional characters can have such a meaningful real world impact?

DN The role these characters can play is bringing awareness to the broadest audience with key messages of social responsibility. And it can be done authentically because many of these issues are integral to the DC world and its top characters.

LB Do you think the current interest in superheroes is sustainable, and what does the future hold for superheroes from a cross-platform perspective?

DN As long as we continue to be committed to great storytelling, there will always be room for these characters and their stories. And DC's library of characters and stories goes well beyond traditional superheroes, allowing us a broad array of characters and genres in which to tell these stories.

Part 3

Becoming the Superhero

10

Arkham Knave

The Joker in Game Design

STEVEN CONWAY

> To be awkward or unkempt, to talk or move wrongly, is to be a dangerous giant, a destroyer of worlds. As every psychotic and comic ought to know, any accurately improper move can poke through the thin sleeve of immediate reality.
>
> —Erving Goffman

"So much more fun with ME at the controls!" cackles the Joker as he takes over Batman's consciousness, Batmobile, and narrative trajectory in Rocksteady Studios' 2015 videogame *Batman: Arkham Knight*. Games in the *Arkham* series, beginning with 2009's *Batman: Arkham Asylum*, are action-adventure experiences providing third-person control of Batman's physicality, gadgets, and vehicles. Each game presents a central crisis, triggered by one of the supervillains in the rogues gallery, which must be resolved by the player-as-Batman, alongside a selection of side quests and activities. Since its inception, the series has toyed with the technical foundations of digital games. For example, in *Arkham Asylum* Scarecrow's fear toxin triggers a (fake) software crash sequence. The Joker's above announcement in *Arkham Knight* is similarly metaleptic, transgressing many levels of the game's diegesis in an assertive wink toward the digital game player. The "controls" the Joker speaks of are not simply the Batmobile's instrumental devices; the Joker also jeopardizes the very concept of avatars as frequently used within the digital game medium. As the Joker asserts, to perform as Batman is restrictive, rigid, even boring. Why not have a taste of freedom as the Joker?

To continue playing the game is to play along, leashed to the Joker's fantasy. As hermeneutic phenomenologist Hans-Georg Gadamer reminds us, "All playing is a being-played. The attraction of a game, the fascination it exerts, consists precisely in the fact that the game masters the players. . . . Whoever 'tries' is in fact the one who is tried."[1] *Arkham Knight* is indeed a game with a design that plays with the player as much as the player plays with it. As the user shapes the game world through interaction, so the game system enforces, insists upon, and ultimately shapes player identity and motivation in becoming Batman.

Indeed, at its core the game is obsessed with the processes of becoming, whether this is becoming the player, the hero, or the villain. Even the title *Arkham Knight* refers not to Batman but to a mysterious villain's transformation from heroic beginnings. More precisely, the game interpellates hero, villain, and player simultaneously. This strategy pervades the entire design, as the interwoven identities of Batman, the player, and the supervillains become the subject of a neurotic riddle, realized both narratively and ludically. At various points in the game the user takes control of Catwoman and Nightwing. Preorder bonus and later downloadable content (DLC) also provide control of Harley Quinn, Batgirl, and Red Hood, each interacting with superheroes and villains across a personal narrative. Player identity is insistently provoked: Whose game is this? Batman's? The Joker's? The Arkham Knight's? Catwoman's?

This chapter explores *Arkham Knight*'s game design of becoming both hero and villain, blurring the line between playing and being played. To unpack such design, three theoretical strands are interwoven: the concept of the Trickster, drawn from Jungian analytical psychology and anthropology; the theory of Benign Violation within social psychology; and the notion of "role" and its accompanying features from Erving Goffman's sociological oeuvre. Before we move to concrete analysis, let us attend to a brief overview of each of these theoretical strands.

The Trickster

The Trickster is an archetypal figure evident across numerous cultures, described by psychoanalyst Carl Jung as "both subhuman and superhuman, a bestial and divine being, whose chief and most alarming characteristic is his unconsciousness."[2] The Trickster is the Native American Wakdjunkaga, the Greek god Hermes, the Norse god Loki, the African Ananse, and the Christian fool. In modern times the comedian, the troll, the clown, the celebrity, or even a head of state can fulfill this role. The Trickster's common traits are paradox, absurdity, grotesquery, and subversion.[3] Yet through capricious activity, the Trickster is also a catalyst of personal, social, cultural, and political transformation; as cultural anthropologist Paul Radin's classic work outlines, "[The] Trickster is at one and the same time creator and destroyer, giver and negator, he who dupes the others and who is always duped himself. He wills nothing consciously. At all times he is constrained to behave as he does from impulses over which he has no control. He knows neither good nor evil yet he is responsible for both. He possesses no values, moral or social . . . yet through his actions all values come into being."[4] While the archetype has been previously used to analyze Batman's rogues gallery, this chapter investigates the Trickster not just as individual character but also as the ethos of game design.[5] The Trickster archetype is evident throughout *Arkham Knight*'s design via its construction and destruction of narrative expectation, its integration and disintegration of player-avatar identification, and its playing with and against the conventions of the digital game medium.

Benign Violation

Currently, the most robust theory of humor is the Benign Violation thesis.[6] A violation is "any stimulus that seems threatening, wrong, or negative,"[7] while a benign phenomenon is "when a person feels that there is nothing to worry about. In other words, everything seems okay."[8] Humor is experienced when a violation of physical, social, cultural norms occurs, yet this disruption is understood as benign, as being harmless or inconsequential to the perceiver.

For a simple example, falling over is a physical and cultural violation as society expects most people to walk with ease. If a person is sufficiently young or old, or appears injured, no humor is found in the situation. Yet if the occupant possesses adequate motor skills and appears unharmed from the fall, laughter often occurs: this is a benign violation. This laughter facilitates many positive outcomes for the person, and sometimes a connected group, such as learning and comprehension, coping with trauma, improving creativity, accentuating social cohesion, and accelerating enjoyment.[9] Of course this sense of benignity is not objective, but better understood phenomenologically as bounded by corporeal, social, cultural, and historical parameters. For example, psychologists Caleb Warren and Peter McGraw found that a Western heterosexual white male is more likely to view sexist or racist jokes as benign and therefore more likely to laugh than a woman or African American.[10] The entire concept of benign violation assumes knowledge: one *knows* the parameters, what is in or outside these borders, and therefore recognizes when a violation occurs, understanding whether it is benign or malign based upon the social, cultural and political situation.

Similarly, Rocksteady Studios' use of the Joker in *Arkham Knight* is positioned toward the *knowing* player, that is, the highly literate member of digital game culture who understands its conventions and therefore comprehends its violations. Furthermore, the design is also positioned toward the *knowing* Batman fans, those who understand the role of the Joker in the Batman universe and his Trickster motivations and behaviors: to divert, undermine, and ridicule Batman's goals, such as to enact "justice" or "save Gotham" and so on.

In many situations, one can emphasize the benign motivation behind the forthcoming violation through an array of *augmentations*, such as body language, tone of voice, eye contact, or disclaimer utterances such as "I'm only joking" or "Not to be sexist but. . . ." All these features shape the benignity, or malignity, of communication. Following his Trickster nature, the Joker famously offers benign augmentations while enacting malign violations, such as articulating the benefits of massage therapy while torturing a character or dancing comically while shooting someone.

As we will see, within *Arkham Knight* this paradoxical benign-malign relationship takes on a distinctly ludic accent. The Joker deploys a variety of augmentations matching the polyvalence of the character's nature, many directed toward helping the player cope with ludic failure. He sometimes playfully subverts user expectations and is periodically a catalyst for the narrative's trajectory. For example, midway through the game, the player-as-Batman confronts Scarecrow. From the player's perspective, this is a standard "boss fight."[11] Yet due to the impact of Scarecrow's fear toxin, the Joker is able to take control of Batman's psyche during the fight, and he pushes Batman's "no killing" policy to its breaking point; the player is now player-as-Joker-as-Batman. Such benign violations playfully alter the user's experience of both the immediately occurring battle and larger narrative encompassing the Joker-Batman relationship.

Role Playing

Finally, we draw from sociology via sociologist Erving Goffman's concept of role distance.[12] "Role" describes the separation between one's entire existential sense of self, and the social performance one is currently tasked with. For example, John plays the role of John "the cashier." Such roles are cued via the innumerable contexts we are socialized into: workplaces, schools, malls, homes, leisure facilities, and games all insist the participants select a correct role and perform it adequately. Even walking down the street a role is demanded, that of being the "public citizen." Public citizens can walk or stand, but running will draw anxious attention. They can speak, but must do so quietly, as shouting incurs avoidance or admonishment. Their eye contact should be employed judiciously, as to negotiate movement or acknowledge a request.

Clearly, in playing a social role, one must conform to the sociocultural configuration of that subject position, performing in line with its expectations. For example, John "the cashier" will speak, dress, move, and altogether behave in a way that John "the dad" or John "the romantic partner" does not (or at the least *should* not). All such roles are connected, in essence, to this larger existential John who manages, selects, and performs these separate roles for different contexts. Put simply, the existential "John" acts as a holding company for the many roles modern society requires of its subjects, selecting and enacting these roles based on the social cues perceptible.

Role Distance

Yet as knowledge configures perception, unknowing actors can make all sorts of social faux pas as they simply do not perceive the blunder that is so obvious to actors quite literally "in the know." More frequently, unknowing actors know *just enough*, cued by others' reactions, to understand their performance is inadequate. Hence, the fulfilling of a role can prove extremely tense if one feels underqualified or even overqualified to enact it. If the role feels too big to fill anxiety and panic occur; if the role feels too small frustration occurs.

As panic or frustration grows, the performance of the role is in danger of complete breakdown. For example, performing the role of Natalie "the lecturer" allows Jennifer to enact Jennifer "the student," which is conducted through a performance of engagement with the lecture, such as attentive posture, perfect silence, and consummate eye contact. Yet if Natalie shows complete disinterest or incompetence in playing the lecturer role, Jennifer's maintenance of the student becomes increasingly difficult. For example, her body language will convey disengagement, her eyes will wander, and she might turn and speak to other students in hushed tones. Such behavior by enough actors may escalate to complete disintegration of the social frame in a matter of minutes.

Indeed, this disintegration is sometimes the goal, as the person or people wish disassociation from the role. Yet if motivated to save the social frame and role therein, the central performer will often conduct "role distance," announcing to the audience a degree of separation, a larger, existential self, from the narrow social role currently on display. The role is not completely abandoned, but a tension is displayed for the audience, between existential self (Natalie) and performed role (Natalie the lecturer). This is often embodied in a person's sarcastic or cynical commentary on her performed role or admissions of unfamiliarity and worry concerning her performance.

In doing so, complete breakdown of the social frame is avoided, as one encourages acknowledgment of the foundational strain between the larger existential self and the current performed role, eliciting sympathy, empathy, and understanding, often embodied in smiles, jokes, laughter, nods, and encouraging statements. Goffman refers to such rehabilitative actions, if performed by the authority figure within the social frame (such as Natalie above), as "poise," which is an attempt to maintain equilibrium within an otherwise teetering social frame.

Role-playing holds especially true of games that provide for the player a fixed or "closed avatar," which is an avatar whose characteristics are predetermined by the game developers and, in cases such as Batman, the larger history of the fictional character.[13] Batman is a big role to play, a mythic figure of supreme martial competence and intellect. He is unrelentingly serious and committed, and, of course, Batman always wins, though sometimes a pyrrhic victory. How then do we ameliorate player frustration when they fail to fill the role: how can design lessen their frustration at ludic incompetence, or a lack of mastery?

Even if the player is highly competent, how do we account for the postmodern impulse for irony, for cynicism, for breaking conventions, for pushing back against the narrative and ludic rigidity embodied by Batman's well-defined role? How do we surprise and delight a player in an era of pervasive intertextuality and spectacle? The Joker, as a Trickster, as benign violation, as embodying role distance, provides an effective and efficient solution for game design by playfully thwarting the player's expectations. Let us now look at the Joker's introduction within *Arkham Knight*, and how it toys with narrative and ludic expectation in a manner pleasurable for the knowing user.

The Killing Joke

Sociologist Don Handelman regards the ritual clown, that is, a buffoonish figure involved in sacred ceremonies, as a "dissolver of structure, indicative of its in-between or transitional state of being."[14] Cultural anthropologist Alfonso Ortiz similarly defines clowns as "permanently equivocal and liminal characters."[15] Finally, Jungian therapist Michael Bala outlines the clown's realms as "humor and play, order and disorder, the sacred and the profane."[16] Such definitions accord with RockSteady's deployment of the Joker. Dissolution, liminality, and obscenity permeate various aspects of *Arkham Knight* via the Joker. The Joker is a character both alive and dead,

Figure 10.1. The Joker as he appears in *Arkham Knight*. Rocksteady Studios.

both inside Batman's psyche and outside toying with the world and characters. Finally, the Joker is a constant source of *profane* commentary and action, literally an attack upon any idolization of Batman as hero.

At the beginning of *Arkham Knight* events from the series are obliquely summarized via an interactive cutscene where the Joker's body is cremated, having died in the previous game *Arkham City*. RockSteady Studios' first use of the Joker is therefore to set up audience expectations: the Joker will not be in this game. This is also the first use of Trickster subversion—the construction and destruction of narrative—and the punchline soon follows. In the first mission of the central quest line, Batman attempts to shut down an overloading reactor at the infamous ACE chemical plant, set in motion by Scarecrow. Knowing fans of the Batman universe will be cognizant of this plant as the birthplace of the Joker, the liminal space where he was transformed from Red Hood into the Clown Prince of Crime.

The player-as-Batman must navigate a puzzle involving the careful insertion of "neutralizing agent" cylinders into receptacles within the core of the plant. As the player moves to place the last cylinder, camera control is taken away, panning across Batman's shoulder. A blood-drenched Joker is suddenly standing on screen, reborn with gun in hand. "Miss me?" he grins, unloading the pistol onto Batman's skull. Fade-out occurs, with no explanation proffered. This is of course not only a subversion of audience expectation, but very much, in ludic terms, a violation of player control. Indeed, the literate player is led to believe, momentarily, this is a classic "game over" scenario, that they have performed somehow incorrectly to receive this game state.

As social anthropologist Klaus-Peter Koepping explains, the Trickster is "not a figure of resolution of paradoxes but merely a signpost pointing out these paradoxes, bringing them to the conscious mind."[17] Thus begins one of many paradoxes in *Arkham Knight*: how is the Joker alive? Explained in Jungian terms, the Joker is an irruption emanating from the unconscious mind, the liminal figure achieving materiality within the perception of the traumatized Batman. The cutscene continues via fade-in: the Joker stands looking down into the camera. He offers his own diagnosis delivered in lascivious timbre, "Don't act all surprised Bats. You knew this was going to happen sooner or later. Me . . . stuck deep inside you." The violation of player control, the unexpected cutscene and fade to black, is revealed as benign: Batman lives, which, importantly, is also to say the game still lives for player interaction. Batman stands silently as the Joker continues his repartee, admonishing him: "You need to look out for yourself. After all, you're brooding for two now."

It is ultimately revealed in flashbacks that Batman received the Joker's infected blood in a transfusion. This narrative device allows the villain to haunt Batman's body and mind. Throughout the game the Joker represents what, in Jungian terminology, is known as the Shadow archetype, immanent within every Trickster. The Shadow archetype contains latent aspects of character one avoids acknowledging, commonly through repression, suppression, avoidance, denial, or, as Batman performs, stoic silence. In the Jungian view, employing these defense mechanisms is ultimately harmful: whether I repress, suppress, or sublimate, that unconscious aspect of my character simply grows in strength, eventually leading to some form of psychosis.

Indeed, this lesson is symbolized through the Joker's evolving appearance: upon his first manifestation (see Figure 10.1) he appears blood soaked. Yet across his numerous appearances, the blood slowly disappears, his vitality restored. Simply, the more Batman resists, the stronger the Joker becomes, eventually leading to the psychotic break described within the introduction where the Joker takes over Batman's agency. Concordantly, such breaks are sometimes experienced internally as an entirely separate self or as unconscious impulses and behaviors. Sometimes, they are experienced externally as perceptual hallucinations.

If the Batman metanarrative represents the Jungian notion of individuation, a gradual, continuous integration of one's personal and collective unconscious aspects into one's conscious sense of self, symbolized through the relationship between Bruce Wayne and Batman, Batman and Gotham City, Batman and his rogues gallery, then the deeply egoistic Shadow demands, "What about me?!" Or indeed, as the Joker aptly puts it, "What about *us*?!" again interpellating not only Batman and the Joker's increasingly fused identities, but the player too: what about *their* desires, *their* needs, and *their* expectations for control, freedom, power, and pleasure, all of the implicit promises of the digital game medium.

The Joker introduces himself therefore as both advocate for *and* attacker of the player, as both serious trauma and frivolous interjector, as living but dead, as violation but benign. Yet it is this "dialectic interplay of structure and antistructure" that is once more the hallmark of the Trickster.[18] Let us now discuss how the Joker moves between these poles and what this means for the postmodern player experience.

Send in the Clown

One of the gestural hallmarks of postmodernity within the Western world is laughter.[19] As Western belief in metanarratives began to dissolve in postmodernity, key Trickster characteristics such as paradox, irony, and spectacle became prominent structuring features of Western culture.[20] Laughter's antistructure, "unlaughter," which is the refusal to perform the expected audience role in a comedic situation, became increasingly taboo.[21] Librarian Moira Smith ponders the example of the cartoon depiction of the prophet Muhammad in Danish newspapers and the controversy that ensued to illuminate the importance of "having a sense of humor" to Western civilization. Judged on this singular criteria, the Islamic world's failure to laugh was seen to illuminate "serious deficiencies in personality and a symptom of inability to adjust to group norms."[22] As Smith further describes, "The ancient philosopher said, 'Know thyself,' but in the contemporary world the equivalent injunction is 'Laugh at thyself.' To laugh at oneself requires a capacity for self-objectification, the ability to perceive the incongruity between our subjective and objective selves, between our interior estimation of ourselves and the way we appear to others. Thus defined, humor is able to mediate between the paradoxes inherent in the contemporary idea of selfhood and the conflicting demands of psychological versus social modes of being."[23]

Let us now consider how the laughter of the Joker, directed at Batman's steadfast commitment to ideals such as justice and order, works in the design of *Arkham Knight*.

The Man Who Laughs

If one of the key characteristics of the Joker is his laughter, then Batman's is "unlaughter," a quality evident across his appearances in film, television, and the comics. Batman is the "straight man" in even the most absurd of situations. Batman does not negotiate paradox, illustrate the many incongruities between the subjective and objective self, or accept the fluid "social modes of being" that Smith points toward.[24] Instead, Batman adroitly, obdurately, and consistently applies his strict ethical code. This rigidity opens up a phenomenological gap between the contemporary player's fluid, self-reflexive understanding of selfhood and morality, versus Batman's resoluteness. Indeed this may be part of the attraction of Batman, and superheroes in general to Western audiences: their unflinching, high modernist commitment to ideals is perhaps a reassuring fantasy for one drenched in the existential uncertainty of liquid modernity.[25]

This fluidity and reflexivity is hardwired into our body's innate capacity for adaptation, that is, to attune to a phenomenon and neutralize its affective qualities. For entertainment experiences, this is known as hedonic adaptation: our ability to adjust, through repeated exposure to the stimuli, to pleasure and pain in such a way that our response is lessened.[26] Simply put, as we continuously engage with the same content, its psychological impact lessens. For example, playing the thirtieth hour of *Super Mario Bros.*, squashing yet another Goomba lacks the excitement felt during my first hour of play, when I first encountered and learned to overcome a variety of enemies.[27] Further, every encounter with content raises the "baseline level" for future stimuli to elicit a heightened response. We refer to this as experience or literacy. For example, as a competent digital game player, I am less likely than someone inexperienced in the medium and genre to find *Pac-Man* novel, challenging, and therefore pleasurable. Of course hedonic adaptation is a constant danger for games since the basis of any game is repetitive action: whether kicking a football in a soccer match, or aligning tetrominoes in *Tetris*, games demand repetition from the player.

In a society and culture of exuberant spectacle, we are extraordinarily literate in all kinds of media. Hedonic adaptation, as bound up with repetition, literacy, and experience, is founded upon expectation, for example, knowing that in a genre's narrative B usually follows A, which together equals C. As musicologist David Huron's work outlines, if these expectations are met too closely, fulfillment results in the boredom of absolute hedonic adaptation, and the person seeks new experiences elsewhere.[28] One method of keeping this adaptation at bay, and henceforth ennui and eventual rejection, is to violate expectation. Once more, as outlined, these violations should not be serious, such as game-breaking glitches and bugs, but benign, which will be experienced as harmless and within the boundaries of the user's literacies.

The average gamer is familiar with the medium, genre, control scheme, narrative, mechanics, dynamics, and aesthetics present within the *Arkham* series. Furthermore, as mentioned earlier, the player may also be literate in various aspects of the Batman universe, knowledgeable on Batman's history and code of ethics, the cohort of heroes and villains, and the city of Gotham. While, for new and veteran players alike, this can promote excitement through the novelty of exploring this well-known fictional locale through a game medium, it can also turn to apathy when the player goes through *yet another* brawl with gang thugs, such as when Batman *once again* refuses to kill or when Robin and Batgirl *predictably* whine because Batman refuses to include them in his plans. As these tropes inevitably occur within *Arkham Knight*, the Joker's laughter, his constant mocking of Batman's code, his ridiculing of Batgirl and Robin's whimpering work to stave off this ever-present threat of boredom, constantly winking at and surprising the player with playful interjections, embodying the cynicism of the postmodern subject.

The Joker's Wild

Not only is Batman unrelenting in his commitment to his code; he is also an implacable master of the martial arts and virtuoso detective. This is where the Joker once more serves as player advocate, as the antistructure to modernity, and the Trickster of the digital game medium. For example, when ludic failure occurs the player is greeted with the classic fade-to-black screen, signifying "game over" since early arcade games. Yet this traditional admonishment is quickly undercut by the Joker, who suddenly walks onto the black screen, addressing the player-as-Batman with one of many quips, "Oops. You're dead! Wait . . . does this mean I'm dead?! GET UP BRUCE! GET UP!" or "What the? Why has everything gone dark? Are we dying? We better not be dying, Bruce!" Player failure is transformed into a benign violation: not only is it harmless, it is spectacular.

Simultaneously, such design keeps poise. If one continuously fails to enact the "player" role adequately, the silent condemnation of the conventional "game over" screen exacerbates breakdown; the player throws down the controller, switches games, or perhaps turns off the computer entirely. Yet the Joker intervenes, strolling onto the "game over" screen in mock exasperation, "Now, if I was in charge, this never would have happened!" a model poise statement directed toward recovering an unsteady social frame. Frustration lessens and one's habitation of the player role, so close to rupture a moment ago, may stabilize for another attempt.

Conclusion

We can understand the Joker's many violations of Batman, and by extension the player, as benign violations: ultimately harmless disruptions of the narrative, game mechanics, characters, and player identification. Indeed, these violations move beyond benignity to provide the spectacle, pleasure, and surprise demanded by a highly literate postmodern audience. The Joker's presence in *Arkham Knight* is therefore an excellent design solution for the commercial game, which must provide failure to qualify *as* a game, and yet avoid frustrating the player-as-consumer. Even when the player loses, the Joker's spectacular appearance on the "game over" screen makes it feel like a win.

The use of the Joker also targets the jaded, postmodern videogame player, whose default hermeneutic position is skepticism, embodied in ironic, sarcastic, or otherwise derisive behavior indicative of role distance. Such behaviors are essentially defense mechanisms against metanarratives, against the anxiety of being "duped" yet again by giving oneself over to any rigid belief system, which Batman as a character represents.[29] The Joker is therefore catharsis: he is the incompetent, frustrated, and cynical player given voice. Instead of the player throwing up their hands in irritation, making a sarcastic comment about Batman's rigid code, or providing ironic commentary on his dealing with criminals, the Joker takes over and turns the dial to eleven. The player in this manner is not only given voice but also placated through constant spectacle.

Hence through role distance, as embodied by the Joker, the sometimes-suffocating mask of Batman is alleviated. Furthermore, game developer Rocksteady's deployment of the Joker maintains poise, providing a benign avenue to channel the player's frustration and anxiety, indeed even leveraging such negative emotion to generate laughter. Building upon the idea explicit in this chapter's opening quote, by the very act of "poking through the thin sleeve of immediate reality" with absurdity and grotesquery, the Joker is not in fact a "destroyer of worlds," but instead allows the often unskilled, ironic, and skeptical player to inhabit the world of Batman.[30]

Notes

Epigraph: Erving Goffman, *Encounters: Two Studies in the Sociology of Interaction* (Harmondsworth: Penguin, 1972), 72.

1 Hans-Georg Gadamer, *Truth and Method*, ed. Joel Weinsheimer and Donald G. Marshall (London: Sheed & Ward, 2004), 106.

2 Carl Gustav Jung, *Collected Works of C.G. Jung, Volume 9 (Part 1)* (Princeton: Princeton University Press, 2014), 263.

3 Klaus-Peter Koepping, "Absurdity and Hidden Truth: Cunning Intelligence and Grotesque Body Images as Manifestations of the Trickster," *History of Religions* 24, no. 3 (1985): 191–214.

4 Paul Radin, *The Trickster: A Study in American Indian Mythology* (London: Routledge, 1956), ix.

5 See Robert Moses Peaslee and Robert G. Weiner, *The Joker: A Serious Study of the Clown Prince of Crime* (Jackson: University Press of Mississippi, 2015).

6 Caleb Warren and A. Peter McGraw, "Differentiating What Is Humorous from What Is Not," *Journal of Personality and Social Psychology* 110, no. 3 (2015): 407–430.

7 Warren and McGraw, "Differentiating What Is Humorous," 410.
8 Warren and McGraw, "Differentiating What Is Humorous," 412.
9 Warren and McGraw, "Differentiating What Is Humorous."
10 Warren and McGraw, "Differentiating What Is Humorous."
11 A "boss fight" is a delimited space and time within a game where the player character faces another major character, often incorporating unique mechanics and cinematic sequences to drive the narrative or reward the player.
12 Goffman, *Encounters*.
13 Daniel Kromand, "Avatar Categorization," in *Proceedings from DiGRA 2007: Situated Play* (Tokyo: DiGRA, 2007), 400–406.
14 Don Handelman, "The Ritual Clown," *Anthropos* 76 (1981): 333.
15 Alfonso Ortiz, "Ritual Drama and the Pueblo World View," in *New Perspectives on the Pueblos*, ed. Alfonso Ortiz (Albuquerque: University of New Mexico Press, 1972), 155.
16 Michael Bala, "The Clown: An Archetypal Self-Journey," *Jung Journal: Culture & Psyche* 4, no. 1 (2010): 51.
17 Koepping, "Absurdity and Hidden Truth," 191–197.
18 Koepping, "Absurdity and Hidden Truth," 191–199.
19 Moira Smith, "Humour, Unlaughter, and Boundary Maintenance," *Journal of American Folklore* 122, no. 484 (2009): 166.
20 Jean-François Lyotard, *The Postmodern Condition: A Report on Knowledge* (Manchester: Manchester University Press, 1984); Smith, "Humour."
21 Michael Billig, *Laughter and Ridicule: Towards a Social Critique of Humour* (London: Sage, 2005).
22 Smith, "Humour," 166.
23 Smith, "Humour," 158.
24 Smith, "Humour," 158.
25 Zygmunt Bauman, *Liquid Modernity* (Oxford: Polity, 2000).
26 Shane Frederick and George Loewenstein, "Hedonic Adaptation," in *Well-Being: The Foundations of Hedonic Psychology*, ed. Daniel Kahneman, Ed Diener, and Norbert Schwarz (New York: Russell Sage Foundation, 1999), 302–329.
27 Nintendo R&D4, *Super Mario Bros.* (Kyoto: Nintendo, 1985), digital platformer game.
28 David Huron, *Sweet Anticipation: Music and the Psychology of Expectation* (Cambridge, MA: MIT Press, 2006).
29 Lyotard, *Postmodern Condition*.
30 Goffman, *Encounters*, 72.

Bibliography

Bala, Michael. "The Clown: An Archetypal Self-Journey." *Jung Journal: Culture & Psyche* 4, no. 1 (2010): 50–71.

Batman: Arkham Asylum. Playstation 3 game. Directed by Sefton Hill. London: Rocksteady Studios, 2009.

Batman: Arkham Knight. Playstation 4 game. Directed by Sefton Hill. London: Rocksteady Studios, 2015.

Bauman, Zygmunt. *Liquid Modernity*. Oxford: Polity, 2000.

Billig, Michael. *Laughter and Ridicule: Towards a Social Critique of Humor*. London: Sage, 2005.

Frederick, Shane, and George Loewenstein. "Hedonic Adaptation." In *Well-Being: The Foundations of Hedonic Psychology*, edited by Daniel Kahneman, Ed Diener, and Norbert Schwarz, 302–330. New York: Russell Sage Foundation, 1999.

Gadamer, Hans-Georg. *Truth and Method*. Edited by Joel Weinsheimer and Donald G. Marshall. London: Sheed & Ward, 2004.

Goffman, Erving. *Encounters: Two Studies in the Sociology of Interaction*. Harmondsworth: Penguin, 1972.

Handelman, Don. "The Ritual Clown." *Anthropos* 76 (1981): 321–370.

Huron, David. *Sweet Anticipation: Music and the Psychology of Expectation*. Cambridge, MA: MIT Press, 2006.

Jung, Carl Gustav. *Collected Works of C.G. Jung, Volume 9 (Part 1)*. Princeton, NJ: Princeton University Press, 2014.

Koepping, Klaus-Peter. "Absurdity and Hidden Truth: Cunning Intelligence and Grotesque Body Images as Manifestations of the Trickster." *History of Religions* 24, no. 3 (1985): 191–214.

Kromand, Daniel. "Avatar Categorization." In *Proceedings from DiGRA 2007: Situated Play*, 400–406. Tokyo: DiGRA, 2007.

Lyotard, Jean-François. *The Postmodern Condition: A Report on Knowledge*. Manchester: Manchester University Press, 1984.

Ortiz, Alfonso. "Ritual Drama and the Pueblo World View." In *New Perspectives on the Pueblos*, edited by Alfonso Ortiz, 135–161. Albuquerque: University of New Mexico Press, 1972.

Peaslee, R. M., and Robert G. Weiner. *The Joker: A Serious Study of the Clown Prince of Crime*. Jackson: University Press of Mississippi, 2015.

Radin, Paul. *The Trickster: A Study in American Indian Mythology*. London: Routledge, 1956.

Smith, Moira. "Humour, Unlaughter, and Boundary Maintenance." *Journal of American Folklore* 122, no. 484 (2009): 148–171.

Warren, C., and A. Peter McGraw. "Differentiating What Is Humorous from What Is Not." *Journal of Personality and Social Psychology* 110, no. 3 (2015): 407–430.

11

Being Super, Becoming Heroes

Dialogic Superhero Narratives in Cosplay Collectives

CLAIRE LANGSFORD

This is a tale of two Batman cosplays. At first glance the outfits of U.S. cosplayer Charles Conley and Irish cosplayer Julian Checkley are almost identical. In their respective portraits the two tall, well-built men pose dramatically in intricately molded masks, battle-damaged plated armor and flowing black capes. Both cosplayers re-created a specific version of the character Batman as presented in the Warner Bros. Interactive videogame *Batman: Arkham Origins*. However, as this chapter reveals, the narratives surrounding these two performances of the Batman character were very different. One Batman costume was represented as a technical feat worthy of a Guinness World Record; the other was framed as a political protest against the whiteness of globalized popular media. One superhero and two performances promoted very different interpretations with different implications for cosplay communities. Whether they are inspiring Hollywood blockbusters and best-selling videogames, materialized as children's playthings, or being remixed in fanfiction and memes, fictional superheroes have considerable power in our world. Can the power of superhero imagery and narratives be successfully harnessed to affect actual political change? In his recent work noted fan scholar Henry Jenkins has highlighted the use of narratives and imagery from popular culture in Western social justice activism.[1] In particular Jenkins has argued that superheroes, as highly recognizable cultural icons associated with diverse and malleable narratives and sets of meanings, can provide inspiration for political action, and a means for communication of political ideas across broad potential audiences—an argument he further expounds in his contribution to this

Figures 11.1 and 11.2. Batman cosplayer Charles Conley (above) is an example of the quest for justice narratives found in the cosplay community, while Julian Checkley (opposite), who also cosplays as Batman, is more typical of epic feat narratives.

collection.[2] As Jenkins points out, globalized figures like Spider-Man or Superman, with their recognizable visual designs and histories of associated myths and meanings, can facilitate communication between diverse actors, and they can provide a rallying point for collective action on issues like racial equality and global poverty.[3] In a phenomenon Jenkins terms "the civic imagination," the tropes and narratives of superhero media may enable individuals or collectives to imagine better futures, empathize with others, and enact change.[4]

However, existing anthropological studies of social movements highlight the complexity of collective political action, and these can be used to highlight two main concerns with Jenkins's argument. First, in Jenkins's work and other emerging discussions of fan activism, the social movements that these various authors describe, such as the globalized nonprofit organization the Harry Potter Alliance, tend to be treated as homogenous collectives acting in unison.[5] In these accounts fan activists are depicted as sharing common interests, goals, and rhetoric that is provided by their shared understanding of a popular media text. In groups like the Harry Potter Alliance, shared understandings of a mythology like J. K. Rowling's wizarding world become a framing device for understanding political issues—werewolves can provide insight into marginalization and stigma, wizard and non-wizard conflicts can represent racial tensions.[6] Shared readings can produce social bonds and a sense of collectivity that can be marshalled toward particular causes as diverse as fair trade or protection of the Affordable Care Act.[7]

However, ethnographic accounts of social movements have shown that these collectives are, in fact, heterogeneous.[8] In their analysis of social movements across North America, Europe and Asia anthropologist Dorothy Holland and collaborators argue that the collective identities of social movements are not stable but are instead produced and reproduced by dialogues and conflicts within the group and with those outside of the group.[9] Drawing on concepts of dialogics developed by the philosopher Mikhail Bakhtin and expanded by anthropologists Dennis Tedlock and Bruce Mannheim, Holland et al. argue that contradictory goals, beliefs, and meanings exist within social movements.[10]

The scholarly emphasis on cohesion in fan activism also contradicts existing fan studies' literature, which recognizes that like social movements, fan communities are heterogeneous. Media scholars such as Matt Hills and Daisuke Okabe have recognized that hierarchies exist within specific fan collectives, hierarchies that are often in tension with a community's self-description as open and inclusive.[11]

Furthermore, while Jenkins recognizes the multiple nature of the superhero as a cultural artifact that is open to many different uses and interpretations by diverse actors, he does not fully consider how this multiplicity may impact on the potential uses of superheroes in social movements. Holland et al. argue that cultural artifacts such as narratives and symbols are interpreted or experienced differently by different actors or subgroups within a social movement.[12] These different experiences and interpretations may even shape the structure and actions within a social movement.[13] As polyvalent cultural symbols, different fan activists interpret superheroes differently. These multiple interpretations could act as points of difference and contention between potential activists rather than as points of connection.

As a counterpoint to fan activism's emphasis on shared understandings of symbols and mythologies in social movements, this chapter explores how fans can hold very different interpretations of character and mythology. These different interpretations complicate the use of popular culture icons as marshalling points for civic participation. To gain a greater understanding of how popular culture icons like superheroes may play a role in diverse and heterogeneous collectives and social movements, fan scholarship can learn much from studying examples where superhero imagery and myths are already woven into the communities' narratives and practices. One such context is the fan practice of costume role-play (cosplay) in which practitioners re-create preexisting character designs in the form of a wearable costume. Cosplay can be considered a "figured world," which is, according to Holland et al., a socially constructed context in which particular actors, symbols, and actions are interpreted through a shared framework, and identities (collective *and* individual) are constructed.[14] Superheroes play an important role in this figured world; their images are re-created materially on cosplayers' bodies and costumes, and the rhetoric of the superhero genre influences the way the practice is discussed. Indeed, media coverage of cosplay frequently draws direct parallels between cosplayers and the heroes/

villains they portray in articles such as "Superheroes and Villains Living among Us to Descend on Melbourne Convention Centre."[15]

Cosplayers use superhero imagery as a source of inspiration for their costumes and embedded performances, but they also draw upon superhero narrative tropes in their own storytelling practices. Stories, oral and written, play an important role in the construction of collectives and identities, and they can be used to effect transformations. In telling stories, outsiders can become insiders and insiders can gain or lose status within the collective.[16] Storytelling is also heteroglossic, as narratives can be interpreted in multiple ways, and certain stories or types of stories can contradict or negate others.[17] Cosplayers are great storytellers: they tell stories about themselves, their creations, and the subjects of their fandom in oral performances, in news articles, and in personal anecdotes on blogs and social media. These oral and written narratives frequently act as paratexts—devices and conventions that guide the interpretation of a text, for visual and temporal works such as costumes, photographs, and performances.[18] Cosplayers tell stories to explain their motivations for character choices or to reveal the processes that went into costume creation. In telling these stories cosplayers draw upon superhero tropes to explain their own participation in cosplay and to discuss and debate the values practiced and celebrated within cosplay communities.

Examining cosplayer narratives collected from publicly accessible profiles and posts on social media and from onstage interviews during cosplay competitions, this chapter explores the use of superhero rhetoric in the construction of cosplay communities and identities. In particular, the chapter explores the dialogic tensions in cosplayers' use of two different superhero tropes: the quest for justice and the performance of epic feats. In one set of narratives cosplayers invoke the idea of a quest for justice to position their dress activities as a struggle for representation and inclusion. In the other set of narratives cosplayers describe their own craft activities as superheroic feats as a means of gaining personal distinction within the cosplay community. Radical fan activism or elite craft practice? Superhero tropes are used to support both imaginings of cosplay, to create connections between specific kinds of cosplay performers and cosplay values, and to establish oppositions between others.

Heroic People: Quest for Justice Narratives

Why This "Brown Batman" Meant So Much to One Little Boy[19]

In 2016 the story of U.S. cosplayer Charles Conley's Batman costume and its impact on a young convention attendee was shared online by many cosplayers. Conley's story, which started as a post he wrote on Facebook and was later covered by multiple international news sources, described how the black cosplayer's performance had inspired a small boy to believe that he too could be a "brown superhero." The performance could be viewed as a form of fan activism as described by Jenkins, Kligler-Vilenchik, and others because Conley explicitly framed his cosplay as a critique of the dominance of white superhero figures in mainstream media.[20] In his original Facebook post Conley described his performance of the Batman character as both an expression of fandom and a deliberately political act: "Well I cosplay batman [*sic*] because I love the character and because representation matters."[21]

Like many classic superheroes, there are cosplayers who explicitly position their actions and performances as contributing to an ongoing quest for social justice. Within superhero narratives the quest or mission trope plays an important role because it demonstrates that the protagonist is willing to use their abilities for a cause greater than their own prestige or empowerment.[22] In cosplay narratives the quest most often involves advocating for more diverse representation of bodies and sexualities within cosplay and more broadly, in the comics, novels, films, and television series that inspire cosplay. According to this view unequal power structures found in societies are reproduced in the depictions of characters in popular texts. The dominance of particular character types legitimizes the hegemonic power of particular actors and marginalizes others.[23] As alternative cultural products, cosplay performances may provide a form of protest against cultural forms that support social inequality. As cosplayer Priya Rehal, a self-described "disruptive cosplayer," explains in an online article for *GUTS* magazine, "While I used cosplay mostly to explore gender, I've become interested in using cosplay to challenge the future and the whiteness of the media that I enjoy."[24] Dressing up can be a deeply political act. Anthropologists have noted that the dressed body is an important site for the negotiation of power, cultural values, and ideologies as clothing enables the intersection of private bodies, beliefs, and practices with public values and expectations.[25] Clothing can be the materialization of particular policies and power structures and can convey symbolic meanings, and dress practices can be practical constructions of self in relation to religious, ethnic, and gender norms.[26] Cosplay in particular has a number of unique aspects that enable it to be adopted as a mode of political expression. As many cosplay scholars have noted, the playful act of re-creating a character design as a wearable object enables practitioners to remix recognizable visual and material symbols in new and surprising ways.[27] Among the many established forms of remix in cosplay are race bending—performing the character as having an alternate ethnicity; crossplaying—performing characters whose identified gender differs from the cosplayer's own; and gender flipping—performing the character as being an alternate gender.

While some cosplayers may intend their performances to be disruptive to gendered, heteronormative, or racialized power structures, these performances are not always read in this way by audiences. Cosplay performances are open to many different interpretations—including those that differ from the performer's intentions. In her article Rehal argues that audience members misread or misinterpreted the intentions of her performance:

> For example, when I cosplayed as Rogue from X-Men, I heard whispers:
>
> "Is that a brown Rogue?"
> "Look, a brown Rogue!"
>
> Men (fellow guests and vendors) interrogated my legitimacy as a racialized woman who is a fan and a racialized woman who is a cosplayer; they ceaselessly informed me of "missing" components of my cosplay when I had intentionally combined comic book and screen adaptations of the character.[28]

Texts such as articles, interviews, blogs, vlogs, and other social media posts provide cosplayers with an opportunity to frame the meaning of their visual and material cosplay performances. These paratexts enable cosplayers to narrate their own practices and to articulate their positions within fan and cosplay communities. For some cosplayers this includes explaining how their performances engage with social justice concerns about diversity of representation in popular media.

These narratives are deeply dialogic. The cosplayer defines his or her performances in relation to the actions, beliefs, or opinions of others. These others include globalized corporate cultural producers such as Disney, Marvel, Electronic Arts, and Nintendo. Cosplayers use paratexts to frame their performances as a rejection of or correction to what they perceive as inadequately diverse character representations in films, television, comics, and other media. In blog posts, articles, and social media cosplayers discuss the representation of characters' gender and sexuality: "The prevalence of cosplays that cross gender lines like this is, I think, attributable to two things. First, there is a widespread lack of characters who aren't cis men in popular art. Second, characters who aren't cis men are often not multidimensional in any way."[29] They also discuss disability: "With so little disability representation in media, whom should we cosplay?"[30]

These texts also speak back to other participants in cosplay communities. In some instances cosplayers position their performances as aesthetically similar to the work of other cosplayers, as a commentary on the work of others, or as following a tradition established by other cosplayers. In her online article cosplayer Sam de Leve pays tribute to the works of other cosplayers who live with a significant physical disability, and she provides hyperlinks to images of their work: "And many wheelchair construction cosplays are absolutely stonking brilliant: Ben Carpenter's Mad Max "Blood Bag Mobile," Mica Bethea's Tyrion Lannister on the Iron Throne, and countless adorable children in TIE fighters."[31] De Leve goes on to explain that while she admires these works where the cosplayers have incorporated their wheelchairs or other assistive technologies into their costumes, she wishes to take an alternative approach to performance in which her wheelchair is incidental to her costume rather than a focus. De Leve's article positions her work alongside works by other cosplayers, both able-bodied and those living with disability, explaining the similarities and differences in their approaches and practices. She highlights approaches that she views as inclusionary and empowering to cosplayers living with disability and criticizes approaches that trivialize or appropriate the experiences of cosplayers with a disability such as the use of wheelchairs as character props by able-bodied cosplayers.

Paratext narratives are used to reject or oppose the views of other community members who hold alternative understandings of text or practice. In his Facebook post Conley describes experiencing rejection from others while cosplaying Batman as a black man: "As many of you know I've had to deal with issues regarding bigots who can't seem to wrap their mind around the idea of a black guy cosplaying Batman, because 'Batman is historically white, there are plenty of black characters you could do instead.'"[32] In his account Conley positions his actions and beliefs against unnamed others in the community who denigrate his performance on the grounds that it does not visually re-create the look of Batman found in the source material. Rehal's account of her experiences while playing Rogue echoes the concern that more radical forms of cosplay are not accepted by all members of the cosplay community. While Kligler-Vilenchik in her examination of the Harry Potter Alliance emphasizes the way that shared mythologies around specific texts can be used to create shared forms of resistance, practices such as race-bending, gender-flipping, and other remix forms of cosplay seem to promote multiple readings of superhero texts and provoke uncertainty in the community around the definition and identity of cosplay itself.[33]

"Quest for justice" narratives also speak to future fans and cosplayers. At the heart of these concerns, "quest for justice" narratives emphasize the affective potential of cosplay performances. By challenging or inspiring others, these cosplayers express the hope that their performances will transform these communities. Conley's Facebook post centers on the idea that through his performance he has been able to inspire a young boy to be able to imagine himself as Batman. Misa on Wheels, aka Amanda Knightly, a cosplayer performing while living with a disability speaks explicitly about her hopes to inspire others living with disability to participate in cosplay: "'I get a lot of anonymous mail on Tumblr from people, and those looking to cosplay, with disabilities,' she said. 'Maybe the anonymity shows that disability is still an issue that is not as openly discussed as it should be in today's world. And I am doing my best to change that.'"[34]

Stories like Conley's position particular cosplay performances as heroic acts in an ongoing quest for increased diversity of representation in popular media. However, as the dialogic nature of these stories reveals, this is far from the only interpretation of superhero narratives and imagery present within cosplay communities. While Conley and others incorporate the superheroic quest trope into their fan activism, other cosplayers use heroic language and imagery for quite different purposes. The following section describes how cosplayers construct stories of epic cosplay feats to legitimize their practice and to establish aesthetic standards for the community.

Super People: Epic Feat Narratives

Batman Cosplay Suit Sets World Record with 23 Gadgets[35]

In 2016, the Guinness World Records awarded their first cosplay-related record to Irish costumer Julian Checkley for a costume with the most functioning gadgets. Checkley's Batsuit featured "smoke bombs, a grapnel gun and a bat sign projector," among its working parts.[36] Checkley demonstrated that like the fictional masked vigilante, he too was capable of achieving epic feats—albeit feats of craftsmanship rather than feats of fighting prowess. Photographs and news articles describing Checkley's achievement were promoted on many online cultural sites, including *Rolling Stone*.[37]

Articles like these highlight particular costumes, performers, or individuals as spectacular or exemplary representations of cosplay and cosplayers. Popular culture media sites like *Kotaku* frequently post galleries of the "best" cosplays performed at recent events and interview features with cosplayers whose work has been recognized in competitions or online. The trend of highlighting cosplay's spectacular works and practitioners has extended to television with programs such as SyFy's *Heroes of Cosplay*, which showcased the activities of experienced U.S.-based cosplay practitioners. More recently, SyFy introduced the show *Cosplay Melee*, which explicitly emphasizes competition and evaluation. *Cosplay Melee* positions cosplayers against each other in the search for winning costumes and performances. Collectively, these narratives promote the idea that there exists a hierarchy of cosplay works and creators who stand apart and above the thousands of other cosplayers who attend events or post images and videos of their works online. Extraordinary figures like Batman or Superman standout from the ordinary citizens of Gotham or Metropolis; "super" cosplayers, in their detailed and handcrafted outfits, stand apart from others in the cosplay community. While cosplayers evoke the heroic quest trope to promote inclusivity within and without cosplay communities, another superheroic trope—the story of the epic feat—is used to create exclusivity and hierarchies between cosplayers.

One of the most enduring tropes of the superhero genre is the hero's ability to perform extraordinary feats beyond the capability of the everyday person.[38] These feats may be achieved through the use of paranormal powers as in the case of Superman, Spider-Man, or the X-Men, or through the use of assistive technologies as in the case of Iron Man or Batman. The trope endures even in revisionist works such as the *Kick-Ass* franchise, where the everyman protagonist is able to achieve unlikely feats through an ability to endure pain. In these texts, superheroic feats provide readers, viewers, and players with an opportunity to enjoy empowerment fantasies or to take pleasure in a carnivalesque inversion of their everyday realities.

Superheroic feats also feature heavily in cosplayer storytelling. In his exploration of Japanese cosplayers, Okabe identifies "cosplay versions of heroic tales" circulating among the community.[39] In these stories the protagonist cosplayer displays some "extraordinary effort" to create or wear their costume. This could be performing some amazing craft skill, spending a large amount of time and money on a particular costume, or recreating every detail of a design. These tales about epic cosplay feats serve not only to entertain but also to provide a model of an idealized super-cosplay to which other cosplayers should aspire.

The heroic tales Okabe records bear a striking similarity to epic feat narratives told in Australian cosplay competitions. During many competition events participants are interviewed by hosts or judges while onstage. Most interview narratives describe the processes of the transformation of objects. Through the use of questioning, the host or judge attempts to elicit the story of the costume the cosplayer is wearing, such as how and why it was created. Anthropologist Shalini Shankar has argued that verbal narratives about objects can be used by individuals as a means of potentially enhancing personal status within a community.[40] In their narratives of cosplay assembly, competitors attempt to articulate the effort and love that has gone into the costumes they are wearing in order to portray their efforts as an epic feat. Through their responses to questions, cosplayers verbally connect their onstage presentation with offstage processes and labor that are invisible to competition audiences and judges. In their stories of creative processes, cosplayers strategically present themselves as competent amateurs, deserving of attention and acclaim for their loving efforts.

Competitors may describe their processes with dramatic understatement. A cosplayer at the Supanova convention in Melbourne used this technique to emphasize his amazing skill and speed at prop creation. The contestant walked onstage carrying a prop katana that was taller than himself. It was accurately re-created with an elegant curved blade and tsuka ito–style cord wrappings around the tang.

> HOST Tell us about the sword, obviously. . . .
> A Thursday afternoon.
> HOST What? [a pause as the contestant smiles] What?
> A I did this on Thursday afternoon. It's a record-breaking ten dollars spent on this. [crowd cheers] And it's my second largest prop.
> HOST Yeah. It's awesome.[41]

The juxtaposition between the beautiful presentation of the prop and the understatement of the contestant's verbal delivery emphasizes the creation of the sword as a heroic cosplay feat, achievable only by a highly experienced cosplayer. The host's surprised reactions emphasize to the audience that it is amazing that such a large and detailed prop could have been created in such a short time frame. Epic feat narratives not only emphasize the creativity and craftsmanship of the competitor but also celebrate the willingness of cosplayers to endure pain and discomfort:

> HOST Check out these shoes that are currently coming to the stage. . . . [Kathy walks onto the stage wearing stilt-like "merchant geta" that require her to balance each foot on a wooden spike. The audience exclaims.] Now I just want to make a point, just right here, Kathy, who is currently standing up on those shoes—one, she's had leg surgery, two, she sprained her ankle yesterday. It is a miracle that she can walk let alone in those shoes and do a flip in a fight scene. Ladies and gentlemen, a round of applause right about now for effort![42]

In the instance described the cosplayer was onstage, visible to the audience, wearing a detailed costume, and had just moments prior performed a skit involving acrobatics. The juxtaposition of the magical and apparently effortless visual performances of the competing cosplayer with the story of embodied pain and effort in the host's narrative serves to enhance the competing cosplayer's prestige as it demonstrates that not only can the competitor apparently overcome the demands of her body; she can make it appear to the audience as if she is in no pain.

In an onstage interview during a major competition the host and contestant Mel discussed the body shaping activities Mel used to achieve a taut, flat stomach, reminiscent of her chosen male character:

> HOST You've said you like miso soup. What's the story there with miso soup?
>
> M I used to drink like three glasses of Pepsi for breakfast but when I realized that I would have to do a costume that bares my stomach I thought ah yeah, better stop that. So I've cut out the Pepsi and replaced it with miso soup for breakfast instead so now I have a miso addiction instead of a Pepsi addiction [audience cheers]. But I've lost like an awful lot of weight so I'm happy [audience cheers].[43]

In these stories it is body transformation for the sake of character accuracy that is celebrated. Super cosplayers diet or bulk up, endure heavy or constricting outfits, or even risk further injury to wear certain items in order to look and perform like their chosen characters. This narrated suffering demonstrates the cosplayers' dedication to the character, to their fandom, and to their audience.

Super and/or Heroic? Dialogic Tensions in Cosplay Narratives

Conley's and Checkley's respective Batman cosplays and the paratexts surrounding these performances demonstrate the variety of meanings, interpretations, and values that are attributed to superhero characters and cosplay performances. In his Facebook blog post and other paratexts Conley frames his Batman performance as an attempt to highlight the importance of ethnically diverse portrayals of character and to inspire young black people. The paratexts around Checkley's Batman performance instead highlight the cosplayer's individual talents in re-creating the look and functionality of a preexisting character design.

Epic feat and quest for justice narratives present different ways of positioning cosplayer actors within communities of practitioners. Quest for justice authors create a discursive world in their paratexts where cosplayers as activists, radicals, and disrupters are positioned in opposition to cosplayers and fans who promote and defend hegemonic power structures. In epic feat narratives cosplayers are portrayed as competing individuals whose prominence and value in the community are determined by their technical skills and personal motivation.

The examples provided also demonstrate the different ways that cosplayer bodies are interpreted. In epic feat narratives, the ideal cosplay body is one that is molded to resemble the character as depicted in the source text. The emphasis here is on physical transformation as an individual skill and a materialization of fannish effort. In contrast quest for justice narratives centered on issues of race and disability cosplayers perceive physical characteristics such as race or body shape as intrinsic to their conception of self. Their physical body and any adornments are not merely an expression of self: they are the self. For some cosplayers body transformation is the epitome of cosplay excellence. For other cosplayers altering one's skin color or body shape for a cosplay is a betrayal of self.

Both epic feat and quest for justice narratives act as forms of discursive gatekeeping. The competition interviews and activist social media posts both attempt to define the nature of cosplay—what the practice is or should be, what meanings it should hold, how it should be performed, and who should be permitted to practice. Quest for justice texts argue that cosplay and cosplayers should broadly support social justice concepts of racial, gender, and sexual equality. Good cosplay are performances and actions that work toward a greater social good. Epic feat narratives instead support an almost capitalist model of cosplay predicated on individualism, personal enterprise, and competition. Here good cosplay is defined as performances and objects that emulate spectacular aesthetics and highlight the varied skills of the performer-creator.

Conclusion

Superhero narrative tropes are interpreted and employed in a variety of ways by different actors within the figured world of cosplay. For some cosplayers the superheroic idea of a quest for justice provides inspiration and a means of framing their own costuming activities as an explicit form of political action. In these narratives the cosplayers portray their embodied performances as a means of resisting the hegemonic values of an imagined mainstream culture or as creating a diversity of representation that is perceived as absent from commercially produced popular media.

However, for other cosplayers the superheroic trope of epic feats—the demonstration of extraordinary physical, mental, or emotional acts—is used in the micro-political narratives of cosplayers seeking to gain prestige and social standing within cosplay communities. In telling stories about epic feats of construction, endurance, and body transformation cosplayers perform themselves or others as super-cosplayers worthy of recognition and influence. These superheroic narratives also serve to define and rank cosplay objects, acts, and actors as superior or inferior.

Within cosplay communities different aspects of the superhero are used to embody, enact, and counter the various discourses and ideologies existing within and without the figured world of cosplay. For some cosplayers' superheroic narratives are used to frame their costuming activities as political resistance to broader hegemonic discourses, enacting the kind of "civic imagination" envisioned by Jenkins. These narratives portray cosplay as a practice that should be furthering an agenda of social equality and providing resistance to hegemonic power structures. Conversely, cosplayers' use of the epic feat superheroic trope creates distinctions and hierarchies between practitioners and focuses on the micropolitics of a smaller community than a broader political sphere.

The differing uses of superheroic narratives within the figured world of cosplay demonstrate the complexity of using superhero characters to define social action, be it political or micro-political, individual or collective. Superheroes as cultural artifacts can be used and interpreted in myriad ways even within an individual fan community. The narratives of cosplayers serve as a cautionary tale for those wishing to explore the role of superheroes in political action; social movements are composed of diverse actors with diverse intentions, who use cultural artifacts in diverse ways. Future explorations of fan activism need to recognize this heterogeneity in their analyses.

Notes

1 Henry Jenkins, "'Cultural Acupuncture': Fan Activism and the Harry Potter Alliance," in "Transformative Works and Fan Activism," ed. Henry Jenkins and Sangita Shresthova, special issue of *Transformative Works and Cultures*, no. 10 (2012): 206–229.

2 Henry Jenkins, "Youth Voice, Media, and Political Engagement: Introducing the Core Concepts," in *By Any Media Necessary: The New Youth Activism*, edited by Henry Jenkins, Sangita Shresthova, Liana Gamber-Thompson, Neta Kligler-Vilenchik, Arely M. Zimmerman, and Elisabeth Soep (New York: New York University Press, 2016), 32–35.

3 Jenkins, "Youth Voice, Media, and Political Engagement," 32–33.

4 Jenkins, "Youth Voice, Media, and Political Engagement," 29.

5 See, for example, Neta Kligler-Vilenchik, "'Decreasing World Suck': Harnessing Popular Culture for Fan Activism," in Jenkins et al., *By Any Media Necessary*, 102–148.

6 Kligler-Vilenchik, "'Decreasing World Suck,'" 107; Ashley Hinck, "Theorizing a Public Engagement Keystone: Seeing Fandom's Integral Connection to Civic Engagement through the Case of the Harry Potter Alliance." In "Transformative Works and Fan Activism," ed. Henry Jenkins and Sangita Shresthova, special issue of *Transformative Works and Cultures*, no. 10 (2012).

7 Kligler-Vilenchik, "'Decreasing World Suck,'" 107.

8 Dorothy Holland, Gretchen Fox, and Vinci Daro, "Social Movements and Collective Identity: A Decentered, Dialogic View," *Anthropological Quarterly* 81, no. 1 (2008): 95–98.
9 Holland, Fox, and Daro, "Social Movements," 99.
10 Mikhail Bakhtin, *The Dialogic Imagination: Four Essays* (Austin: University of Texas Press, 1981); Dennis Tedlock and Bruce Mannheim, *The Dialogic Emergence of Culture* (Chicago: University of Illinois Press 1995); Holland, Fox, and Daro, "Social Movements," 99.
11 Matt Hills, *Fan Cultures* (London: Routledge, 2005): 50–51; Daisuke Okabe, "Cosplay, Learning, and Cultural Practice," in *Fandom Unbound: Otaku Culture in a Connected World*, edited by Mizuko Ito, Daisuke Okabe, and Izumi Tsuji (New Haven, CT: Yale University Press, 2012), 234–235.
12 Holland, Fox, and Daro, "Social Movements," 118.
13 Holland, Fox, and Daro, "Social Movements," 118.
14 Dorothy Holland, William Lachicotte Jr., Debra Skinner, and Carole Cain, *Identity and Agency in Cultural Worlds* (Cambridge, MA: Harvard University Press, 1998), 49.
15 Mikey Cahill, "Superheroes and Villains Living among Us to Descend on Melbourne Convention Centre," *Herald Sun*, June 10, 2016, www.heraldsun.com.au/news/oz-comiccon-superheroes-and-villains-living-among-us-to-descend-on-melbourne-convention-centre/news-story/2caa9abe8b99dbd9b5774dbe52a5aa29.
16 Holland et al., *Identity and Agency in Cultural Worlds*, 66–67.
17 Tedlock and Mannheim, *Dialogic Emergence of Culture*, 16–17.
18 Gérard Genette, *Paratexts: Thresholds of Interpretation*, vol. 20 (Cambridge: Cambridge University Press, 1997), 1–2; Jonathan Gray, *Show Sold Separately: Promos, Spoilers, and Other Media Paratexts* (New York: New York University Press, 2010), 5–6.
19 Caroline Bologna, "Why This 'Brown Batman' Meant So Much to One Little Boy," *Huffington Post*, October 12, 2016, www.huffingtonpost.com.au/entry/why-this-brown-batman-meant-so-much-to-one-little-boy_us_57f7d92ee4b0e655eab3d029.
20 Kligler-Vilenchik, "'Decreasing World Suck,'" 107.
21 Bologna, "Why This 'Brown Batman.'"
22 Peter Coogan, "The Definition of the Superhero," in *A Comics Studies Reader*, edited by Jeet Heer and Kent Worcester (Jackson: University Press of Mississippi, 2009), 77.
23 For further discussions of this issue, see Stacy L. Smith, Marc Choueiti, and Katherine Pieper, "Gender Bias without Borders" (Geena Davis Institute on Gender in Media, 2014), http://seejane.org/research-informs-empowers; GLAAD, "Where We Are on TV Report 2016–2017: GLAAD's Annual Report on LGBTQ Inclusion," https://glaad.org/files/WWAT/WWAT_GLAAD_2016-2017.pdf.
24 Priya Rehal, "I Fight White Supremacy by Cosplaying," *GUTS*, May 18, 2016, http://gutsmagazine.ca/cosplaying/.

25 Carola Lentz, "Ethnic Conflict and Changing Dress Codes: A Case Study of an Indian Migrant Village in Highland Ecuador," in *Dress and Ethnicity: Change across Space and Time*, edited by J. B. Eicher (Oxford: Berg, 1995), 107–119; Susan Woodward, *Why Women Wear What They Wear* (Oxford: Berg, 2007), 153–158.
26 Jean Allman, *Fashioning Africa: Power and the Politics of Dress* (Bloomington: Indiana University Press, 2004); Heather M. Akou, *Politics of Dress in Somali Culture* (Bloomington: Indiana University Press, 2011).
27 Larissa Hjorth, "Game Girl: Re-imagining Japanese Gender and Gaming via Melbourne Female Cosplayers," *Intersections: Gender and Sexuality in Asia and the Pacific* 20 (April 2009): 5; Frenchy Lunning, "Cosplay, Drag, and the Performance of Abjection," in *Mangatopia: Essays on Manga and Anime in the Modern World*, edited by Timothy Perper and Martha Cornog (Santa Barbara, CA: Libraries Unlimited, 2011), 71–89.
28 Rehal, "I Fight White Supremacy by Cosplaying."
29 Rehal, "I Fight White Supremacy by Cosplaying."
30 Sam de Leve, "I Cosplay More Than Just 'Wheelchair Costumes' and Here's Why," *Medium*, November 1, 2016, https://medium.com/@DeLeve/i-cosplay-more-than-just-wheelchair-costumes-and-heres-why-bd2fdf86cbe.
31 de Leve, "I Cosplay."
32 Bologna, "Why This 'Brown Batman.'"
33 Kligler-Vilenchik, "'Decreasing World Suck,'" 107.
34 Lauren Rae Orsini, "Misa on Wheels Rolls into Cosplay," *Daily Dot*, February 8, 2012, www.dailydot.com/upstream/amanda-knightly-misa-on-wheels-cosplay/.
35 Ryan Reed, "Batman Cosplay Suit Sets World Record with 23 Gadgets," *Rolling Stone*, August 26, 2016, www.rollingstone.com/culture/news/batman-cosplay-suit-sets-world-record-with-23-gadgets-w436345.
36 Reed, "Batman Cosplay Suit Sets World Record."
37 Reed, "Batman Cosplay Suit Sets World Record."
38 Coogan, "Definition of the Superhero," 77.
39 Okabe, "Cosplay, Learning, and Cultural Practice," 240.
40 Shalini Shankar, "Metaconsumptive Practices and the Circulation of Objectifications," *Journal of Material Culture* 11, no. 3 (2006): 293–317.
41 Supanova Melbourne Competition, author's video and transcript, 2012.
42 Madman National Cosplay Championship, author's video and transcript, 2011.
43 Madman National Cosplay Championship, author's video and transcript, 2011.

Bibliography

Akou, Heather M. *Politics of Dress in Somali Culture*. Bloomington: Indiana University Press, 2011.

Allman, Jean. *Fashioning Africa: Power and the Politics of Dress*. Bloomington: Indiana University Press, 2004.

Bakhtin, Mikhail. *The Dialogic Imagination: Four Essays*. Austin: University of Texas Press, 1981.

Bologna, Caroline. "Why This 'Brown Batman' Meant So Much to One Little Boy." *Huffington Post*, October 12, 2016. www.huffingtonpost.com.au/entry/why-this-brown-batman-meant-so-much-to-one-little-boy_us_57f7d92ee4b0e655eab3d029.

Cahill, Mikey. "Superheroes and Villains Living among Us to Descend on Melbourne Convention Centre." *Herald Sun*, June 10, 2016.

Coogan, Peter. "The Definition of the Superhero." In *A Comics Studies Reader*, edited by Jeet Heer and Kent Worcester, 77–93. Jackson: University Press of Mississippi, 2009.

de Leve, Sam. "I Cosplay More Than Just 'Wheelchair Costumes' and Here's Why." *Medium*, November 1, 2016. https://medium.com/@DeLeve/i-cosplay-more-than-just-wheelchair-costumes-and-heres-why-bd2fdf86cbe.

Genette, Gérard. *Paratexts: Thresholds of Interpretation*. Vol. 20. Cambridge: Cambridge University Press, 1997.

GLAAD. "Where We Are on TV Report 2016–2017: GLAAD's Annual Report on LGBTQ Inclusion." https://glaad.org/files/WWAT/WWAT_GLAAD_2016-2017.pdf.

Gray, Jonathan. *Show Sold Separately: Promos, Spoilers, and Other Media Paratexts*. New York: New York University Press, 2010.

Hills, Matt. *Fan Cultures*. London: Routledge, 2005.

Hinck, Ashley. "Theorizing a Public Engagement Keystone: Seeing Fandom's Integral Connection to Civic Engagement through the Case of the Harry Potter Alliance." In "Transformative Works and Fan Activism," edited by Henry Jenkins and Sangita Shresthova, special issue of *Transformative Works and Cultures*, no. 10 (2012). http://dx.doi.org/10.3983/twc.2012.0311.

Hjorth, Larissa. "Game Girl: Re-imagining Japanese Gender and Gaming via Melbourne Female Cosplayers." *Intersections: Gender and Sexuality in Asia and the Pacific* 20 (April 2009): 5.

Holland, Dorothy, Gretchen Fox, and Vinci Daro. "Social Movements and Collective Identity: A Decentered, Dialogic View." *Anthropological Quarterly* 81, no. 1 (2008): 95–126.

Holland, Dorothy, William Lachicotte Jr., Debra Skinner, and Carole Cain. *Identity and Agency in Cultural Worlds*. Cambridge, MA: Harvard University Press, 1998.

Jenkins, Henry. "'Cultural Acupuncture': Fan Activism and the Harry Potter Alliance." In "Transformative Works and Fan Activism," edited by Henry Jenkins and Sangita Shresthova, special issue of *Transformative Works and Cultures*, no. 10. (2012): 206–229. http://dx.doi.org/10.3983/twc.2012.0305.

———. "Youth Voice, Media, and Political Engagement: Introducing the Core Concepts." In *By Any Media Necessary: The New Youth Activism*, edited by Henry Jenkins, Sangita Shresthova, Liana Gamber-Thompson, Neta Kligler-Vilenchik, Arely M. Zimmerman, and Elisabeth Soep, 1–60. New York: New York University Press, 2016.

Kligler-Vilenchik, Neta. "'Decreasing World Suck': Harnessing Popular Culture for Fan Activism." In *By Any Media Necessary: The New Youth Activism*, edited by Henry Jenkins, Sangita Shresthova, Liana Gamber-Thompson, Neta Kligler-Vilenchik, Arely M. Zimmerman, and Elisabeth Soep, 102–148. New York: New York University Press, 2016.

Lentz, Carola. "Ethnic Conflict and Changing Dress Codes: A Case Study of an Indian Migrant Village in Highland Ecuador." In *Dress and Ethnicity: Change across Space and Time*, edited by J. B. Eicher, 107–119. Oxford: Berg, 1995.

Lunning, Frenchy. "Cosplay, Drag, and the Performance of Abjection." In *Mangatopia: Essays on Manga and Anime in the Modern World*, edited by Timothy Perper and Martha Cornog, 71–89. Santa Barbara, CA: Libraries Unlimited, 2011.

Okabe, Daisuke. "Cosplay, Learning, and Cultural Practice." In *Fandom Unbound: Otaku Culture in a Connected World*, edited by Mizuko Ito, Daisuke Okabe, and Izumi Tsuji, 225–248. New Haven, CT: Yale University Press, 2012.

Orsini, Lauren Rae. "Misa on Wheels Rolls into Cosplay." *Daily Dot*, February 8, 2012. www.dailydot.com/upstream/amanda-knightly-misa-on-wheels-cosplay/.

Reed, Ryan. "Batman Cosplay Suit Sets World Record with 23 Gadgets." *Rolling Stone*, August 26, 2016. www.rollingstone.com/culture/news/batman-cosplay-suit-sets-world-record-with-23-gadgets-w436345.

Rehal, Priya. "I Fight White Supremacy by Cosplaying." *GUTS*, May 18, 2016. http://gutsmagazine.ca/cosplaying/.

Shankar, Shalini. "Metaconsumptive Practices and the Circulation of Objectifications." *Journal of Material Culture* 11, no. 3 (2006): 293–317.

Smith, Stacy L., Marc Choueiti, and Katherine Pieper. "Gender Bias without Borders." Geena Davis Institute on Gender in Media, 2014. http://seejane.org/research-informs-empowers.

Tedlock, Dennis, and Bruce Mannheim, eds. *The Dialogic Emergence of Culture*. Chicago: University of Illinois Press, 1995.

Woodward, Susan. *Why Women Wear What They Wear*. Oxford: Berg, 2007.

12

From Pages to Pavements

A Criminological Comparison between Depictions of Crime Control in Superhero Narratives and "Real-Life Superhero" Activity

VLADISLAV IOUCHKOV AND JOHN MCGUIRE

Control of street crime has been central to superhero stories since their introduction on the comic book page, continuing into their adaptation across multiple media platforms (movies, TV shows, videogames, etc.). Reflecting this interest, recent social phenomena have seen the methods of fictional superheroes appropriated into real-world efforts, albeit not without societal concerns for the risks inherent in these unorthodox approaches to the management of street crime. This phenomenon is known as the real-life superhero (RLSH) movement, where individuals with superhero identities intervene in street crimes and social welfare injustices.

The purpose of this chapter is twofold. First, this chapter performs an analysis of Batman, Captain America, and Superman hero narratives with an emphasis on the relationship between the protagonists and their motivations and duties as superheroes. The chapter then draws on current research into the RLSH phenomenon and utilizes a thematic analysis of interviews with actual RLSHs in order to identify the differences and similarities between the fictional approaches and their nonfictional counterparts. It also examines how some RLSHs view the police as well as how their activities relate to the sanctioned actions of formal law enforcement.

A Brief Introduction to Real-Life Superheroes

The RLSH movement is a global community of individuals who create original superhero-inspired identities and utilize them for prosocial action, primarily in the forms of crime prevention patrols and social outreach initiatives. These two approaches are often combined. While it is largely an American phenomenon, there are active RLSHs based in Canada, Australia, and throughout Europe. There is currently a small but growing body of academic research concerning RLSHs and their activities.[1] This chapter draws primarily on data from a doctorate research project, conducted by Vlad Iouchkov, which includes semistructured interviews with forty-five RLSHs.[2] Participants for this research were recruited online via private messages to their social media accounts, and interviews were almost exclusively conducted online using Facebook Messenger, except for one face-to-face interview with a Sydney-based RLSH in Australia. Using this method, participants would instantly retain copies of the raw interview data to use in the event of any ethical discrepancies from the researcher. The researcher left it to the discretion of participants whether they wished to disclose any personal information in the interviews. As this is largely exploratory research, the collected data were then put through a thematic analysis in order to identify the relevant themes that would emerge from participant responses and provide an indication of the motivations and methods of RLSHs.[3]

While RLSHs could easily be mistaken for cosplayers, it is crucial to highlight four key distinctions between these two approaches to superheroes. These distinctions are primarily found in dimensions of identity, activities, secrecy, and gender representation. First, RLSHs and cosplayers differ in the sense that cosplayers replicate, rework, or combine preexisting fictional characters of trademarked franchises and assume these identities as such. While having clear inspirations from superheroes, RLSH identities are entirely original creations. Second, cosplayers utilize these identities largely for attending pop culture conventions, special events, and fundraisers; RLSHs can and do attend conventions, but their activities are primarily focused on community safety and welfare, through a combination of neighborhood watch-like patrols and social outreach/charity initiatives.[4] Third, cosplayers tend to be very open about their true identities and can build professional careers from cosplay. RLSHs, however, often use their "superhero" personas in place of providing their "real" identities when engaging in RLSH activity (usually masked), and their activities remain purely voluntary with no evident financial recompense (although heroes like Phoenix Jones have become local celebrities). Finally, there tend to be vast differences in gender representation in the cosplay and RLSH communities.

Results from a simple Internet search will show an overwhelming number of female cosplayers, whereas the research this chapter draws on managed to successfully recruit only two female RLSHs out of a total of forty-five participants.

What the above research has found is that perceptions about RLSHs generally remain mixed among the public and police. While support is drawn from the public in that they appreciate having a bystander willing to intervene in a critical situation while waiting on police presence, they also question the integrity and sincerity of RLSHs, voicing concerns about the onset of vigilante action. The police share a similar concern, albeit complemented with the potential risk of harm done to the RLSHs themselves and whether this could disrupt ongoing police activity. RLSHs, however, broadly expressed that they desire an open dialogue with their local police to ensure that their efforts do not conflict. Finally, the media largely follow a single narrative of RLSHs as "vigilantes," without drawing distinctions between the various facets of RLSH activity; while some RLSHs do engage in crime prevention patrols and may be likely to engage in some degree of violence, others engage merely in community outreach initiatives including environmental cleanups, food drives for the homeless, and even superhero-themed workshops and magic shows for children in the community.

Hyperreality and the Endurance of Superheroes as Crime Control Mechanisms

In his theory of "hyperreality," philosopher Jean Baudrillard describes a cyclical relationship between "simulations" (objects, images, or discourses that have no discernible origin point) and "simulacra" (representations, reproductions, or copies that are merely *depicting* the simulations).[5] For Baudrillard, the media's proliferation of simulacra has reduced the simulation to a spectacle that creates a version of reality that is more accessible and thus more "real," shattering the simulacra's relationship with simulation. Simulacra once *reproduced* simulations; now, it *produces* them. In other words, that which was merely a "copy" of the real has become the "real" itself, and clear distinctions between what is "reality" and what is "fiction" have collapsed.

When applied to social life, hyperreality presents itself in the realm of "hyper-real religions." Coined by sociology professor Adam Possamai, "hyper-real religions" refers to the social phenomenon of religions, spiritualities, and their associated praxes that are borne of popular culture: "a simulacrum of religion partly created out of popular culture which provides inspiration for believers/consumers at a metaphorical level."[6] Yet these phenomena do not exist in a vacuum and over time have demonstrated real implications for the social world. A notable example would be that of Jediism and the Temple of the Jedi Order, which draws inspiration from the *Star Wars* franchise and has gathered attention for being a recurring response to religious affiliation questions within census statistics in Australia, New Zealand, the United Kingdom, and Canada—this alone has affected statistical representations of religious affiliation in Western countries. While this could well be understood as satirical in nature, this is not exclusively the case when examining its followers who engage in spiritual practices derived from the Eastern traditions that inspired the *Star Wars* mythos, including Buddhism, Hinduism, Daoism, and Samurai, among others, yet frame their experiences, beliefs, and praxes through "Jediism."[7] In a similar vein, RLSHs are utilizing the mythos of superhero fiction in order to engage in their own varieties of social, and in some cases spiritual, practices.[8]

With reference to comic books, criminal justice professor Jarett S. Lovell notes the hyperreality in a nostalgic resurgence for popular justice (i.e., forms of justice dished out by the public) that had a brief but impactful presence in post–World War II American comic books, mainly between 1946 and 1950.[9] Comic books such as *Justice Comics* (1947), *Murder Incorporated* (1948), *Crime Case Comics* (1950), and notably *War Against Crime!* (1948) incorporated real-life crime stories with fictional embellishments, by which "the pages of the 1940s comic strip became a terrain for the hyperreal where actual law enforcement successes and their simulated counterparts inevitably become one."[10] The escapist use of contemporary popular culture to channel this nostalgia, according to Lovell, represents a sociocultural response to the rapidly growing complexities of the modern world, which, for better or for worse, cause individuals to long for a historical period in which crime and its control were simplified in the eyes of the public, merely "good versus evil." Lovell does note, however, that such a practice can have problematic effects, as it not only resurrects sociocultural attitudes from which society has progressed but also illustrates one's willingness to neglect the status of the present. Indeed, such a parallel is clear when examining the integration of superheroes into the real world as a criminal justice mechanism, with consideration of the fact that superhero comic books have endured, albeit inconsistently, since the 1930s and continue to permeate new forms of media, such as film, television, and videogames. With rapid growth in technological sophistication, the twenty-first century marks an important change in how superheroes are consumed. Indeed, the Modern Age of superhero fiction retains a focus on character psyches and a response to cultural anxieties in a post-9/11 world as well as deeper explorations of criminal justice and depictions of control, prevention, and justifications of violence.[11]

Heroic Motivations and Social Control in Superhero Fiction

Superheroes are an American invention of the late 1930s, bringing together concepts and ideals of ancient mythology with the science fiction and pulp magazines of their time. They were an early part of the comic book industry, one of the first popular culture consumer products that targeted American youth.[12] Published in *Action Comics* #1 in 1938, Superman is widely acknowledged as the very first superhero.[13] Richard Reynolds has noted that Superman thus established the archetypal definition of a superhero. The superhero is marked out from society and has some type of superpower, although the scope of superpower can be quite broad. At one end it can be god-like abilities, while at the lower end it can be simply peak physical fitness or superior intelligence. In either case the superpower separates the superhero from the rest of society and the abilities of ordinary citizens. In regard to values, the superhero often has a devotion to justice that overrides their devotion to the law. While above the law, the superhero is often dedicated to patriotism or is morally loyal to the state. Reynolds states that the extraordinary nature of the superhero is contrasted to the ordinariness of their environment and the mundane nature of the alter ego/secret identity. The narratives of the superhero are mythic and use both science and magic to create a sense of wonder.[14] In his work on superheroes (specifically the nationalist superhero) Dittmer makes the point that there have been academic definitions of the character of a superhero within the genre, specifically Reynolds's Superman archetype and Coogan's work that emphasizes the prosocial mission of the superhero and the generic conventions of costumes and secret identities.[15] Coogan's idea of a prosocial mission links directly with Reynolds's idea of a devotion to justice over law. The prosocial superhero works in the interests of society over those of the state; the prosocial mission is beyond the limitations of the state and aligns the superhero more closely with the social values of society over the laws of the state.

The prosocial mission of the superhero is an integral element of the superhero origin story. Origin stories tend to focus on the transformation of the ordinary citizen into the superhero and often detail a spectacular event involving the ordinary citizen, such as a gamma bomb explosion, a radioactive spider bite, or the tragic death of a loved one, which sets the stage for the superpower and the specific prosocial mission of the superhero. The event is the catalyst that leads to the superhero making a moral choice to embrace the prosocial mission that truly creates the superhero. Without that moral decision there is no hero. While the prosocial mission and the moral decision are open to reinterpretation by different superhero creators and can change over time for the character, essentially they represent an articulation of good versus evil.

The crucial nature of the moral choice can be seen in the comparison of the superhero to the supervillain. Like the superhero the supervillain is marked out from society and has some type of superpower. *Unlike* the superhero the supervillain lacks devotion to justice. Whereas the superhero makes a moral decision to use their powers for the good of society, the supervillain choses to use their powers for more selfish ends, and they reject the sacrifice of the hero. For instance, the Batman mythos includes supervillains like Hush and Wrath who share a similar traumatic event to Bruce Wayne, the death of a parent, but make a different moral choice. For example, *Batman* #601 introduced a new villain, Nicodemius, who carries out a campaign of terror, burning to death certain individuals and threatening to destroy the whole of Gotham City, a place he sees as evil.[16] After Batman foils Nicodemius's attack on the mayor of Gotham, it is revealed that Nicodemius is actually Councilman Thomas Hart, who targets those who contributed to his tragic childhood. It is in Hart's motivation that a clear comparison is made to Batman, reinforcing the caped crusader's prosocial mission and moral choice. Like those of Bruce Wayne, Hart's parents were murdered when he was a child. However, this motivated him not to become a *hero* but to seek revenge, not only on those who killed his parents but also on all those involved in the botched investigation. In the end Hart comes to blame not only the individuals responsible but the whole city itself. The lesson for the reader is clear: be like Batman and protect the innocent, and do not be like Nicodemius and seek revenge. The difference between the two is the moral decision to become a superhero and support the community versus the decision to become a villain and seek revenge.

Captain America represents another type of moral choice to become a superhero, but there is no tragic event as a catalyst. Steve Rogers had already embraced the heroic mission of the soldier by volunteering to serve in the army before he became Captain America. However, his prosocial mission, which is beyond the limits of the state, is clarified by the historical context of the first Captain America comics. In the comics Captain America began his battle against the Red Skull and other Nazis working on American soil a full year before America entered the war and was still following a policy of isolation and neutrality. The Captain America comic differed from those depicting other patriotic superheroes of the time because it took a clear and overt political stand on America's need to enter World War II.[17] While Captain America works in the interest of the state, it is Captain America, not the chain of command, who decides what his mission will be. Thus, Captain America's creators, who were second-generation European immigrants, outfitted the hero with his prosocial mission.

The last example of the moral choice to become a superhero is the character of Superman. Unlike the other superheroes covered here, Superman starts his narrative already with his superpowers. One of the most recent retellings of the Superman mythos, the movie *Man of Steel*, presents Superman's decision to be a superhero in a way that combines concepts of identity with a search for broader meaning.[18] Clark Kent navigates two very different visions of his identity from his two fathers, Jonathan Kent from Earth and Jor-El of Krypton. Kent asks his son to keep his powers hidden, even to the point of allowing himself to die in a tornado rather than have his son save him and reveal his powers to others. In the end it is Jor-El's vision of his son's mission that wins over Superman. Jor-El explains to Superman that he sent him to guide his adoptive planet's people rather than live a normal life and challenges Superman to represent an ideal to the people of Earth and to lead them to accomplish wonders. The prosocial mission is more than a commitment to justice. It is presented as a quasi-spiritual drive to lead the people to a new promised land. In this way, for Superman the moral choice is internalized. The choice to be a superhero is depicted as an act of self-discovery, with Superman exploring where he is from and who he is meant to be. The prosocial mission is the identity that his father always planned for him. Such prosocial missions are an integral part of the superhero origin story, but are these motivations echoed by RLSHs?

Motives and Methods of Real-Life Superheroes

The "origin stories," or range of motivators, behind RLSH activities within the research can be divided into two forms: intrinsic and extrinsic. Intrinsic motivators refer to deeper personal or individual factors in becoming and being an RLSH, commonly associated with themes of trauma and/or inspiration; a history of victimization; physical and mental/emotional health issues; a personal connection to superhero fiction; and/or "higher" callings of a religious/spiritual nature. Extrinsic motivators encompass contextual or social factors, with two key emergent themes: first, prior involvement in community service, social outreach, or crime prevention initiatives; and second, participant self-awareness as bystanders (intervening or nonintervening) in response to ongoing trends of bystander inaction (i.e., reluctance to intervene) rather than individualized instances of inaction. Intrinsic and extrinsic motivators are simultaneously present in most cases.

Detailing his inspiration to become an RLSH, Australian-based RLSH-45 described a combination of victimization and health issues as well as viewing a documentary about RLSHs.[19] His involvement was accelerated after he became the victim of an act of violence, which served as the impetus for his newfound confidence:

> Just after I restarted training in martial arts, I was attacked in the street. Before that, I already had posttraumatic stress disorder [PTSD], and it was very shame-oriented; and after I was attacked and managed to fight off my attacker, and have him locked up, he got 250 hours of community service—actually, that was the first time in my life that I had actually put my defense skills into practice, and being able to defend myself against a much bigger attacker who attacked without warning gave me a new sense of confidence. I went from this post-traumatic shame to more of a sense of vigilance and strength.

RLSH-20, one of two female participants, drew direct inspiration from X-Men character Storm in order to cope with anxiety issues:

> The better part of my life I have struggled with social anxiety, everything caused fear, and I was in a constant state of distress. At a young age, I remember turning to Marvel comics and cartoons as an escape. I remember admiring the strong female characters; Storm particularly.
>
> Storm epitomizes what I yearned for at that age. If you look at her character from the nineties X-Men, Storm rarely has personal problems, aside from the obvious duties of her position in Xavier's school. She was perfect to me, and I wanted to be her because she had it together, and I didn't. I still don't sometimes, it's a daily struggle, but such is life.

Yet the most diverse embodiment of intrinsic and extrinsic motivators came from Canadian-based RLSH-38. His "origin story" commences with being a victim of a violent hate crime, a near-death experience (NDE), which left him with a traumatic brain injury and consequent dreams, hallucinations, and visions that led him to become an RLSH:

> I received a vision of resistance and solidarity that in any other terms would be the proverbial "white light" of NDEs. Upon waking I realized I had a newfound conviction, but could no longer remember the clear path to the end goal of my vision.
>
> I found the RLSH community when I was looking for a framework to understand and present the kind of work I wanted to do in my community. These weirdos seemed to be the best fit for what I was thinking about.

RLSH-38 later conceptualized his "transformation" with explicit reference not to any specific superhero but to Joseph Campbell's "monomyth," which argues that hero narratives follow the same basic structure of the hero answering a "calling" and experiencing death, rebirth, and transformation along the adventure before triumphantly returning to the "ordinary world."[20] For RLSH-38, this "adventure" is not a spiritual calling to uncover the meaning of his dream and the "visions" associated with them but serves as the basis of his RLSH activity as an outreach worker in response to macrosocial and political issues that he has identified:

> I am not quite sure I'm out of the labyrinth (and the narrative of a queer, disabled vegan outreach worker doesn't exactly have a clear analogy). But, even in the context of my dream visions, that structure is there. I am trying to uncover more and more of what the dream meant.
>
> We see increased militarization of police on a global scale, a continued occupation of indigenous lands and the resources contained within, as well as massive movements protesting neoliberal austerity; the more this all plays out the more my dream returns to me. I have a vision of resistance, and it looks a little like [his superhero identity].[21]

Participants also expressed that being an RLSH was simply another outlet for their prior involvement in social outreach. Australian-based RLSH 19 stated that being an RLSH was a means of "getting more mileage out of my altruism." Similar sentiments were expressed by RLSH-22, who moved into RLSH activity once they felt competent in their ability to defend themselves in violent situations: "I've always been actively trying to involve myself in what's going on around me. And I've always been actively desirous to help others if I can. I think the natural evolution was after years of training and study and wondering, 'what can I do?' I think adding a mask and gloves was the natural next step once I felt competent to hold my own." In the original research, twenty-nine of the forty-five participants explicitly expressed that their activities combined safety patrols (in the spirit of neighborhood watch programs) and social outreach initiatives (such as charity drives, first aid assistance, and pickups of litter and drug paraphernalia). RLSHs would often also patrol their local nightlife areas as a means of intervening in and attempting to deescalate instances of alcohol-fueled violence.

Australian-based RLSH-19 described the variety of RLSH activity as follows: "In general terms, being part of the VERY broad community that comes under the ['RLSH'] label means being active in some ways in terms of fighting the culture of indifference, be that crime, homelessness, or other issues, either directly or in a more activistic way." Although participants also expressed differing opinions about the relationships between superheroes and police in comic books, as acting either in accordance with police procedures or irrespective of them, the data demonstrated no evidence of hostility toward police officers or their work. While some participants, such as RLSH-19, were critical of policing, noting, "I am not anti-police so much as I see flaws in the system that controls them," no participants expressed any desire to act against the law.

RLSH-28, in fact, makes use of his professional background in his crime-fighting activities:

> My experience as an officer, as well as my other career positions in investigations, has given me a definite edge in crime fighting. I know what evidence matters, doctrines of law, statutes that the police and the district attorney runs on, uses, understands. I know their language, both courtroom procedural, to radio traffic. I know how their system works, and I know what they need for an arrest, a conviction, etc.
>
> Just as importantly, I know what will and will not get me in trouble with the law. My degree, academy training, and experience allows me to be at full capacity.

RLSH-24 and RLSH-31—both patrolling RLSHs—expressed similar sentiments about their experiences with law enforcement in the line of RLSH activity:

> As RLSHs, we don't have as much authority as cops, so it is helpful to have law enforcement in the area because situations usually deescalate really fast when people see police officers. Some people will still keep fighting even after seeing RLSHs, but once people see a cop, they magically stop fighting. [The RLSH's faction] has had a history of being pulled over by the cops, but since I joined, we never had problems with the cops. I do wish the cops would respect us more sometimes, but usually we are neutral with them. (RLSH-24)

> In my experience, local law enforcement has been an essential asset when dealing with these drunken brawls. As soon as we come across a violent situation, one of our first reactions is to have the member on phone duty call police dispatchers to inform them of the situation. The quicker we can get the cops over to help, the more likely it is the situation will be resolved without anyone getting hurt. Police attitudes towards us, as far as I've seen, ranges from neutral to supportive. It isn't completely uncommon to hear a cop thank us for what we're doing. (RLSH-31)

Indeed, RLSHs bear close similarities to other volunteer crime-fighting efforts, most notably those of the Guardian Angels—a neighborhood watch group known for patrolling New York City subways and streets since the late 1970s, extending their efforts into raids on local drug dealers. However, some of the historically direct and violent means associated with the Guardian Angels have not yet been identified in RLSH activity.[22]

Discussion and Conclusion

The data show some clear similarities and distinctions between superheroes in fiction and RLSHs in reality. The motivators behind *becoming* an RLSH reflect some of the same patterns and moral choices of fictional superheroes: physical and/or emotional trauma, spiritual callings, and dissatisfactions with being bystanders. While the participants are certainly more grounded than their fictional counterparts insofar as (in the original research) the vast majority indicated no allusions to superpowers of a physical nature, their circumstances of trauma yielded similar consequences.

The key differences between RLSHs and fictional superheroes, then, lie in their activities, a finding that departs from what Phillips and Strobl suggest informs the bulk of superhero fiction—vigilantism.[23] While RLSHs may appear to be the "hockey pad" vigilantes found in Christopher Nolan's *The Dark Knight*, the nature of "vigilantism" itself is in fact more complicated than individual moral justice merely superseding criminal policies and processes.[24] Activities of RLSHs are not entirely consistent with what the (limited) criminological literature defines as "vigilantism," which has no clear consensus on "vigilante" criteria, with variables including planning, premeditation, and organization; voluntary engagement by private citizens; autonomous citizenship and distrust of procedural justice; use or threatened use of force (violence); reaction to crime and social deviance; and/or an aim to control crime by improving personal and "collective" security.[25] This is not to say that meeting these criteria is unlikely for certain RLSHs, but given the limited criminological research on RLSHs and vigilantism itself as well as the responses provided by some of the research participants in this chapter, "vigilantism" indeed may not be the most appropriate term to describe RLSH activity as a whole.

Despite differing attitudes, participants expressed a desire to work with and within the law rather than attract the ire of local law enforcement—indeed, for the effective functioning of RLSH activity alongside police activity, this may be at once a desire and a necessity. While these data certainly cannot account for legal differences between the vast respective jurisdictions of the participants and therefore cannot reliably comment on whether or not RLSH activities are illicit behaviors, they *can* account for a general desire among participants to cooperate with formal social control agents.

This chapter has illuminated the numerous similarities and differences across the origins and activities of fictional superheroes and participants from the RLSH community. Trauma, inspiration, and a desire to "fight the culture of indifference" coalesce to produce a new form of neighborhood watch with a superhero cape and cowl. While the authors would be remiss to not acknowledge the valid concerns surrounding volunteer crime control groups that have an affinity for masks and superhero outfits, this research does prompt an important discussion about the frontiers of social control and the strength of fiction in inspiring social action and individual healing.

Notes

1 See E. Fishwick and H. Mak, "Fighting Crime, Battling Injustice: The World of Real-Life Superheroes," *Crime, Media, Culture* 11, no. 3 (2015): 335–356; V. Iouchkov, "Kickin' Ass and Taking Identities: Understanding the Phenomenon of the Real-Life Superhero Movement" (honors diss., Western Sydney University, 2012); V. Iouchkov and P. Birch, "'Masked Crusader': A Case Study of 'Crime-Fighting' Activities By a 'Real-Life Superhero,'' *Journal of Criminological Research, Policy, and Practice* 1, no. 2 (2015): 56–64; H. Mak, "The Amazing Everyday Man: A Study on Real-Life Superheroes" (honors diss., University of New South Wales, 2010); A. Possamai and V. Iouchkov, "An Implicit Hyper-real Religion: Real-Life Superheroes," in *Fiction, Invention, and Hyper-reality*, edited by C. Cusack and P. Kosnac (New York: Routledge, 2017), 272–290; and D. White et al., "Look Up in the Sky: Latent Content Analysis of the Real Life Superhero Community," *Qualitative Report* 21, no. 2 (2016): 178–195.

2 Semistructured interviews entail a series of preset questions while also allowing the researcher to ask impromptu questions in light of specific topics or themes arising from participant responses.

3 This doctorate research (H10447) was approved by the Western Sydney University Human Research Ethics Committee (HREC) on February 27, 2014.

4 It must be recognized that cosplay can be used as a vehicle for social justice activism, however it is the inherent risk of physical harm that separates RLSH's brand of civic participation from cosplay's. In her contribution to this collection Claire Langsford identifies cosplayer "quest for justice" narratives that are centered on social justice issues such as representation and inclusion; RLSH "quests for justice," on the other hand, are more pragmatic, with participants voluntarily placing themselves in their respective neighborhoods for the purpose of directly addressing emergent problems such as acts of violence as well as attempting to alleviate broader social ills such as homelessness.

5 See Jean Baudrillard, *Simulacra and Simulations* (New York: Semiotext(e), 1983) and Jean Baudrillard, *Jean Baudrillard: Selected Writings* (Cambridge: Polity, 1988).

6 Adam Possamai, *Religion and Popular Culture: A Hyper-real Testament* (Brussels: Peter Lang, 2007), 79.
7 Debbie McCormick, "The Sanctification of Star Wars: From Fans to Followers," in *Handbook of Hyper-real Religions*, edited by Adam Possamai (Leiden: Brill, 2012), 165–184; A. Williams, B. Miller, and M. Kitchen, "Jediism and the Temple of the Jedi Order," in *Fiction, Invention, and Hyper-reality*, edited by C. Cusack and P. Kosnac (New York: Routledge, 2017), 119–133.
8 Possamai and Iouchkov, "Implicit Hyper-real Religion."
9 Jarret S. Lovell, "Nostalgia, Comic Books, and the 'War Against Crime!' An Inquiry into the Resurgence of Popular Justice," *Journal of Popular Culture* 36, no. 2 (2002): 333–351.
10 Lovell, "Nostalgia," 341.
11 N. D. Phillips, "The Dark Knight: Constructing Images of Good vs. Evil in an Age of Anxiety," in *Popular Culture, Crime and Social Control*, ed. M. Deflem (Bingley, UK: Emerald, 2010), 25–44; B. W. Reyns and B. Henson, "Superhero Justice: The Depiction of Crime and Justice in Modern-Age Comic Books and Graphic Novels," in Deflem, *Popular Culture, Crime and Social Control*, 45–66; J. McGuire, "With Us or Against Us? Hegemony and Ideology within American Superhero Comic Books 2001–2008" (PhD diss., Western Sydney University, 2014).
12 Bradford W. Wright, *Comic Book Nation: The Transformation of Youth Culture in America* (Baltimore: Johns Hopkins University Press, 2001).
13 Gerard Jones, *Men of Tomorrow: Geeks, Gangsters and the Birth of the Comic Book* (London: William Heinemann, 2005).
14 Richard Reynolds, *Super Heroes: A Modern Mythology* (Jackson: University Press of Mississippi, 1994), 16.
15 Jason Dittmer, *Captain America and the Nationalist Superhero: Metaphors, Narratives and Geopolitics* (Philadelphia: Temple University Press, 2013); Peter Coogan, *Superhero: The Secret Origin of a Genre* (Austin, TX: MonkeyBrain Books, 2006).
16 Ed Brubaker, Scott McDaniel, et al., *Batman* #601–2 (New York: DC, May–June 2002).
17 Joe Simon and Jim Simon, *The Comic Book Makers* (Middlesex, NJ: Lebanon, 2003).
18 *Man of Steel*, dir. Zack Snyder (Warner Bros., 2013).
19 All participants are referred to by "RLSH" and their numbered position in the research.
20 Joseph Campbell, *The Hero with a Thousand Faces*, 3rd ed. (Novato, CA: New World Library, 2015).
21 The participant self-referenced his superhero name, which is not disclosed to maintain his confidentiality.
22 Although partnerships are not common between RLSHs and Guardian Angels, since late 2016 New York–based RLSH "Dark Guardian" has been consistently publishing Facebook photos on his public profile that show his own recent joining with the Guardian Angels and participating in their ongoing activities.

23 N. D. Phillips and S. Strobl, "Cultural Criminology and Kryptonite: Constructions of Crime and Justice in Comic Books in America," *Crime, Media, Culture* 2, no. 3 (2006): 304–331.
24 *The Dark Knight*, dir. Christopher Nolan (Warner Bros., 2008).
25 L. Johnston, "What Is Vigilantism?," *British Journal of Criminology* 36, no. 2 (1996): 220–236. See also Iouchkov and Birch, "'Masked Crusader.'"

Bibliography

Baudrillard, Jean. *Jean Baudrillard: Selected Writings*. Cambridge: Polity, 1988.

———. *Simulacra and Simulations*. New York: Semiotext(e), 1983.

Brubaker, Ed (writer), and S. A. McDaniel (artist). "Bruce Wayne: Fugitive, Part Three: Turning the Town Red, Part One of Two." *Batman* 1, no. 601. New York: DC Comics, 2002.

———. "Turning the Town Red, Part Two of Two." *Batman* 1, no. 602. New York: DC Comics, 2002.

Campbell, Joseph. *The Hero with a Thousand Faces*. 3rd ed. Novato, CA: New World Library, 2015.

Coogan, Peter. *Superhero: The Secret Origin of a Genre*. Austin, TX: MonkeyBrain Books, 2006.

Dittmer, Jason. *Captain America and the Nationalist Superhero: Metaphors, Narratives, and Geopolitics*. Philadelphia: Temple University Press, 2013.

Finger, Bill (writer), and B. Kane (artist). "The Batman Wars Against the Dirigible of Doom." *Detective Comics* 1, no. 33. New York: Detective Comics, 1939.

Fishwick, Elaine, and H. Mak. "Fighting Crime, Battling Injustice: The World of Real-Life Superheroes." *Crime, Media, Culture* 11, no. 3 (2015): 335–356.

Iouchkov, Vlad. "The Hero with a Thousand Graces: A Socio-criminological Examination of the 'Real-Life Superhero' Phenomenon." PhD dissertation, Western Sydney University, forthcoming.

———. "Kickin' Ass and Taking Identities: Understanding the Phenomenon of the Real-Life Superhero Movement." Honors dissertation, Western Sydney University, 2012.

Iouchkov, Vlad, and P. Birch. "'Masked Crusader': A Case Study of 'Crime-Fighting' Activities by a 'Real-Life Superhero.'" *Journal of Criminological Research, Policy, and Practice* 1, no. 2 (2015): 56–64.

Johnston, Les. "What Is Vigilantism?" *British Journal of Criminology* 36, no. 2 (1996): 220–236.

Jones, Gerard. *Men of Tomorrow: Geeks, Gangsters and the Birth of the Comic Book*. London: William Heinemann, 2005.

Lovell, Jarret S. "Nostalgia, Comic Books, and the 'War Against Crime!' An Inquiry into the Resurgence of Popular Justice." *Journal of Popular Culture* 36, no. 2 (2002): 335–351.

Mak, Heusen. "The Amazing Everyday Man: A Study on Real-Life Superheroes." Honors dissertation, University of New South Wales, 2010.

McCormick, Debbie. "The Sanctification of Star Wars: From Fans to Followers." In *Handbook of Hyper-real Religions*, edited by Adam Possamai, 165–184. Leiden, Netherlands: Brill, 2012.

McGuire, John. "With Us or Against Us? Hegemony and Ideology within American Superhero Comic Books 2001–2008." PhD dissertation, Western Sydney University, 2014.

Phillips, Nickie D. "The Dark Knight: Constructing Images of Good vs. Evil in an Age of Anxiety." In *Popular Culture, Crime and Social Control*, edited by M. Deflem, 25–44. Bingley, UK: Emerald, 2010.

Phillips, Nickie D., and S. Strobl. "Cultural Criminology and Kryptonite: Constructions of Crime and Justice in Comic Books in America." *Crime, Media, Culture* 2, no. 3 (2006): 304–331.

Possamai, Adam. *Religion and Popular Culture: A Hyper-real Testament*. Brussels: Peter Lang, 2007.

Possamai, Adam, and V. Iouchkov. "An Implicit Hyper-real Religion: Real-Life Superheroes." In *Fiction, Invention, and Hyper-reality*, edited by C. Cusack and P. Kosnac, 272–290. New York: Routledge, 2017.

Reynolds, Richard. *Super Heroes: A Modern Mythology*. Jackson: University Press of Mississippi, 1994.

Reyns, Bradford W., and B. Henson. "Superhero Justice: The Depiction of Crime and Justice in Modern-Age Comic Books and Graphic Novels." In *Popular Culture, Crime and Social Control*, edited by M. Deflem, 45–66. Bingley, UK: Emerald, 2010.

Rucka, Greg (writer), and R. Burchett (artist). "Vacancies." *Detective Comics* 1, no. 765. New York: DC Comics, 2002.

Simon J (writer) and J Kirby (artist). "Meet Captain America." *Captain America Comics*, no. 1. New York: Timely Publications, 1941.

Simon, Joe, and Jim Simon. *The Comic Book Makers*. Middlesex, NJ: Lebanon, 2003.

White, Daniel, M. Szabo, N. Tiliopoulos, P. Rhodes, M. Spurrier, and S. Griffiths. "Look Up in the Sky: Latent Content Analysis of the Real Life Superhero Community." *Qualitative Report* 21, no. 2 (2016): 178–195.

Williams, A., B. Miller, and M. Kitchen. "Jediism and the Temple of the Jedi Order." In *Fiction, Invention, and Hyper-reality*, edited by C. Cusack and P. Kosnac (New York: Routledge, 2017): 119–133.

Wright, Bradford W. *Comic Book Nation: The Transformation of Youth Culture in America* Baltimore: Johns Hopkins University Press, 2001.

13

An Interview with *Dark Night: A True Batman Story* Writer Paul Dini

LIAM BURKE

Paul Dini is the Emmy–, Eisner–, and Annie Award–winning writer of many fan-favorite superheroes stories across animation, film, comics, and videogames. He is one of the writers of *Batman: The Animated Series* and related shows and films, including *Batman: Mask of the Phantasm*, *Superman: The Animated Series*, and *Batman Beyond*. Dini cocreated with artist Bruce Timm the antihero Harley Quinn and wrote the best-selling Batman videogames *Arkham Asylum* and *Arkham City*.

Other credits in Dini's career include *Lost*, the Star Wars spin-offs *Ewoks* and *Clone Wars*, as well as *Tiny Toon Adventures*, *Animaniacs*, *Freakazoid!*, *Ultimate Spider-Man*, and DC Comics' *The Batman Adventures: Mad Love* and *Superman: Peace on Earth*.

His 2016 graphic novel *Dark Night: A True Batman Story* debuted on the *New York Times* best-seller list and is a harrowing autobiographical tale of Dini's courageous struggle to recover from a vicious mugging and how the figure of Batman helped him to come to terms with the trauma.

LIAM BURKE As a writer you have worked on a huge number of characters across a range of platforms, but who is your favorite superhero?

PAUL DINI As far as heroes go, probably my all-time favorite superhero is Captain Marvel [a.k.a. Shazam] and that might be an odd choice, but he was the first superhero I was ever really aware of. My father would tell me stories about the original Captain Marvel. This was years before I saw him in the comic books, but

Figure 13.1. Writer Paul Dini recalls how the figure of Batman helped him recover from a brutal attack in the graphic novel memoir *Dark Night: A True Batman Story*. Photo by Alan Weissman.

he always had this sort of amazing allure to me because I never saw him, he was handed down in verbal form from my father who'd tell me the stories of Billy Batson and the wizard Shazam and that incredible world. When I finally read the comics, I knew who they were from hearing about them from my dad and I found them just as delightful reading them.

LB Since 2000 superheroes have moved to center of popular culture. What do you attribute this popularity to?

PD I think superheroes are more popular than ever because we seem to have entered a stage of eternal childhood for better or for worse. Our parents, who were from the thirties to the fifties, were products of a TV age and of radio and of the first wave of superheroes and I think they really embraced those characters and that was passed on to their kids. But at some point our parents put it on a shelf: "Okay, *Captain Marvel*, *Orphan Annie*, *Dick Tracy*, they all stay here and now I'm going to be interested in other things." Luke Skywalker, Darth Vader, and Spider-Man, however, are still part of a forty-year-old dad's zeitgeist and consciousness and he's passing that on to his kids.

I don't know if that's going to endure. I don't know if when the kids who are ten now start having kids, if those kids are going to embrace *Iron Man* and *Thor* and *Harley Quinn* in the way that their parents have. It'll be interesting to see.

LB How would you define a superhero?

PD The question of what makes a superhero is interesting. It goes far beyond what a normal person can do. I think that there are plenty of people who are heroic in everyday life, certainly parents who sacrifice their happiness or their dreams for their child are heroic. However, the traditional definition of a superhero is someone who does things a human being just can't do. Through extra effort or through the blessings of power or circumstance or science or magic, they're able to do things that a human being can only dream of: to lift up incredible weights, to fly through the air, to avenge wrongs.

And more than just physical strength, they choose to put their powers and abilities in the service of others. Somebody like Batman, for instance, I think of as mostly like a monk. Even though he's wealthy and he has great resources, in my mind when I write him, it is like he's saying, "I can't embrace those elements. I can't use my wealth to make myself happy. I have to use it to facilitate my war on crime. I have to use it to save people." So somebody who has that form of altruism combined with tremendous powers or skills, is, to me, a superhero.

LB What do you see as the central difference between Batman and Superman?

PD I think that Batman is a much more selfish character. I think that he likes to believe that what he is doing is for the benefit of the city, and that's certainly true on some level. But I think Batman deals with an incredible amount of guilt over the fact that as a nine-year-old boy he watched his parents murdered in front of him and he couldn't stop it, and so his whole life is apologizing for that.

I don't think Superman has that gravitas. Granted his family is dead, too, but it was something that could never be prevented. He realizes that he has these abilities and he realizes that humans are not as advanced as perhaps the Kryptonians were, but he also thinks that "I can be as good an example as possible for people to find what's good in themselves and extend that to other people," which is really the definition of a hero.

I don't think a lot of people are *that* altruistic, but it's nice to think that Superman and Batman to a degree have that in them and I think that's what makes those characters endure. The same with Wonder Woman also. There's an honesty to Wonder Woman. She encourages people to tell the truth or she encourages people to extend a loving feeling toward people, so that they will have love back in return. So those three characters are tremendously powerful in that triumvirate.

LB Talking about Wonder Woman, why do you think it took seventy-five years for a feature film to be produced?

PD I think that a lot of times people have not understood what it is about Wonder Woman that is compelling. I think that Wonder Woman means a lot of different things to a lot of different people. I think sometimes she's looked upon as a figure of fun and camp and sometimes she's looked upon, in reference to the man [William Moulton Marston] who created her, as a sexual figure. I also feel that there has to be somebody for girls to identify with. They have to see a reflection of themselves in somebody who is strong and powerful and loving and brave.

I feel that once you've got that image of Wonder Woman and you know how to extend that to people in a positive way, it gets easier to tell the story. And I'll be crass here, for a long time people said: "Well, male heroes sell. We're dealing in superheroes, we're dealing in power fantasy and girls would rather not be a part of that." And I think that that's something that has changed radically in the last few years. With more female characters coming into the light they're showing that female characters are a much-needed element in heroic fantasy and you can't rely on princesses forever.

LB How would you then define a supervillain and have you a favorite?

PD Basically it's somebody who has such a lack of empathy that their selfish needs supersede even the thought of anybody else around them. The Joker has always been a personal favorite of mine simply because of the madness element. [*Batman* director] Tim Burton had a good take on him and it's like a bizarre performance artist and I kind of ascribe to that, too. He's very theatrical and to quote the original Batman movie, he "makes art until someone dies" and I've always sort of liked that, the fact that you could be that cruel, that funny and that, I don't know, nonchalant about it, I've always thought, was terrific.

LB Would you consider Harley Quinn to be a villain?

PD Probably more to herself than anybody else. I think that she falls into the same category where she just doesn't think about the ramifications of her actions. I feel that there are times she will undertake a cause that makes sense to her alone and that might ultimately have a benefit to whoever or whatever she's trying to help, but there's carnage all around her even though she accomplished what she set out to do.

LB How would you characterize her relationship with the Joker?

PD That is a difficult relationship to define. It's not healthy, but there is passion and I think there is affection there from both parts. The question that I get asked the most is "Does the Joker love Harley?," and I say to a point, but he's such an odd creature that love doesn't really exist for him in the way it would in another relationship. I think he loves what she is or what he has made her. He got into her head, twisted her. It's almost like *Pygmalion*, she became the idealized vision of what he wanted to the point where she's now her own entity and she constantly surprises him. I think the relationship works when they're both into it, but ultimately it's an unhealthy one and it's a sort of passion that burns itself out or could become abusive very quickly. You can't deny that when they're together and when they're both on the same track the sparks really do fly.

LB In your memoir, *Dark Night: A True Batman Story*, you describe how you were in a number of one-sided relationships. Did you channel some of that frustration into Harley's relationship with the Joker?

PD Yes. Harley comes from me in a lot of ways. I could empathize very much with what she was going through with the Joker and with these feelings of abandonment or rejection and I did find myself putting that into a lot of her dialogue. In fact, there's one where the Joker kicks her out and she says, "Face it Harl, you're a certified nutso wanted in twelve states." She knows what she is. She'd rather not acknowledge it, but there were times when I was trying to get a person to notice me by making myself available to them and then going home by myself or getting a pat on the head after paying for dinner. I would realize that I'm not getting what I want out of this, but the next day I would go into work and say, "I had a great date with this wonderful girl and she was fabulous and everything's great" and everybody would kind of go, like, "Really? If that's what you think." It was a process of self-deception and self-delusion and I recognized it and I interpreted some of that through Harley.

LB In your *Batman: The Animated Series* episode "Trial" the District Attorney describes Batman as "a drug the city keeps taking to avoid facing reality." Do you think superheroes in the real world could be criticized for being an escapist fantasy that we use to avoid real issues?

PD I think superhero fandom is escapist. Certainly. Is it a drug or a narcotic? I don't know. I think that's something each person has to answer individually; to what degree does it rule their life? You can make the same comment about people who play *World of Warcraft*, are into *Game of Thrones*, or anything that has a big fan following. I think that superheroes are very important as an extension of the better part of a person. If they think of Superman or Spider-Man or Batman at a moment of trial or conflict and they're able to say, well, I'm going to do it this way because Batman did it this way, I think they can inspire.

I received a letter from a police officer, I think, in North Carolina, who said that he had realized he could never be Batman, but he could be a policeman. He was inspired by Batman, especially the *Batman: The Animated Series*, to become a policeman. That was his chance to do good in that role and reach out to people and take the better elements of what he felt a superhero was to make a difference within his community. And I think that that's great. That's why you read heroic fantasy, myths, and legends. To some degree you can argue that's why you go to church, to take on the better qualities of a being that you have faith in that has a message, and you want extend that message. If it's Jesus Christ, that's fine, if it's Superman, that's fine.

LB In *Dark Night: A True Batman Story*, you recount an incident in your life where you needed a heroic figure and one wasn't there for you. So maybe, in as much detail as you want to go into, tell us what happened on that night.

PD *Dark Night* deals with my life at the time, which was around 1993, when I was working on the *Batman* series and the show had come on the air and we were getting a good response from it. Right around that time I was walking home one night from a date that didn't go particularly well and two men assaulted me on the street. They grabbed me and held me down and smashed me in the face and kicked me and it was a full-on battering assault. They were threatening to kill me. Ultimately they robbed me and left me there and I was bleeding and torn up and I had to walk home. It was terrifying and it was humiliating because I felt like there was nothing I could do to get out of it and you sometimes fantasize: "if I'm ever attacked, I'm going to do this and that" and it's like, no, you really can't, not in a situation like this.

It was a hard time and at that point I felt like I just don't want to write *Batman*, I don't want to write a guy who avenges people because there's nobody here to avenge anything for me. It was followed by months of staying home and drinking and doubt and misery and trying to work myself through it and ultimately I realized there is no one. There is no one who's going to help you out of this unless you help yourself and you either help yourself or you don't. And it reached the point where I realized I have to help myself because I don't want to live this way.

LB In the book you use Batman and his Rogues Gallery to represent certain doubts, confusions, and anxieties you had. How did you decide on that narrative device?

PD Well, I've always been somebody who has existed to a great degree in their imagination and that goes back to when I was a child. There's a scene in the book of me getting bullied on a bus and then going home and opening the door and there are all these characters that I like from comics or movies or books just waiting in my room and that was my Sanctum Sanctorum where I could go in and write stories and read stories and have a moment's peace and that moment of peace was inside my imagination.

I remember seeing the play when I was young, *Play It Again, Sam* by Woody Allen where he plays a film critic whose wife has left him and he likes Humphrey Bogart and Humphrey Bogart is kind of a voice in his head. So when I came up with *Dark Night* I referred back to that. I liked that Batman would be a stronger and very unwavering element in my head. He's somebody you can't look away from; he's like a tough dad. There was no Adam West in him;

it's more like, "Get up. I need you to just get on your feet again. And then once you're up there, I'm going to leave because I've got a lot more things to do than worry about you." Whereas the Joker and the Penguin are more indulgent. They're easier voices to listen to and to respond to because they're the voice of self-pity, they're the voice of doubt and derision and it gets very easy for somebody with wavering self-esteem sometimes to tap into those voices, to listen to the devil on your shoulder.

LB When did things turnaround for you where you felt you could write Batman again?

PD When *Batman: The Animated Series* came on TV I had other offers from other studios to go and write for them. I was under contract with Warner Bros. at that time and if I had gone to them and said, "I am really miserable and I can't do this job, please release me" they would have understood and they would have released me and I had plenty of opportunities to go out there and write other stuff like comedy where I could turn my brain off and hide. I recognized after a while it was a form of retreat and if I wasn't happy where I was I wouldn't be happy anywhere.

It was also one night where I was with my sister at a record store and I was wearing a Warner Bros. animation jacket and one of the sales people started talking about cartoons and he told me that his wife had cancer and that they really loved watching cartoons because it got their minds off of dealing with this illness. And he liked *Batman*, but he also liked *Tiny Toons* and we wound up talking about certain episodes. He started telling me, "You know what, one, you're lucky to have a job doing anything, two, you're lucky to have a job working on something that people enjoy."

I don't think I can contribute anything more to the overall benefit of mankind and still make myself happy than telling silly stories and doing what I do and that's work with cartoon characters and working with fantasy and imagination and if I give up on that the bad guys win. Those two guys, they win more than the money they stole from me or the fact they put me in the hospital for a week. They've taken something and really destroyed it and they can't win. They just can't.

Part 4

Superheroes and National Identity

14

Captain America, National Narratives, and the Queer Subversion of the Retcon

NAJA LATER

Captain America (aka Steve Rogers) is a towering figure in the American imagination. Yet his extensive comic book history complicates an easy reading of his relationship with national ideologies. While all long-running comics use repetition and revision to sustain canon, in *Captain America* this process is often overtly textual and political, as rewriting Captain America's backstory can involve rewriting America's war history.[1] Steve Rogers's inescapable link to World War II requires an unusual approach to narration and retelling, as, unlike other superheroes, his origin story cannot be periodically revised to "he got powers a few years ago." Flashbacks, revisions, retcons, and *mise en abyme* are fundamental to narrating *Captain America* and understanding his subversive potential. This chapter explores how *Captain America* comics combine these narrative devices in order to open a valuable vein of counterhegemonic readings with significant political allegory. Ultimately this chapter demonstrates how the dominant narratives of American ideology, particularly those linking the nation at war to ideals of heroism, are increasingly subverted in *Captain America* through unreliable narratives and queer subtext.[2]

Cap Canon and Canon Cap

Captain America, as a pop culture icon, a war hero, and a representative of the American dream, is an inherently political character whose narratives always function to some degree as political allegories.[3] On the surface Cap appears open to a nationalist reading. His name, the flag uniform, and his origins in World War II bear the markers of propaganda. He affirms—or seems to affirm—key facets of the American heroic monomyth as described by media scholar J. Richard Stevens: he has an inherent moral goodness, wages war righteously, and presents hypermasculine ideals.[4] However, Rogers's Cap has endured for generations partly due to his availability for polysemic readings. In his contribution to this collection, "America Is a Piece of Trash," Neal Curtis acknowledges that "different, often competing stories about a nation . . . have the potential to destabilize an idea that many hold to be true, certain, and incontrovertible" and that Cap is "an ongoing exercise in this narrative ambivalence." Analyzing Superman, cultural studies scholar Alex Evans argues "the real signs of splinter and dissent, are to be found at the coal face of hegemonic, mainstream, populist texts."[5] In the case of Rogers, Curtis has suggested that "the biography of Captain America reveals him to be a New Deal Democrat and a social liberal, so it is difficult to make the charge of (big 'C') Conservative stick."[6] Curtis and Jason Dittmer have explored significant *Captain America* arcs that support a progressive reading of Rogers.[7] Why these arcs should be considered significant among the decades of comics is integral to understanding the validity of the progressive reading these narratives can encourage.

Evans notes that the repetition that forms a long-running superhero's mythology "is not *just* a tool of hegemony and imperialism but also a site of considerable resistance and conflict. What close study shows . . . is just how fraught—and, perhaps, fragile—the ideological unity of *mainstream* American popular culture is."[8] This fraught and fragile process of distinguishing meaning from canon is an integral part of why we may read *Captain America* as a commentary on the instability of America's mythic narratives. Dittmer argues, "Ultimately, national identity is not a static and timeless concept, as national mythmaking would have it, but instead a continually changing discourse that structures the nation's sense of collective self and its relationship with others."[9] The repetitions and revisions that have shaped Rogers's canonical narrative critically articulate how America's national narrative itself is shaped through repetition and revision. Evans uses this theoretical framework to demonstrate a critique of hegemonic narratives by superhero mythology:

> Hegemony itself is constantly fragmented, fraught, and in danger of losing its grip. As such, it requires constant reinforcement, realignment, and defense, since, at the same time, we find that counter-hegemonic influences themselves are always struggling to achieve

> dominance. . . . In popular culture in particular we are able to see this process in action, and most of all, perhaps, in those cultural texts which repeat—texts we might call myths, archetypes, or "generic." The reason is that their persistent (but flexible) shape and clear structural delineation allow us to see more clearly the points of breakage and shift in ideological formation that inevitably occur over the period of repetition.[10]

This analysis identifies an inherent weakness in the repetition ironically necessary to uphold hegemonic narratives. Self-conscious instances of narrative instability invite subversive and progressive readings of *Captain America* and the American national narrative.

The narrative of *Captain America* is a collaborative, ongoing, and unreliable work.[11] Making sense of the enormous *Captain America* canon requires a complex process of selective, critical, and subjective reading that renders impossible any monolithic narrative for the character, similar to historian Ian Gordon's framework of Superman "as a process, rather than as a static, fixed phenomenon."[12] This chapter does not aim to reduce the "true" Cap to a "progressive" Cap; instead, it explores how *Captain America* instills counternarratives that encourage a challenge to American hegemonic narratives, especially those concerning the rigid and continuous righteousness of soldiers.

To better understand how Captain America can challenge these narratives, the iconic superhero can be read through literary scholar Alan Sinfield's model of the "faultline story."[13] Sinfield examines canonical texts such as Shakespeare by seeking "the faultlines and breaking points through which they enable dissident reading."[14] Evans, who applied Sinfield's approach to Superman, highlights how repetition is key to understanding superheroes as cultural faultlines: "Culture itself produces its own problems and contradictions, which manifest themselves in culture as sites of anxious repetition: the stories must be retold, reworked, rethought. At this point, they may be either returned to, and recuperated by, hegemonic ideology, or, instead, may be sizably re-figured by non-hegemonic readings—or rewritings—in such a way that they actually produce some kind of cultural change."[15] As will be demonstrated, the strategic use of repetition in *Captain America* creates unreliable narrators. This unreliable narration is a faultline that articulates the unreliability of America's narrativization of itself as a unified nation. When Captain America is presented as a fragmentary, subjective, curated narrative, America—the nation, the fixity of its heroic ideals, and especially its history in war— becomes a fragmentary, subjective, curated narrative.

Framing Flashbacks

Captain America comics are preoccupied with memory, history, narrative, and image. Repetitions and revisions keep readers familiar with Rogers's history as a World War II soldier. Unlike most other Marvel heroes, whose origin stories are revised to keep them young, Rogers's origin has remained fixed within World War II. A number of titles and arcs since the Silver Age tell new tales of Rogers's wartime adventures. On the surface, these new World War II–set stories might seem to reinforce an idealized Cap and an idealized America: a Golden Age hero shaped by the "Good War." However, as English scholar Matthew Vernon argues, nostalgia for World War II is a process of subjective storytelling and tailored memory.[16] Vernon states that the Captain America movies engage in "subversive nostalgia," which he defines as "nostalgia [deployed] to question national narratives."[17] Similarly, one could argue that every repetition—of World War II and other major events in Rogers's life—is also engaged in this self-reflection.

A flashback is never quite the same as the original. Each narrator adds details to Rogers's history, creating hairline fractures in the cohesion of the canon. These fractures can grow deeper and darker, exposing truths that Rogers's narration tells us have been hidden under a dominant narrative. Flashbacks muddy the Manichean extremes of the Golden Age, reducing the racist caricatures typical of the time, while confronting Rogers with the ethical horrors of war.[18] Every flashback engenders excess: surely more time has passed in Rogers's cumulative World War II adventures than could fit into the real war. Something, then, must be untrue: something about the heroic war narrative is inconsistent. Every affirmation undermines itself, demanding we agree that constructing World War II as a cohesive narrative involves curation and selective memory. The war cannot be easily memorialized as what historian Studs Terkel called "The Good War."[19] Fraught with inconsistencies, Rogers cannot embody a cohesive ideal of America's role in World War II as ministering angels. Instead, flashbacks are an opportunity for Rogers to expose and criticize these ideals, narrating his complicity, regrets, and failures as a soldier and a superhero.

Retconning Bucky, and Retconning Bucky's Retcons

No flashback to Rogers's experiences during World War II is a true repetition of past comics' events. The further a flashback strays, the more it questions *why* the original narrative was different. The closer it adheres, the more it questions *why* this narrative needs repeating. The most repeated

Figure 14.1. Bucky's fall as it was first presented in *Avengers* #4 (March 1964).

story in the *Captain America* canon is his second "origin" story, which, like other superhero origin stories, is regularly retconned to have occurred within a decade of the issue's publication to explain Captain America's youthfulness. Stan Lee and Jack Kirby first published the narrative in *Avengers* #4 in 1964. The comic details how in the last days of World War II Rogers and his sidekick Bucky must stop a plane laden with explosives.[20] Rogers falls from the plane, witnessing the plane exploding and killing Bucky.[21] Rogers's body lands in the north Atlantic Ocean and becomes frozen, only to be discovered and defrosted by the newly formed Avengers decades later.

This retcon serves myriad functions: it preserves Rogers's World War II origin by making his time in the ice flexible. It erases the unsuccessful postwar comics from the canon, in particular the 1953 revival of Cap as a "Commie Smasher."[22] It invites critical contrast between American narratives of heroism, masculinity, and nationalism in World War II and the contemporary age. For instance, from the 1960s to the 1970s this second origin enabled Rogers to candidly engage in the civil rights movement. It also excused Rogers from the obligation to intervene in the bombing of Hiroshima. Furthermore, the reworked origin allowed Stan Lee to write out the passé sidekick.[23] This retcon brought to light the trauma, complicity, and regret of an American soldier in World War II.[24] Its periodic repetition reflects Rogers's inner trauma and his attachment to Bucky: its slight variation with each repetition is narrated by Rogers to be evidence of his own unreliable memory.[25] This second origin also gives Rogers a tragic past where his grief over Bucky damages his subsequent romances, highlighting the queer subtext between hero and sidekick. It inspired a revival of Bucky in 2005 as the antihero Winter Soldier, forging a compromise between the original timeline in which Bucky survived and the 1964 retcon. Repetitions of Rogers's fall recur with exponential frequency, emphasizing the event as iconic but also expressing and exacerbating its destabilizing force. In the "original" timeline the event *never happened*—and in the frequent retellings of the event it never happens the same way twice. Ed Brubaker, writer of the Winter Soldier arc, describes his own response: "I'd always been angry as a kid when I found out that Bucky dying was some huge retcon that they did because Stan Lee didn't want to have sidekicks."[26] Rogers's memory of World War II's climax fragments with the increasing pressure of every flashback and every retcon. America's own mythic hero undercuts a national narrative that relies on linearity and continuity.

In these flashbacks Rogers's personal memories of World War II deviate from the comic books that readers may remember. Significantly, this point of instability centers on Bucky. The bond between Rogers and Bucky, with its endless repetitions and variations, is one of the deepest faultlines in the *Captain America* canon. Their relationship is opened to a queer reading by the profound unreliability of Bucky's narrative, and this reading exemplifies ways to trace subversions of conservative narratives in *Captain America*. As artist Rob Lendrum argues, nationalist narratives preclude queer comic characters from representing American iconography and heroism: "Typified as unloyal to the nation, homosexuals were also seen as a security risk."[27] According to Lendrum, queer subtext in superhero comics thus "challenges the assumed hetero-normative 'ownership' of cultural iconography."[28] Bucky's presence has always troubled Rogers's continuity, ethical framework, and heterosexuality, complicating a reading of Rogers's and Bucky's narrative as straightforward or straight. The ideal of a clear continuity, without the problems Bucky causes, not only is a myth naturalized by hegemony but also may be read as a heterosexist concept. Working from film scholar Vivian Sobchack's theories, Jessica Balanzategui reads linear continuity as aligned with a conservative narrative, rooted in familial continuity and the continuity of the status quo.[29] Thus, reading a queer narrative in the retcons of Rogers and Bucky's relationship is more than simply the potential to better represent marginalized identities: it is a disruptive force to both narrative and conservative continuity.[30]

The idea of a queer Bucky emerges from his original role as a sidekick, deeply informs his return as an antihero, and explains much of his popularity within fan communities. Media scholars Andy Medhurst and Neil Shyminsky present compelling readings of the sidekick-hero relationship as queer coded.[31] Lendrum, who recognizes the retcon as a queering device, politicizes the potential for queer narratives in Marvel comics. Focusing on Marvel's heavily publicized 2000s retconning of the Rawhide Kid—a camp but closeted cowboy character from the 1950s—as gay, Lendrum notes how despite Marvel's promotional narratives, the Rawhide Kid's sexuality is never acknowledged beyond innuendo in the actual comics. Lendrum argues that Marvel thus permits and encodes the dominant reading of all camp and innuendo-laden comics as queer since no "canonical" acknowledgment was needed for Marvel to promote the Rawhide Kid as a groundbreaking gay title.[32] This imbues queer-coded American icons, whether cowboys or supersoldiers, with the mythical power necessary to challenge the hegemonic narrative that exclusively links heroism with heterosexuality.[33] The requirement that American soldiers remain closeted was, after all, a real-world law until 2011. The necessity of introducing and enforcing this ban suggests that the nationalist-heterosexist narrative requires the same reinforcement as any hegemonic paradigm. The repeated closeness of Rogers and Bucky regularly goes beyond camaraderie, falling into story tropes usually reserved for romance narratives.[34] Their homoerotic subtext is a multilayered and deeply politicized challenge to narratives of heterosexuality in war heroes. Bucky's revival and brainwashing as a Cold War assassin echoes Lendrum's characterization of real Cold War moral panics that conflated nationalist disloyalty and homosexual tendencies.[35] The 2000s' comic book story arc "Winter Soldier" conspicuously ages Bucky up to sixteen-to-twenty years old during World War II, alleviating the pederastic overtures of the relationship, but also calling attention to those same overtures by revising them. During this arc both Rogers and Bucky disclose to the reader that more occurred between them than may be apparent: Bucky's image as a sidekick was "the official story" hiding "a darker truth underneath."[36] This example typifies the characters' self-conscious knowledge of their potential to be read conservatively, and it challenges a reader to search for misdirection and subtext in the dominant narratives of World War II.

Mise en Abyme

To further the idea of repetition as subversive, *Captain America* often frames its repetitions with reminders of their destabilizing power. This is done through mise en abyme, with diegetic characters problematizing or denying the events of a flashback within their narration.[37] In the aforementioned example Rogers describes how, during World War II, Bucky dressed as Rogers's sidekick but acted as his "advanced scout," while illustrations show Bucky slitting Nazi throats. The discontinuity between what readers remember of Bucky as a sidekick, and what Rogers now claims was merely propaganda, demonstrates the unreliability of narration.[38] It compels reading with the assumption that more is occurring between characters than the "official story," whether "official" refers to the U.S. government or Marvel publishing.

Rogers's new narration acknowledges the directly political connotations of Cap's persona, and how those connotations may have altered the surface narrative via propaganda and censorship. A reader is invited to revisit Golden Age comics and World War II flashbacks in the *Captain America* canon critically for this "darker truth underneath." This device explicitly frames *Captain America*'s flashbacks not simply as affirmations of World War II heroism but also as a framework to deconstruct convention and censorship in earlier comics. World War II is framed through this device as deliberately tailored and historicized to exclude unsavory details: the mise en abyme invites a reader to critically contextualize the popular narrative.

Examples of critical mise en abyme in *Captain America* occur in the Golden and Silver ages and frequently during Brubaker's run from 2004 to 2012. In Brubaker's books Rogers is plagued with corrupted memories and Bucky struggles with induced amnesia. This self-reflexively addresses the frailty of our cultural memory of the *Captain America* canon, especially around the retcon of Bucky's death—which Brubaker himself was plagued by as a fan.[39] Before Rogers realizes Bucky has returned, he is plagued with nightmares and hallucinations of Bucky during World War II, telling the reader none of them are consistent with his usual memories. Rogers muses, "Sometimes I think *I'm* not even sure what really happened anymore. Did I ever *really* remember it, or was I just filling in blanks?"[40] Rogers seems reflexively aware that in the original *Captain America* comics Bucky *didn't* die in 1945. Even his enhanced memory is unreliable, allowing the events of 1964/1945 to be pried open, renarrated, and subverted. Brubaker returns to this unreliability in his final issue of *Captain America*. Rogers gives Bucky a comic book: a diegetic, in-universe issue of *Captain America Comics* #1 from 1941.[41] Bucky is unimpressed, dismissing the book as heavily censored propaganda.[42] This confirms, canonically, a difference between what we read in *Captain America Comics* #1 and a version of Rogers and Bucky not "for kids." The scene is a reminder of the pervading unreliability of narrative, deepening the faultline and subverting all of the *Captain America* canon, including Brubaker's own.

Figure 14.2. The "Official Story" from *Captain America* #5 (New York: Marvel, May 2005).

Between the Lines

The mise en abyme of *Captain America* poses questions: What has been omitted from the comic we hold in our hands? And what might we later discover was censored, curated, or misremembered? We learn in 1964 that Bucky died in 1945; we learn in 1972 that the 1953 Commie Smasher was an impostor; we learn in 2005 that Bucky was revived after 1964/1945; we learn in 2012 that the narrative of 1941 was heavily censored. These moments pry open *Captain America* for subversive readings, furthering the progressive politics already on the page. What could another Marvel team bring to the surface in future comics? Long-running comics have a revolving door of official writers and artists to revise and repeat *Captain America* narratives, and Cap is not, of course, limited to official creators. Evans notes of Superman, "The primary texts are still to play for, can be changed, reproduced and rewritten directly. There are political battles of reading—performatively, publicly—between fans, bloggers, journalists, but there are also those between, say, traditionalist and revisionist writers and artists."[43] Fans already participate in narrating *Captain America*, from selecting which version of the canon to accept to creating and sharing their own transformative works. This trajectory of fans-as-narrators is increasingly converging, as Marvel hires creators such as Kevin Wada from fan communities where

Figure 14.3. Kristafer Anka's "Best Pals" Instagram post, March 6, 2017.

transformative queer works are popular. Wada and fellow artist Kristafer Anka, both of whom regularly draw Marvel characters "officially" and "unofficially," are at the forefront of crafting an iconic queer aesthetic for Captain America and Bucky. The liminal zones between official and unofficial narrators, where a queer context is flourishing, demonstrate the extent to which *Captain America* is an open, collaborative mythology. The potential for the on-page, superficially heterosexual narration of Captain America to be unreliable has been written into the comics from its earliest issues and has become a prevalent negotiated reading in fan communities pushing for more progressive representation in popular media.[44]

This potential to read subversively is embedded in all conventional comics. For *Captain America*, its significance lies in the character's inherent political allusions and the sustained attempts to direct attention beyond the mediating forces of censorship and propaganda to truths we may yet find "underneath."

Conclusion

It would be difficult to claim a progressive reading of *Captain America* as against the grain: the grain, as this chapter has demonstrated, has always run with radical potential. As long as Rogers functions as an allegory—indeed the *longer* he functions as an allegory—the more cracks appear on the surface of his narrative. Every repetition, flashback, retcon, and use of mise en abyme that *Captain America* relies upon to sustain the narrative inherently subverts the narrative, making unreliability a characteristic trope attached to the character. Accordingly, the dominant narratives of American ideology are shown through *Captain America* as unreliable. The function of any cultural memory that upholds nationalist narratives is, through the powerful iconography of the superhero, rendered fragmentary. Hegemonic ideals attached to heroism, war, and nationalism are denaturalized through the comics, which call deliberate critical attention to how these ideals are constructed through strategic repetition. This makes a queer reading of the Rogers/Bucky relationship, as it emerges through crises of continuity, a criticism of continuity's ideological function. The potential to read retcons as faultlines increasingly opens Captain America to narratives that powerfully challenge the status quo.

Notes

1 *Captain America* in italics refers to any Marvel comics that feature the character Captain America. The comics discussed in this chapter are set in Marvel's main canonical timeline, called "616." Alternate-universe comics, movies, and television fall outside this chapter's scope; however, each adaptation complements the framework of repetitions as a destabilizing force for national narratives.

2 The superhero and war hero, conflated in Captain America, champion hegemonic ideals in part through a continuous heterosexuality. The preclusion of queerness from both is not simply ideological: historian Christina S. Jarvis discusses how military bans and checks for homosexuality arose during World War II. Queerness was perceived as a threat to American moral values and incompatible with the mythic masculinity of the American military. Thus, when the possibility of queerness in *Captain America* appears in the cracks of the "official" narrative, it demonstrates the frailty of both a heterosexist narrative and the dominant narrative of America at war. Jarvis, *The Male Body at War: American Masculinity during World War II* (DeKalb: Northern Illinois University Press, 2004), 75–77.

3 Jason Dittmer extensively argues that all *Captain America* comics are inherently political allegories, an approach shared by this chapter. Dittmer, "Captain America's Empire: Reflections on Identity, Popular Culture, and Post-9/11 Geopolitics," *Annals of the Association of American Geographers* 95, no. 3 (2005): 626–643.

4 J. Richard Stevens, *Captain America, Masculinity and Violence* (Syracuse, NY: Syracuse University Press, 2015), 18, 28.
5 Alex Evans, "Superman *Is* the Faultline: Fissures in the Monomythic Man of Steel," in *Reframing 9/11: Film, Popular Culture and the "War on Terror,"* ed. Jeff Birkenstein, Anna Froula, and Karen Randell (New York: Bloomsbury, 2014), 117.
6 Neal Curtis, *Sovereignty and Superheroes* (Manchester: Manchester University Press, 2016), 35.
7 Curtis, *Sovereignty and Superheroes*, 34–57; Dittmer, "Captain America's Empire," 626–643.
8 Evans, "Superman *Is* the Faultline," 117.
9 Jason Dittmer, "Retconning America: Captain America in the Wake of World War II and the McCarthy Hearings," in *The Amazing Transforming Superhero! Essays on the Revision of Characters in Comic Books, Film and Television*, ed. Terrence R. Wandtke (Jefferson, NC: McFarland, 2007), 36.
10 Evans, "Superman *Is* the Faultline," 122.
11 "Narrator" is used in this chapter to refer to the creative teams of *Captain America* titles as well as characters whose inner monologues fill caption boxes, and, as will be discussed later, the reader.
12 Ian Gordon, *Superman: The Persistence of an American Icon* (New Brunswick, NJ: Rutgers University Press, 2017), 5–6.
13 Evans, "Superman *Is* the Faultline," 122.
14 Alan Sinfield, *Faultlines: Cultural Materialism and the Politics of Dissident Reading* (Berkeley: University of California Press, 1992), 9.
15 Evans, "Superman *Is* the Faultline," 122–123.
16 Matthew Vernon, "Subversive Nostalgia, or Captain America at the Museum," *Journal of Popular Culture* 49, no. 1 (2016): 116.
17 Vernon, "Subversive Nostalgia," 120.
18 *Captain America* comics produced during World War II featured villains such as "Monstro the Mad Jap," a grotesque example of contemporary stereotypes. Subsequent stories of Rogers's World War II exploits made efforts to improve racial representation, such as the introduction of Japanese American soldier Jim Morita in 1967. Vince Alascia, *All Winners Comics* #14 (New York: Timely, January 1945); Roy Thomas, Dick Ayers, and John Tartaglione, *Sgt Fury and His Howling Commandos* #38 (New York: Marvel, January 1967).
19 Studs Terkel, *The Good War* (New York: Pantheon Books, 1984).
20 Stan Lee, Jack Kirby, et al., *Avengers* #4 (New York: Marvel, March 1964).
21 Even in the 2005 retcon of Captain America's second origin that brings Bucky back, it is revealed that Bucky still died but was resuscitated by Russian military scientists who turned him into the Winter Soldier. Ed Brubaker and Steve Epting, *Captain America* #11 (New York: Marvel, November 2005).
22 The 1950s' Captain America comics removed from continuity by Captain America's second origin were later incorporated back into the canon. A 1972 retcon shows that while Steve Rogers and James "Bucky" Barnes were indeed lost in 1945, the "Cap" and "Bucky" roles passed to William Naslund and Fred Davis from 1945 to 1949, then William Burnside ("Commie Smasher" / "Bad

Cap") and Jack Monroe in 1953. Bad Cap—who had been written out of existence by a 1964 retcon—becomes a recurring villain, exemplifying how nationalist *Captain America* arcs are not simply erased from canonical memory but brought to light to be critically addressed. Fan letters from the age show canny responses to this retcon: "You're about to explain that the super-commie hater . . . of the 1950s was not *our* Cap, but a nut who was out to protect the USA in the big commie witch hunt!" Curtis's chapter in this collection explores a similar case in which Rogers was retconned to be a long-term agent of Nazi-affiliated terrorist organization Hydra—and then retconned back to his original self after poor fan reception. Hank Chapman, Russ Heath, and Carl Burgos, *Young Men* #24 (New York: Atlas, December 1953); Steve Englehart, Sal Buscema, and Jim Mooney, *Captain America* #153 (New York: Marvel, September 1972); Walt Podrazik in Steve Englehart, Sal Buscema, and John Verpoorten, *Captain America* #158 (New York: Marvel, February 1973); Roy Thomas, George Tuska, Pablo Marcos, and George Roussos, *Captain America* #215 (New York: Marvel, November 1977).

23 For a closer study of Bucky's problematizing role as a sidekick archetype, see Naja Later, "A Darker Truth Underneath: Captain America and Bucky," in *The Dark Side: A Superhero Reader*, ed. Robert Peaslee and Robert G. Weiner (Jackson: University Press of Mississippi, forthcoming).

24 Robert G. Weiner, "Sixty-Five Years of Guilt Over the Death of Bucky," in *Captain America and the Struggle of the Superhero: Critical Essays*, ed. Robert G. Weiner (Jefferson, NC: McFarland, 2009), 90–103.

25 Ed Brubaker, Steve Epting, Michael Lark, et al., *Captain America* #1–60, #600–619, #1–19 (New York: Marvel, January 2005–December 2012).

26 Ed Brubaker, interview by Oliver Sava, *AV Club*, October 7, 2011, www.avclub.com/ed-brubaker-1798226673.

27 Rob Lendrum, "Queering Super-Manhood: Superhero Masculinity, Camp and Public Relations as a Textual Framework," *International Journal of Comic Art* 7, no. 1 (2005): 287.

28 Lendrum, "Queering Super-Manhood," 287.

29 Jessica Balanzategui, *The Uncanny Child in Transnational Cinema: Ghosts of Futurity in the Twenty-First Century* (Amsterdam: Amsterdam University Press, 2018).

30 Another example of a retcon using Rogers as a site for more diverse representation is discussed in Liam Burke's chapter in this collection, "Apes, Angels, and Super Patriots." In 2012 Rogers's parents are retconned as Irish immigrants. While this could be read as a retcon casting Rogers as an outsider, problems persist: Burke notes Rogers's parents are caricatured as negative Irish stereotypes, while Rogers himself now affirms the national myth of the successfully assimilated first generation. The retcon creates another inconsistency in Rogers's hegemonic characterization, suggesting ways to revise Rogers—since for better or worse he remains the "original" Cap.

31 Andy Medhurst, "Batman, Deviance and Camp," in *The Superhero Reader*, ed. Charles Hatfield, Jeet Heer, and Kent Worcester (Jackson: University of

Mississippi Press, 2013), 237–251; Neil Shyminsky, "'Gay' Sidekicks: Queer Anxiety and the Narrative Straightening of the Superhero," *Men and Masculinities* 14, no. 3 (2011): 288–308.

32 Lendrum, "Queering Super-Manhood," 295.

33 Lendrum, "Queering Super-Manhood," 298.

34 In the front matter and back matter for the *Captain America: White* collection, the book's consulting editor Richard Starkings, as well as Christopher Markus and Stephen McFeely (writers of the 2014 film *Captain America: The Winter Soldier*), describe Cap and Bucky's narrative as "a love story." Jeph Loeb and Tim Sale, *Captain America: White* (New York: Marvel, 2016).

35 Lendrum, "Queering Super-Manhood," 287.

36 Brubaker and Lark, *Captain America* #5.

37 *Mise en abyme* describes the narrative device of a story within a story. It is often used to destabilize the diegesis and self-reflexively challenge the authority of both reader and narrator. In *Captain America* it appears as comic book issues, newsreels, and other media present within the diegesis: Bucky can pick up a comic book about himself. They are framed as promotional media for the real-life superhero and are often direct copies of comics and memorabilia from *our* universe.

38 Fan letters during this arc reveal enthusiasm for these darker retcons of Bucky and his revival as an antihero. John Nicklos in Brubaker and Epting, *Captain America* #4; Mary Borsellino in Brubaker, Epting, and Lark, *Captain America* #12.

39 Brubaker interview.

40 Brubaker and Epting, *Captain America* #6.

41 Brubaker and Epting, *Captain America* #19.

42 On many occasions Bucky reflexively derides his public image when confronted with it in diegetic newsreels and propaganda.

43 Evans, "Superman *Is* the Faultline," 124.

44 Cap and Bucky's Golden Age superhero-sidekick dynamic has a similar queer subtext to that between Batman and Robin. Shyminsky and Gareth Schott research this subtext extensively: the emotional intimacy, close domestic arrangements, and deferred heterosexuality, along with the sidekick often falling into a damsel role, produce queer overtones between the superhero and sidekick. These may also be applied to *Captain America*, with such tropes found in the fourth issue. Joe Simon and Jack Kirby, *Captain America Comics* #4 (New York: Timely, June 1941). Shyminsky, "'Gay' Sidekicks," 294. Schott, "From Fan Appropriation to Industry Re-appropriation: The Sexual Identity of Comic Superheroes," *Journal of Graphic Novels and Comics* 1, no. 1 (2010): 19.

Bibliography

Anka, Kristafer. "Best Pals." Instagram post, March 6, 2017. www.instagram.com/p/BRRo6N9FQWr/.

Balanzategui, Jessica. *The Uncanny Child in Transnational Cinema: Ghosts of Futurity in the Twenty-First Century.* Amsterdam: Amsterdam University Press, 2018.

Brubaker, Ed, Steve Epting, Michael Lark, et al. *Captain America* #1–60, #600–619, #1–19. New York: Marvel, January 2005–December 2012.
Chapman, Hank, Russ Heath, and Carl Burgos. *Young Men* #24. New York: Atlas, December 1953.
Curtis, Neal. *Sovereignty and Superheroes*. Manchester: Manchester University Press, 2016.
Dittmer, Jason. "Captain America's Empire: Reflections on Identity, Popular Culture, and Post-9/11 Geopolitics." *Annals of the Association of American Geographers* 95, no. 3 (2005): 626–643.
———. "Retconning America: Captain America in the Wake of World War II and the McCarthy Hearings." In *The Amazing Transforming Superhero! Essays on the Revision of Characters in Comic Books, Film and Television*, edited by Terrence R. Wandtke, 35–51. Jefferson, NC: McFarland, 2007.
Englehart, Steve, Sal Buscema, and Jim Mooney. *Captain America* #153. New York: Marvel, September 1972.
Evans, Alex. "Superman *Is* the Faultline: Fissures in the Monomythic Man of Steel." In *Reframing 9/11: Film, Popular Culture and the "War on Terror,"* edited by Jeff Birkenstein, Anna Froula, and Karen Randell, 117–126. New York: Bloomsbury, 2014.
Gordon, Ian. *Superman: The Persistence of an American Icon*. New Brunswick, NJ: Rutgers University Press, 2017.
Jarvis, Christina S. *The Male Body at War: American Masculinity during World War II*. DeKalb: Northern Illinois University Press, 2004.
Later, Naja. "A Darker Truth Underneath: Captain America and Bucky." In *The Dark Side: A Superhero Reader*, edited by Robert Peaslee and Robert G. Weiner. Jackson: University Press of Mississippi, forthcoming.
Lee, Stan, Jack Kirby, et al. *Avengers* #4. New York: Marvel, March 1964.
Lendrum, Rob. "Queering Super-Manhood: Superhero Masculinity, Camp and Public Relations as a Textual Framework." *International Journal of Comic Art* 7, no. 1 (2005): 287–303.
Loeb, Jeph, and Tim Sale. *Captain America: White*. New York: Marvel, 2016.
Medhurst, Andy. "Batman, Deviance and Camp." In *The Superhero Reader*, edited by Charles Hatfield, Jeet Heer, and Kent Worcester, 237–251. Jackson: University Press of Mississippi, 2013.
Schott, Gareth. "From Fan Appropriation to Industry Re-appropriation: The Sexual Identity of Comic Superheroes." *Journal of Graphic Novels and Comics* 1, no. 1 (2010): 17–29.
Shyminsky, Neil. "'Gay' Sidekicks: Queer Anxiety and the Narrative Straightening of the Superhero." *Men and Masculinities* 14, no. 3 (2011): 288–308.
Simon, Joe, and Jack Kirby. *Captain America Comics* #1. New York: Timely, March 1941.
———. *Captain America Comics* #4. New York: Timely, June 1941.
Sinfield, Alan. *Faultlines: Cultural Materialism and the Politics of Dissident Reading*. Berkeley: University of California Press, 1992.
Stevens, J. Richard. *Captain America, Masculinity and Violence*. Syracuse, NY: Syracuse University Press, 2015.

Terkel, Studs. *The Good War*. New York: Pantheon Books, 1984.

Thomas, Roy, George Tuska, Pablo Marcos, and George Roussos. *Captain America* #215. New York: Marvel, November 1977.

Vernon, Matthew. "Subversive Nostalgia, or Captain America at the Museum." *Journal of Popular Culture* 49, no. 1 (2016): 116–135.

Weiner, Robert G. "Sixty-Five Years of Guilt over the Death of Bucky." In *Captain America and the Struggle of the Superhero: Critical Essays*, edited by Robert G. Weiner, 90–103. Jefferson, NC: McFarland, 2009.

15

Apes, Angels, and Super Patriots

The Irish in Superhero Comics

LIAM BURKE

When former Marvel Comics editor Stan Lee was asked whether he had ever thought about creating an Irish superhero, the onetime *Captain America* writer responded, "I don't know how to make a superhero specifically Irish."[1] Indeed, while there are enough heroes clad in the stars and stripes, Union Jack, and maple leaf for political geographer Jason Dittmer to recognize nationalist superheroes as a "subgenre," there have been comparatively few Irish-themed heroes.[2] Nonetheless, superhero comics regularly feature Irish supporting characters, set adventures in Ireland, or expand their hero's backstory to include Irish immigrant origins.

However, these comics often perpetuate prejudices that stem, in part, from Victorian era efforts to undermine Irish Home Rule.[3] This chapter traces the Irish stereotypes that still pervade superhero stories in the hope of unmasking their origins and understanding why they circulate so freely. It also demonstrates how the recent growth of Ireland's comic book community is serving as a corrective to wider representations of the Irish in superhero comics.

Victorian Cartoons and Irish Home Rule

During the late 1800s Irish efforts to gain Home Rule were gathering pace with British prime minister William Ewart Gladstone publicly supporting the cause. Nonetheless, many British people feared that an independent Ireland would lead to the dissolution of the empire. This anxiety was articulated in cartoons that appeared in British satirical magazines like *Punch*,

Fun, and *Judy*. Although many of the visual conventions for depicting the Irish predate the Home Rule movement, sociolinguist Shane Walshe describes Victorian era publications as the "zenith" of such portrayals.[4] Typical of these cartoons was the 1881 piece "Two Forces" created by *Alice's Adventures in Wonderland* illustrator John Tenniel for the magazine *Punch*. In the satirical image the female personification of Britain, Britannia, protects her meek sister from across the Irish Sea, Hibernia, from a rock-wielding Irish anarchist. Extrapolating from images such as this, the American historian L. Perry Curtis observed in his book *Apes and Angels* that in Victorian cartoons the Irish tended to fall into two categories: Neanderthal-like beasts who could not be reasoned with and demure ladies who needed protection from Irish nationalists.[5] As the media scholar Michael de Nie notes, "These images ultimately reinforced long-standing prejudices about the people of Ireland and undercut their claims for self-government."[6]

Curtis also describes how this "apes and angels" dichotomy crossed the Atlantic, where it became an "ethnic fixture in cartoons about Irish-Americans in New York."[7] Curtis goes on to describe how in the satirical magazine *Puck* the artist Frederick Burr Opper "excelled at simianizing Irish-Americans."[8] Opper would later become one of the pioneers of the newspaper comic strip with his popular character Happy Hooligan, an imbecilic Irish itinerant. Much of the humor in *Happy Hooligan* was derived from the Irish stereotypes Opper had spent years cultivating in satirical magazines, and which he now helped embed into the grammar of the fledgling comic strip.[9] Indeed, Curtis describes how the "convention of bestializing or simianizing faces of villains in the twentieth century may be seen repeatedly in such comic strips and pulp crime-and-adventure books as *Batman*, *Superman*, *Spiderman* [*sic*], *Dick Tracy*, and *Rex Morgan*."[10]

However, with their political roots obfuscated, modern representations of the Irish in comics have gone largely unanalyzed, an oversight Walshe identifies in his 2012 chapter on representations of Irish English speech in the Marvel Universe.[11] Even those studies that one might expect to engage with the topic skirt the issue. For instance, Chris Murray briefly acknowledges the "uprising in Ireland and the calls for independence" in his book *The British Superhero*. However, by emphasizing the book's focus on the relationship between American and British comics, the study does not interrogate how "British" identity often chafes with national and regional identities within Britain including Scotland, Wales, and Northern Ireland.[12] Yet the representation of the Irish in comics is an area worthy of analysis; as de Nie noted of Victorian comics, "By analysing them and discovering what made them intelligible and amusing, we can appreciate how traditional stereotypes

Figure 15.1. "Two Forces" cartoon by artist John Tenniel in the magazine *Punch*, October 29, 1881.

and contemporary concerns informed popular perceptions of the Irish question."[13] To that end this chapter examines representations of the Irish in superhero comics by international and local creators to better understand where and why these stereotypes continue to be used, and also when they have been challenged.

Figures 15.2 (above) and 15.3 (opposite). The villainous and heroic version of Banshee in *X-Men* #28 (New York: Marvel, January 1967) and *Uncanny X-Men* #94 (New York: Marvel, August 1975), respectively, conform to Victorian conventions for depicting the Irish.

Angels

Film scholar Martin McLoone observed that the "most positive (or at least less negative) face of Irish primitivism" is the depiction of Ireland as a "Garden of Eden, populated by a simple, musically gifted, loquacious and happy (if quarrelsome) peasantry."[14] While these "Stage Irish" stereotypes might be dismissed as benign, even affectionate, they were employed in Victorian cartoons to suggest the Irish were unable to rule themselves. These condescending conventions have been maintained in modern superhero comic books, as evident by the most explicitly Irish superhero, Banshee.

The mutant Sean Cassidy, better known as Banshee, was first introduced as a villain in *X-Men* #28 using his supersonic scream to steal a "Gaelic landscape" painting of "the utmost serenity."[15] When X-Men was relaunched in 1975 with *Giant-Size X-Men* #1 the character was added to the book's new international team.[16] However, not only had the mutant changed his

affiliation, but his physiognomy was also altered to better match his new role. In his introduction to the revised edition of *Apes and Angels: The Irishman in Victorian Caricature* Curtis identifies a "topography of Irish facial features" used by Victorian era artists to depict the Irishman. This taxonomy includes the acceptable "rustic male" Pat who "displayed no overt interest in politics" and "a prognathous and somewhat hairy or unshaven plebeian Irishman, better known as Paddy, who supported the cause of repeal or Irish home rule."[17] When first introduced as a villain Banshee displayed the "protrusive mouth and jaw" of the "primitive" and "degenerate" Paddy, but when he joined the X-Men Banshee moved from a Paddy to a Pat, with the character's facial features dramatically reworked to a more classic hero's profile.[18] However, while the hero was now a more acceptable Irishman, his pastoral simplicity was emphasized through costuming, accent, and setting.

Following his first mission as an X-Man, Banshee doubts his usefulness to the team, describing himself as "a barely literate ex-cop" while clutching his clay pipe. In this moment he is positioned as the good-natured Pat: not particularly intelligent or useful but well meaning.[19] Curtis notes how the clay pipe was a signifier of Irish ethnicity in late 1800s U.S. cartoons, while de Nie identifies the most common stereotype for the Irish as Paddy the Peasant, who "was typically depicted wearing breeches, a shabby or patched coat, and a distinctive hat, usually with a clay pipe in its band."[20] Indeed, Banshee is never far from his clay pipe, with the mutant breaking into a tobacconists to satisfy his habit in his first appearance.[21] Banshee often completes the look with other symbols of his Irish identity, including a flat cap and green jumper. Cassidy even wears these signifiers to a formal dinner he hosts for the X-Men at his home, prompting Wolverine to criticize this fashion faux pas by suggesting Banshee looks "like a stablehand," to which Cassidy counters, "Since I happen t' be Lord o' this manor, I get t' come t' dinner dressed however I please."[22] It seems in Ireland even lords dress like peasants and Paddies.

As that near incompressible dialogue suggests, accent is another means of signifying Banshee's Irish identity, yet this also serves to diminish the character. As part of wider research on representations of Irish speech, Shane Walshe provides a detailed analysis of Irish English speech in Marvel comics. Walshe identifies the types of phrasing used to distinguish Irish characters in mainstream comics such as "elision, reduction, and weak forms" that are typically not used for other vernacular English, and which he argues are "meant to reflect the common perception of Irish people speaking quickly and unclearly."[23] Walshe identifies these conventions across 150 Marvel comic books, and many more examples can be found in DC Comics titles. For instance, in *All-Star Batman & Robin, The Boy Wonder* the hero Black Canary was reworked by the Irish American writer Frank Miller as an immigrant who had "left County Monaghan and her sweet mother." The leather-clad hero is introduced with the caption "the lilt in her voice is sweet Irish." This lilting Irish accent is realized in a patois made up of the types of interjections and exclamations Walshe identified: "You know, you're a fine man, Mister Batman. A right hero, you are. A hero, to be sure."[24]

In addition to physiognomy, costume, and accents, Banshee's primitivism is illustrated through the depiction of Ireland as a premodern paradise. For instance, during the intergalactic conflict of "The Phoenix Saga" the X-Men were sent on vacation by Professor X, with Banshee offering his childhood home, located "in a remote part o' County Mayo . . . few conveniences, fewer people." The X-Men reach this ancient location by increasingly archaic modes of transport, before it is ultimately revealed that Banshee grew up in a castle infested with leprechauns. Similar depictions of Ireland as a preindustrial utopia can be found across a range of comics. For instance, in the 2000 A.D. comic *Sláine*, which reworks Irish mythological hero Cú Chulainn as a Conan the Barbarian–style warrior, foreign invaders promise to bring "civilisation" to Ireland, which Sláine describes as a threat to their "freedom" designed to "steal" their "souls."[25] Similarly, in *Ultimate Wolverine vs. Hulk* Bruce Banner hides out in this backward land hoping that its pastoral simplicity will keep the Hulk at bay.[26] However, as McLoone notes this "ideological construction" of Ireland as a Garden of Eden owes "more to the culture of the centre than to the realities of life on the periphery" and is in keeping with infantilizing tendencies that many scholars have identified in colonial representations of Ireland.[27]

Apes

While the good-natured peasants living in an untouched Garden of Eden is one set of conventions associated with the Irish, much like Bruce Banner, these images often transform into a violent shade of green. Describing the second dominant trend in media representations of the Irish, McLoone notes that Ireland is often "presented as a society torn asunder by violence . . . where a proclivity to violence was seen as a tragic flaw of the Irish themselves. This again was often presented as the result of ignorance and a lack of progress."[28]

Among the many descendants of the Victorian Ape is the convention of the "Fighting Irish." Writing about regional stereotypes in British comics, media scholar Mike Catto notes that Ireland was synonymous with "large male maniacs. . . . In war comics both Scots and Irish soldiers were other rankers, heavy drinkers and as much of a danger to their own side as to the enemy."[29] Similar examples can be found in superhero books with characters such as Black Canary, Sláine, and Hitman regularly depicted getting into bar brawls.

These conventions became more overt in comics that engage with Irish conflicts, particularly those centered on the sectarian violence or Troubles that dogged Northern Ireland from the late 1960s to the 1990s.[30] Curtis notes how the conflict prompted some British newspaper cartoonists to "revive the gorilla guerrilla image."[31] While superhero books stopped short at such extreme character types, they did widely participate in the "myth of atavism," which Ruth Barton describes as a "'two tribes' interpretation of Loyalist-Republican sectarianism" with violence "seen as endemic to the human condition" and in particular Irish nature.[32] On this topic McLoone adds, this tradition "ends up denying the historical, social and political roots of such violence."[33]

For instance, the 1982 Captain Britain story "Friends and Neighbours" was intended by writer Dave Thorpe to engage directly with the Troubles, but artist Alan Davis felt that "it was inappropriate to have a guy dressed in the Union Jack flying over to Ireland and sorting out the entire Northern Ireland situation."[34] Following editorial pressure Thorpe left the book with the story changed to an anonymous gang conflict. Nonetheless, the original concept is clear. Captain Britain lands in a city center street to save a teenager, Jeff, from a gang attack. Jeff's friend explains, "We met on holiday, but he's not from around here and there's a war going on." The gang does not understand why Captain Britain is not on their side (loyalists), while Jeff's neighborhood (nationalist) greet his savior with suspicion. Conflict erupts only for Captain Britain's sidekick Jackdaw to use his telepathic powers to bring about a peace brokered over a shared love of tea. Even under the thin veneer of metaphor this story perpetuates the myth of atavism that pervades many media by reducing the Troubles to a localized conflict, ignoring the colonial history and complicated political landscape underlying the violence.

Similarly, in the *Justice League Quarterly* story "Flight," the Irish hero Jack O'Lantern helps a pregnant fourteen-year-old girl from Northern Ireland get to London so that she can have an abortion, after a mob of "hardline Catholics" surround her home with flaming torches and later place a bomb on her plane. While the storyline is an extreme abstraction of the real-world conflict, it also fails to account for the roots of the division, with Jack O'Lantern reflecting, "This is what I'm up against in this community. Not a pack of evil super-villains like my cousin used to fight. Just your average citizen with a bad idea."[35] Moving to television, a similar example can be found in an episode of the environmentalist superhero show *Captain Planet and the Planeteers.*[36] In the episode titled "If It's Doomsday, This Must Be Belfast" one of the heroes, Wheeler, finds himself in Northern Ireland and "miles into Protestant territory." After observing the conflict Wheeler summarizes, "You got to be kidding, you beat each other up because of your names?" to which the leader of a Protestant gang responds, "It's as good a reason as any." Film scholar Ruth Barton describes how such simplifications of sectarian violence have allowed the British government "to be represented as honest broker in a battle between two sides of warring fanatics. Why those fanatics should have arrived at that point is considered to be a matter in the so far distant past as to be unworthy of consideration."[37]

Apes and Angels

These two broad traditions for depicting the Irish—the ape and the angel—are often employed simultaneously by creators to achieve dramatic contrast. For instance, in *Web of Spider-Man* #20–22 photojournalist Peter Parker is sent by the *Daily Bugle* newspaper to investigate terrorism in the

United Kingdom. Following the trail to Ireland, Peter travels "through some of the most beautiful countryside on the face of the Earth" before arriving on a scene that he describes as "more like Berlin during World War II."[38] These exaggerated moments achieve a stark juxtaposition by playing on widely recognized conventions: ape and angel, war zone and Eden, and hawk and dove.[39]

Often these conventions are realized in a single hero. For instance, Shamrock (aka Molly Fitzgerald) was an Irish superhero created for Marvel's *Contest of Champions* comic book series. In her first panel the caption reads, "In Northern Ireland, a group of school children stare as their lives are saved from a terrorist bomb" with the image depicting the emerald avenger throwing the explosive into the air. Thus, from her very first appearance Shamrock was rooted in sectarian violence.[40] In later appearances it is revealed the Shamrock gained her superpowers when her father, a Republican terrorist, asked the heavens to grant his son the abilities to defeat his enemies. However, it was Molly who was gifted with "luck" powers. Yet Shamrock is described as a "reluctant superhero," eventually retiring to "teach grammar school in Dublin." A red-haired maiden who speaks in the now conventional Irish accent—"Begorrah! Tisn't Ireland we've been sent to teammates"—and whose powers are blind luck rather than ability, Shamrock conforms to Curtis's angel while her terrorist father evokes the ape.[41]

This apes and angels dichotomy is so embedded in the DNA of Irish superheroes that even those characters identified as Irish American continue the theme. Paul Young notes in his book *Frank Miller's Daredevil and the Ends of Heroism* that from the first issue Daredevil's father, the boxer Battlin' Jack Murdock, had "a working-class Irish vibe."[42] When Irish-American writer-artist Frank Miller began his celebrated run on the character he relied on familiar stereotypes to emphasize Daredevil's Irish American roots. For instance, Jack became a hard-drinking wreck who was physically abusive to the young Matt Murdock, while the hero's previously deceased mother was revealed to be alive and living as a nun. If Miller's apes and angels contrast was not obvious enough, the first appearance of Murdock's mother re-creates the Pietà with Margret Murdock as the Virgin Mary in full habit.[43]

As Naja Later notes in her chapter that opens this part, Captain America's origin is particularly prone to revisions and expansions. In 2012 the star-spangled hero's background was revisited in a storyline that detailed Steve Rogers's childhood as the son of Irish immigrants growing up in a New York tenement. Conforming to type, Steve's father is an abusive drunk who believes that his inability to find work is because "the foreman hates Irish," while his mother is a paragon of virtue.[44] Similarly, when Miguel O'Hara, the Spider-Man of 2099, was introduced in 1992 he also had an abusive Irish

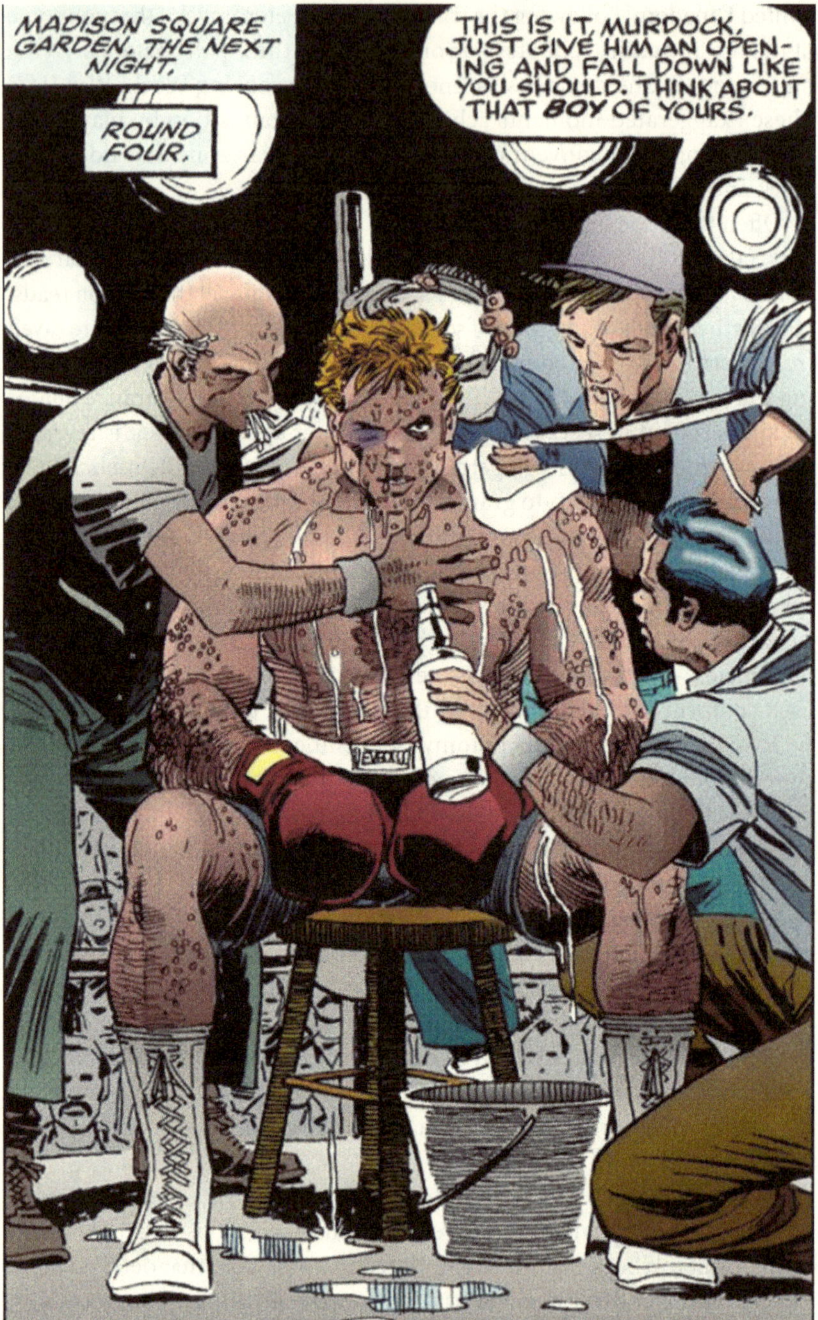

Figures 15.4 (above) and 15.5 (opposite). Frank Miller's Daredevil is the son of the apes and angels dichotomy often used to depict the Irish. *Daredevil: The Man Without Fear* #1 (New York: Marvel, October 1993) and *Daredevil* #229 (New York: Marvel, April 1986), respectively.

father, suggesting that Marvel had anticipated that the Irish would continue to be apes and angels well into the twenty-first century.[45]

Irish Cultural Nationalism and Comics

The Spirit creator Will Eisner describes comic book stereotypes as an "accursed necessity," which are used to succinctly convey a message to the reader.[46] Nonetheless, Scott McCloud warns in *Making Comics* that "some prejudices can creep in" when using such seemingly innocuous character types, explaining that "every stereotype comes from somewhere, and that place may not always be obvious."[47] Indeed, the conventions for depicting the Irish used by today's comic book creators are rarely politically charged, but rather, as Walshe argues, they are designed to lend the Irish characters "a greater degree of verisimilitude."[48]

However, as superhero comics featuring Irish characters tend to be produced by international creators, they frequently rely on outdated, often atavistic, conventions. For instance, following the X-Men storyline that depicted Ireland as a premodern paradise, one Dublin-based reader wrote in a letter that was published in a subsequent issue, "I did spot one big mistake. We don't have steam locomotives any more in Ireland," to which the editor responded, "[The writer] Chris [Claremont] was so shocked by your statement that Ireland has no more steam locomotives that he decided to fly over there to check things out for himself. And, sure enough, Kevin, you're absolutely right; the locos are either diesel or electric," with the reader being awarded a "No-Prize," Marvel's honor for those readers who identify story errors and continuity gaffes.[49]

Yet much of the responsibility for perpetuating these simplistic conventions rests with the Irish themselves. At the time of Victorian cartoons a cultural nationalist movement emerged in Ireland to augment political efforts. To emphasize a distinct Irish national identity this cultural movement defined itself in opposition to the modern, urban Britain by focusing on tradition, rural life, and the Catholic religion. However, as McLoone notes, "In accepting and promoting a romantic rural sense of Irish identity, therefore, cultural nationalism ironically accepted one of the great stereotypes of Ireland produced by imperialism."[50] The influence of the cultural nationalist movement is still evident in Ireland today. Local media often position the country for what sociologist John Urry describes as the "tourist gaze" with promotional materials, films, and other aspects of culture making use of widely recognized, but antiquated conventions.[51] Thus, it would be myopic to criticize international comic creators for using the stereotypes the Irish themselves often employ to promote the country and its various outputs.

This irony is deftly satirized in Garth Ennis's 1991 Judge Dredd story arc "Emerald Isle." As an Irish creator Ennis was well positioned to subvert the stereotypes and misconceptions held about Ireland, while also highlighting the role that the Irish play in promoting them. In the story future lawman Dredd investigates the death of an ambassador killed with a roast potato. Dredd's search brings him to the Emerald Isle (formerly Ireland), which was developed as a "theme park" littered with stereotypes from Ireland's past including leprechauns, thatched cottages, and potatoes. Ultimately the assassins are revealed to be the terrorist group Sons of Erin, whose aim is "no more patronising our entire nation for the stereotyped garbage in a tourist brochure."[52] "Emerald Isle" raises oft-ignored questions about the disconnect between the stereotypes of Ireland and the reality, as well as the complicity of the Irish in fostering the images they so often condemn.

Super Patriots and Irish Comic Book Creators

Discussing Irish cinema, McLoone observed how the absence of local filmmakers has allowed overseas images and conventions to circulate "in culture generally as markers of 'Irishness.' As such, they have been as influential at the point of consumption in Ireland as they have been elsewhere."[53] Similarly, in the past Irish comic creators have been rare, with the few comics that did appear often relying on wider stereotypes. For instance, *Our Boys*, an Irish version of British magazine *Boys' Own*, featured the Irish-language strip *Tír na nÓg*, which, conforming to type, had a leprechaun as the hero.[54]

Originally from County Down in Northern Ireland, *Preacher* creator Garth Ennis was arguably the first Irish comic book professional to gain an international reputation. His breakout book was *Troubled Souls*, which first appeared in the short-lived but critically acclaimed British comics anthology *Crisis*. The Belfast-set drama tells the story of a young man caught up in sectarian violence. When interviewed about his intentions for the 1989 story, Ennis explained, "Certainly I wanted to avoid the usual comic book treatment of Northern Ireland, although even at that point there was precious little. I think it did crop up now and again in Batman and Spider-Man [on being shown the Belfast-set Spider-Man story described earlier] I remember someone showing me this, it might even have been [*Troubled Souls* artist] John McCrea, and thinking 'Well we won't do it like this.'"[55] *Troubled Souls* challenged representations of Ireland, providing a story where Eden is an illusion, revolutionaries are rarely romantic, and modern conflicts defy Manichean simplifications. Following this success, Ennis maintained an interest in his homeland peppering his U.S. comics with

Irish characters such as the vampire Cassidy (*Preacher*), *Hitman* Tommy Monaghan, and Constantine love interest Kit Ryan (*Hellblazer*). Yet Ennis was a lone voice throughout the 1990s and the early 2000s, a shortfall that was redressed in the 2010s when Ireland finally began to enjoy a period of sustained comic production.

Irish creator Will Sliney attributes Ireland's increased comic book production to the web's ability to narrow boundaries: "I think it basically boiled down to people realizing here that you could do those kind of jobs; I would imagine there was plenty of generations of artists before us that would have had the same interest, but they wouldn't have had had the same reach because they weren't able to show their work online."[56] The key publishers in this recent growth include Atomic Diner, the publishing arm of the Irish comic book chain Sub City, which has built a shared superhero universe that incorporates titles such as *The League of Volunteers*, *Black Scorpion*, and *Glimmer Man*.[57] Button Press Publications describes itself as the home of "All-ages Irish superhero action and adventure!!" with interrelated titles like *The Wren*, *Artos*, and *Thimble*.[58] Other publishers include Mayo Print, which focuses on Irish language titles, and O'Brien Press, which made tentative steps into comics by publishing historical graphic novels like *Blood upon the Rose: Easter 1916, the Rebellion That Set Ireland Free*, but later moved into mythological action with books such as Sliney's *Celtic Warrior: The Legend of Cú Chulainn*.[59]

These Irish books regularly emphasize their status as local titles. For instance, the cover of the first issue of *The League of Volunteers* features a blurb from BBC News that announces, "After 72 years of importing characters from America, the emerald age of superheroes may be about to dawn."[60] Similarly, the introduction to the first collection of *The Wren* reads, "Button Press staff like all sensible people love comic books, especially superhero action and adventure! We wanted to see this same adventure happen above the streets of Irish cities."[61] One of the ways that these local books articulate their Irish identity is through national-themed heroes.

When U.S. publisher Marvel Comics introduced the Irish hero Shamrock in *Contest of Champions*, she appeared alongside a cadre of other international heroes including Blitzkrieg (Germany), Collective Man (China), and Talisman (Australia).[62] Dittmer argues that this is a "false equivalency" that "elides the role of American power in producing its global hegemony" as "these superheroes never get their own comics in 'our' world."[63] However, the recent development of an Irish comic book industry has seen nationally themed heroes receive their own titles. For instance, the lineup for the superhero team the Celtic Clan includes an axe-wielding St Patrick, a mutated former boxer the Celtic Tiger, and a domino-mask-wearing version of real-life Irish revolutionary leader Michael

Collins.[64] Demonstrating their compatibility with the national heroes that were the focus of Dittmer's research, the Celtic Clan made their first appearance in the international crossover series *The War of the Independents*, where they teamed up with Canada's Captain Canuck.[65]

In fact, Dittmer suggests that Captain Canuck and other "Canadian attempts at superhero publishing tend to be much more self-consciously nationalist; perhaps as a result of Canadian concern over being subsumed within American culture."[66] Similarly, the heroes created by Irish comic book professionals are often explicitly nationalistic in part to distinguish the characters from international examples. For instance, in *Celtic Knights* the villain is a bowler-hat-wearing British "arms trader" who plans to "take control of the British Isles," only to be reminded by the hero Rubenette that "Ireland isn't Britain."[67]

Sovereignty is a recurring theme across these books. The formation of the Irish superhero team League of Volunteers is positioned in the first issue as a necessary step to maintain Ireland's independence and neutrality during World War II, with the Emerald Scorpion, remarking, "I've heard all about our apparent need for mystery men now that we're under pressure from both sides [i.e., Allied and Axis forces]."[68] Yet, there is an inevitable tension in adopting a U.S. trope, the superhero, in books that claim to be "100% Irish."[69] This uncertainty is acknowledged on the page, with a degree of skepticism expressed by many characters and the larger books. For instance, in the 1939-set *Glimmer Man* Irish taoiseach (prime minister) Éamon de Valera attempts to recruit former solider James Quinn as a costumed hero, explaining, "Our friends in America have shown how a super patriot can inspire a generation to give their all for their country" to which James responds, "If Ireland needs heroes . . . why do you feel the need to have them hide who they are?"[70] Reinforcing the view prevalent in superhero comics and cultural nationalism alike that symbols are more important than the people behind them, the politician counters, "You wouldn't be hiding in the uniform you'd be wearing a symbol of Ireland." Although James accepts the mantle of the Glimmer Man he refuses a U.S.-provided supersolider serum. As he later reflects, "The only conscious thought I had in that tunnel was that Ireland would have its symbol that night . . . and that symbol would be an Irishman . . . and nothing other than an Irishman."[71] Thus, while the comic utilizes the convention of the American super patriot, like many Irish titles it draws on local politics and history to maintain a distinct identity.

Another way creators have mollified this tension between Irish identity and perceived American cultural imperialism is to root these characters in Irish mythology. As a comparatively new nation, the United States lacked an obvious folkloric tradition, a vacuum superheroes helped fill. However, as Grant Morrison notes of British heroes, "Local legend could always be relied upon to produce superheroes from whole cloth."[72] Similarly, Irish creators have frequently drawn on local myth to develop their heroes. For instance, the Irish legendary warrior Cú Chulainn not only gets a Kirby-esque biography in *Celtic Warrior* but also is evoked in comics such as *The Wren*, *Hound*, and *Big Bastard*.

In the final pages of *Celtic Warrior* creator Sliney links the mythological Cú Chulainn with Irish revolutionary leader Michael Collins, over a montage of heroes "who fought for us so that every generation of the Irish people can assert their right to freedom and sovereignty."[73] In *On the Origin of Superheroes* Chris Gavaler demonstrates the close proximity of the superhero to the revolutionary, explaining, "Oppression is radiation. It's the original cosmic gamma ray bomb [or] spider-bite mutation that births the superhero," later adding, "Superheroes love oppression. It justifies their revolutionary instincts."[74] The boundary between the superhero and revolutionary collapses completely in Irish comics, with real-life Republican figures such as Michael Collins, Wolfe Tone, and Countess Markievicz reimagined as superheroes in books like *The League of Volunteers*, *Celtic Clan*, and *The Crimson Blade*.[75] Reflecting on the parallels, Atomic Diner publisher and writer Robert Curley noted how revolutionaries, like superheroes, "operate outside the given law at the time for what they see as the betterment of society, sometimes under the cover of night, and they are not always popular with the general public. . . . I do see a lot similarities."[76]

Although Irish comics rework the revolutionary as a superhero, they also highlight the political and historical issues omitted or glossed over by international titles. In this manner many contemporary Irish comics, particularly those from Atomic Diner, challenge the atavistic portrayals of Ireland identified earlier. For example, the first issue of *The Crimson Blade* focuses on the influence of the American and French revolutions on the Irish Rebellion of 1798. There is also a sustained effort to unpack the dichotomies that pervade depictions of Ireland. *Glimmer Man* and *The League of Volunteers* acknowledge that Irish people served on both sides of the Spanish Civil War. Further dispelling lazy contrasts, Protestant characters in *The Crimson Blade* are among the staunchest supporters of an Irish Free State.

Similarly, while these books engage with the Irish Republican struggle, they often avoid unabashed celebration. For instance, superhero books *Black Scorpion* and *The League of Volunteers* highlight how many Irish people fought as part of the British forces during World War I. This part of Irish history is often ignored due to the celebration of the 1916 Easter Rising.[77] Writer Curley notes, "We seem to have brushed [Irish involvement in World War I] under the carpet and created our own mythology around 1916, and obviously not all of it was true. When the League came out and we acknowledged that Irish people fought in the war it was amazing the amount of emails we got from people saying, it was great because their grandfather had done that and it was nice to see something positive about it."[78]

To conclude, it is useful to return to the Victorian examples that opened this chapter. Curtis notes how Irish artists during the Home Rule movement would attempt to challenge the stereotypes found in British magazines, but these nationalist cartoons were "blunt banderillas that failed to puncture John Bull's tough old hide. Few Englishmen ever saw Dublin's weekly complement of political cartoons."[79] Unfortunately, due to their limited print runs and distribution, the influence of these Irish comics beyond Ireland's borders (or even within) is similarly limited.

However, while locally produced comics may not have much international impact, they are a breeding ground for new creators. As Will Sliney, who transitioned from his early Irish comics to drawing Spider-Man for Marvel, explained, "As the industry here is growing, and people's reputations are growing, [international publishers] are coming here to find our stories," with the artist suggesting that "per capita, we probably have more people working in Marvel than anyone else."[80] Indeed, Sliney joins a host of Irish creators such as Stephen Byrne, Declan Shalvey, and Maura McHugh who began their careers working for Irish publisher Atomic Diner before moving on to U.S. superhero titles like *Justice League*, *Deadpool*, and *Hellboy*.

These creators are now in a position to redress outdated conventions in international publications. For instance, Shalvey recently published the Limerick-set graphic novel *Savage Town* with U.S. publisher Image Comics. Shalvey described how he wanted "to show how Ireland is a great place but . . . not the picturesque tourist postcard image that everybody has gotten used to seeing."[81] Shalvey, like his contemporaries, has never been better positioned to dismantle outdated conventions and allow a more balanced depiction of Ireland to flourish on the page. In the future, perhaps, Irish superheroes will no longer simply be apes and angels but rounded characters that challenge simple stereotypes and the prejudices that they conceal.

Notes

1 Stan Lee, telephone interview by author, November 25, 2007.

2 Jason Dittmer, *Captain America and the Nationalist Superhero: Metaphors, Narratives, and Geopolitics* (Philadelphia: Temple University Press, 2013), 3.

3 The Irish Home Rule movement formally began in 1870 with the founding of the Home Government Association pressure group by Irish barrister Isaac Butt. The goal was to achieve Irish self-government within the United Kingdom of Great

Britain and Ireland. The Home Rule movement continued until the War of Independence (1919–1921), which concluded with the signing of the Anglo-Irish Treaty. The treaty led to the partition of Ireland's thirty-two counties. The Irish Free State of twenty-six counties was established on 6 December 1922, while the six counties of the loyalist-dominated Northern Ireland remained in the United Kingdom.

4 Shane Walshe, "'Ah, Laddie, Did Ye Really Think I'd Let a Foine Broth of a Boy Such as Yerself Get Splattered . . . ?' Representations of Irish English Speech in the Marvel Universe," in *Linguistics and the Study of Comics*, ed. Frank Bramlett (Houndmills: Palgrave Macmillan, 2012), 264.

5 L. Perry Curtis, *Apes and Angels: The Irishman in Victorian Caricature*, rev. ed. (Washington, DC: Smithsonian Institution Press, 1997).

6 Michael de Nie, "Pigs, Paddies, Prams and Petticoats: Irish Home Rule and the British Comic Press, 1886–93," *History Ireland* 13, no. 1 (2005): 43.

7 Curtis, *Apes and Angels*, xxiv.

8 Curtis, *Apes and Angels*, 64.

9 On the *Happy Hooligan* website Max Sparber notes how some have argued that Happy Hooligan was not explicitly Irish. Yet as Sparber points out, "Happy borrows from a well-established Vaudeville tradition, the Irish tramp, and in his earliest illustrations he looks perilously similar to one of Thomas Nast's anti-Irish cartoons, with brutish, almost simian features." Similarly, Curtis traces the origin of the term "hooliganism" to a "notorious family of East End Irish roughs named Houlihan." Sparber, "Happy Hooligan by Frederick Burr Opper," *Happy Hooligan*, August 19, 2014; Curtis, *Apes and Angels*, 174.

10 Curtis, *Apes and Angels*, 179.

11 Walshe, "'Ah, Laddie,'" 266.

12 Chris Murray, *The British Superhero* (Jackson: University Press of Mississippi, 2017), 15.

13 De Nie, "Pigs, Paddies, Prams and Petticoats," 42–43.

14 Martin McLoone, *Irish Film: The Emergence of a Contemporary Cinema* (London: British Film Institute, 2000), 36.

15 Roy Thomas, Werner Roth, et al., *X-Men* #28 (New York: Marvel, January 1967).

16 Len Wein, Dave Cockrum, et al., *Giant-Size X-Men* #1 (New York: Marvel, May 1975).

17 Curtis, *Apes and Angels*, xxi–xxii.

18 Curtis, *Apes and Angels*, xxii.

19 Len Wein, Chris Claremont, Dave Cockrum, et al., *Giant-Size X-Men* #1 (New York: Marvel, May 1975).

20 De Nie, "Pigs, Paddies, Prams and Petticoats," 44.

21 Thomas et al., *X-Men* #28.

22 Chris Claremont, Dave Cockrum, et al., *X-Men* #101 (New York: Marvel, October 1976).

23 Walshe, "'Ah, Laddie,'" 281.

24 Frank Miller, Jim Lee, et al., *X-Men* #3–7 (New York: DC Comics, December 2005–November 2007).

25 Pat Mills and Clint Langley, *Sláine: Books of Invasions* (Oxford: Rebellion / 2000 A.D., 2012).
26 Damon Lindelof, Francis Yu, et al., *Ultimate Wolverine vs. Hulk* #2 (New York: Marvel, February 2006).
27 McLoone, *Irish Film*, 34; de Nie, "Pigs, Paddies, Prams and Petticoats," 46; Ruth Barton, *Irish National Cinema* (London: Routledge, 2005), 150–151.
28 McLoone, *Irish Film*, 34.
29 Mike Catto, "Them & Them Us & US: Regional and National Stereotypes in British Comics," *Circa* 44 (1989): 23.
30 The Troubles was the term used locally to describe the often violent conflict in Northern Ireland from the late 1960s until the Good Friday Agreement of 1998. Key participants included the paramilitary groups the Provisional Irish Republican Army (IRA) and Ulster Volunteer Force (UVF). Much of the conflict was fueled by Northern Ireland's status as part of the United Kingdom and the tensions between those who wanted Northern Ireland to remain as part of the United Kingdom (loyalist) and those who wished to see the six counties return to a united Ireland (nationalist).
31 Curtis, *Apes and Angels*, 174.
32 Barton, *Irish National Cinema*, 158.
33 McLoone, *Irish Film*, 4.
34 Eric Nolen-Weathington, *Modern Masters Volume 1: Alan Davis* (Raleigh, NC: TwoMorrows, 2006), 33.
35 Steven T. Seagle, Frank Squillace, et al., "Flight," in *Justice League Quarterly* #14 (New York: DC Comics, March 1994).
36 Doug Molitor (writer), "If It's Doomsday, This Must Be Belfast," in *Captain Planet and the Planeteers*, season 3, episode 12, TBS, November 28, 1992 .
37 Barton, *Irish National Cinema*, 169.
38 David Michelinie, Marc Silvestri, et al., *Web of Spider-Man* #20–22 (New York: Marvel, November 1986–January 1987).
39 Another popular motif for representing Irish conflicts is the hawk and the dove, a violent figure and the more peaceful alternate. In *Web of Spider-Man* #22 Peter Parker, while in Northern Ireland, befriends a pacifist, Liam, who is searching for his brother, Rory, who has been taken by the Black Hoods terrorist cell. Although Liam does not find his brother, he is forced to shoot one of the Black Hoods to save the life of Peter's partner Joy. However, when Liam unmasks the terrorist he discovers that it is his brother Rory, who has become a terrorist. This convention, the hawk and the dove, is frequently used in depictions of sectarian violence to demonstrate the futility of conflict.
40 Mark Gruenwald, John Romita Jr., et al., *Marvel Super Hero Contest of Champion* #1 (New York: Marvel, June 1982).
41 Michael Gallagher, Collen Doran, et al., *Guardians of the Galaxy Annual* #3 (New York: Marvel, August 1993).
42 Paul Young, *Frank Miller's Daredevil and the Ends of Heroism* (New Brunswick, NJ: Rutgers University Press, 2016), 23.

43 Frank Miller, David Mazzucchelli, et al., "Born Again," in *Daredevil* #227–231 (New York: Marvel, February–June 1986); Frank Miller, John Romita Jr., et al., *Daredevil: The Man Without Fear* #1 (New York: Marvel, October 1993).
44 Rick Remender, John Romita Jr., et al., *Captain America* #1 (New York: Marvel, November 2012).
45 Peter David, Rick Leonardi, et al., *Spider-Man 2099* #10 (New York: Marvel, August 1993).
46 Will Eisner, *Graphic Storytelling and Visual Narrative* (Tamarac, FL: Poorhouse Press, 1996), 17.
47 Scott McCloud, *Making Comics: Storytelling Secrets of Comics, Manga and Graphic Novels* (New York: Harper, 2006), 124.
48 Walshe, "'Ah, Laddie,'" 270.
49 Chris Claremont, Dave Cockrum, et al., *X-Men* #104 (New York: Marvel, April 1977).
50 McLoone, *Irish Film*, 37.
51 John Urry, *The Tourist Gaze: Leisure and Travel in Contemporary Societies* (London: Sage, 1990), 1.
52 Garth Ennis, Steve Dillon, et al., "Emerald Isle," in *2000 A.D.* #727–732 (London: Egmont UK, April–May 1991).
53 McLoone, *Irish Film*, 4.
54 Catto, "Them & Them Us & US," 24.
55 Garth Ennis, interview by author, August 20, 2011.
56 Will Sliney, interview by author, June 9, 2014.
57 Robert Curley and Barry Keegan, *League of Volunteers* #1 (Dublin: Atomic Diner, February 2011); Robert Curley and Stephen Downey, *Black Scorpion* #1 (Dublin: Atomic Diner, July 2012); Robert Curley, Darrin O'Toole, et al., *The Glimmer Man* #1 (Dublin: Atomic Diner, September 2013).
58 Jason Connors, Mark Kirwan ,et al., *The Wren* #1 (Dublin: Button Press, August 2012); Mike Lynch, Jason Conor, et al., *Artos* #1 (Dublin: Button Press, October 2012); Jason Browne, Sarah Roe, et al., *Thimble* #1 (Dublin: Button Press, April 2015).
59 Gerry Hunt, *Blood upon the Rose: Easter 1916, the Rebellion That Set Ireland Free* (Dublin: O'Brien, 2010); Will Sliney, *Celtic Warrior: The Legend of Cú Chulainn* (Dublin: O'Brien, 2013).
60 Curley and Keegan, *League of Volunteers* #1.
61 Connors et al., *The Wren* #1.
62 Gruenwald et al., *Marvel Super Hero Contest of Champion* #1.
63 Dittmer, *Captain America*, 21.
64 Nigel Flood, Frank J. Right, et al., *Celtic Clan* #1 (Bray: Punt Press, October 2012).
65 Dave Ryan, Aurelio Mazzara, et al., *War of the Independents* #3 (New Jersey: Red Anvil, May 2012).
66 Dittmer, *Captain America*, 20.
67 Stephen Coffey, Mike Kennedy, et al., *Celtic Knights*, vol. 1 (CreateSpace, December 2014).

68 Curley and Keegan, *League of Volunteers* #1.
69 Button Press Publications, "About Button Press," www.buttonpresspublications .com/about.
70 Robert Curley, Darrin O'Toole, et al., *The Glimmer Man* #1–3 (Dublin: Atomic Diner, September 2013–May 2015).
71 Curley et al., *The Glimmer Man* #1–3.
72 Grant Morrison, *Supergods: Our World in the Age of the Superhero* (London: Jonathan Cape, 2012), 51.
73 Sliney, *Celtic Warrior*, 125.
74 Chris Gavaler, *On the Origin of Superheroes: From the Big Bang to Action Comics No. 1* (Iowa City: University of Iowa Press, 2015), 52–55.
75 Even a children's comic such as *The Wren* is informed by this interest in revolutionary history, with the comic's Avengers-like superhero team named the Flying Column in an allusion to the guerrilla groups that fought the Irish War of Independence.
76 Robert Curley, telephone interview by author, October 23, 2017.
77 The Easter Rising was an armed rebellion that took place primarily in Dublin in 1916. Hoping to take advantage of Britain's focus on World War I, Irish rebels occupied key strategic locations and proclaimed an Irish Republic. Although the rebellion would last only one week, the execution of its leaders by the British government changed public sentiment, giving rise to the Irish War of Independence and ultimately leading to the establishment of an Irish Free State in 1922.
78 Curley telephone interview.
79 Curtis, *Apes and Angels*, 82.
80 Will Sliney, interview by author, June 9, 2014.
81 Joe Leogue, "New Crime Comic Book from Irish Artist to Be Set in Limerick," *Examiner* (Cork), March 8, 2017, www.irishexaminer.com/ireland/new-crime -comic-book-from-irish-artist-to-be-set-in-limerick-444618.html.

Bibliography

Barton, Ruth. *Irish National Cinema*. London: Routledge, 2005.

Button Press Publications. "About Button Press." www.buttonpresspublications.com /about.

Catto, Mike. "Them & Them Us & US: Regional and National Stereotypes in British Comics." *Circa* 44 (1989): 22–24.

Curley, Robert. Telephone interview by author, October 23, 2017.

Curtis, L. Perry. *Apes and Angels: The Irishman in Victorian Caricature*. Revised ed. Washington, DC: Smithsonian Institution Press, 1997.

de Nie, Michael. "Pigs, Paddies, Prams and Petticoats: Irish Home Rule and the British Comic Press, 1886–93." *History Ireland* 13, no. 1 (2005): 42–47.

Dittmer, Jason. *Captain America and the Nationalist Superhero: Metaphors, Narratives, and Geopolitics*. Philadelphia: Temple University Press, 2013.

Eisner, Will. *Graphic Storytelling and Visual Narrative*. Tamarac, FL: Poorhouse Press, 1996.

Ennis, Garth. Interview by author, August 20, 2011.

Ennis, Garth, and John McCrea. *Troubled Souls*. London: Fleetway Publications, 1990.

Gavaler, Chris. *On the Origin of Superheroes: From the Big Bang to Action Comics No. 1*. Iowa City: University of Iowa Press, 2015.

Hunt, Gerry. *Blood upon the Rose: Easter 1916, the Rebellion That Set Ireland Free*. Dublin: O'Brien, 2010.

Lee, Stan. Telephone interview by author, November 25, 2007.

Leogue, Joe. "New Crime Comic Book from Irish Artist to Be Set in Limerick." *Examiner* (Cork), March 8, 2017. www.irishexaminer.com/ireland/new-crime-comic-book-from-irish-artist-to-be-set-in-limerick-444618.html.

McCloud, Scott. *Making Comics: Storytelling Secrets of Comics, Manga and Graphic Novels*. New York: Harper, 2006.

McLoone, Martin. *Irish Film: The Emergence of a Contemporary Cinema*. London: British Film Institute, 2000.

Mills, Pat, and Clint Langley. *Sláine: Books of Invasions*. Oxford: Rebellion / 2000 A.D., 2012.

Molitor, Doug (writer). "If It's Doomsday, This Must Be Belfast." In *Captain Planet and the Planeteers*. TBS, November 28, 1992.

Morrison, Grant. *Supergods: Our World in the Age of the Superhero*. London: Jonathan Cape, 2012.

Murray, Chris. *The British Superhero*. Jackson: University Press of Mississippi, 2017.

Nolen-Weathington, Eric. *Modern Masters Volume 1: Alan Davis*. Raleigh, NC: TwoMorrows, 2006.

Sliney, Will. *Celtic Warrior: The Legend of Cú Chulainn*. Dublin: O'Brien, 2013.

———. Interview by author, June 9, 2014.

Sparber, Max. "Happy Hooligan by Frederick Burr Opper." *Happy Hooligan*. August 19, 2014.

Tenniel, John. "Two Forces." Cartoon. *Punch*, October 29, 1881.

Urry, John. *The Tourist Gaze: Leisure and Travel in Contemporary Societies*. London: Sage, 1990.

Walshe, Shane. "'Ah, Laddie, Did Ye Really Think I'd Let a Foine Broth of a Boy Such as Yerself Get Splattered . . . ?' Representations of Irish English Speech in the Marvel Universe." In *Linguistics and the Study of Comics*, edited by Frank Bramlett, 264–290. Houndmills: Palgrave Macmillan, 2012.

Young, Paul. *Frank Miller's Daredevil and the Ends of Heroism*. New Brunswick, NJ: Rutgers University Press, 2016.

16

Missing in Action

The Late Development of the German-Speaking Superhero

PAUL M. MALONE

The skies and streets of German-speaking Europe are suddenly teeming with superheroes. *Captain Berlin* battles madmen and Nazis in the German capital; to the south, *Tracht Man* dons a Bavarian costume to combat evil.[1] Next door Captain Austria, Jr., leads the *Austrian Super Heroes* against rampaging monsters.[2] In Switzerland William Tell has returned to fight new oppressors; and even former East Germans, thirty years after the Wall fell, can rejoice that the "Border Angel," who once teleported defectors to the West, still lives among them.[3]

However, these are recent developments. Long after the Second World War, economic, social, and political factors hindered the creation of German-speaking superheroes. Indeed, for three decades the small, import-dominated comic market hardly published comics by German creators. Original German-language comics began appearing regularly only in the 1980s, but not until the turn of the century was it possible to envision a German superhero; it took longer still for the idea to find an audience.

The roots of these issues lie in the war and its aftermath. The original American superhero, Jerry Siegel and Joe Shuster's *Superman*, was still young in the spring of 1940, when *Das schwarze Korps*, weekly newspaper of the SS, published the article "Jerry Siegel Goes on the Attack."[4] This was a response to Superman's appearance in a strip for *Look* magazine, in which the hero delivered both Hitler and that *other* man of steel, Joseph Stalin, to the international court for trial.[5] Gunter d'Alquen's article describes writer Siegel as "circumcised in mind and body" and suggests that Superman, far from being an Aryan *Übermensch* (the Nietzschean "superman" appropriated by the Nazis), is a brainless goon who ought to be speaking Yiddish.

Anti-Semitism aside, the article's contempt for the supposedly superficial, commercialized nature of American culture echoed the sentiments of many Germans who otherwise rejected Nazi ideology but nonetheless believed in the innate superiority of German *Kultur*. Despite d'Alquen's attempt to disavow any connection between Superman and the ideals of the master race, this connection, combined with anti-American sentiment, was used after the war to argue against the acceptance of superhero comics.

It was possible, of course, to transfer the superhero into other national contexts. In his study *The British Superhero*, Chris Murray observes, "The range of modes of representation found in British superhero comics, from reverence to parody, illuminates the complexity of British feelings toward America, its foreign policy, and the dominance of its culture, as well as positioning the superhero as a figure that can be appropriated and reshaped as a tool of resistance to American political and military authority."[6] British superheroes, however, developed in a preexisting comic industry, which Germany lacked; and postwar Britain still saw itself as America's political equal and partner in victory. Germany was the loser, occupied and divided into the Federal Republic of Germany in the west and the German Democratic Republic in the east, with the Iron Curtain running between them.[7]

Defeated Germany was surrounded by neighbors whom it had recently invaded, subjugated, and plundered and millions of whose citizens it had murdered. From this point, "Germany's Nazi past provided the 'basic narrative' of the Federal Republic between 1949 and 1990, making any identification with the nation contentious as well as difficult."[8] West Germany not only needed to be rebuilt economically; the country also had to be relegitimized politically through acts of restitution and reconciliation. The 1950s' "economic miracle" enabled the country to enter the Common Market, agree to reparations to Israel, and rearm to support NATO against Soviet expansion. However, for West Germans at least the "patriotic narratives" that Murray ascribes to American superhero comics, and which British superheroes were free to appropriate, parody, or subvert,[9] were no longer permissible. Rather, "the question of guilt became part of the self-image of the emerging new Germany."[10] Furthermore, "resistance to American political and military authority" was impossible in a Federal Republic occupied by the United States and its allies. Only in the cultural realm could American hegemony be resisted.

Conservative West German chancellor Konrad Adenauer feared Americanization—with its "materialism" (*Materialismus*) and "massification" (*Vermassung*)—as much as he feared socialism or communism.[11] Left-wing Germans, meanwhile, also felt that American-style capitalism was dehumanizing and could slide into oligarchy and resurgent fascism.[12] Few American cultural phenomena seemed to embody this dilemma more than the comic book superhero, who fought in the name of justice for all yet embodied specifically American values of individualism and vigilantism. Germans nervous about American comics took heart, however, to see even critics in the United States raising doubts regarding the superhero's value. For instance, in his 1954 book *Seduction of the Innocent*, psychiatrist Fredric Wertham describes Superman as a fascist "with the big S on his uniform—we should, I suppose, be thankful that it is not an S.S."[13] Wertham repeatedly draws attention to "the Nietzsche-Nazi myth of the exceptional man who is beyond good and evil," "the superman philosophy," "ideology," "conceit," or "cult."[14] Wertham even quotes a letter to the *New York Times* criticizing the use of Marshall Plan funds to distribute American comics in Germany, which asks, "Have the Germans not had enough of supermen?"[15] German authorities, unaware that Wertham was German-born and educated and shared many of their own cultural attitudes, cited him as an American witness that comics were pernicious; his warnings against "re-Nazification" set the tone for the critical reception, and rejection, of superheroes in Germany and Austria.[16]

However, actual sales of superhero comics in West Germany hardly warranted such angst. In 1950, before Wertham's warnings crossed the Atlantic, Superman had already made this journey under the title *Supermann*. His Metropolis was a German city, where reporters Klaus Kent and Luise Lang work for Peter Weiss.[17] With two-color covers, black-and-white interiors, and cheap paper, *Supermann* was overpriced for young readers' budgets before Germany's economic recovery. Furthermore, only one short Superman story in each issue, taken from contemporary DC comics, was insufficient to acquaint German readers with what had become a complex mythos; and the rotating cast of second-string heroes in the backup features offered no continuity. The comic lasted only three issues before the publisher folded.

The Danish Aller Verlag then revived *Supermann* in an anthology comic, *Buntes Allerlei* (Colorful Assortment), which originally featured American newspaper comic strips. From October 1953 Aller licensed Superman, Batman, and other DC characters. Supermann was now mild-mannered Karl Kent, working with Linda Lane. However, superheroes did not sell comics. *Buntes Allerlei* went from weekly to biweekly publication and the price rose from forty-five to fifty pfennigs, to no avail. By the comic's final issue in August 1954, it had resorted to DC's now-forgotten funny animal series, such as *Fox and Crow*, *Flippity and Flop*, and *Tito and His Burrito*.[18]

It would seem that Germans had indeed had enough of supermen, or at least of supermen pretending to be Germans. Yet at the same time Danish publisher Ehapa Verlag's license to import Disney's *Micky Maus* was reaping huge profits; Walter Lehning Verlag and Gerstmayer Verlag were successfully selling comics about the knightly *Sigurd* and *Robinson Crusoe*, respectively; and Western series such as *Pecos Bill* and *Texas* were also popular. However, strict censorship of even mild violence and sexual imagery in children's books was brought in after May 1954, causing increasing difficulties for the smaller publishers of adventure comics. By the mid-1960s Lehning and Gerstmayer had gone under, leaving international giant Ehapa with its family-friendly Disney comics and a market dependent upon foreign firms and imported licenses.

Thus in 1965, when literary scholar Alfred C. Baumgärtner criticized adventure heroes as fascists along Wertham's lines in his book *Die Welt der Comics* (The World According to Comics), there had been no German superhero comics for a decade.[19] Baumgärtner's fears that children's books might inculcate fascism reflected the reemergence of the past in West German society, as the Frankfurt Auschwitz trials had begun in 1963. After two years, seventeen of twenty-two former Auschwitz extermination camp officials were convicted and sentenced.[20] However, this engagement with history was quickly suppressed; trial judges and media alike treated the defendants as amoral outliers, reassuring the public that normal Germans could not have committed such atrocities.[21]

Only a year after Baumgärtner's book, with censorship somewhat relaxed, Ehapa Verlag—home of *Micky Maus*—made a renewed attempt in 1966 to publish DC superheroes, while new rival Bildschriftenverlag (later Williams Verlag) began importing Marvel material. Neither publisher localized these stories: from this point on American superheroes in German translation remained comfortably far away in the exotic land of gangsters, skyscrapers, and yellow taxi cabs. However, it was difficult winning fans when these comics were frustrating to read. DC and Marvel had developed complex continuities among their various series, but the German licensees published stories out of order; shortened them by omitting panels or entire pages; and released different series out of sync, making cross-references so obscure that they required footnotes. At the same time, the colloquial dialogue, especially in Marvel Comics, often stumped translators, resulting in bizarre misunderstandings, such as the infamous rendering of Marvel editor Stan Lee's traditional sign-off "'Nuff said!" as "Das sagte Nuff!" (literally, "That's what Nuff said," whoever Nuff might be).[22] Finally, different translators, working in isolation, sometimes gave characters different German names or reverted to their English names within the same issue. Thus, the Flash might appear as *Roter Blitz* (Red Lightning) or *Blitzmann* (Lightning Man); Iron Man could be *Eisenmann*, *Der Eiserne* (The Iron One), or *Erzkämpfer* (Ore Fighter); and Daredevil did business as *Devil-Man* or *Der Dämon* (The

Demon). Though Ehapa's *Superman* (with one "n") lasted over four hundred issues, sales in general remained lukewarm, and both DC and Marvel licenses hopped from publisher to publisher for the next two decades.

By comparison, German publishers began licensing Franco-Belgian *bandes dessinées* in the mid-1960s. Creators of *bandes dessinées* were treated as *auteurs*, and their works were published in order, uncut, and faithfully translated. This wave imported Germany's first ersatz superhero: Willy Vandersteen's *Wastl*, "the strong man with the heart of gold" (in the original Flemish *Jerom*, and in French *Jérôme*).[23] A humorous character, Wastl is a caveman brought to the present by time travel, where he fights evil in gold tights and a cape. Clearly not only Germans but Europeans in general had difficulty taking the superhero trope seriously. In his four-year publishing career in Germany in the early 1970s, Wastl outlasted some of his serious American counterparts, yet neither he nor they inspired local imitators.

The 1970s saw considerable changes, however, in West Germany's relationship to its history, as two decades of conservative leadership gave way to the socialist governments of Willy Brandt and his successor Helmut Schmidt. On December 7, 1970 Brandt spontaneously fell to his knees in contrition at the monument to the 1943 Warsaw Jewish ghetto uprising in Poland, which German studies scholar Ingrid Laurien describes as "a symbolic gesture that set the tone for the whole younger generation."[24] From that moment education about the Nazi era increased, until the January 1979 broadcast of the 1978 American television series *Holocaust* placed the question of German responsibility at the center of public discourse.[25] In this climate the first postwar generation embraced a critical counterculture that eschewed pro-establishment superheroes in favor of provocative underground comics, both American and homegrown.

This underground sensibility informed the first German-speaking superhero in the 1980s: *Flattermann*. Interestingly, this hero hailed not from West Germany but from Austria. Austria's attitude to its history long depended on the *Opfermythos* or "victim myth." In 1943 the Allies' Moscow Declaration had proclaimed Austria—annexed by Germany in March 1938—the Nazis' first victim. As a result, although individual Austrian Nazis were punished, there was little sense of collective guilt or responsibility prior to the "Waldheim affair."[26] Without these pressures Kurt and Wenzel Kofron's *Flattermann* was free to satirize contemporary issues such as the energy crisis, championship football, and the nuclear arms race.[27] Beer-bellied Johannes Flattermann is the last in a line of superheroes in Metropolis, a city much like Vienna. Not terribly intelligent, he is incapable of solving crimes without the aid of his would-be adversary, Professor Irrwahn Grausewitz (Madmania Gruewit), whose sole ambition is to win the Nobel Prize at any cost. Grausewitz could easily defeat Flattermann, but instead finds himself continually dragooned into helping the good-natured dullard. The three-volume series ends with the world destroyed by nuclear war and the protagonists trapped in the past, where Grausewitz at least gets to meet Alfred Nobel. As with *Wastl*, *Flattermann* depends on a recognition of American models for its basic premise; the hero wears a costume like Batman's, but like Superman he has superhuman strength and can fly. Unlike the toothless Belgian strip, however, *Flattermann* savages Austrian society's officiousness, the violent competitiveness that lies under its polite veneer (personified by Grausewitz), and the incompetence of its intelligence service and police force. Although the country's name is never mentioned, Flattermann is positioned as the superhero Austria deserves.[28] It is unfortunate that the series, and the publisher, did not continue into the post-Waldheim era.

It was the Americans who would be the first to demonstrate the challenge of creating a serious German superhero. In 1991, in a recurring backup feature in Marvel's *Captain America*, Hauptmann Deutschland (Captain Germany) and his teammates Blitzkrieger and Zeitgeist kidnap the evil Red Skull and transport him home for trial and execution.[29] The Hauptmann is a mirror image of Captain America as "nationalist superhero," which political geographer Jason Dittmer describes as a subgenre in which American political hegemony is justified by "false equivalency": every country has its own national hero and therefore appears to participate on a level playing field.[30]

However, this example demonstrates the difficulty of constructing a German nationalist superhero on the American model when the "Golden Age" of such American superheroes corresponds to Germany's darkest hour morally.[31] Indeed, Captain America himself debuted delivering a roundhouse punch to the jaw of Adolf Hitler.[32] This difficulty became particularly acute following the collapse of the German Democratic Republic and the rapid reunification of Germany. In the light of conservative chancellor Helmut Kohl's 1982 remark that "the grace of late birth" meant that his generation "no longer had to bear the burden of collective guilt personally,"[33] both Germany's neighbors and many Germans began to worry that economically powerful West Germany would now disrupt the European order; these concerns intensified in 1991 when the Eastern Bloc fell, the Cold War ended, and the occupying forces left the new, expanded, and sovereign Germany.[34] The reunification inspired the creation of Marvel's Hauptmann Deutschland and his team, but it also made them potentially explosive.

For example, with their military overtones, Hauptmann Deutschland and Blitzkrieger are offensive as superhero names, the latter particularly so.

Moreover, *Hauptmann*, the army rank of "captain," lacks the prestige of the English term—Germans would use the naval/airline rank of *Kapitän*, or simply English "captain." The newspaper *Süddeutsche Zeitung* complained that the Hauptmann's flag-themed uniform makes him look "a bit like an eccentric football fan."[35] The Hauptmann's behavior is not eccentric, however, but villainous: pointing out that the chair restraining the Red Skull converts into an electric chair, he intones, "We Germans are known for our *efficiency*, are we not?" Although he speaks in terms of a reckoning with the past ("Until we have *purged* ourselves of you, the *world* will never let us live down that *ignoble period of history*!"), Hauptmann Deutschland's superhero vigilantism becomes a human rights abuse, at a time when Germany was more than ever obligated to emphasize its commitment to liberal democracy.[36]

When these stories were translated for German readers,[37] Hauptmann Deutschland was blandly renamed Freiheitskämpfer (Freedom Fighter) and Blitzkrieger had to be rechristened first Generator and then in later stories Elektro-Blitz, or E-Blitz. The German Marvel licensee at the time, Condor Verlag, was infamous for shoddy production and poor translations, but its attention to these details demonstrates just how inappropriate the original character names were for a German readership.[38]

Hauptmann Deutschland perfectly encapsulated the anxiety that many Europeans—including Germans—felt regarding the potential abuses of power of which a reunified Germany, given its dominant position in the European Union, might be capable free of Cold War constraints.[39] Partly to assuage these fears, Chancellor Kohl made a surprising about-face in 1992 and began supporting the construction of a proposed Holocaust Memorial for Berlin—support that he maintained until he left office in 1998.[40] The result was that "since reunification in 1989, the Holocaust has turned into a kind of official litmus test of national identity."[41] In place of division and containment, Kohl offered contrition as a guarantee of Germany's good behavior, a policy carried on by Kohl's socialist successor Gerhard Schröder, whose government constructed the memorial in 2003–2004 and who entered office proclaiming, "Germany is now a normal state with similar values to its neighbours in Europe."[42]

Some German comic book fans believed "normality" entailed Germany having its own superheroes and took matters into their own hands. However, the German comic book industry had virtually collapsed following reunification due to an oversaturated market and little interest in comics among East Germans. Moreover, the unexpected costs of reunification led to nationwide recession. As comic sales plummeted, many smaller firms went under, while the largest companies survived the 1990s largely by licensing Japanese *manga*. However, while the professional comic industry had been decimated, technological advances had made self-publishing possible. Thus the first "German superheroes" were independently published.

These heroes were indebted aesthetically to Image Comics, home of Todd McFarlane's *Spawn*, licensed in Germany by the short-lived Infinity Verlag in the late 1990s. Despite appropriating Image's formula of hypertrophied musculature and bombast, none of them attracted many readers. Jörn Krug's *Cool Patrol*, for example, declares itself as "the first genuinely completely German-conceived and drawn superhero comic,"[43] but both plot and layouts are incoherent, and it is unclear whether any of the characters are superheroes. One reviewer exulted, "There is justice in the world after all. ;) There will be no second issue, because Jörn Krug has broken it off with his publisher."[44] Copies remain for sale after almost two decades, even though most of the print run was returned unsold and pulped.[45] Two years later, Santiago and Enrique Ruiz's *Power Freaks*, set in a dystopian future where corporations have replaced nations and employ battling superheroes to advertise their products, also ended with a single issue.[46] Even less professionally drawn than *Cool Patrol*, *Power Freaks* is described by journalist Stefan Pannor as "the biggest flop in [G]erman comic publishing and . . . the most bizarre comic ever published by a [G]erman comic artist," selling about two hundred of twelve thousand self-published copies.[47]

Longer-lived and better drawn were Maximilian Pfeffer's *New Arden Chronicles* and Ralf Paul's *Der Morgenstern, bekannt als Dorn* (The Morningstar, Known as Thorn).[48] The former takes place in a pseudo-American urban fantasy milieu and features an English-named hero, Red Shadow; the latter is consciously set in contemporary Cologne. This dichotomy reflects a lack of agreement among fans and creators as to whether superheroes, even those made in Germany, *belonged* in Germany. Setting stories in America or in an unspecified future sidestepped questions of what a German superhero might represent; while a German location entailed facing just those questions—an issue that *Dorn*, described on the comic's website as "A German SUPERHERO," wrestles with on the page.[49]

In *Dorn* virtual reality technology somehow turns skinny technology magnate Paul Paker into the muscular barbarian from his own role-playing game. Paker first realizes that he now has a huge penis; then that he is now the perfect superhero. Inspired by his framed collection of classic American superhero comics, he constructs a new identity. The first name on his short-list is "Super*er* Man"; runner-up is "Mr. Germany," though as he writes he wonders whether he ought to dress as a bat or a spider. He almost becomes "Captain Deutschland," and even sews a tricolor uniform to match, but his own muscles rip the costume's seams.[50] Finally, he names himself after his weapon of choice—a medieval morningstar—and creates a

Spawn-like masked costume, defining himself as a superhero for Cologne. Throughout this process, both text and pictures continually refer to American models as the starting point for constructing a superhero identity. When, however, he tries to become Captain Deutschland, Chancellor Schröder's claims of German normality notwithstanding, this identity is too constraining: the costume literally cannot contain him. Thus he *refuses* to become a national(ist) superhero and settles instead for a regional identity, which carries less baggage. After four issues, however, *Dorn* was discontinued.

The only German superhero comic to appear from a major publisher at the end of the 1990s was Martin Frei's *Superbabe*, from the Danish-owned Carlsen Verlag. However, Superbabe is depicted as an American hero with roots in the Golden Age. For instance, her first appearance in 1999 is labeled her sixtieth anniversary.[51] The comic parodies the sexist depictions of female superheroes, but without the critical function of satire: the heroine is an unlucky bimbo who is objectified by every male in her world. Superbabe is subjected to constant, humiliating sexual harassment, which is played for laughs. Despite Frei's peppy, cartoony style, which resembles the art of Bruce Timm, Pannor has described the series' sophomoric sexual humor as "belaboring" its theme.[52] *Superbabe* eventually moved to a smaller publisher, where it lasted three further issues.

Unlike earlier attempts at German-speaking heroes, *Dorn* and *Superbabe* were better able to play off of American models because Hollywood superhero films had reached a wider global audience. With the success of the *X-Men* (2000–present) and *Spider-Man* (2002–present) franchises, and then later a new *Batman* cycle (2005–2012), superheroes finally became viable in the German-language comic market. In 2003 both DC and Marvel licenses landed at a single publisher: the Italian-owned Panini Verlag, which also acquired the rights to Image Comics, as well as a number of popular cross-media hits, including *The Simpsons*, *Star Wars*, and *Buffy the Vampire Slayer*. As a result of its lucrative licensing, however, Panini has shown little inclination to publish original German-language comics of any kind.

When Angela Merkel won the German chancellorship in 2005, there were fears that renewed conservative leadership would mean a return to early Helmut Kohl-style revisionism. However, Merkel has instead continued Schröder's policy of contrition, acknowledging that the Holocaust is singular and "an irrevocable part of German memory and identity," while emphasizing in positive terms Germany's responsibility to prevent such catastrophes from recurring and its achievement in overcoming forty years of division.[53] On this basis a new sense of affirmative patriotism has begun to develop—though there are also increased manifestations of chauvinist

Figure 16.1. Golden Age U.S. comics serve as a reference point in *Der Morgenstern, bekannt als Dorn*. Copyright Ideenschmiede Paul & Paul GbR.

nationalism. Particularly given that comics are still largely seen as children's entertainment, the new German superhero comics of the last few years, all from independent publishers, have had to clearly avoid the appearance of nationalism.

Jörg Buttgereit's *Captain Berlin*, for instance, is a "biologically manipulated" supersoldier created by the German resistance to capture Hitler, an operation

Figure 16.2. Captain Berlin as Nazi fighter. Copyright Jörg Buttgereit/Weissblech Comics/Levin Kurio.

ironically thwarted by the July 20, 1944, Stauffenberg assassination attempt.[54] In subsequent issues the ageless hero goes undercover as reporter Fritz Neumann ("new man") and survives to fight evil down to the present day. Meanwhile, Harald Havas's *ASH: Austrian Super Heroes* are led by Kurt Kogler, alias Captain Austria, Jr., whose father Alfred (originally known as Kapitän Österreich) was recruited in postwar Vienna by the American occupation forces and artificially enhanced to combat both Nazism and the Soviets. Kurt has inherited a reduced form of Alfred's strength and stamina and a host of issues connected with his emotionally distant father, which both symbolize the quasi-generational contrast between pre- and post-Waldheim Austria and set up emotional conflicts and hinted-at revelations in issues to come.[55]

Both series thus define a German-speaking superhero identity in explicitly antifascist terms. Indeed, the Koglers are even Jewish: Alfred bears an Auschwitz tattoo on his forearm. At the same time, both leaven the absurdity of European superheroics with humor. *Captain Berlin* veers into camp melodrama ("Ilse von Blitzen . . . my archenemy, transformed into a Nazi gargoyle?!!") with textual and visual inside jokes for popular culture fans, while *Austrian Super Heroes* features heroes like Der Bürokrat, a supernerd who embodies the power of the Austrian legal code, Donauweibchen (Danube Maiden), a water nymph, and Grüner Panther (Green Panther), whose power is combustible flatulence. Such humor enables both captains to wear the colors of their respective national flags without evoking the specter of fascist nationalism or looking like "eccentric football fans."[56]

Recent German-speaking superhero titles also include examples from regions where the past has historically been less of an issue. Switzerland, for instance, developed a "myth of resistance" that has prevented sustained discussion of Swiss collusion with the Nazi regime and obstruction of Jewish heirs' access to family accounts.[57] David Boller's comic *Tell* is set in a near-future Zurich, where the Illuminati, led by Mr. X, have engineered Switzerland's economic collapse and now seek to control the populace with a supercyborg cloned from the medieval hero William Tell.[58] However, when Tell's historical adversary Governor Gessler returns as a radioactive, superpowered zombie, and Mr. X clones Tell's son Walter to give him a sidekick, the hero's dormant rebellious memories are reawakened and he prepares to lead a revolution against his creators, forging a new myth of resistance without the need to deal with World War II. A relative lack of cultural pressures did not mean that there were no financial pressures: the series ceased publication at this point.[59]

A more original example is Sascha Wüstenfeld and Ulf S. Graupner's *Das Upgrade*, the only East German superhero story in this recent wave.[60] Thanks to the combination of alien intervention and an experimental socialist fertility pill, Ronny Knäusel is born in Dresden in 1966 with the ability to teleport himself and others when he hears a certain song performed by American pop star Cosmo Shleym. As a young adult Ronny becomes *Der Grenzengel*, the "Border Angel," teleporting defectors into West Germany in an act of nonviolent resistance. After reunification, how-

Figure 16.3. *ASH—Austrian Super Heroes*: Humor and local color. Copyright Harald Havas/ASH—Austrian Superheroes.

ever, the hero's life lacks direction, until the reclusive Shleym contacts him in the hope that Ronny's power can help bring back his dead wife. The German Democratic Republic dealt with the Nazi past in only a cursory fashion, and since its demise has become another aspect of the past to master.[61] *Das Upgrade* can thus construct a German superhero identity that brackets out Nazism in favor of the more recent East German dictatorship. In keeping with this focus, *Das Upgrade*'s bright, psychedelic style owes little to American comics; rather, it is an *hommage* to the rounded, organic style of the 1960s GDR comic *Mosaik*, reinforcing their protagonist's specifically East German identity while balancing criticism and nostalgia.[62]

The combination of local color and a light touch that *Das Upgrade* shares with *Captain Berlin* and *Austrian Super Heroes* has inspired yet more creators: Captain Berlin has gained a Bavarian counterpart in Christopher Kloiber's *Tracht Man*, a comic that asks, "Can a hero in Lederhosen be taken less seriously than one in a bat suit?"[63] Meanwhile, in an unusual reversal of the cultural relationship between Germany and Austria, in which the much larger German market usually takes the lead, the *Austrian Super Heroes* have led to a German spin-off, the *Liga deutscher Helden* (League of German Heroes), led by a mysterious holographic figure known only as "Der Captain."[64] Der Captain eventually turns out to be the Captain

Deutschland whose absence has repeatedly marked the vacuum in the German national identity.

The superhero is a marginal, if growing, aspect of the German-language comic industry, and the German-speaking superhero even more so. The center remains dominated by humor, European adventure and fantasy, historical drama, and *manga*; and aside from humor and the narrow range of history and biography that deals with the East German dictatorship, all of these genres continue to be dependent upon foreign licenses. The arrival of the first generation of German superheroes who may be commercially viable has coincided with an apparent rightward turn in both German and Austrian politics;[65] however, under the present conditions, the "re-Nazification" that Fredric Wertham once feared appears doubtful, and even more unlikely is that superhero comics will be its advance guard.

Notes

1 Jörg Buttgereit et al., *Captain Berlin* #1–5 (Schönwalde: Weissblech Verlag, 2013–2016); and Christopher Kloiber, *Tracht Man* #0 (Bamberg: Plem Plem Productions, 2017).

2 Harald Havas et al., *ASH: Austrian Superheroes* #0–4 (Vienna: Contentkaufmann, 2016).

3 David Boller, *Tell* #1–2 (Zurich: Zampano/Virtual Graphics, 2010–2011); and Sascha Wüstenfeld and Ulf S. Graupner, *Das Upgrade* #1–3 (Berlin: Zitty/Cross Cult, 2012–2016).

4 Gunter d'Alquen, "Jerry Siegel greift ein," *Das schwarze Korps*, April 25, 1940, 3, as cited in Ralf Palandt, "'Blühender Blödsinn' an der Propagandafront," in *Deutsche Comicforschung 2006*, ed. Eckart Sackmann (Hildesheim: Verlag Sackmann und Hörndl, 2005), 83–91. All translations from the German are the author's.

5 Jerry Siegel and Joe Shuster, "How Superman Would End the War," *Look*, February 27, 1940, 16–17.

6 Chris Murray, *The British Superhero* (Jackson: University Press of Mississippi, 2017), 277.

7 Austria, a German province under the Nazis, had been restored to sovereignty on condition of political neutrality.

8 Ruth Wittlinger and Steffi Boothroyd, "A 'Usable' Past at Last? The Politics of the Past in United Germany," *German Studies Review* 33, no. 3 (2010): 489; Ingrid Laurien, "Germany: Facing the Nazi Past Today," *Literator* 30, no. 3 (2009): 96–98.

9 Murray, *British Superhero*, 277–279, 3–4.

10 Laurien, "Germany," 97.

11 Michael Ermarth, "Counter-Americanism and Critical Currents in West German Reconstruction 1945–1960: The German Lesson Confronts the American Way of Life," in *Americanization and Anti-Americanism: The German Encounter with American Culture after 1945*, ed. Alexander Stephan (New York:

Berghahn Books, 2005), 44–45. *Materialismus* and *Vermassung* were essentially antimodernist terms and could be leveled in different contexts against either American capitalism or Soviet-style state socialism.

12 Ermarth, "Counter-Americanism," 38, 41–42.

13 Fredric Wertham, *Seduction of the Innocent* (Port Washington, NY: Kennikat Press, 1972), 34.

14 Wertham, *Seduction of the Innocent*, 15, 34, 88, 96, 97, 382.

15 Wertham, *Seduction of the Innocent*, 292.

16 Wertham, *Seduction of the Innocent*, 293.

17 *Supermann* #1–3 (Stuttgart: Verlag "Supermann," 1950). *Verlag* is German for "publishing house."

18 Siegmar Wansel, *Illustrierte Deutsche Comic Geschichte*, vol. 14 (Cologne: ComiCZeit Verlag, 2004), 2–53.

19 Alfred C. Baumgärtner, *Die Welt der Comics: Probleme einer primitiven Literaturform*, 4th ed. (Bochum: Kamp, 1971), 37–47.

20 Laurien, "Germany," 100.

21 Volker Wagener, "Auschwitz Trial Ensured That Germany Would Never Forget," *Deutsche Welle*, August 18, 2015, www.dw.com/en/auschwitz-trial-ensured-that-germany-would-never-forget/a-18654790.

22 Daniel Wamsler, "1974—Das Jahr der Superhelden: Wie Williams neue Helden ins Rennen Schickte," in *Comic Report 2015: Der deutschsprachige Comicmarkt*, ed. Volker Hamann and Matthias Hofmann (Heederbrook: Verlag Volker Hamann, 2015), 6.

23 Willy Vandersteen, *Wastl* #1–173 (Cologne: Bastei Verlag, 1968–1972). "Wastl" is a Bavarian nickname for Sebastian.

24 Laurien, "Germany," 100.

25 Laurien, "Germany," 102; Andrei S. Markovits and Rebecca S. Hayden, "'Holocaust' Before and After the Event: Reactions in West Germany and Austria," *New German Critique* 19, no. 1 (1980): 74–79.

26 Austrian complacency began to crumble after the 1985 revelation that president-elect Kurt Waldheim had neglected to mention his wartime service in the Balkans, when the German Army was committing atrocities against partisan fighters. See Matthew P. Berg, "Commemoration versus *Vergangenheitsbewältigung*: Contextualizing Austria's *Gedenkjahr* 2005," *German History* 26, no. 1 (2008): 48.

27 Kurt Kofron and Wenzel Kofron, *Flattermann* #1–3 (Vienna: Pollischansky Verlag, 1981–1983). Pollischansky was Austria's only comic publisher, best known for reprinting American comic strips. It left the comic market in 1987.

28 "Flattermann im Bauch" is the German equivalent of "butterflies in the stomach."

29 Mark Gruenwald et al., "The Masque Club/Slaughterhouse/Kidnaped/Sneak Attack/The Skeleton Key/Skullbound," *Captain America* #387–393 (New York: Marvel Comics, 1991).

30 Jason Dittmer, *Captain America and the Nationalist Superhero: Metaphors, Narratives, and Geopolitics* (Philadelphia: Temple University Press, 2013), 21–22.

31 Markus Engelns, "Der Dritte Weltkrieg als Reifeprüfung: Struktur und Funktion von Weltkriegsszenarien in aktuellen Superheldencomics," *Medienobservationen*, September 7, 2009, www.medienobservationen.lmu.de/artikel/comics/comics_pdf/engelns_weltkrieg.pdf.

32 Joe Simon and Jack Kirby, "Meet Captain America," in *Captain America Comics* #1 (New York: Timely Publications, March 1941).

33 Laurien, "Germany," 103.

34 Jill Stephenson, "Anniversaries, Memory and the Neighbours: The 'German Question' in Recent History," *German Politics* 5, no. 1 (1996): 43–44.

35 Benedikt Frank, "Marvels Matadore: Wir sind Helden," *Süddeutsche.de*, July 22, 2015, www.sueddeutsche.de/kultur/popkultur-wir-sind-helden-1.2577919. Soccer matches have only recently become the rare occasions when Germans wave their flag; surprised by the show of flags at the 2006 World Cup, Ingeborg Majer-O'Sickey writes, "Growing up, I would have had trouble telling you what the German flag's colors were. I believed, as so many of the post World War II generation of Germans did, that Germany's national flag was anathema to all that was ethical and moral." "Out of the Closet? German Patriotism and Soccer Mania," *German Politics and Society* 24, no. 3 (2006): 83. Draping the Hauptmann in the flag in 1991 thus did not necessarily signal moral rectitude to a potential German reader.

36 Stephenson, "Anniversaries," 55. The Hauptmann's actions are particularly unconscionable given that the Federal Republic had abolished the death penalty in 1949.

37 *Captain America Comic-Taschenbuch* #18–19 (Hamburg: Condor Verlag, 1994).

38 Marvel later addressed this problem by rechristening Hauptmann Deutschland *Vormund*, or "Guardian." However, *Vormund* means "legal guardian for a minor or incapable person," which reflects even more poorly on Germany.

39 Stephenson, "Anniversaries," 45.

40 Alison Lewis, "Germany's Metamorphosis: Memory and the Holocaust in the Berlin Republic," *Cultural Studies Review* 9, no. 2 (2003): 111–113.

41 Hanno Loewy, "A History of Ambivalence: Post-Reunification German Identity and the Holocaust," *Patterns of Prejudice* 36, no. 2 (2002): 4.

42 Lewis, "Germany's Metamorphosis," 109.

43 Jörn Krug, *Cool Patrol* #1 (Hannover: Karicartoon Verlag, 1998), inside cover.

44 "Stephan," "Cool Patrol No. 1," *ComicRadioShow*, November 30, 1998, www.comicradioshow.com/ Article393.html.

45 "Cool Patrol # 01—Krug, Jörn," *Phantastische Zeiten Comic-, SF- und Fantasy Versand*, June 24, 2006, www.phantastische-zeiten-shop.de/product_info.php?products_id=49. The current price is 0.99 euros, about one-fifth of the cover price.

46 "Sanchez" and "Subzero" [Santiago and Enrique Ruiz], *Power Freaks* # 1 (Ludwigsburg: Kerosin Comics, 2000), www.power-freaks.de/sites/start.html.

47 Stefan Pannor, comment on Heidi MacDonald, "Awesome Horrible Comics of the 80s and Beyond," *The Beat*, March 4, 2015, www.comicsbeat.com/awesome-horrible-comics-of-the-80s-and-beyond/.

48 Maximilian Pfeffer et al., *New Arden Chronicles* #0–7 (Saulheim: Final Art Comics, 1999–2002); Ralf Paul, *Der Morgenstern, bekannt als Dorn* #1–4 (Stuttgart: IPP Comix, 2001–2004).

49 "Dorn," IPP-World: Comics und Illustrationen, www.ipp-world.de /eigenproduktionen-de/dorn-de/. Krug, in *Cool Patrol*, dodges the issue of what a German superhero might represent by failing to even identify any of his characters as the protagonist, but this appears to be unintentional.

50 Paul, *Der Morgenstern, bekannt als Dorn* #2 (2001).

51 Martin Frei, *Superbabe* (Hamburg: Carlsen Comics, 1999); *Superbabe* #1–3 (Esslingen: Gringo Comics, 2002–2003).

52 Stefan Pannor, "Raketenhelden und Puddingmonster: 'Der Held,'" *Stefan Pannor: Journalist, Übersetzer, Lektor, PR-Texter*, January 29, 2009, www.pannor .de/?p=279.

53 Wittlinger and Boothroyd, "A 'Usable' Past at Last?," 494.

54 Buttgereit et al., *Captain Berlin*. Claus Schenk Graf von Stauffenberg led a circle of aristocratic military officers who conspired to kill Hitler. Their motivations are disputed; after their plot failed, they were all executed. The conspiracy was the basis for the 2008 film *Valkyrie*, starring Tom Cruise as Stauffenberg.

55 Havas et al., *ASH*.

56 Notably, due to German laws forbidding the display of Nazi symbols, whenever Hitler or Nazis appear in *Captain Berlin*, they are not allowed to wear swastikas, but rather are depicted with the "double cross" symbol from Charlie Chaplin's 1940 film *The Great Dictator*.

57 Regula Ludi, "Demystification or Restoration of Neutrality? Confronting the History of the Nazi Era in Switzerland," *Holocaust Studies* 11, no. 3 (2005): 42–43.

58 Boller, *Tell*.

59 A hardcover reprinting of the two issues of *Tell* was announced for 2018; however, Boller has moved on to other projects, including graphic novels about the historical William Tell.

60 Wüstenfeld and Graupner, *Das Upgrade*.

61 Laurien, "Germany," 104; Jan-Werner Müller, "Just Another *Vergangenheitsbewältigung*? The Process of Coming to Terms with the East German Past Revisited," *Oxford German Studies* 38, no. 3 (2009): 334–335.

62 Further cementing the link between *Das Upgrade* and the 1960s GDR comic *Mosaik*, the protagonist, Ronny, is a *Mosaik* fan, while the series' creators, Wüstenfeld and Graupner, worked as *Mosaik* artists following the reunification.

63 Kloiber, *Tracht Man* #0, 2.

64 Jan Dinter et al., *LDH: Liga deutscher Helden* #0 (Vienna: Contentkaufmann, 2017).

65 In their respective 2017 federal elections, Germany saw a far-right nativist party, Alternativ für Deutschland (AfD), gain Bundestag seats for the first time since 1949, while Austrians elected as chancellor Sebastian Kurz, who seems set to move his conservative People's Party into an alliance with the much further

right Freedom Party (FPÖ). Both AfD and FPÖ members have made statements praising the Nazi era and minimizing or denying the Holocaust.

Bibliography

Baumgärtner, Alfred C. *Die Welt der Comics: Probleme einer primitiven Literaturform.* 4th ed. Bochum: Kamp, 1971.

Berg, Matthew P. "Commemoration versus *Vergangenheitsbewältigung*: Contextualizing Austria's *Gedenkjahr* 2005." *German History* 26, no. 1 (2008): 47–71.

Boller, David. *Tell* #1–2. Zurich: Zampano/Virtual Graphics, 2010–2011.

Buttgereit, Jörg, Levin Kurio, Rainer F. Engel, Martin Trafford, Fufu Frauenwahl, The Lep, Roman Turowski, and Geier [Jürgen Speh]. *Captain Berlin* #1–5. Schönwalde: Weissblech Verlag, 2013–2016.

Captain America Comic-Taschenbuch #18–19. Hamburg: Condor Verlag, 1994.

"Cool Patrol # 01—Krug, Jörn." *Phantastische Zeiten Comic-, SF- und Fantasy Versand*, June 24, 2006. www.phantastische-zeiten-shop.de/product_info.php?products_id=49.

Dinter, Jan, Harald Havas, Oliver Naatz, Martin Frei, and Stefan Dinter. *LDH: Liga Deutscher Helden* 0. Vienna: Contentkaufmann, 2017.

Dittmer, Jason. *Captain America and the Nationalist Superhero: Metaphors, Narratives, and Geopolitics*. Philadelphia: Temple University Press, 2013.

"Dorn." IPP-World: Comics und Illustrationen. www.ipp-world.de/eigenproduktionen-de/dorn-de/.

Engelns, Markus. "Der Dritte Weltkrieg als Reifeprüfung: Struktur und Funktion von Weltkriegsszenarien in aktuellen Superheldencomics." *Medienobservationen*, September 7, 2009. www.medienobservationen.lmu.de/artikel/comics/comics_pdf/engelns_weltkrieg.pdf.

Ermarth, Michael. "Counter-Americanism and Critical Currents in West German Reconstruction 1945–1960: The German Lesson Confronts the American Way of Life." In *Americanization and Anti-Americanism: The German Encounter with American Culture after 1945*, edited by Alexander Stephan, 25–50. New York: Berghahn Books, 2005.

Frank, Benedikt. "Marvels Matadore: Wir sind Helden." *Süddeutsche.de*, July 22, 2015. www.sueddeutsche.de/kultur/popkultur-wir-sind-helden-1.2577919.

Frei, Martin. *Superbabe*. Hamburg: Carlsen Comics, 1999.

———. *Superbabe*. Esslingen: Gringo Comics, 2002–2003.

Gruenwald, Mark, Dan Panosian, Larry Alexander, Bud La Rosa, Rik Levins, and Danny Bulanadi. "The Masque Club/Slaughterhouse/Kidnaped/Sneak Attack/The Skeleton Key/Skullbound." *Captain America* #387–393. New York: Marvel, 1991.

Havas, Harald, Andi Paar, Thomas Aigelsreiter, Lenny Grosskopf, Jörg Vogeltanz, Michael Liberatore, Leo Koller, Michael Wittmann, and Lisa Heschl. *ASH: Austrian Superheroes* #0–4. Vienna: Contentkaufmann, 2016.

Kloiber, Christopher. *Tracht Man* #0. Bamberg: Plem Plem Productions, 2017. www.trachtman.de/app/download/13208844829/TRACHT_MAN_0.pdf?t=1489587382.

Kofron, Kurt, and Wenzel Kofron. *Flattermann* #1–3. Vienna: Pollischansky Verlag, 1981–1983.
Krug, Jörn. *Cool Patrol*. Hannover: Karicartoon Verlag, 1998.
Laurien, Ingrid. "Germany: Facing the Nazi Past Today." *Literator* 30, no. 3 (2009): 93–114.
Lewis, Alison. "Germany's Metamorphosis: Memory and the Holocaust in the Berlin Republic." *Cultural Studies Review* 9, no. 2 (2003): 102–122.
Loewy, Hanno. "A History of Ambivalence: Post-Reunification German Identity and the Holocaust." *Patterns of Prejudice* 36, no. 2 (2002): 3–13.
Ludi, Regula. "Demystification or Restoration of Neutrality? Confronting the History of the Nazi Era in Switzerland." *Holocaust Studies* 11, no. 3 (2005): 24–52.
MacDonald, Heidi. "Awesome Horrible Comics of the 80s and Beyond." *The Beat*, March 4, 2015. www.comicsbeat.com/awesome-horrible-comics-of-the-80s-and-beyond/.
Majer-O'Sickey, Ingeborg. "Out of the Closet? German Patriotism and Soccer Mania." *German Politics and Society* 24, no. 3 (2006): 82–97.
Markovits, Andrei S., and Rebecca S. Hayden. "'Holocaust' Before and After the Event: Reactions in West Germany and Austria." *New German Critique* 19, no. 1 (1980): 53–80.
Müller, Jan-Werner. "Just Another *Vergangenheitsbewältigung*? The Process of Coming to Terms with the East German Past Revisited." *Oxford German Studies* 38, no. 3 (2009): 334–344.
Murray, Chris. *The British Superhero*. Jackson: University Press of Mississippi, 2017.
Palandt, Ralf. "'Blühender Blödsinn' an der Propagandafront." In *Deutsche Comicforschung 2006*, edited by Eckart Sackmann, 83–91. Hildesheim: Verlag Sackmann und Hörndl, 2005.
Pannor, Stefan. "Raketenhelden und Puddingmonster: 'Der Held.'" *Stefan Pannor: Journalist, Übersetzer, Lektor, PR-Texter*, January 29, 2009. www.pannor.de/?p=279.
Paul, Ralf. *Der Morgenstern, bekannt als Dorn* #1–4. Stuttgart: IPP Comix, 2001–2004.
Pfeffer, Maximilian, et al. *New Arden Chronicles* #0–7. Saulheim: Final Art Comics, 1991–2002.
"Sanchez" and "Subzero" [Santiago Ruiz and Enrique Ruiz]. *Power Freaks* #1. Ludwigsburg: Kerosin Comics, 2000.
Siegel, Jerry, and Joe Shuster. "How Superman Would End the War." *Look*, February 27, 1940, 16–17.
Simon, Joe, and Jack Kirby. "Meet Captain America." In *Captain America Comics* #1. New York: Timely Publications, March 1941.
"Stephan." "*Cool Patrol* No. 1." *ComicRadioShow*, November 30, 1998. www.comicradioshow.com/ Article393.html.
Stephenson, Jill. "Anniversaries, Memory and the Neighbours: The 'German Question' in Recent History." *German Politics* 5, no. 1 (1996): 43–57.
Supermann #1–3. Stuttgart: Verlag "Supermann," 1950.
Vandersteen, Willy. *Wastl* #1–173. Bastei Verlag, 1968–1972.

Wagener, Volker. "Auschwitz Trial Ensured That Germany Would Never Forget." *Deutsche Welle*, August 18, 2015. www.dw.com/en/auschwitz-trial-ensured-that-germany-would-never-forget/a-18654790.

Wamsler, Daniel. "1974—Das Jahr der Superhelden: Wie Williams neue Helden ins Rennen Schickte." In *Comic Report 2015: Der deutschsprachige Comicmarkt*, edited by Volker Hamann and Matthias Hofmann, 5–28. Heederbrook: Verlag Volker Hamann, 2015.

Wansel, Siegmar. *Illustrierte Deutsche Comic Geschichte*. Vol. 14. Cologne: ComiC-Zeit Verlag, 2004.

Wertham, Fredric. *Seduction of the Innocent*. Port Washington, NY: Kennikat Press, 1972.

Wittlinger, Ruth, and Steffi Boothroyd. "A 'Usable' Past at Last? The Politics of the Past in United Germany." *German Studies Review* 33, no. 3 (2010): 489–502.

Wüstenfeld, Sascha, and Ulf S. Graupner. *Das Upgrade* #1–3. Berlin: Zitty/Cross Cult, 2012–2016.

17

Chinese Milk for Iron Men

Superhero Coproductions and Technological Anxiety

SHAN MU ZHAO

In 2002 Indian filmmaker Shekhar Kapur wrote an article in the *Guardian* titled "The Asians Are Coming." It begins with a prediction: "Ten years from now, *Spider-Man* will make $1bn in its first week. But when Spider-Man takes off his mask, he'll probably be Chinese. And the city in which he operates will not be New York, it will be Shanghai. And yet it will be an international film, it will still be *Spider-Man*."[1] To a certain extent this prediction has come true. The People's Republic of China (PRC) has been investing heavily in its film industries, including coproduction with Hollywood. These coproductions tend to be action and adventure blockbusters, including superhero films such as *Iron Man 3* and *X-Men: Days of Future Past*, with Stan Lee even attempting to create original heroes with Chinese producing partners.[2] Although the superhero genre has uniquely American origins, Hollywood's reach has helped internationalize these films. At the same time Hollywood's production is undergirded by newly liberalized film markets in countries such as China.[3] These trends reinforce each other in such a way that there is now a boom in international superhero films, where the conventions and meaning of the genre are subject to global re-creations.

Iron Man 3 was partially funded by China's DMG Entertainment, stars Chinese actors Wang Xueqi and Fan Bingbing as doctors who help Tony Stark, and includes product placement from Yili, a Chinese dairy company. Upon its release, the film received a lukewarm reception from both Chinese officials and audiences, although for different reasons. The main objection was that Wang and Fan's few scenes were mostly cut from the film's international release. Chinese audiences expressed disappointment, while SARFT (then China's State Administration of Radio, Film, and Television) released statements that *Iron Man 3* did not meet the state's standards for Chinese input.[4] Government officials and audiences also responded negatively to Yili's product placement. SARFT officials argued that Chinese merchandise does not stand for China as a whole, while Chinese audiences ridiculed Iron Man–themed advertisements that Yili released on other platforms. In light of frequent food safety scandals in China, many of which occur in the dairy industry, Chinese "netizens" popularized the meme "Only iron men can drink Chinese milk without getting diarrhea."[5]

The coproduction of *Iron Man 3* demonstrates that the internationalization of superheroes engenders various adoption strategies, even within the same national community. For *Iron Man 3* the government of the PRC, its businesses, and its audiences constitute at least three parties with divergent interests and interpretations. While the state invested in the film as a part of its developmentalist and soft power goals and the dairy industry sought greater advertising reach, audiences used the trope of a superpower to articulate concerns about the cost of unbridled development. These avenues of Chinese input into Iron Man demonstrate both a general phenomenon where superheroes are remade as they travel worldwide via American media and a specific case where multinational input into Iron Man actually engenders local opposition to the technopositivist principles that he stands for.

In the early 1960s Stan Lee and Marvel Comics created a new crop of superheroes who begin as ordinary people and acquire their abilities due to accidents. Two attendant tropes were that these accidents occur during the course of scientific development and the resulting superpower also comes with a cost, such as physical distortions or blindness. Thus, scholars demarcate this era of comics as the "atomic age," where origin stories reflect anxieties regarding science in the wake of the atomic bomb.[6] Though Iron Man was created in 1963, he is a uniquely technopositive superhero. Iron Man's alter ego, Tony Stark, is a millionaire industrialist motivated by a desire to invent. In addition, while various versions of Stark refuse to weaponize his inventions for the American military, *Iron Man* narratives are aligned with discourses that American innovation is necessary to maintain global order, even as they cast doubt on whether the U.S. government should deploy them.[7] This is illustrated in *Iron Man 2*, where insurgencies around the world have fallen due to Iron Man's interventions and Stark tells a senate committee that he has "successfully privatized world peace."[8]

Whenever the Marvel Cinematic Universe (MCU) films introduce an element of technological anxiety to Iron Man, it is quickly dispelled. In the *Iron Man* comics Stark invents a transistor in captivity to keep his heart beating after shrapnel reaches it;[9] the twenty-first-century Stark invents an "arc reactor" that not only prevents shrapnel from reaching his heart but also becomes the energy source for the Iron Man suit. In *Iron Man 2* Stark finds that the element powering the reactor—palladium—is toxic and slowly killing him. However, this threat is quickly assuaged as Stark discovers a new element in his deceased father's research, which he synthesizes as a replacement for palladium.

The technopositivism synonymous with Iron Man also provided an opportunity for the PRC's new goals for its national film industry. Before the 1980s films were treated mainly as ideological vehicles. Even in the 1990s, many Chinese officials and intellectuals resisted importing Hollywood films.[10] However, economic reforms beginning in the late 1970s meant that film was subject to commercialization and international exchange. The Motion Picture Association of America (MPAA) lobbied for access to the Chinese market, and upon China's bid to join the World Trade Organization (WTO) in 2001, American negotiators in the Sino-U.S. bilateral treaties focused heavily on promoting film as a part of international trade.[11] After WTO accession, the PRC increased the foreign film quota from ten to twenty films per year.[12] Despite opening up film exhibition, PRC policy-makers prioritized domestic film production by funding them with box office revenue from foreign films.[13] A financial crisis in state-owned film studios in the 1990s also prompted the first efforts at international coproductions, which have been counted as domestic films and are therefore exempt from the foreign film quota.[14]

Coproductions have become an optimal vehicle for the PRC to balance the development of Chinese content while staying connected to global film industries. Media scholar Stephanie DeBoer introduced the term "scale convergence" to describe the phenomenon in which multinational industries and investment converge with new filmmaking technology to produce a film with intense drama and sweeping visuals, so as to appeal to a wide audience.[15] *Iron Man 3* fits these criteria well, as it features a titular character who embodies innovation, tells a grand adventure story, and contains spectacular visual effects that would draw audiences and provide opportunities for technology sharing. Global appeal alone is not enough, however. According to media and cultural studies scholar Wendy Su, the PRC's stance regarding Hollywood has shifted from "containment to competitive cooperation," but even so the state sees itself in a "post–Cold War cultural war" where the PRC needs to maintain hegemony in global discourse.[16] Currently, official coproductions involving the PRC require government review from production to exhibition.[17] Thus, a coproduction would have high production values while carrying positive representations of China to international audiences, thereby boosting China's soft power.[18]

Hollywood makes concessions to the PRC's ideological interests and also self-censors in the hope of accessing China's large audiences. In 2013, the year *Iron Man 3* was released, the Chinese box office grew by 27 percent.[19] *Iron Man 3* earned $64.5 million in China on its opening weekend, accounting for a third of the international opening weekend revenue.[20] One of the biggest changes for *Iron Man 3* was the film's villain, the Mandarin. In the comics the Mandarin was originally a half-Chinese warlord realized through Asian stereotypes such as despotism, mysticism, and inscrutability—a negative representation for which Stan Lee later expressed regret.[21] However, the Mandarin's threat to Iron Man and to the world came from crafting ten rings from an alien spaceship and misusing this technology for world domination, which provided a contrast with Stark's more altruistic use of technology to better the world.[22] Such a Cold War image of a Chinese villain had become untenable in the 2010s, especially in a coproduction with an industrialized China that sees itself engaging in a "post–Cold War cultural war."[23] Accordingly, in *Iron Man 3* the Mandarin, as played by British actor Ben Kingsley, became a character staged by Stark's rival and actual villain of the film, Aldrich Killian (Guy Pearce).

Furthermore, two prominent Chinese actors, Wang Xueqi and Fan Bingbing, were cast in the film as original characters: the Chinese cardiologist Doctor Wu and his assistant. Their new roles cemented a shift in the discourse about the fallibility of progress and who has a right to technology and its benefits. Although Stark finds a safe replacement for palladium, he must still wear the reactor to prevent shrapnel from reaching his heart. Surgery could remove the shrapnel, but Stark delays the operation due to the procedure's high risk. The events of *Iron Man 3* convince Stark to take the risk. Over a montage of surgery scenes with Dr. Wu, Stark's voiceover discusses his decision. "Of course there are people who say progress is dangerous, but I'll bet none of those idiots had to live with a chest full of shrapnel. And now neither will I." Wang Xueqi reported in an interview that he refused to play a villain, a character who gets killed off quickly, or a groveling subordinate, and he was told that his character would be a friend of Stark's and save him partly through traditional Chinese medicine.[24] Due to the input of the PRC's film industry, the Chinese characters of the *Iron Man* franchise are not villains who misuse technology but heroes who share and even advance Stark's technopositivism by getting rid of the last burden of his innovation, a process that Stark and the film present as a necessary danger of progress.

Various privately owned industries in China are also capitalizing on the commercial possibilities of the expanding film industry to assert that they are also agents of progress. China's dairy companies, especially Yili, have utilized product placements in international coproductions to reach a large

Chinese viewership. Although Yili's product placement was restricted to the Chinese cut of *Iron Man 3*, it was widely seen in *Transformers: Dark of the Moon*.[25] In the Chinese release of *Iron Man 3*, Dr. Wu drinks a Yili product called Guliduo before performing Stark's surgery.[26] In addition, Yili used scenes from the film in prescreening commercials. In the commercial, scenes of a wounded Iron Man in the snow are presented with a voiceover saying that he has run out of energy, asking rhetorically what would save him, and answering that it is the comprehensive nutrition of Guliduo. The advertisement also includes an image where Guliduo's logo is superimposed on Iron Man's glowing arc reactor.[27]

In addition to advertising a product, the commercial can also be seen as a metaphor for Chinese financial input, with a Chinese product fueling the arc reactor paralleling Chinese investment in the production of *Iron Man 3*. However, the film satisfied neither SARFT nor audience expectations. It was pulled from official coproduction status, most likely after the government saw that the film differed from what they had approved.[28] Actor Wang Xueqi stated in an interview that he did not even know that there would be different international and Chinese releases and expressed disappointment at his reduced role, especially after the care he took to ensure that his character was positively represented.[29] Indeed, *China Daily* quoted the deputy chief of SARFT, Zhang Pimin, as saying, "A completely US story, some Chinese money, a few Chinese faces and some Chinese elements—these kinds of films are not real coproductions." Zhang also cautioned viewers against equating product placement with Hollywood truly being receptive to Chinese culture.[30] Statements such as this echo Su's analysis of the state's motivations for developing its film industry, which is ultimately not about economic gain but boosting soft power.

Audience experiences of the Chinese release seem to agree with how Zhang characterized the film, but they differ with him regarding what is to be done. Chinese audiences were dissatisfied with the clumsy addition of Dr. Wu's scenes and reported feeling as though they were watching two films.[31] On Chinese social networking site Douban.com, nonfiction writer Nai Xia wrote a negative review in which he addressed the character of the Mandarin extensively, writing that the film clearly showed how state interests in presenting China as one of the good guys overshadowed all other concerns.[32] One interpretation of these audience responses is that they come from a consumer rather than a patriotic standpoint, as Xia and other Chinese audiences wanted better storytelling. However, Xia also expresses a desire for Wang's character to be central to the plot, rather than simply be on the side of good. He writes, "It's not like we'd blast you just for playing a villain okay! We want to see the Mandarin as a Chinese person okay, a reincarnation of Sun Yat-sen okay, what does it take to create a screenplay—imagination my dear."[33] Xia demonstrates knowledge of the comic book character in his review and would know that the Mandarin isn't really comparable to Sun Yat-sen—revolutionary and founding father of the Republic of China in the early 1900s—but this comment asks that the state and producers find more creative ways to express national concerns, rather than a complete lack of regard for them.

Despite concerns from SARFT deputy chief Zhang, Chinese audiences seem to be in no danger of mistaking product placement as a representation of Chinese culture. New generations of Chinese media consumers are also avid social media users, and memes and colloquialisms based on both domestic and foreign media content frequently go viral. In *Transformers*, the character Jerry Wang (Ken Jeong) draws attention to Yili's product placement by saying "May I finish my Shuhua milk, Donny?" which became a frequent online response in situations where the speaker wanted to fend off interruptions.[34] While the Transformers meme further advertises Shuhua milk, for *Iron Man 3* some online responses were not so benign. For instance, the meme "Only iron men can drink Chinese milk without getting diarrhea" referred to scandals where Chinese dairy companies consistently failed to meet food safety standards. The most prominent incident occurred in 2008, when Sanlu knowingly put dangerous amounts of melamine (otherwise a common dairy additive) into their products, resulting in the deaths of a number of infants.[35] A year before *Iron Man 3*'s release, Yili itself had to recall baby formula containing dangerous levels of mercury.[36]

The dairy industry has been under particular scrutiny due to its effects on children, but Chinese food industries often use unsafe levels of additives and pesticides to reduce production costs.[37] In this context, instead of seeing Yili's advertisement as an assertion of China's role in the film, much of the Chinese audience for *Iron Man 3* ridiculed the ad. The meme itself seemed to have come from a short review left on Douban's page for the film, which in its entirety reads, "From Shuhua milk to Guliduo, from *Transformers* to *Iron Man*, it seems only iron men can drink Chinese dairy products without getting diarrhea." This comment has over a thousand "useful" votes and is ranked second out of 70,877 comments on the film.[38] Similarly, one commenter stated that when this advertisement appeared among the pre-show advertisements, there was laughter among the entire theater.[39] Another commenter went a step further than the meme to reference palladium: "If Iron Man drank Yili he'd be poisoned right, even more severely than in the second film."[40]

As anthropologist Yunxiang Yan writes regarding food safety in China, large-scale production and distribution of unsafe food involve the authorities. For example, Sanlu had been granted a waiver from inspection and quarantine by the General Administration of Quality Supervision, Inspection, and Quarantine.[41] As Yan writes, "Because many problems of unsafe food are actually derived from modern farming and food-processing technologies as well as from a modern consumerist ideology, the food-safety problems at this level are an inherent and reflexive part of modernity."[42] However, because China has modernized only recently, much of society regards science, technology, and modernization as the solution to food safety problems, even in the face of evidence to the contrary.[43] Yan cites numerous studies showing the prevalence of this philosophy in Chinese society, yet the jokes around *Iron Man 3* and Yili show that social belief in modernization clearly coexists with an acknowledgment of its shortcomings. Chinese netizens are extremely active and vocal across numerous social networking platforms such as microblogs and WeChat, but audience critiques were especially trenchant because Yili's product placement in the coproduction of *Iron Man 3* constituted a blatant conjunction of technopositivism and financial motives.

For these audiences, *Iron Man 3* was not simply a vehicle to display soft power or earn money for China but also a vehicle for mounting a social critique. As communications scholar Eric Kit-wai Ma writes, strong ideological control in the PRC has actually not made Chinese audiences into dupes; rather, audiences have become very skilled at reading between the lines and coming up with subversive interpretations.[44] Although scholarship has emphasized active Chinese audiences in response to state broadcast media rather than entertainment or consumerism, audience discussions around *Iron Man 3* implicitly address the interconnectedness of these spheres in contemporary China and reveal the hypocrisy in which the Chinese state micromanages ideological content in international coproductions yet cannot enforce safety regulations for domestic industries.

While these critiques are specific to China, they also have implications for superheroes as a genre. The technopositivism in Iron Man narratives has been sustainable in the United States, a country that has largely enjoyed the benefits of technological progress and contained its hazards. Aside from Iron Man, arguably figures such as the Fantastic Four and Spider-Man also neutralize post–World War II and early Cold War anxieties regarding radiation and nuclear power, as these characters are in the end able to derive an unexpected benefit from the accidental transformations they undergo. However, in an Iron Man coproduction with a China still experiencing the growing pains of rapid modernization, conflicting stances regarding technological progress emerge more clearly. The response of Chinese audiences to *Iron Man 3* restores some of the technological anxiety visible in heroes of the atomic age, which Iron Man specifically has not expressed. As media scholar Peter Coogan writes, superheroes can be seen as aspirational stories about the ability to enforce personal justice without danger to oneself, and "this vision of power fits quite well with the position America finds itself in after the Cold War. America is the only superpower in the world, something like Superman in the days before other superheroes and supervillains."[45] While the PRC aims to be a superpower, the Chinese cultural context does not have a tradition of superheroes.[46] "Only iron men can drink Chinese milk" does not suggest abilities so powerful that they allow individuals to directly confront the authorities, nor does the meme reflect attitudes so technopositivist that calamities in the course of progress actually engender special abilities. Rather, it suggests that a superpower would merely allow people to withstand the calamities that authorities and unbridled progress have created.

Chinese audiences do not seem to be responding to the validity of technopositivism in the American Iron Man, but rather an Iron Man made even more technopositivist by the materialistic aspirations of their state and commercial enterprises. However, the overlapping interests of Hollywood and the PRC make it even more difficult than ever to clearly demarcate an American Iron Man from global interpretations. Iron Man has become different versions of iron men who are at the center of discussions regarding technopositivism around the world. There is an official international release of *Iron Man 3*, however there is also the Chinese release with Wang and Fan, and the Iron Man of Yili commercial advertisements. Most importantly, there is also the hypothetical iron men in the imagination of Chinese audiences who have changed the nature of a superpower to fit their social reality.

Notes

1 Shekhar Kapur, "The Asians Are Coming," *Guardian*, August 22, 2002, www.theguardian.com/film/2002/aug/23/artsfeatures1.

2 *Iron Man 3*, dir. Shane Black (Marvel Studios, 2013); *X-Men: Days of Future Past*, dir. Brian Singer (Twentieth Century Fox, 2014). In 2015 Lee announced that he was developing ideas for a new superhero story, *Realm*, and had cast actress Li Bingbing as a Chinese superheroine (Rebecca Ford, "Li Bingbing to Star as Superhero in 'Realm,'" *Hollywood Reporter*, October 28, 2015, www.hollywoodreporter.com/heat-vision/li-bingbing-star-as-superhero-835088), and in 2016 he announced *Monkey Master*, a coproduction with China and India (Nyay Bushan, "Stan Lee Unveils India-China Co-Production 'Monkey Master,'" *Hollywood Reporter*, September 21, 2016, www.hollywoodreporter.com/news/stan-lee-unveils-india-china-931431).

3 The superhero genre has also traveled without the aid of Hollywood blockbusters. For example, Japan has a strong tradition of adapting superhero conventions, with Batman reimagined as a Japanese comedy manga series by Jiro Kuwata in the 1960s, and many Japanese franchises feature heroes with

secret identities fighting evil in a contemporary setting, from *Ultraman* to *Sailor Moon*.

4 As of 2013 SARFT had merged with the General Administration of Press and Publication to form the State Administration of Press, Publication, Radio, Film, and Television (SAPPRFT).

5 The Chinese character for "man" does not stand in for all people as in English, and Iron Man's name in Chinese (钢铁侠) literally translates to "steel iron hero," with the gender unspecified. The meme uses the character for "person/people," which this chapter translates as "man/men" as the meme primarily refers to Iron Man.

6 For further discussion, see David Genter, "'With Great Power Comes Great Responsibility': Cold War Culture and the Birth of Marvel Comics," *Journal of Popular Culture* 40, no. 6 (2007): 953–978, and Matthew J. Costello, *Secret Identity Crisis: Comic Books and the Unmasking of Cold War America* (New York: Continuum, 2009).

7 *Iron Man*, dir. Jon Favreau (Marvel Studios, 2008). For analysis of Iron Man's transformations across time, see Joseph J. Darowski, ed., *The Ages of Iron Man: Essays on the Armored Avenger in Changing Times* (Jefferson, NC: McFarland, 2015).

8 *Iron Man 2*, dir. Jon Favreau (Marvel Studios, 2010).

9 Stan Lee, Don Heck, et al., "Iron Man Is Born!," *Tales of Suspense* #39 (New York: Marvel, March 1963).

10 Wendy Su, *China's Encounter with Global Hollywood: Cultural Policy and the Film Industry, 1994–2013* (Lexington: University Press of Kentucky, 2016), 51.

11 Aynne Kokas, *Hollywood Made in China* (Oakland: University of California Press, 2017), 27; Shujen Wang, *Framing Piracy: Globalization and Film Distribution in Greater China* (Lanham, MD: Rowan & Littlefield, 2003), 65.

12 Su, *China's Encounter*, 62.

13 Su, *China's Encounter*, 20.

14 Su, *China's Encounter*, 90; Weiying Peng, "Sino-US Film Coproduction: A Global Primer," *Global Media and China* 1, no. 4 (2016): 308.

15 Stephanie DeBoer, *Coproducing Asia: Locating Japanese-Chinese Regional Film and Media* (Minneapolis: University of Minnesota Press, 2014), 152.

16 Su, *China's Encounter*, 10, 44.

17 Kokas, *Hollywood Made in China*, 32.

18 Joseph Nye, *Soft Power: The Means to Success in World Politics* (New York: PublicAffairs, 2004). The idea of soft power has been extremely influential in China. Its cultural cachet has also increased since President Xi Jinping stated in 2014, "We should increase China's soft power, give a good Chinese narrative, and better communicate China's messages to the world." David Shaumbaugh, "China's Soft Power Push: The Search for Respect," *Foreign Affairs*, July/August 2015, www.foreignaffairs.com/articles/china/2015-06-16/china-s-soft-power-push.

19 Motion Picture Association of America, "Theatrical Marketing Statistics 2013" (March 2014), www.mpaa.org/wp-content/uploads/2014/03/MPAA-Theatrical-Market-Statistics-2013_032514-v2.pdf.

20 "Iron Man 3," Box Office Mojo, November 5, 2017, www.boxofficemojo.com/movies/?page=intl&id=ironman3.htm.

21 Stan Lee, *Son of Origins of Marvel Comics* (New York: Simon & Schuster, 1975), 45.

22 Richard A. Iadonisi, "Fu Manchu Meets Maklu-4: The Mandarin and Racial Stereotypes," in Darowski, *Ages of Iron Man*, 44–45.

23 Su, *China's Encounter*, 44.

24 Shuang Chen [陈爽], "Wang Xueqi Discusses Part Being Cut: The Role had Seemed Important" [王学圻谈戏份被删：当时看角色分量很重要], Phoenix New Media Limited, May 2, 2013, http://ent.ifeng.com/a/20130502/24848967_0.shtml. The surgery scenes do show acupuncture, but it is not prominently featured.

25 *Transformers: Dark Side of the Moon*, dir. Michael Bay (Paramount, 2011).

26 FilmIsNow Movie Bloopers & Extras, "Iron Man 3 (2013) #3 'Chinese Version' Deleted, Extended & Alternative Scenes," YouTube, November 10, 2013, www.youtube.com/watch?v=39m85puOQok&t=17s.

27 Madisonboom, "Iron Man 2 YiliGuliduo Preview Commercial" [钢铁侠2 伊利谷粒多贴片广告], Youku.com, May 8, 2013, http://v.youku.com/v_show/id_XNTUzNzcwNzcy.html.

28 Peng, "Sino-US Film Coproduction," 301.

29 Chen, "Wang Xueqi Discusses Part Being Cut."

30 Liu Wei, "Co-productions Facing Up to Some Awkward Realities," *China Daily USA*, April 22, 2014, www.chinadaily.com.cn/culture/2014-04/22/content_17452769.htm.

31 "*Iron Man 3* Elicits Ire from Audiences: We Can Do without This Kind of Chinese Co-productions" [《钢铁侠3》引观众吐槽：这种中国特供版不要也罢], *People.cn*, May 2, 2013. http://media.people.com.cn/n/2013/0502/c40606-21336425.html.

32 Nai Xia [夏奈], "I'm Not Holding a Bucket of Popcorn So That I Could Watch Wang Xueqi Drink Guliduo" [我捧着一桶爆米花，不是为了看王学圻喝伊利谷物多的]," *Douban*, May 4, 2013, https://movie.douban.com/review/5918053/.

33 Xia, "I'm Not Holding a Bucket of Popcorn."

34 Lei Wang [王磊], "Product Placements Beware Rejection" [电影植入广告小心 '排异反应], Phoenix New Media Limited, July 21, 2011, http://culture.ifeng.com/1/detail_2011_07/21/7839494_0.shtml.

35 Yunxiang Yan, "Food Safety and Social Risk in Contemporary China," *Journal of Asian Studies* 71, no. 3 (2012): 717.

36 "China's Yili Recalls Mercury-Tainted Baby Formula Milk," *BBC*, June 15, 2012, www.bbc.com/news/world-asia-china-18456795.

37 Yan, "Food Safety," 710, 712.

38 Laohuang [老晃] [pseudonym], May 1, 2013, in response to "钢铁侠3 Iron Man 3 (2013)," *Douban*, n.d., https://movie.douban.com/subject/3231742/. The highest upvoted entry describes the experience of watching *Iron Man 3* as watching two different films.

39 mob_3781486463935938532, May 14, 2013, in response to madisonboom, "Iron Man 2 YiliGuliduo Preview Commercial."

40 Youkuuserw0131486463407241467 [优酷用户w0131486463407241467], May 8, 2013, in response to madisonboom, "Iron Man 2 YiliGuliduo Preview Commercial."

41 Yan, "Food Safety," 717.

42 Yan, "Food Safety," 715.

43 Yan, "Food Safety," 721.

44 Eric Kit-wai Ma, "Rethinking Media Studies: The Case of China," in *De-Westernizing Media Studies*, ed. James Curran and Myung-Jin Park (London: Routledge, 2000), 24.

45 Peter Coogan, *Superheroes: Secret Origins of a Genre* (Austin, TX: MonkeyBrain Books, 2006), 231.

46 Arguably, a Chinese equivalent to the superhero genre is the martial arts genre. Similar to superheroes, warriors and martial arts masters in legends and folklore have superhuman abilities, and while they have their own code of honor, they are not beholden to the state. The last character in Iron Man's Chinese name, 侠 (xiá), has historically been used to denote these heroes, and more recently they have been used in translation of superhero names.

Bibliography

Appadurai, Arjun. *Modernity at Large: Cultural Dimensions of Globalization*. Minneapolis: University of Minnesota Press, 1996.

Bushan, Nyay. "Stan Lee Unveils India-China Co-Production 'Monkey Master.'" *Hollywood Reporter*, September 21, 2016. www.hollywoodreporter.com/news/stan-lee-unveils-india-china-931431.

Chen Shuang [陈爽]. "Wang Xueqi Discusses Part Being Cut: The Role had Seemed Important" [王学圻谈戏份被删：当时看角色分量很重要]. Phoenix New Media Limited, May 2, 2013. http://cnt.ifeng.com/a/20130502/24848967_0.shtml.

"China's Yili Recalls Mercury-Tainted Baby Formula Milk." *BBC*, June 15, 2012. www.bbc.com/news/world-asia-china-18456795.

Coogan, Peter. *Superheroes: Secret Origins of a Genre*. Austin, TX: MonkeyBrain Books, 2006.

Costello, Matthew J. *Secret Identity Crisis: Comic Books and the Unmasking of Cold War America*. New York: Continuum, 2009.

Darowski, Joseph J., ed. *The Ages of Iron Man: Essays on the Armored Avenger in Changing Times*. Jefferson, NC: McFarland, 2015.

DeBoer, Stephanie. *Coproducing Asia: Locating Japanese-Chinese Regional Film and Media*. Minneapolis: University of Minnesota Press, 2014.

Denison, Rayna, and Rachel Mizsei-Ward, eds. *Superheroes on World Screens*. Jackson: University Press of Mississippi, 2015.

FilmIsNow Movie Bloopers & Extras. "Iron Man 3 (2013) #3 'Chinese Version' Deleted, Extended & Alternative Scenes." YouTube, November 10, 2013. www.youtube.com/watch?v=39m85puOQok&t=17s.

Ford, Rebecca. "Li Bingbing to Star as Superhero in 'Realm.'" *Hollywood Reporter*, October 28, 2015. www.hollywoodreporter.com/heat-vision/li-bingbing-star-as-superhero-835088.

Genter, Robert. "'With Great Power Comes Great Responsibility': Cold War Culture and the Birth of Marvel Comics." *Journal of Popular Culture* 40, no. 6 (2007): 953–978.

Hassler-Forest, Dan. *Capitalist Superheroes: Caped Crusaders in the Neoliberal Age*. Winchester, UK: Zero Books, 2012.

Iadonisi, Richard A. "Fu Manchu Meets Maklu-4: The Mandarin and Racial Stereotypes." In *The Ages of Iron Man: Essays on the Armored Avenger in Changing Times*, edited by Joseph J. Darowski, 39–50. Jefferson, NC: McFarland, 2015.

Iron Man. Directed by Jon Favreau. Marvel Studios, 2008.

Iron Man 2. Directed by Jon Favreau. Marvel Studios, 2010.

Iron Man 3. Directed by Shane Black. Marvel Studios, 2013.

"Iron Man 3." Box Office Mojo, November 5, 2017. www.boxofficemojo.com/movies/?page=intl&id=ironman3.htm.

"*Iron Man 3* Elicits Ire from Audiences: We Can Do without This Kind of Chinese Co-productions" [《钢铁侠3》引观众吐槽：这种中国特供版不要也罢]. *People.cn*, May 2, 2013. http://media.people.com.cn/n/2013/0502/c40606-21336425.html.

Jenkins, Henry. *Fans, Bloggers and Gamers: Media Consumers in a Digital Age*. New York: New York University Press, 2006.

Kapur, Shekhar. "The Asians Are Coming." *Guardian*, August 22, 2002. www.theguardian.com/film/2002/aug/23/artsfeatures1.

Kokas, Aynne. *Hollywood Made in China*. Oakland: University of California Press, 2017.

Lee, Stan. *Son of Origins of Marvel Comics*. New York: Simon & Schuster, 1975.

Lee, Stan (editor), Archie Goodwin (writer), and George Tuska (artist). "What Price Life?" *Iron Man* #19. New York: Marvel, November 1969.

Lee, Stan (plot), Larry Lieber (script), Don Heck (art), and Art Simek (lettering). "Iron Man Is Born!" *Tales of Suspense* #39. New York: Marvel, March 1963.

Lürzer's Archive. "Hollywood and Chinese Advertising." N.d. www.luerzersarchive.com/en/features/audiovisual/hollywood-and-chinese-advertising-198.html.

Ma, Eric Kit-wai. "Rethinking Media Studies: The Case of China." In *De-Westernizing Media Studies*, edited by James Curran and Myung-Jin Park, 17–28. New York: Routledge, 2000.

Madisonboom. "钢铁侠2伊利谷粒多贴片广告." Youku.com, May 8, 2013. http://v.youku.com/v_show/id_XNTUzNzcwNzcy.html.

Motion Picture Association of America. "Theatrical Marketing Statistics 2013." March 2014. www.mpaa.org/wp-content/uploads/2014/03/MPAA-Theatrical-Market-Statistics-2013_032514-v2.pdf.

Nye, Joseph. *Soft Power: The Means to Success in World Politics*. New York: PublicAffairs, 2004.

Peng, Weiying. "Sino-US Film Coproduction: A Global Primer." *Global Media and China* 1, no. 4 (2016): 295–311.

Roh, David S., Greta A. Niu, and Betsy Huang. "Technologizing Orientalism: An Introduction." In *Techno-Orientalism: Imagining Asia in Speculative Fiction, History, and Media*, edited by David S. Roh, Betsy Huang, and Greta A. Niu, 1–19. New Brunswick, NJ: Rutgers University Press, 2015.

Shaumbaugh, David. "China's Soft Power Push: The Search for Respect." *Foreign Affairs*, July/August 2015. www.foreignaffairs.com/articles/china/2015-06-16/china-s-soft-power-push.

Su, Wendy. *China's Encounter with Global Hollywood: Cultural Policy and the Film Industry, 1994–2013*. Lexington: University Press of Kentucky, 2016.

Transformers: Dark Side of the Moon. Directed by Michael Bay. Paramount Pictures, 2011.

Wang Lei [王磊]. "Product Placements Beware Rejection" [电影植入广告小心 "排异反应"]. Phoenix New Media Limited, July 21, 2011. http://culture.ifeng.com/1/detail_2011_07/21/7839494_0.shtml.

Wang, Shujen. *Framing Piracy: Globalization and Film Distribution in Greater China*. Lanham, MD: Rowan & Littlefield, 2003.

Wei, Liu. "Co-productions Facing Up to Some Awkward Realities." *China Daily USA*, April 22, 2014. www.chinadaily.com.cn/culture/2014-04/22/content_17452769.htm.

Xia Nai [夏奈]. "I'm Not Holding a Bucket of Popcorn So That I Could Watch Wang Xueqi Drink Guliduo" [我捧着一桶爆米花，不是为了看王学圻喝伊利谷物多的]. *Douban*, May 4, 2013. https://movie.douban.com/review/5918053/.

X-Men: Days of Future Past. Directed by Brian Singer. Twentieth Century Fox, 2014.

Yan, Yunxiang. "Food Safety and Social Risk in Contemporary China." *Journal of Asian Studies* 71, no. 3 (2012): 705–729.

Yúdice, George. *The Expediency of Culture: Uses of Culture in the Global Era*. Durham, NC: Duke University Press, 2004.

18

Age of the Atoman

Australian Superhero Comics and Cold War Modernity

KEVIN PATRICK

"Are 'Comic' Books Harmful to the Minds of Young Readers?" This was the question that the *Sydney Morning Herald* posed to its readers on December 28, 1948. A staff correspondent purchased twenty comic books from a newsstand, and discovered that modern-day comic magazines were no longer content with "illustrated whimsy or slapstick." Three-quarters of the comics examined were preoccupied with "arbitrary justice, futuristic fantasy, bulk slaughter, and sadism." Leading the fray were the so-called "supermen" comics, featuring characters who battled tyrants and criminals alike against a lethal backdrop of "death rays" and "atomic devastators." The newspaper quoted a Sydney psychiatrist who saw this new breed of "superheroes" as authoritarian figures dishing out vigilante justice and who were every bit as tyrannical as their macabre opponents. "This is the technique of dictatorship," the psychiatrist warned. "It is something against which we should guard ourselves."[1]

The reporter claimed that "the language used in many of the comics . . . shows an unmistakable United States origin." Yet many of the so-called "supermen" comics denounced in the article were not, in fact, American. For instance, of the six individual comic books cited by the *Sydney Morning Herald*, only *Captain Triumph* and *Hurricane Hawk* were of American origin (albeit printed under license in Australia). The remaining four comics were either British (*Garth—Man of Mystery*) or Australian titles (*Captain Atom*, *The Phantom Knight*, and *Tim Valour Comic*). This journalistic oversight, however, highlights an intriguing aspect of Australia's nascent comic book industry. While the publication rights for many popular American comics were held by large Australian publishers, smaller firms capitalized on this booming market by commissioning locally drawn superhero comics that deliberately emulated their American counterparts. Thus, Australian artists became responsible for some of the most popular "American-style" superhero comics published in Australia during the post–World War II era.

This chapter investigates this cultural paradox by studying the exploits of some of Australia's most popular comic book superheroes, such as Captain Atom and the Crimson Comet, and how they invoked broader anxieties about the fragility of Australian culture in an era of American media hegemony. It also looks at how these superheroes mirrored Australia's embrace of Cold War modernity, by articulating the possibilities and perils of new technologies, set amid the affluence of postwar consumerist society. However, these costumed superheroes did not monopolize the imagination of Australian readers. This chapter also considers how a rival cohort of so-called "mystery men"—masked adventurers like the Grey Domino and the Shadow—also resonated with Australian readers, not least because their comparative "realism" evoked memories of an earlier generation of popular British heroes, whose exploits predated the comic book revolution. Understanding this triangulation of cultural influences between Australia, Britain, and the United States not only highlights the complexities of Australia's postwar comics culture but also deepens our understanding of how the American superhero became a transnational phenomenon.

Australia's "Accidental" Comic Book Industry

Historian Richard White argues that American influences on Australian society have been most evident in those aspects of popular culture that are readily subject to technological change or most open to commercial exploitation.[2] This was reflected in the changing complexion of mass-market literature available to Australian readers throughout the 1930s. By the middle of the decade, it was estimated that a hundred thousand backdated American "pulp-fiction" magazines were being exported to Australia every month.[3] These illustrated story magazines were being joined by growing numbers of imported American comic books, which were sold through railway station bookstalls, newsagents, and selected discount retail chains.[4]

The popularity of imported American comics was not lost on Australian magazine publishers, which began producing their own variants of "American-style" comic books for the domestic market. But these publishers initially confined themselves to issuing magazine compilations of American newspaper comic strips that were already proven favorites with local audiences. Thus, Australia's first successful ongoing comic magazine was *The*

Adventures of Buck Rogers, released in November 1936 by Fitchett Bros. (Melbourne), which capitalized on the strip's exposure in the company's top-selling women's magazine the *New Idea*. From the outset, however, American comics provoked heated response from some quarters of Australian society. The Cultural Defence Committee, organized by the Fellowship of Australian Writers, denounced cheaply syndicated American comic strips, not only for undermining the economic livelihoods of Australian authors and illustrators but for propagating "cultural ideas which are entirely and literally foreign to Australian sentiment and British-Australian traditions."[5]

However, the birth of Australia's comic book industry was accelerated by the nation's entry into World War II. In 1940 the Australian government enforced import licensing restrictions that prohibited the importation of printed matter from non-sterling currency markets (i.e., United States and Canada), to preserve national currency reserves for the war effort.[6] The ban applied to all imported comic magazines and comic strip art intended for publication in Australia. This policy handed domestic publishers a captive market, but their capacity to exploit these favorable circumstances was hindered by the introduction of newsprint rationing and exacerbated by wartime prohibitions on the launch of new, ongoing periodicals.[7]

Frank Johnson Publications (Sydney) was one of a handful of firms eager to satisfy readers' demand for escapist reading material. The company overcame Australia's publishing restrictions by issuing comic books that were ostensibly "one-off" magazines. Unlike their American counterparts, Australian publishers could not call upon any local equivalent of the dedicated comic art studios that generated much of the content for America's wartime comic book industry. Instead, they often relied on individual writer-illustrators to produce an entire comic book.

The Superhero Deficit

It was under these straitened circumstances that Moira Bertram (1913–ca. 1993) forged her reputation as an outstanding comic book illustrator by creating Australia's first female superhero. Bertram originally created *Jo and Her Magic Cape* as a comic strip serial for Sydney's *Daily Mirror* newspaper in 1945. She subsequently repackaged the series as a comic book feature for several publishers (including Frank Johnson Publications) in the mid-1940s. *Jo and Her Magic Cape* distilled the creative and cultural paradoxes that underscored Australian-drawn superhero comics. Jo was a curvaceous Broadway dancer who owned a magician's cape that gave her the power of flight. Whenever danger threatened Jo would shed her civilian garments to reveal her skimpy, sequined stage costume and took to the skies after donning her cape (Figure 18.1). Bertram went to great lengths to portray Jo as an American, rather than Australian, superhero. Jo frequently joined her American fighter pilot boyfriend, Serge Shawn, in battling Japanese troops throughout the Asia-Pacific theater.

Unlike many of her peers Bertram had firsthand experience of American culture, having traveled to New York with her father, who was a Sydney wool-shipping agent. However, Bertram was not alone in her enthusiasm for all things American. Wartime Australia was transformed by the influx of nearly one million American servicemen stationed throughout the country. One Australian author, working as a stenographer for the U.S. Army, recalled the magnetic appeal of these "friendly invaders": "They were the neatest and most glamorous soldiers we had ever laid eyes on . . . the entire keynote of this amazing army seemed to be enthusiasm. . . . This was the feature that made us believe, after a time, in the identities like Flash Gordon and Superman."[8] Even at this anecdotal level, the dynamism and exuberance of American culture were associated with such fantastic creations as Superman. Little wonder that comic book superheroes came to be regarded by many Australians as a uniquely American idiom.

The relative dearth of wartime superheroes in Australian comics may be attributable to the creative dispositions of local artists. Many of Australia's earliest comic book illustrators were newspaper cartoonists who had difficulty adapting their style for comic books. This is evident in two early Australian examples of superheroes from the 1940s—*Powerman*, drawn by Norm Rice (1913–1956), and *Dr Mensana*, drawn by Tom Hubble (ca. 1903–1960). Neither artist fully grasped the medium's visual demands, as evidenced by their dull, unvarying panel compositions, overcrowded with word balloons. They belonged to an older generation of Australians raised on juvenile British "penny comics" and children's papers. The following account from Tony Rafty (1915–2015), a newspaper cartoonist who produced *Jimmy Rodney on Secret Service* (1940), the first Australian-drawn comic book, is revealing: "One day in 1940, [Brendan] Dowling [of NSW Bookstall Company] said to me, 'Will you do a comic strip for us? We'll print it.' I'd not read many comic books before then, maybe a few Yankee things . . . but I used to enjoy those English tabloid comics, which had lots of humor in them."[9]

Moira Bertram, by contrast, was enamored of the medium. "I wanted to do [comics] from the moment I first saw them," she later recalled. "There's just something fascinating about them."[10] Bertram, therefore, was well schooled in the visual dynamics of the comic book page and displayed an artistic virtuosity that eluded many of her male contemporaries. While Bertram discarded *Jo and Her Magic Cape* in favor of romance and science fiction/fantasy comics after the war, she proved that Australian cartoonists

Figure 18.1. "Jo and the Werewolf" (Dandy Comics, ca. 1946).

could successfully adapt superheroes to local conditions by retaining the genre's American trappings. But her approach, widely emulated by subsequent Australian-drawn superhero comics, was a harbinger of what architect and social commentator Robyn Boyd denounced as the "culture of Austerica." Australian society, he argued, was "mesmerized by the appearance of Americana" but was only capable of producing an austere, threadbare imitation of American popular culture.[11]

The Postwar Comics Explosion

Many of Australia's pioneering wartime comic book publishers were gradually squeezed out of the market by the reappearance of American comics on Australian newsstands. American publishers circumvented the ban on imported comic magazines by supplying Australian publishers with print-ready artwork (often at artificially low prices) that could be reproduced in locally printed comic books. The end of newsprint rationing in 1949, coupled with resurgent public demand for leisure reading, saw new comic magazines flood the Australian market. In 1949 there were already 90 comic book titles being published in Australia; that number had swelled to over 170 titles by 1954—but two-thirds of these were American titles printed under license by local publishers.[12] Despite the intense competition for readers' attention, comic book sales in Australia continued to climb at astonishing rates. By 1952, the number of comic books sold in Australia had reached 50 million copies annually, generating estimated revenues of A£2.4 million.[13]

Children undoubtedly composed the largest readership segment for comic books in Australia. A study of 455 school children in Perth, Western Australia, discovered that most thirteen-year-olds were reading more than ten comics per week.[14] Another study of Sydney adolescents claimed that thirteen-year-old boys read twice as many comics as girls and that "superhuman stories" were the most popular comic book genre.[15] The exponential growth of Australia's comic book industry during the late 1940s and early 1950s occurred just as Australia's postwar "baby boom" generation came of age during a period of relative economic prosperity. Comic books provided consumer brands with a direct marketing conduit to children and routinely featured advertisements for clothing, confectionery, and toys. Australian children, according to Mark Finnane, stood at the center of a "growing youth-oriented market for consumer goods," of which comic books, intended for "an audience exclusive of adults," were but one element.[16]

American superhero comics found new life on Australian shores following the end of the war. The inaugural series of *Superman Color Comics*, launched by K. G. Murray (Sydney) in 1947, was posting record sales of 150,000 copies per issue at a time when dozens of wartime-era superhero comics were facing cancellation in the United States due to declining sales.[17] While Americans had grown weary of superheroes, they had become an exciting new phenomenon to young Australian readers. And it was at this moment when *Captain Atom*, destined to become Australia's most popular "homegrown" superhero comic book, made its debut.

The origin of Australia's own "Atoman" bore the hallmarks of the dawning nuclear age. An infant child, trapped aboard a makeshift vessel, is washed ashore on a remote Pacific island, where he is found by a young woman named Lai. Lai discovers a note, which explains that the child and his twin brother were born on Bikini Atoll during the American atomic bomb tests held there after the war. Her father names the child Bikini Rador, and together they discover his strange secret: whenever danger threatens, Bikini utters the word "Exenor" and swaps places with his superpowered twin, Captain Atom.

Captain Atom was the brainchild of writer Jack Bellew (1907–1957), a former journalist and cofounder of Atlas Publications (Melbourne), and freelance cartoonist Arthur Mather (1925–2017). The series borrowed elements from rival American superheroes, including the magic word gimmick used by Captain Marvel ("Shazam!"), and the twin brother device from Captain Triumph. And just like Superman, Captain Atom could fly great distances, possessed superhuman strength, was impervious to bullets, and utilized x-ray vision. The comic strived to pass itself off as "American" in every way, even to the point where Mather granted Bikini Rador a new civilian identity—Larry Lockhart, FBI agent.

Captain Atom's exploits imbued atomic energy with magical qualities, while barely acknowledging its destructive potential. In one episode he is pitted against Rigor Mort, a supervillain who uses a radioactive disc implanted on his chest to absorb Captain Atom's atomic powers. He eventually thwarts Rigor Mort's plans to extract the secrets of atomic energy from the Prophet of Exenor ("You may kill me if you wish, but you will never learn the secret of atomic strength from my lips!").[18] The fairytale dimensions of this story, likening atomic power to a magic spell jealously guarded by mystical figure, stands as a bizarre counterpoint to the destructive realities of the British nuclear weapons tests conducted on Australian soil throughout the 1950s.[19]

The series' frenetic charm proved hugely popular with Australian readers. *Captain Atom* debuted in January 1948 and sold over one million copies by the end of its first year of publication.[20] By the mid-1950s, the Captain Atom Club boasted over seventy-five thousand members. In exchange for their glow-in-dark Captain Atom rings, new club members were instructed to be "truthful and honest" and "be kind and helpful always to other people."[21]

Australian Superheroes and the Cold War

The earliest American comic book superheroes were born during the waning years of the Great Depression, but their symbolic potential as expressions of American exceptionalism was truly realized only during World War II. The stark delineation of good and evil between the combatant nations allowed the United States to cast its war effort as the struggle for (American) democracy against the fascist ambitions of the Axis Powers. The war provided the perfect opportunity for superheroes to unleash their martial energies against the collective might of foreign invaders. Timely Comics, the forerunner of Marvel Comics, routinely pitted their headline superheroes—Captain America, the Human Torch, and the Sub-Mariner—against hordes of bestial German and Japanese soldiers. But peacetime robbed many superheroes of their moral purpose, while the complexities of the dawning "Cold War" between the United States and the Soviet Union made them unfit for service in a conflict indirectly waged through "dirty wars" fought in faraway lands. Even Atlas Comics' attempt to relaunch Captain America as a "Commie Smasher" in 1954 fell flat with American audiences and was promptly cancelled.

Ironically, the Cold War furnished several Australian comic book characters with the perfect opportunity for undertaking dangerous adventures in exotic locales, which reflected Australia's growing military engagements with communist forces throughout Southeast Asia. One example was *Char Chapman—The Phantom of the East*, written and illustrated by Kevan Hardacre (b.1927), for Young's Merchandising Co. (Sydney), in 1950. Char Chapman was a big-game hunter in the British protectorate of Malaya who donned the guise of the Phantom of the East. The hero was a supernatural figure revered by the "native" populace and fought cabals of slave traders, poachers, and scheming tribal chieftains commonly found in both American pulp-fiction magazines and British story papers during the interwar decades. However, at the height of the Malayan Emergency (1948–1960), when British Commonwealth forces (including Australia) fought communist guerillas, Char Chapman also battled communist insurgents. Creator Kevan Hardacre ruefully acknowledged that the series reflected prevailing Western attitudes toward anticolonial uprisings: "The Malay people were then trying to stop the British from regaining control (of the country) after World War II. . . . The press (was) demonizing them and, back then, I naively believed in the media services—and so Chapman was forever defeating the independence fighters. . . . Today, I would portray Char Chapman . . . as a champion of the people—a freedom fighter, certainly not an agent for neo-imperialism."[22] Clad in a skin-tight jersey and jodhpurs, with his face partly concealed by a bandana and aviator-styled goggles, the Phantom of the East cut an eccentric but strangely impressive figure. Yet because he chiefly relied on his hunting knife, revolver, and physical strength to overcome his opponents, the Phantom was not a true "superhero" in the modern sense of the word.

The Crimson Comet, by comparison, was the near-perfect embodiment of the American-styled superhero, who overcame the strangest origin story ever recorded in the annals of Australian comics. A brilliant surgeon, rendered insane by his wife's murder, grafts a pair of eagle's wings onto the back of his only child, a boy named Ralph Rivers. Growing to manhood, Rivers reinvents himself as the famous "hunch-backed private detective," known for solving baffling crimes. What his clients never realize is that Rivers's "hunchback," concealed by his trench coat, is the eagles' wings grafted onto his back. But when special measures are called for, Ralph Rivers discards his civilian guise and dons the red-and-yellow uniform of the Crimson Comet, who soars skyward, armed with a deadly ray pistol.

The Crimson Comet, launched in 1949, was created by John Dixon (1929–2015), who had developed the top-selling adventure series, *Tim Valour Comic*, for publisher H.J. Edwards (Sydney). The Crimson Comet's early exploits were conventional crime-detection stories, tinged with science-fiction elements, which saw him battle submarine pirates (#2), followed by a crime syndicate that used saber-tooth tigers to terrorize an entire city (#4).

Dixon handed *The Crimson Comet* over to artist Albert De Vine to focus on *Tim Valour Comic*. But when Dixon resumed control of the series in the early 1950s it took on the dramatic urgencies of the Cold War. At a time when Australian military forces were on the frontlines of the Korean War (1950–1953) Ralph Rivers was appointed Special Intelligence Agent by the United Nations to carry out clandestine missions against Sino-Korean forces. One assignment sees Rivers parachuted behind enemy lines to discover the whereabouts of a secret Chinese rocket base. Rivers sheds his military fatigues to become the Crimson Comet, and quickly discovers the rocket range, concealed in an abandoned village. The Crimson Comet is captured by the corpulent Colonel Wang, who sentences him to death. He is tied to a stake in the middle of the base's aerial firing range but manages to escape being strafed by the incoming MiG-15 jet fighters and redirects the next salvo of atomic warhead-tipped rockets back to the Chinese base, which is engulfed in a dreadful mushroom cloud.[23]

Dixon's decision to insert the Crimson Comet into a Korean War narrative was, admittedly, the exception rather than the norm for the relative handful of Australian-drawn superhero comics. But it does reflect Australian popular culture's historical preoccupation with the Chinese "Yellow Peril"—a fear that gathered force following China's entry into the Korean War in 1950.[24] The Crimson Comet's wartime exploits were made relatively plausible by the character's physical limitations. Although he was an undeniably fantastic superhero, he was not omnipotent in the way that Superman or, indeed, Captain Atom were. His presence, however fanciful, could not feasibly tip the military balance of power in a war that would end only in a bitter stalemate.[25]

Catman—Superhero Redux

The complex provenance of the superhero known as Catman further underscored the extent of the commercial and editorial links between American comic book publishers and their Australian counterparts in the postwar era. Cat-Man and his shapely female sidekick, Kitten, were created by Charles Quinlan and Irwin Hasen for *Crash Comics* (United States) in 1940. The duo proved so popular that *Crash Comics* was eventually renamed *Cat-Man Comics*, which rode out the superhero craze until its cancellation in 1946.

But Cat-Man was resurrected in Australia, after Frew Publications (Sydney) bought the rights to the character, and relaunched Catman (as he was now known) in *Super Yank Comics* (ca. 1951). The company's newest title continued an informal tradition, dating back to the early 1940s, when Australian publishers often gave their comic magazines such titles as *Popular Yank Comics* and *Famous Yank Comics*. They would often affix cover labels, such as "Price in Australia—6d," to reinforce the impression that these domestically printed comics were "genuine," imported American comic books.

It is doubtful whether such marketing ploys deceived Australian readers. Nor did Frew's new version of Catman compare favorably with the violent dynamism of the original American series. For starters Catman's original sidekick, Kitten, was replaced by a prepubescent boy named Kit—presumably in the hopes that younger (male) readers would identify with a character closer to their own age. The series was drawn in a simplistic style by the Australian artist Lloyd Piper (1923–1983), who later conceded his early comic book work was produced under "treadmill conditions."[26] But Catman and Kit proved no match for Batman and Robin—on whom they were clearly modeled (and who now starred in their own Australian-edition comic)—and the feline crime fighters disappeared after the abrupt cancellation of *Super Yank Comics* in 1952.

Ironically, the economic downturn that shook Australia's comic book industry following the advent of television broadcasting in 1956 proved fortuitous for both Frew Publications and Catman. One of the industry's casualties was H.J. Edwards Pty Ltd (publishers of *The Crimson Comet*), which closed its doors in 1957. As John Dixon later recalled, the circulation figures for many Australian-drawn comics plummeted from eighty thousand to just ten thousand copies per issue soon after the arrival of television.[27] Undeterred by such tough business conditions, Ron Forsyth

(1907–1991), the cofounder of Frew Publications, commissioned Dixon to revive Catman in an all-new series.

Catman and Kit were revamped as high-tech superheroes, clad in colorful, streamlined costumes that sported utility belts and infrared visors. Their secret headquarters, bristling with the latest crime-fighting equipment, was located atop their mountain stronghold, known as "Cat Rock." From their cliff-top hangar they would board their supersonic Cat Jet, and take off to their next dangerous assignment. The resemblance between Catman and Kit and Batman and Robin thus became even more pronounced under Dixon's hands.[28] But he altered the series dynamic by introducing Catman's fiancée, Terry West. The vivacious blonde was more than a match for many of Catman's opponents. In one episode a seafaring gang of thieves kidnap Terry, but she uses her wits to overpower one of her amorous captors and commandeers the ship's radio to notify Catman of her whereabouts ("They didn't expect trouble from a mere girl," she mused).[29] Unlike many female protagonists featured in Australian comic books, Terry was portrayed as a resourceful and capable ally during Catman and Kit's dangerous assignments.

Mystery Men: The Anglo-Australian Alternative

In 1954, the novelist Norman Bartlett complained that comic magazines now eclipsed the British public-school yarn and John Buchan thrillers, which were once staple reading for millions of Australians.[30] However, the British-styled "children's paper" enjoyed a brief resurgence in Australia during the 1950s. This renewed interest was partly in response to the deluge of American-style comics swamping the local market. The *Australian Boy* (1952–1955), for example, featured a mixture of illustrated short stories, puzzles, and factual articles, which made it "the comic that newsagents are proud to sell."[31] But even ostensibly "wholesome" publications like the *Australian Boy* were forced to acknowledge contemporary readers' tastes by including comic strip serials. Those children's papers that did not acquiesce to the appetite for comics soon vanished from newsagents' shelves.

Superheroes were undeniably popular, but they were not the only comic book heroes to captivate Australian readers' imagination. The 1950s ushered in a new a cohort of "mystery men" comics, featuring masked vigilantes who used their wits and their fists to combat evildoers. Aside from their distinctive code names and facial masks, they bore little resemblance to superheroes. Instead, they invoked an earlier generation of fantastic crime fighters (and antiheroes), which flourished in British story papers of the 1920s and 1930s. Many of these characters, according to comic book historian Chris Murray, could be legitimately described as British "protosuperheroes," which anticipated many of the defining elements of the American superhero genre.[32] However, it is also entirely possible that these comparatively realistic adventure comics appealed to older (adolescent) readers, who still craved escapist entertainment but now dismissed American-style superheroes as childish.

The Grey Domino, created by Terry Trowell (1918–1964) for Atlas Publications (Melbourne), was a leading example of the genre. The Grey Domino was the secret wartime guise of former British commando, Hugh Standish, who later became an "ace racing motorist." But the rise of organized crime and the threat of foreign espionage compelled Standish to once more don the mantle of the Grey Domino, "hooded crime breaker [and] relentless enemy of the underworld." Whereas many American superheroes operated outside the law, the Grey Domino frequently worked on behalf of the authorities. The War Office invites Standish to participate in road tests of a revolutionary new armored car, based on his military record, and his reputation as "one of our leading racing motorists." Standish naturally complies, but when the armored car is stolen he assumes the guise of the Grey Domino and eventually captures the foreign agents responsible for its disappearance.[33] Despite the character's Australian genesis, the Grey Domino—like so many British heroes of popular fiction—frequently works on behalf of the state, in defense of British interests. This stance further sets the Grey Domino apart from the vigilante justice practiced by American superheroes.[34]

The Shadow, created by Jeff Wilkinson (1924–2007) for Frew Publications in 1950, bore little resemblance to the famous American pulp magazine hero of the 1930s with whom he shared the same name. To the world at large Jimmy Gray is the "gay, charming (and) useless" heir to the fortune left by his industrialist father. Even his closest friend, Inspector Drummond of Scotland Yard, never suspected that Gray was the Shadow, the elusive crime fighter who terrorized the underworld. Many of the character's defining motifs were borrowed from the American pulp character, Jimmie Dale (aka the Gray Seal), first penned by Frank L. Packard for *People's Magazine* in 1914. But Wilkinson, a Royal Navy veteran who emigrated to Australia after the war, cast the Shadow as a British rather than American hero. Jimmy Gray often posed as "Limpy" Olsen, a small-time cockney thief, allowing him to move among London's gangland circles undetected. The Shadow also found himself embroiled in Cold War–era intrigue. In one episode he prevents a high-ranking War Office bureaucrat from being assassinated by Soviet troops inside Berlin's "Red Zone." The Shadow stops his pursuers in their tracks by lobbing a grenade into the turret of a Russian tank: "This is the best tin-opener I know!"[35]

These and other Australian "mystery men" comics, including Monty Wedd's *The Scorpion* (1954–1955) and Paul Wheelahan's *The Raven* (1962–1963), all cast their protagonists as British rather than American characters. Their intriguing similarities allude to the unspoken rivalry between the British and American influences over Australian popular culture throughout the 1950s. Together, they embodied the tough-but-fair ethos that typified past champions of British popular fiction, such as Richard Hannay and Sexton Blake. These Anglo-Australian "mystery men" therefore stood as a symbolic bulwark against the brash excess of the American superhero.

Conclusion

The American superhero once stood at the epicenter of Australian comic book culture. These powerful, bombastic figures excited children's imaginations, and their commercial success fueled the explosive postwar growth of Australia's comic book industry. Locally drawn equivalents, such as Captain Atom and the Crimson Comet, matched their popularity, but they were not "Australian" superheroes in any meaningful sense. Not only did they imitate the outward trappings of American comic book superheroes, but they were deliberately portrayed as American rather than Australian characters. The superhero was so readily identified as a uniquely American phenomenon that to cast the likes of Captain Atom as anything other than American would have tested the credulity of Australian audiences.

The same distortions were evident in the parallel genre of "mystery men" comics, which featured masked vigilantes who pursued gangsters, foreign spies, and other threats to civil society. The Grey Domino and the Shadow, leading exponents of this trend, were created for the Australian market but were nevertheless depicted as British heroes. Just as superheroes were the distinct byproduct of American comic books, these characters owed their inspiration to the "protosuperheroes" once found in British children's papers of the 1930s. The cultural logic of this genre dictated that these Australian-drawn heroes must themselves be "British-to-their-bootstraps."

The undeclared contest between British and American culture, and their respective influence on Australian society, shaped the commercial and creative directions of Australia's nascent comic book industry. For young Australians superheroes embodied the lurid appeal of comic books. For their parents comic book superheroes were emblematic of a violent, alien culture. Superheroes thus became more than symbols of a transnational publishing phenomenon. Their seismic popularity spoke to broader anxieties about the fragility of Australia's own sense of cultural identity, set amid the promise and the perils of the Cold War era.

Notes

1 "Are 'Comic' Books Harmful to Minds of Young Readers?," *Sydney Morning Herald,* December 28, 1948, 2.

2 Richard White, "'Americanization' and Popular Culture in Australia," *Teaching History* 12, no. 2 (August 1978): 7.

3 Peter Coleman, *Obscenity, Blasphemy, Sedition: Censorship in Australia* (Brisbane: Jacaranda Press, 1963), 146.

4 John Ryan, *Panel by Panel: A History of Australian Comics* (Stanmore, NSW: Cassell Australia, 1979), 150, 154.

5 Cultural Defence Committee, *Mental Rubbish from Overseas: A Public Protest* (Sydney: Fellowship of Australian Writers, 1935), 4, 6.

6 S. J. Butlin, *War Economy, 1939–1942* (Canberra: Australian War Memorial, 1955), 115–122.

7 "New Publications: Rationing Order Prohibits," *Canberra Times*, August 15, 1940, 4.

8 Maureen C. Meadows, *I Loved Those Yanks* (Sydney: George M. Dash, 1948), 12, 25–26.

9 Kevin Patrick, "Tony Rafty, OAM—Comic Book Pioneer," *Collectormania* December 2006, 19.

10 Sally McInerney, "Moira, Black Knox, and the Flame Man," *Sydney Morning Herald*, August 6, 1983, 34.

11 Robin Boyd, "The Culture of Austerica," *Quadrant* 2, no. 2 (Autumn 1958): 40.

12 "Comics," *Current Affairs Bulletin* 5, no. 5 (November 21 1949): 71; Norman Bartlett, "Culture and Comics," *Meanjin* 13, no. 1 (1954): 8.

13 W. F. Connell, E. P. Francis, and Elizabeth E. Skilbeck, *Growing Up in an Australian City: A Study of Adolescents in Sydney* (Melbourne: Australian Council for Educational Research, 1957), 155; Brian Fitzpatrick, *The Australian Commonwealth: A Picture of the Community, 1901–1955* (Melbourne: F.W. Cheshire, 1956), 50.

14 "Sixty Comics a Week," *West Australian*, August 30, 1952, 7.

15 "Child Tastes Analysed: 'Comic' Reading and Film-Going," *Sydney Morning Herald*, August 26, 1952, 2.

16 Mark Finnane, "Censorship and the Child: Explaining the Comics Campaign," *Australian Historical Studies* 23, no. 92 (April 1989): 234.

17 Ryan, *Panel by Panel*, 188, 190.

18 Arthur Mather, *Captain Atom* #36 (Melbourne: Atlas Publications, ca. 1951).

19 See Lorna Arnold and Mark Smith, *Britain, Australia, and the Bomb: The Nuclear Tests and Their Aftermath* (Hampshire: Palgrave Macmillan, 2005).

20 "The First Million!" (advertisement), *Newspaper News*, November 1, 1948, 15.

21 "Captain Atom Fan Club" (advertisement), *Captain Atom* #56 (Melbourne: Atlas Publications, ca. 1953).

22 Kevin Patrick, "Interview: Kevan Hardacre," *Comics Down Under*, May 5, 2008, http://comicsdownunder.blogspot.com/2008/05/interview-kevan-hardacre.html.

23 John Dixon, *The Crimson Comet* #59 (Sydney: H.J. Edwards, ca. 1953), 1–11.

24 Alison Broinowski, *The Yellow Lady: Australian Impressions of Asia* (Melbourne: Oxford University Press, 1992).

25 Historian Humphrey McQueen states that anti-Asian sentiment in Australia first gathered force in the mid-1800s, fueled by concerns that cheap Asian laborers (particularly from China), lured by Australia's "gold rush," would undermine Australian workers' economic prospects. These economic concerns soon gave way to broader social condemnation of Asian migrants, based on explicitly racial grounds, and led to growing calls for the preservation of "White Australia" through the introduction of restrictive immigration policies designed to curtail Asian migration from other parts of the British Empire, most notably Hong Kong and India. Humphrey McQueen, *A New Britannia* (St Lucia: University of Queensland Press, 2004), 30–44.

26 Lloyd Piper, "Lloyd Piper," in *Cartoonists of Australia*, ed. Richard Rae (Marrickville, NSW: View Productions, 1983), 76–81.

27 Phillip O'Brien, "John Dixon's *Air Hawk*," *National Library Magazine* 3, no. 4 (December 2011): 29.

28 Dixon produced just twelve issues of *Catman* for Frew Publications in the late 1950s, before leaving the comics industry to focus on his newspaper comic strip, *Air Hawk and the Flying Doctor*. However, the title was subsequently reprinted by Page Publications (Sydney) in the mid- to late 1960s. The company perhaps sensed that the character's similarities to Batman could feasibly exploit the popularity of the *Batman* television series, which began screening in Australia in 1967.

29 John Dixon, *The Adventures of Cat-Man* #16 (Sydney: Frew Publications, ca. 1966), 9.

30 Bartlett, "Culture and Comics," 17.

31 *Australian Boy* #7 (January 9, 1953).

32 Chris Murray, *The British Superhero* (Jackson: University Press of Mississippi, 2017), 38–44.

33 Terry Trowell, *The Grey Domino* #7 (Melbourne: Atlas Publications, ca. 1952).

34 Jason Dittmer, *Captain America and the Nationalist Superhero: Metaphors, Narratives, and Geopolitics* (Philadelphia: Temple University Press, 2013), 15.

35 Jeff Wilkinson, *The Shadow* #83 (Sydney: Frew Publications, ca. 1961), 22.

Bibliography

"Are 'Comic' Books Harmful to Minds of Young Readers?" *Sydney Morning Herald*, December 28, 1948.

Arnold, Lorna, and Mark Smith. *Britain, Australia, and the Bomb: The Nuclear Tests and Their Aftermath*. Hampshire: Palgrave Macmillan, 2005.

Australian Boy #7. January 9, 1953.

Bartlett, Norman. "Culture and Comics." *Meanjin* 13, no. 1 (1954): 5–18.

Boyd, Robyn. "The Culture of Austerica." *Quadrant* 2, no. 2 (Autumn 1958): 39–43.

Broinowski, Alison. *The Yellow Lady: Australian Impressions of Asia*. Melbourne: Oxford University Press, 1992.

Butlin, S. J. *War Economy, 1939–1942*. Canberra: Australian War Memorial, 1955.

"Captain Atom Fan Club" (advertisement). *Captain Atom* #56. Melbourne: Atlas Publications, ca. 1953.

"Child Tastes Analysed: 'Comic' Reading and Film-Going." *Sydney Morning Herald*, August 26, 1952.

Coleman, Peter. *Obscenity, Blasphemy, Sedition: Censorship in Australia*. Brisbane: Jacaranda Press, 1963.

"Comics." *Current Affairs Bulletin* 5, no. 5 (November 21, 1949): 71–83.

Connell, W .F., E. P. Francis, and Elizabeth E. Skilbeck. *Growing Up in an Australian City: A Study of Adolescents in Sydney*. Melbourne: Australian Council for Educational Research, 1957.

Cultural Defence Committee. *Mental Rubbish from Overseas: A Public Protest*. Sydney: Fellowship of Australian Writers, 1935.

Dittmer, Jason. *Captain America and the Nationalist Superhero: Metaphors, Narratives, and Geopolitics*. Philadelphia: Temple University Press, 2013.

Dixon, John. *The Crimson Comet* #59. Sydney: H.J. Edwards, ca. 1953.

———. "Curse of the Diamond." In *The Adventures of Catman* #16. Surry Hills, NSW: Page Publications, ca. 1966.

Finnane, Mark. "Censorship and the Child: Explaining the Comics Campaign." *Australian Historical Studies* 23, no. 92 (April 1989): 220–240.

"The First Million!" (advertisement). *Newspaper News*, November 1, 1948.

Fitzpatrick, Brian. *The Australian Commonwealth: A Picture of the Community, 1901–1955*. Melbourne: F.W. Cheshire, 1956.

Mather, Arthur. "Reflection Racket." In *Captain Atom* #36. Melbourne: Atlas Publications, ca. 1951.

McInerney, Sally. "Moira, Black Knox, and the Flame Man." *Sydney Morning Herald*, August 6, 1983.

McQueen, Humphrey. *A New Britannia*. St Lucia: University of Queensland Press, 2004.

Meadows, Maureen C. *I Loved Those Yanks*. Sydney: George M. Dash, 1948.

Murray, Chris. *The British Superhero*. Jackson: University Press of Mississippi, 2017.

"New Publications: Rationing Order Prohibits." *Canberra Times*, August 15, 1940.

O'Brien, Phillip. "John Dixon's *Air Hawk*." *National Library Magazine* 3, no. 4 (December 2011): 29.

Patrick, Kevin. "Interview: Kevan Hardacre." *Comics Down Under*, May 25, 2008. http://comicsdownunder.blogspot.com/2008/05/interview-kevan-hardacre.html.

———. "Tony Rafty, OAM—Comic Book Pioneer." *Collectormania*, December 2006, 19.

Piper, Lloyd. "Lloyd Piper." In *Cartoonists of Australia*, edited by Richard Rae, 76–81. Marrickville, NSW: View Productions, 1983.

Ryan, John. *Panel by Panel: A History of Australian Comics*. Stanmore, NSW: Cassell Australia, 1979.

"Sixty Comics a Week: A Shock in Perth." *West Australian*, August 30, 1952.
Trowell, Terry. "Terror on the Road." In *The Grey Domino* #7. Melbourne: Atlas Publications, ca. 1952.
White, Richard. "'Americanization' and Popular Culture in Australia." *Teaching History* 12, no. 2 (August 1978): 3–21.
Wilkinson, Jeff. *The Shadow* #83. Sydney: Tricho Publications, ca. 1961.

19

An Interview with *Cleverman* Creator Ryan Griffen and Star Hunter Page-Lochard

LIAM BURKE

One of this collection's central interests is how superheroes have been used to reflect and articulate society's unresolved issues. As superheroes move from American icons to global symbols, they are increasingly expressing local issues within the broadly appealing framework of the genre. Since the colonization of Australia began in 1788, indigenous Australians have suffered a series of social injustices. While attempts have been made in recent years to redress these imbalances, many feel that first nations people are marginalized and disadvantaged in Australia. Reflecting that unease, writer Ryan Griffen created the television series *Cleverman*, which draws on Aboriginal mythology to create an Australian superhero.

Cleverman is set in a near-future Australia in which ancient creatures, the "Hairypeople," have remerged to take their place alongside humans. However, coexistence is not so easy with government agencies denying the Hairypeople (or "Hairies") their civil rights. Navigating this tense climate is Koen (Hunter Page-Lochard), an indigenous Australian who has distanced himself from his community, only to have the ancient power of the Cleverman foisted upon him.

Featuring a largely Aboriginal cast and dealing with themes such as identity, racism, and responsibility, *Cleverman* was met with critical acclaim when it first aired on Australian television in 2016. A wider audience has discovered this uniquely Australian superhero through

Figure 19.1. *Cleverman* creator Ryan Griffen. Photo by Wayne Quilliam and Michelle Grace Hunder.

international broadcasts, such as on Sundance TV in the United States and BBC3 in the United Kingdom. Series creator Ryan Griffen was interviewed prior to the show's broadcast, while star Hunter Page-Lochard was interviewed at the Australian Movie & Comic Expo following the first season.

Ryan Griffen Interview

LIAM BURKE You're obviously a longtime superhero fan. Who is your favorite superhero and why?

RYAN GRIFFEN My favorite superhero is Batman. Batman is a human just like us. He doesn't have any superpowers and he's just as vulnerable emotionally as anyone else. It does help that he's a billionaire, but for me he's just someone who has gone out of his way to pursue something and that's what makes him a superhero.

LB You've created an indigenous Australian superhero with the television show *Cleverman*, where did the idea come from?

RG I came up with the concept almost seven years ago during an afternoon playing Ninja Turtles with my son. We're big Ninja Turtles and Batman fans and I wanted to create something for him that he could connect to on a cultural basis. From that day on I wanted to make an Aboriginal superhero for him.

The premise of this show is about two brothers who are about to be handed down a gift of being the Cleverman and one is chosen over the other and it is sort of a battle between those two of how they deal with that. Mix that into a world where Dreamtime creatures live among us and we follow different journeys throughout that.[1]

LB So you were responding to the shortage of Australian superheroes generally and indigenous Australian superheroes specifically?

RG Cleverman isn't the first Aboriginal superhero. There's several. Not many people know that there's an Aboriginal Avenger, Manifold. For me the difference is that these are superheroes that were created by people outside of Australia and they're just using either stereotypes or what they can quickly Google to help fuel the creation of the characters. We were very much in culture and adhere to cultural sensitivities with our characters, such as what weapons they wield, and all that sort of stuff. I guess for me it was important to create a superhero that is culturally appropriate.

LB Then how would you define a superhero?

RG They come in all different shapes and sizes and abilities. I guess it's on two levels; In the real world superheroes are someone that any normal person could look up to or aspire to be, whether it's about how they live their life or having the ability to give that person strength. Within the fictional world it's a hard to really pin down what actually makes someone a superhero.

LB Do you think we can have superheroes in everyday life?

RG Absolutely. I think a superhero can just be someone who helps someone across the road. People read comics and follow superhero journeys to feel empowered or look up to someone. That could just be someone's brother or sister just helping them out. I think they live with us all the time.

LB How did you use superhero genre conventions in *Cleverman* to address larger issues and topics?

RG I think putting political issues in a superhero world allows people to feel like they're not being preached to. You allow people to fall in love with the character and then learn about how they are treated, and that is something that they may have never gone through in their life. I think we in *Cleverman*, the team, we use the same sort of motifs as *X-Men*. In our case we have the hairy creatures where *X-Men* has the mutants and it allows your audience to impose their own views onto the story, whether that is a black and white story or a gay and straight story or a refugee story.

LB *Cleverman* draws on actual Aboriginal mythology and culture. How did you choose which myths to use and how did you go about making them feel contemporary?

RG We've used our culture, the Aboriginal culture, in different ways. For example, one of our character's story arcs is shaped around the Dreaming story of "Why the Crow Is Black" and the morals and lessons that that bird learned is one of the key things to that character. We also use Aboriginal culture to create our creatures and to open up the spectrum of political issues. It was quite hard to create a story using cultural sensitivities because you'll get to a point where you'll hear a story beat that is amazing in the genre world and you really want to do it. But I'll be sitting in the room and I'll put my hand up and go: "Well look we can't do that because of the cultural sensitivity." You then need to figure out a way to create that story and adhere to the culture, but also give people what they expect from the genre.

LB Given the cultural sensitivity and genre conventions the lead character, Koen, is unconventional in the way that he's quite selfish and removed from his community.

RG I guess for me that was an identity issue and showing an outsider pushing away culture and coming to understand that. The role of a Cleverman in layman terms is kind of like "The Pope of the Dreamtime." It's someone who's appointed as a conduit between the present and the Dreaming and so that's quite a powerful role for someone who is living outside of their culture.

LB Do you think that because the show is in the superhero genre that it will bring aspects of Aboriginal mythology and culture to a wider audience both in Australia and around the world?

RG I think the one thing that keeps our show unique is that these are sixty-thousand-year-old stories that have never been told in this sort of realm, and that's what broadcasters around the world are looking for: something new, something different. People ask the question "how do you think people outside of Australia are going to deal with understanding the Aboriginal culture?," and my response to that is that many people *in* Australia don't understand the Aboriginal culture. There's still a lot to learn here about the mistreatment or cultural law or what it means to be an Aboriginal person in modern day society. I think that's what helps the show reach a wider audience because it's about being treated as the other.

LB In the show the "hairy people" represent the other. Why did you decide on that mythological character and how did you go about conceiving that look?

RG Hairy Men are quite a universal story within all the Aboriginal cultures in Australia. You can go to far north Queensland and they're telling stories of a shorter, more mischievous hairy man. My country they talk about it being a stronger and more aggressive creature. The benefit is then we would go and obtain permission from different places to sort of create a hairy creature that is unique to the show, but still staying true to where the stories came from.

The first time that we teamed up with Weta Workshop to create the creatures, these creatures were really hairy and almost like Wookie-like.[2] For me you lose a little bit of that relatability. You want the audience to connect, and I'd always say that what we want to do is to create these creatures to be as human as possible and it's up to our audience to determine whether they are considered creatures or human?

LB Why do you think Superheroes are so popular now?

RG I think we're breaking past the point where superheroes are associated with comic books. I think cinema and television is the strongest it has ever been. We have the ability to do stuff that you could never think of doing ten or twenty years ago. So you're reaching a bigger audience and people want to be told a story and they're realizing that underneath a lot of superhero stories is a human story. That's what's connecting with people. If you can get that with a whole lot of action and intrigue at the same time, then that's what people start to love.

Hunter Page-Lochard Interview

LIAM BURKE Hunter, you're a big superhero fan, but who is your favorite superhero?

HUNTER PAGE-LOCHARD My favorite superhero is Stan Lee's Spider-Man. I'm sorry I've got to go OG on this one. I've loved Spider-Man from day dot because he's the most similar to us as geeks and nerds, not in the way that he is really smart, but in the way that he is underestimated.

LB How important is it to have an Australian superhero?

HP To have an Australian superhero and to be playing an Australian superhero, especially an indigenous Australian superhero, is probably the biggest privilege I could ever have bestowed onto me in my entire life. The fact that we're telling Dreaming stories to the point where the Dreaming is a part of his powers is magnificent. That we can aesthetically please people with the superhero-ness of the show and then also give them the spirituality is a win-win.

LB You were a superhero fan growing up, can you remember the first superhero that had an impact on you?

HP My early fandom I think started with The Phantom comics. I always loved the purple suit and the mystery and the pizzazz of him riding a horse in the jungle and the whole get-up, I loved it. And then obviously I got straight into Marvel and I got straight into Spider-Man and got into my Hulks and got into my Wolverines and it slowly progressed onto when I was introduced to *Star Wars* and Tim Burton and it just blew up.

LB So how does it feel now being on the other side of the table at this convention?

HP Oh my God, man, it's like a dream come true. Being able to play a superhero on an Australian TV show is like wow! And for that character to be Aboriginal as well and have cultural integrity is amazing. His powers are all about his culture, which is beautiful. Then to be at a convention where I'm sitting next to [G.I. Joe and Wolverine writer] Larry [Hama], there's a Disney princess walking past me [*Aladdin* voice actress Linda Larkin], and I've got a Cyborg next door [*Justice League* actor Ray Fisher] and it's like whoa, this is awesome. But the thing that's sort of awesome about it is little small me from Australia deserves to be here as much as they deserve to be here as well, so it's overwhelming and exciting at the same time.

LB Why do you think superheroes have such resonance in recent times?

HP Superheroes are so popular because I feel like they still, no matter what, keep the authenticity of the classic dream. Everyone wants to be a hero, everyone wants to be able to do something that they can't do, they always want to challenge themselves. And to see superheroes go through that it's a little bit uplifting and then it excites you with things and makes you think outside the box. How many times have you gone, "God, I wish I could just teleport" or something like that and that wouldn't come to your brain unless you were already enveloped into this fantasy world and I think that's what people love is the fantasy aspect of it.

LB You meet a lot of fans at conventions in superhero cosplay. What do you think the appeal is of dressing up as your favorite character?

HP I think it's the attention, but the attention in a good way. It's not like attention seeking or anything like that. Sci-fi fans are people that are introverts and being introvert is not really a bad thing, introverts are very creative and they're very into their passions and their hobbies and stuff. Then when they get a chance to express that and to put a mask on and be in character they feel like they can be the person that they love. I'm sure if I put on a morph suit I feel like I can lift up a car or something like that, you know, the skintight suit or something, I want to be a vigilante and go out there. So I feel the cosplay thing is just another way to step into that fantasy and really step out of their skin, but still feel quite the same.

LB How do you think fan culture in Australia compares with the rest of the world? Do you think Australia can compete so far from the birthplace of superheroes in America?

HP Definitely. I think it's definitely becoming bigger in Australia for sure. We're still competing against the heavyweights that are international and stuff but, look, Australia's still a young country. Australia is so far away from everyone. It's hard to get to guests, when guests have to travel twenty-six hours. So it is a little bit harder for us, but I love how we're still kind of prevailing through that and we're still showing the world that we're a part of this culture and this community as well and we love it. And yet you've got all these Marvel and DC films, *Cleverman*, you've got all these things coming out now that make people feel a part of it on a global level.

LB Cleverman weaves political commentary into the superhero story, how does the show strike the right balance?

HP I think it's because of the genre. I think sci-fi allows anything to weave together whether it be a social political problem or just something that's human nature. To aesthetically give you what you want, but then the subliminal message is something that you need. It gives us a chance to retell our struggles as Aboriginal people through this world whilst still giving you that aesthetic pleasure, and I think they do it in a way where they're not pulling any punches and I feel like that's good because we need to do that more often.

LB Do you think it opens the door for more Australian superheroes?

HP Definitely and hopefully films, hopefully a lot more films. TV is great and TV is taking over the world, but imagine having a superhero film set in Sydney and then there's a big battle at Uluru. Because of the landscape, we've got such great locations in this country and great actors.

Look, at Marvel there have been Aboriginal characters, the X-Man Bishop is Aboriginal you know. I think what is important now is that these characters start being created by Australian people and I feel like *Cleverman* is a great step in that direction. I was always disappointed because I never had a role model that I could look up to that was Aussie and now we have these little kids that are coming to this convention just to see me because there's an Aussie hero, which is amazing. It's amazing, we need more of it.

Notes

1 Dreamtime is a central aspect of Aboriginal spiritual beliefs. In Dreamtime, all life is part of a larger network that can be traced back to the great spirit ancestors of the Dreamtime.

2 New Zealand–based special effects and prop company Weta Workshop, which gained international attention for its work on *The Lord of the Rings* trilogy, designed the Hairy Men for *Cleverman*.

ACKNOWLEDGMENTS

After decades of resting on the fringes of popular culture superheroes have secured their place as a dominant force in political and cultural life. The editors would like to thank the contributors to this collection who brought a range of disciplinary perspectives to help us better understand the superhero's symbolic function. We must also acknowledge the creators who found time in their busy schedules to participate in the interviews that punctuate each section: Trina Robbins, Diane Nelson, Paul Dini, Ryan Griffen, and Hunter Page-Lochard.

A heartfelt thank you to the team at Rutgers University Press, in particular Leslie Mitchner and Nicole Solano, who gave the book a home and were patient and collaborative throughout the process. This book is a research outcome from the Australian Research Council (ARC) Linkage Project Superheroes & Me. We would like to acknowledge the ARC's support of this book and the larger project. We must also thank our industry partner the Australian Centre for the Moving Image (ACMI) for hosting the Superhero Identities Symposium at which many of these chapters were first presented.

We greatly appreciate Swinburne University of Technology's Cinema and Screen Studies discipline for its contribution to the symposium, which made Paul Dini's visit to Melbourne (and his interview for this collection) possible. Thank you to our Superheroes & Me coresearchers Wendy Haslem and Elizabeth MacFarlane for their support, as well as Taylor Hardwick, Samuel Harvey, Mark Hellinger, Cameron Pearce, Henrikk Svensson Dalgren, and Harry Wall. Finally, thank you to Gestalt Editor-in-Chief Wolfgang Bylsma for facilitating the collection's cover image, and super-artist James Brouwer for creating the dynamic art.

NOTES ON CONTRIBUTORS

MITCHELL ADAMS is a research associate at the Centre for Transformative Innovation at Swinburne University of Technology and the Swinburne Law School. His interest is in empirical studies in intellectual property law. His current research projects include examining the registered trademarks system in Australia. He is a registered trademarks attorney and an Australian solicitor with experience in intellectual property and entertainment law. He has worked in the Intellectual Property and Commercialisation group at CSIRO and before that at a prominent entertainment law practice in Melbourne. He graduated from Monash University with LLB(Hons) and BSc degrees, and was awarded first class honors in law in the area of intellectual property law.

JASON BAINBRIDGE is the head of the School of Creative Industries at the University of South Australia. He is a nationally and internationally recognized researcher in popular representations of law; superheroes, justice, and comic book culture; the functioning of popular culture as vernacular theory; and the study of merchandising and material culture in relation to media convergence, particularly the function of toys and play in mainstreaming fan culture. He has also written widely on the relationship between media and journalism, checkbook journalism, and risk communication.

LIAM BURKE is the coordinator of the cinema and screen studies major at Swinburne University of Technology, where he also teaches classes on comic books and cinema. He has written and edited a number of books, including *Superhero Movies* (2008), *Fan Phenomena Batman* (2012), and *The Comic Book Film Adaptation: Exploring Modern Hollywood's Leading Genre* (2015). He is a chief investigator on the Superheroes & Me research project with the Australian Centre for the Moving Image. His other research interests include new media and migration, audience research, and the films of John Ford.

STEVEN CONWAY is director of the games and interactivity program at Swinburne University of Technology. He has presented on many aspects of play, philosophy, aesthetics, and culture and has had a variety of articles published on these subjects in journals such as *Convergence*, *Eludamos*, *Game Studies*, *Journal of Gaming & Virtual Worlds*, *Sociology of Sport Journal*, and *Westminster Papers in Communication & Culture*. He is also coeditor of the first collection in academia on the relationship between policy and digital games, *Video Game Policy: Production, Distribution and Consumption*.

NEAL CURTIS is an associate professor in media and communication at the University of Auckland, where he teaches the course "Comics and Visual Narrative." He is the author of four books on a variety of topics, but most recently published *Sovereignty and Superheroes* in 2016.

DAN GOLDING is a senior lecturer in media and communications at Swinburne University of Technology. He has written on film, music, and videogames for the ABC, *The Australian*, *Metro Magazine*, and *Buzzfeed*, and is the coauthor of *Game Changers*. In 2013 he won the Best Games Journalist award at the Eleventh Annual IT Journalism awards. He regularly works with the Melbourne Symphony Orchestra to present concerts of film music, he made the soundtrack to *Push Me Pull You* (2016), and from 2014 to 2017 he was director of the Freeplay Independent Games Festival.

IAN GORDON is a professor of American history at the National University of Singapore. His books include *Comic Strips and Consumer Culture* (1998), *Superman: The Persistence of an American Icon* (2016), and *Kid Comic Strips: A Genre across Four Countries* (2016), as well as the coedited collections *Comics & Ideology* (2001), *Film and Comic Books* (2007), and *The Comics of Charles Schulz: The Good Grief of Modern Life* (2016). He is an international contributing editor to the *Journal of American History* and on the editorial board of several journals including the *Journal of Graphic Novels and Comics*, *Popular Communication*, *Studies in Comics*, and *ImageText*.

VLADISLAV IOUCHKOV has completed his doctorate thesis at the School of Social Sciences and Psychology at Western Sydney University. His research interests lie at the intersection of crime, risk-taking behavior, religion/spirituality, and identity, with a focus on exploring the impact of popular culture in shaping human behavior. His work is involved in examining the real-life superhero movement and the transformational processes that its participants experience, and how this translates into a variety of social control and welfare initiatives. He has published his research in the *Journal of Criminological Research* and *Policy and Practice* and has coauthored a chapter for *Fiction, Invention and Hyper-reality* (2017).

HENRY JENKINS is the Provost Professor of Communication, Journalism, Cinematic Arts and Education at the University of Southern California. He joined USC from the Massachusetts Institute of Technology, where he was Peter de Florez Professor in the Humanities. He directed MIT's Comparative Media Studies graduate degree program from 1993 to 2009, setting an innovative research agenda during a time of fundamental change in communication, journalism, and entertainment. Some of his many publications include *Convergence Culture* (2006), *Spreadable Media*, with Sam Ford and Joshua Green (2013), *Participatory Culture in a Networked Era*, with Mizuko Ito and danah boyd (2015), and *By Any Media Necessary: The New Youth Activism*, with Sangita Shresthova, Liana Gamber-Thompson, et al. (2016).

CLAIRE LANGSFORD is a visiting fellow at the University of Adelaide's Department of Anthropology and Development Studies. Drawing on material culture and performance approaches, her doctoral thesis explored transformation within the Australian cosplay community of practice, examining the transformations between textual and material, digital and physical, local and global. Her recent writings, including her contribution to *Manga Vision: Cultural and Communications Perspectives* (2016), explore the intersections of performance, materiality, and community in digital spaces and technologies.

NAJA LATER researches and teaches at the University of Melbourne and Swinburne University of Technology. Her PhD researched twenty-first-century American horror movies and their relationship to terror and media cultures. She has published research on superheroes, monsters, and transmedia storytelling. She is a cofounder of the All Star Women's Comic Book Club and organizer of the 2016 Women in Comics Festival.

TARA LOMAX is completing a PhD in screen studies at the University of Melbourne, with research that examines the creative-industrial dynamics of franchise cinema and contemporary Hollywood entertainment. Her research has been published in the edited collection *Star Wars and the History of Transmedia Storytelling*, with forthcoming publications on supervillainy, horror, and seriality. Her other research considers the local-global shifts in the Hollywood visual effects industry. She is also a sessional lecturer in the School of Film and Television at the Victorian College of the Arts, and a sessional tutor in cinema studies at RMIT University. She is a graduate of the Australian Film Television and Radio School, the University of Sydney, and La Trobe University.

PAUL M. MALONE is an associate professor of German in the Department of Germanic and Slavic Studies at the University of Waterloo, Canada. He is the author of *Franz Kafka's* The Trial*: Four Stage Adaptations* (2003) and has also published on performance theory, Faustian rock musicals, German film, and German-language comic books.

JOHN MCGUIRE is a lecturer in sociology and criminology at the School of Social Sciences & Psychology and academic director (Sydney City Campus) at Western Sydney University. He completed his thesis, "With Us or Against Us? Hegemony and Ideology within American Superhero Comic Books 2001–2008," in 2015. His work explores the ability of superhero comic books to reproduce, critique, challenge, and contest dominant ideology. He has published on the Captain America comics' critique of the ideological response to the War on Terror and its contribution to the 2008 presidential election of Barack Obama. More broadly he is interested in social commentary within popular culture and its ability to contribute to societal understanding.

ANGELA NDALIANIS is a research professor in media and entertainment studies at Swinburne University of Technology. Her research focuses on entertainment culture, the history of technologies of vision and embodiment, and neo-baroque aesthetics. Her publications include *Neo-Baroque Aesthetics and Contemporary Entertainment* (2004), *Science Fiction Experiences* (2010), and *The Horror Sensorium; Media and the Senses* (2012), and her edited books include *The Contemporary Comic Book Superhero* (2009), *Neo-baroques: From Latin America to the Hollywood Blockbuster* (with W. Moser and P. Krieger, 2017), *Fans and Videogames: Histories, Fandom, Archives* (with M. Swalwell and H. Stuckey, 2017), and *Baroque to Neo-baroque: Emotion and the Seduction of the Senses* (with L. Beaven, 2018). She is currently working on the book *Batman: The Myth, the Superhero* (forthcoming, Rutgers University Press).

KEVIN PATRICK is an adjunct professor with the Department of Communication and Media Studies at Fordham University. He is the author of *The Phantom Unmasked: America's First Superhero* (2017). He received his doctorate from Monash University (Melbourne, Australia) in 2014 for his thesis titled "The Ghost Who Walks: A Cultural History of *The Phantom* Comic Book in Australia, India and Sweden." Prior to commencing postgraduate studies in 2009, he worked for nearly fifteen years as a communications policy researcher, freelance journalist, magazine editor, children's book author, and comic book publisher. He was appointed guest curator to the State Library of Victoria (Melbourne, Australia), where he staged the exhibition *Heroes and Villains: Australian Comics and Their Creators* (October 2006–February 2007).

SHAN MU ZHAO is a PhD candidate in the Department of American Studies and Ethnicity, University of Southern California. She has contributed essays to *Drawing New Colour Lines: Transnational Asian American Graphic Narratives* and *The Power of Culture: Encounters between China and the United States*, as well as an entry to the *Critical Survey of Graphic Novels* series. Her research examines how meanings associated with the United States circulate in Asia through entertainment media, and she hopes to create her own comic one day.

INDEX